Imperial Masochism

BRITISH FICTION, FANTASY, AND SOCIAL CLASS

John Kucich

PRINCETON UNIVERSITY PRESS

PRINCETON AND OXFORD

Copyright © 2007 by Princeton University Press
Published by Princeton University Press, 41 William Street, Princeton, New Jersey 08540
In the United Kingdom: Princeton University Press, 3 Market Place, Woodstock,
Oxfordshire OX20 1SY

Library of Congress Cataloging-in-Publication Data
Kucich, John.
Imperial masochism : British fiction, fantasy, and social class / John Kucich.
        p.   cm.
Includes bibliographical references and index.
ISBN-13: 978-0-691-12712-5 (hardcover : acid-free paper)
ISBN-10: 0-691-12712-3 (hardcover : acid-free paper)
1. English fiction—19th century—History and criticism. 2. Masochism in literature.
3. Social classes in literature. 4. Imperialism in literature. 5. Great Britain—Colonies—
History—19th century. I. Title.
PR878.M367K83   2006
823′.89353—dc22   2006008917

British Library Cataloging-in-Publication Data is available

This book has been composed in Galliard Typeface

Printed on acid-free paper. ∞

pup.princeton.edu

Printed in the United States of America

1   3   5   7   9   10   8   6   4   2

Imperial Masochism

To Kramer Woods

CONTENTS

ACKNOWLEDGMENTS

MOST OF ALL, I want to thank Dianne Sadoff, whose loving companionship and intellectual camaraderie made this a very different book—a much better one—than it would have been otherwise.

Other vital help came from a few close friends and colleagues. In addition to her unswerving kindness, Martha Vicinus offered me her clarity of vision at crucial junctures as well as practical help with the introduction. Nancy Armstrong, Kerry Powell, and Jenny Taylor gave me the tough advice and savvy coaching one gets only from those who feel like family.

Patrick Brantlinger, James Buzard, Andrew Miller, and Dianne Sadoff gave me extensive commentary on a draft of the whole manuscript.

For reading sections of the book and offering useful feedback at early stages, thanks to James Eli Adams, Joe Bristow, Ginger Frost, Chris Lane, Adela Pinch, Harriet Ritvo, and Molly Rothenberg.

For tangible support, encouragement, and suggestions, I'm grateful to Regenia Gagnier, Daniel Hack, Christopher Herbert, Jason Jones, Gerhard Joseph, Ivan Kreilkamp, George Levine, Jill Matus, John McGowan, Angelique Richardson, Hilary Schor, Sally Shuttleworth, David Wayne Thomas, and Lynn Voskuil. James Hansell gave me reliable advice on psychoanalytic matters, and Mary Childers helped orient me during a memorable conversation as I was just beginning the project.

I owe an enormous debt to the many audiences who heard preliminary versions of parts of the book. But for offering particularly challenging questions, which stimulated much-needed rethinking, thanks to Amanda Anderson, Carolyn Dever, and Helena Michie. I'm also indebted to a number of graduate classes for working through some of the central issues with me.

The National Humanities Center gave me the fellowship year I needed to bring this project to fruition. During the year I spent at the center, Geoffrey Harpham supported and inspired me in ways he probably doesn't even suspect. Thanks also to the University of Sheffield and the University of Houston for giving me extended opportunities to talk with colleagues about my work. I'm grateful to Bill Wortman of the Miami University Library as well as to librarians and staff at the British Library, the Huntington Library, the New York Public Library, University College (London), the University of Michigan, the University of Sussex, and the Writer's Museum (Edinburgh). Caroline Giordano and Casie Legette provided diligent, resourceful research assistance.

Earlier versions of some of this material have appeared as "Melancholy Magic: Masochism, Stevenson, Anti-Imperialism," *Nineteenth-Century Literature* 56 (2001), 364–400; "Masochism, Omnipotence, and Olive Schreiner: Strategies of a Preoedipal Politics," *Novel: A Forum on Fiction* 36 (2002), 79–109; and "Sadomasochism and the Magical Group: Kipling's Middle-Class Imperialism," *Victorian Studies* 46 (2003), 33–68. All three journals have generously given permission to reprint.

A NOTE ON TEXTS

WHENEVER possible, I have used recent, reliable paperback editions of novels and short stories—primarily Oxford World Classics, Norton Critical Editions, and Penguins. Where these were not available, I have used standard collected editions or first editions. For nonfictional writings, I have used standard collected editions if available and, if not, original sources.

More detailed information about texts can be found in the notes to each chapter.

Imperial Masochism

Introduction

———————— ∘⦿⦿∘ ————————

FANTASY AND IDEOLOGY

> Never completely losing its grip, fantasy is always head-
> ing for the world it only appears to have left behind.
> —JACQUELINE ROSE, *States of Fantasy*

MASOCHISM is often regarded as a site of social and cultural intersections. But in late-nineteenth-century British colonial fiction, it focused one particular conjunction more than any other: the relationship
between imperial politics and social class. This relationship has lately been
an unfashionable topic for scholarly analysis, despite the intense scrutiny
being applied to nearly every other aspect of British colonialism and some
noteworthy protests about the imbalance. David Cannadine, for example,
recently claimed that the "British Empire has been extensively studied as
a complex *racial* hierarchy (and also as a less complex *gender* hierarchy);
but it has received far less attention as an equally complex *social* hierarchy
or, indeed, as a social organism, or construct, of any kind."[1] Ann Stoler
has registered a similar complaint, while emphasizing the interdependence
of these categories: "We know more than ever about the legitimating rhetoric of European civility and its gendered construals, but less about the
class tensions that competing notions of 'civility' engendered. We are just
beginning to identify how bourgeois sensibilities have been coded by race
and, in turn, how finer scales measuring cultural competency and 'suitabil-
ity' often replaced explicit racial criteria to define access to privilege in
imperial ventures."[2] Many cultural critics share Stoler's assumptions about
the mediated nature of colonial identities. In Anne McClintock's much
quoted formulation from *Imperial Leather* (1995): "no social category
exists in privileged isolation; each comes into being in social relation to
other categories, if in uneven and contradictory ways."[3] But methodologi-
cally sophisticated imperial studies have persistently marginalized social

---

[1] David Cannadine, *Ornamentalism: How the British Saw Their Empire* (Oxford: Oxford
University Press, 2001), p. 9. Italics in original.

[2] Ann Laura Stoler, *Race and the Education of Desire: Foucault's History of Sexuality and
the Colonial Order of Things* (Durham: Duke University Press, 1995), p. 99.

[3] Anne McClintock, *Imperial Leather: Race, Gender and Sexuality in the Colonial Contest*
(New York: Routledge, 1995), p. 9.

class or have falsely stabilized it in relation to fluid hybridizations of gender, race, sexual orientation, and other forms of social classification. The former is evident in the subtitle of McClintock's book, for example (*Race, Gender and Sexuality in the Colonial Contest*).

Analyzing representations of masochism can help to rectify this imbalance. Although masochism is not usually associated with social class, images of colonial masochism tended to bear with special weight on problems of status hierarchy, no matter how much they were also articulated upon other forms of social identity. These strong correlations between masochism and social class are not the explanatory key to colonial experience, nor can they be studied in "privileged isolation." But they do provide a reminder that class was a more important and a more complicated aspect of colonial life than recent scholarship has recognized. They can also demonstrate that ideologies of social class were intertwined with imperial self-consciousness in immensely variable ways.

The principal contention of this book is that figurations of masochism in British colonial fiction constituted a psychosocial language, in which problems of social class were addressed through the politics of imperialism and vice versa. I am not arguing that masochism had an inherent class or imperial politics. Neither would I wish to claim that social or imperial identity can be understood through collective psychology, masochistic or otherwise. My argument is simply that elements of masochistic fantasy resonated powerfully with both imperial and class discourses in late-nineteenth-century Britain. This discursive resonance presented writers of fiction with an extraordinary opportunity to refashion both imperial and class subjectivities by manipulating the complex intersections between them that masochistic fantasy helped to forge. In this sense, I am arguing that masochism played a vital role in the shaping and reshaping of social identity at the imperial periphery, which had important consequences in domestic British culture as well. I am also arguing that imperial and class ideologies in nineteenth-century Britain exploited a common and very powerful form of affective organization.

Because I regard masochism as a psychosocial language (rather than a fixed set of behaviors or a personality profile), I speak of it throughout this book as a fantasy structure. My emphasis on the centrality of fantasy to masochism—a notion entertained in Sigmund Freud's early studies and sustained by subsequent relational work—has a number of important consequences. For one thing, it circumvents some of the more mechanistic tendencies of psychoanalytic approaches to culture. Critical appropriations of psychoanalytic theory have too often closed off possibilities for cultural interpretation—largely by combining crude, reductive assumptions about psychological causality with hair-splitting terminological distinctions. But psychoanalytic models need not stifle cultural analysis, nor should they provoke unproductive debates about whether the origins of subjectivity lie in private experience, psychobiology, or culture. Important object-relational studies of fantasy, such as Melanie Klein's work on the symbolic status of the mother, deanatomize the body and make it available for figural readings.[4] Poststructural analysts of fantasy, from Jean Laplanche and J. B. Pontalis to Jacqueline Rose, have also insisted on the textualized character of phantasmagoric material.[5] The analysis of fantasy structures has, in fact, served a variety of psychoanalytic approaches seeking to understand the relationship between psychological and social processes without privileging one or the other. Understanding masochism as a fantasy structure means viewing it as a medium in which individual and social experience is intertwined. It also means regarding it as a medium of symbolic transformation that incorporates a wider range of behaviors than is usually conjured up by the term "masochism," which often provokes thoughts only of whips and chains, sexual role reversals, and physical self-mutilation.

Viewing masochism as a fantasy structure has other important methodological consequences. As Laplanche and Pontalis have famously pointed out, fantasy crosses the boundary between conscious and unconscious experience, linking the worlds of daydream and delusion to indecipherable psychic pressures that resist direct apprehension.[6] These pressures can be variously understood as pregiven, socially constructed, or individually developed. For that reason, the analysis of fantasy structures enables the cultural critic to place phantasmagoric forms of conscious awareness in relationship to unconscious material of all kinds, both psychological and social. As Terry Eagleton once observed, the study of ideology means linking together its most articulate with its least articulate levels.[7] Viewing fantasy as a set of psychosocial symbolic structures has the potential to do just that.

By concentrating on processes of discursive mediation, I resist the evaluative urgency that has been so common in the cultural analysis of masochism. Attempts to judge masochism's complicity with or subversion of dominant social power have all too often overwhelmed more nuanced ways of recognizing its powers of symbolic transformation. Masochistic fantasy is an instrument for social action—not an action in itself that has

---

[4] See, in particular, Melanie Klein, "The Importance of Symbol-Formation in the Development of the Ego," *Contributions to Psycho-analysis, 1921–1945* (London: Hogarth Press, 1965), pp. 236–50.

[5] Jean Laplanche and J.-B. Pontalis, "Fantasy and the Origins of Sexuality," *International Journal of Psychoanalysis* 49 (1968), 1–18. Jacqueline Rose, *States of Fantasy* (Oxford: Clarendon Press, 1996), p. 3, claims that fantasy is the fundamental symbolic structure of the social.

[6] Laplanche and Pontalis, p. 11.

[7] Terry Eagleton, *Ideology: An Introduction* (London: Verso, 1991), p. 50.

intrinsic political (or psychological) content. But neither is it an open-ended process of symbolic reversals, resistant to political interpretation. It is, rather, a symbolic language often used to achieve particular, determinate objectives. Of course, reading masochism as an ideological medium is itself a political choice as well as an ethical and aesthetic one. While its evenhandedness may alienate those with polemical views on the politics of masochism, it has the advantage of illuminating a great range of distinct ideological content in very different writers and colonial contexts.

Before venturing further into questions about what masochistic fantasy is and what it is not, I must begin with a brief sketch of the social and cultural contexts that enabled it to link late-Victorian discourses about imperialism and social class. If masochistic fantasy served as an important means for organizing what Cannadine calls the "complex social hierarchy" of British colonial experience, it did so because it was firmly embedded in British imperial and social history.

Masochism in Context

Although we are not used to scrutinizing instances of cherished pain in British imperial iconography very deeply, the glorification of suffering was an enormously important theme well before Victorian evangelicalism tried to Christianize every aspect of the imperial project. British imperialism may have fostered countless narratives of conquest, and it may have celebrated victorious heroes like Wellington, Clive, and Wolseley or great triumphs like Waterloo, Trafalgar, Plassey, and Red River. The arrogance of the British abroad was legendary, too, and often a source of perverse national pride. But British imperialism also generated a remarkable preoccupation with suffering, sacrifice, defeat, and melancholia. As Linda Colley has reminded us, one paradigm of British imperial narrative may well have been Crusoe. But another was Gulliver, a figure whose ordeals of enslavement and humiliation culminate in his subjection to an unquestionably superior race.[8] This subjection compels Gulliver to disavow the sense of legitimacy he had once vested in his nation and in himself, making melancholic abjection, in his case, a vehicle for self-transformation.

What is particularly striking about British imperial culture is how often it mythologized victimization and death as foundational events in the teleology of empire. There was, seemingly, a different crucifixion scene marking the historical gateway to each colonial theater: Captain Cook in the South Pacific, General Wolfe in Canada, General Gordon in the Sudan;

---

[8] Linda Colley, *Captives: Britain, Empire, and the World, 1600–1850* (2002; New York: Random House, 2004), pp. 1–4.

or else there was mass martyrdom (the Black Hole massacre in India) or crucifixion averted (the popular tale of Captain John Smith and Pocahontas in America). When, in 1871, W.H.G. Kingston lionized Cook for "the founding of two nations of the Anglo-Saxon race," for example, he was echoing a long tradition of Cookiana that continued to sustain the cultural identities of Australia and New Zealand well into the twentieth century.[9] This foundational myth, like the others mentioned above, revolved around the sanctification implicit in the imperial martyr's suffering—a sanctification that allied imperial pain with redemption and with the beginning, rather than the end, of history. In short, sanctification transformed the pain and finality of death or defeat into pleasurable fantasies of ecstatic rebirth or resurrection. After Cook's death in 1779, poems by Helen Maria Williams, William Cowper, and Hannah More, along with a famous elegy by Anna Seward, all compared him to Christ and stressed his having been deified by the Hawaiians who killed him (an assertion later contested by British and American missionaries). One of the first important paintings of Cook's death, Philip James De Loutherbourg's *Apotheosis of Captain Cook* (1785), which was used as the backdrop for an immensely successful London pantomime and later published as an engraving, shows Cook being assumed into heaven by the figures of Britannia and Fame. Other influential paintings of the death scene by John Webber, John Cleveley, and Johann Zoffany represent Cook as an icon of emotional and spiritual transcendence—the only serene figure in a scene of chaotic violence.

Wolfe was similarly sanctified in the public imagination. A painting by Benjamin West, viewed by enthusiastic crowds when first exhibited in 1771, possesses, in Simon Schama's words, a "radiance illuminating the face of the martyr and bathing the grieving expressions of his brother officers in a reflection of impossible holiness."[10] The West painting is transparently modeled on Passion scenes, with an upraised British flag standing in for the cross. The Black Hole massacre, which took place in Calcutta in 1756 (helping in some measure to motivate Clive's successful campaign against the French at Plassey), was also transformed into a foundational myth in the second half of the nineteenth century by those who portrayed the victims as saintly martyrs. In 1902, ignoring warnings from the India Council in London against "parading our disaster," Lord Curzon lavishly restored the Black Hole monument in Calcutta and praised the "martyr

---

[9] William H. G. Kingston, *Captain Cook, His Life, Voyages and Discoveries* (London: Religious Tract Society, 1871), p. 319.

[10] Simon Schama, *Dead Certainties (Unwarranted Speculations)* (New York: Alfred A. Knopf, 1991), p. 21.

band" in his dedicatory speech.[11] He defended his actions to the India Council on the grounds that "their death was practically the foundation stone of the British Empire in India."[12]

Many of these foundational scenes of martyrdom were military. The siege of Mafeking, the Mysore disaster, the catastrophic First Afghan War, Gordon's death at Khartoum—all figured in the national imagination as spectacles of military weakness or defeat that also inspired British resurgence. Many contemporary accounts of these military episodes, such as William Thomson's *Memoirs of the Late War in Asia* (1788) or Robert Sale's *A Journal of the Disasters in Afghanistan* (1843), are remarkable excursions into martyrology rather than documentary accounts. But the sanctification of the imperial sufferer was not simply a rallying point for military conquest. Imperial iconography is littered with nonmilitary martyrs as well: missionaries like John Williams and David Livingstone, for example, and explorers like Sir John Franklin, Mungo Park, and, of course, Cook. India was especially rich in civilian martyrs. These included Bishop Heber, whose death in 1826 was widely mourned in both India and Britain, as well as the many young scientists whose lives and work were tragically cut short by disease: William Griffith, Alexander Moon, William Kerr, John Champion, George Gardner, John Stocks, John Cathcart (to name only a few of the botanists).[13] These Keatsian deaths ensured that many a scientific text emerging from India was read as an implicit memorial to its prematurely deceased author. Celebrated instances of self-sacrifice such as these helped stiffen the ethos of martyrdom that underlay even the most ordinary colonial life. In Charlotte Brontë's *Jane Eyre* (1847), St. John Rivers sees in Jane "a soul that revelled in the flame and excitement of sacrifice," which he regards as the supreme qualification for a life—inevitably short—of unheralded colonial service.[14] With a more penitential spirit, Peter Jenkyns in Elizabeth Gaskell's *Cranford* (1853) expiates his youthful sins through the ennobling suffering of colonial service.

Of course, images of imperial martyrdom, self-sacrifice, or even self-abasement cannot be conflated with masochism. The images of cherished imperial suffering I am describing served a great many purposes. In part, they simply reflected the dangerous and often disastrous side of imperial enterprise. From the perspective of the empire at its height, narratives of

[11] Quoted in Zetland, Lawrence John Lumley Dundas, Marquis of, *The Life of Lord Curzon: Being the Authorized Biography of George Nathaniel, Marquess Curzon of Kedleston, K.G.*, 3 vols. (London: Ernest Benn, 1928), 2:158.

[12] Quoted in Zetland, 2:159.

[13] I. H. Burkill, *Chapters on the History of Botany in India* (Delhi: Government of India Press, 1965), makes for chilling reading on these and other untimely deaths.

[14] Charlotte Brontë, *Jane Eyre* (New York: Norton, 2001), p. 344.

conquest may have seemed like the most accurate descriptions of imperial history. But from the perspective of those who could not have anticipated future successes and who either knew of or had themselves experienced harrowing encounters with disease, captivity, enslavement, military defeat, dependence on nonwhites, or sadistic cruelties (whether at the hands of Europeans or non-Europeans), narratives of British suffering may have seemed more honest. Mythologies of imperial suffering also have rather obvious propaganda value, as we know too well in our own time from the political exploitation of the events of 9/11. Indeed, most studies of British imperial pathos regard it simply as a means of legitimating aggression and inspiring vengeance. Mary Louise Pratt has also demonstrated how such images could serve a mythology of anticonquest, engendering the notion that British colonizers were beneficent innocents.[15] On a practical level, representations of imperial suffering were a means of raising money for the redemption of British captives held overseas or the funding of missionary organizations.

But among the many kinds of significance inhering in the iconography of imperial suffering (whatever the intentions of those who promoted it) was the inevitability of its being inhabited by masochistic fantasy. At the very least, the melancholic potentials of imperial suffering were widely indulged. David Arnold has pointed out, for instance, that nineteenth-century India was transformed into a morbid topography, dotted with immense marble funerary monuments commemorating victims of the high colonial mortality rate.[16] Travel writing about India by Emily Eden and James Dalhousie featured mournful, lengthy descriptions of these cemeteries and funeral monuments, a tradition sustained in some of Rudyard Kipling's early journalistic sketches. Similar monuments back home, which introduced exotic Indian place names to British churchyards, helped reinforce a melancholic view of colonial India that had a strong hold from at least the late eighteenth century onwards, as novels like *Jane Eyre*, *Cranford*, or Flora Annie Steel's popular success *On the Face of the Waters* (1896) make abundantly clear. More broadly, encounters with decaying cultures often produced melancholic reflections on the inevitability of British imperial demise. On first contact with Polynesian culture, Robert Louis Stevenson reflected: "I saw their case as ours, death coming in like a tide, and the day already numbered when there should be no more

---

[15] Mary Louise Pratt, *Imperial Eyes: Travel Writing and Transculturation* (London: Routledge, 1992), p. 7.

[16] For this point and for several other observations about India I am indebted to David Arnold, "Deathscapes: India in an Age of Romanticism and Empire, 1800–1856," *Nineteenth-Century Contexts* 26 (2004), 339–53.

Beretani, and no more of any race whatever, and (what oddly touched me) no more literary works and no more readers."[17]

But imperial masochism took more overt forms than melancholia, as we will see in detail throughout this book. The notion that colonial spaces offered opportunities for glorious suicide was deeply conventionalized in British culture, so much so that in *Daniel Deronda* (1876), George Eliot could count on readers recognizing the triteness of Rex Gascoigne's wish to banish himself to the colonies in order to dramatize his having been jilted in love. The rhetoric of histrionic imperial self-destructiveness has entered quite casually into much contemporary analysis of the imperial mind. Thus, James Morris echoes a common theme in writing about Gordon by declaring that he was "trapped by his own death-wish."[18] The unconfirmed but much relished story that Wolfe read Thomas Gray's "Elegy in a Country Churchyard" (1750) to his troops as a way of inspiring them on the eve of battle has helped lionize him as a melancholic fatalist. This rhetoric of histrionic martyrdom is not simply a retrospective imposition. It was often recirculated quite deliberately by military figures and colonists themselves. Robert Baden-Powell's cavalierly desperate dispatches from Mafeking, for instance, were modeled self-consciously on Gordon's from Khartoum. They also titillated the British public with images of endangered women and children that were bound to evoke memories of the massacre at Cawnpore during the 1857 Sepoy Rebellion—itself the single most engrossing spectacle of the British imperialist as victim, with over fifty novels about the rebellion published before the end of the century.

In the late nineteenth century, the masochistic overtones of imperial suffering were amplified by public debates about the rapidly growing but increasingly precarious empire. During this period of "new imperialism," when many Victorian writers sought to bolster public support for expansion, images of the imperialist as willing victim or martyr proliferated. Kipling's "The White Man's Burden" (1899) is perhaps the most famous expression of masochistic jingoism. With its rapturous celebration of sacrifice, toil, and ingratitude, it promotes an apocalyptic vision of history, bestowing on the imperialist the mantle of the Israelites—a chosen people tried by suffering. In "Recessional" (1897), Kipling encouraged a national posture of submissive humility in exchange for divine blessing: "Thy mercy on Thy People, Lord!"[19] More vulgar affirmations of painful self-sacrifice and bravery in the face of death saturated the adventure fiction for

[17] Robert Louis Stevenson, *In the South Seas, The Works of Robert Louis Stevenson*, Skerryvore Edition, 30 vols. (London: Heinemann, 1924–1926), 18:26. "Beretani" was pidgin for Britain.

[18] James Morris, *Farewell the Trumpets: An Imperial Retreat* (London: Faber & Faber, 1978), p. 33.

[19] Rudyard Kipling, "Recessional," *The Five Nations* (New York: Doubleday, 1903), p. 215.

boys that boomed in popularity during the last decades of the nineteenth century: novels by G. A. Henty, R. M. Ballantyne, H. Rider Haggard, Robert Louis Stevenson, W.H.G. Kingston, Gordon Stables, Arthur Conan Doyle, Henry Seton Merriman, and many others. This body of fiction helped foster a fundamentally masochistic ethos of British masculinity, in which the ability to absorb pain stoically—or even ecstatically— was greatly prized.

Late-nineteenth-century narratives of desired or self-inflicted imperial suffering fueled cautionary tales and anti-imperialist allegories as well. Haggard's *She* (1887) described the dangerous, seductive power an exotic dominatrix could exercise over willingly subservient British men. Bram Stoker's *Dracula* (1897) represented the threat of the native "other" in terms of its erotic power to compel the submission of both men and women. These novels portray imperial adventure as an initiation into perverse, willing victimage; symptomatically, Dracula cannot enter his victim's sanctuaries to attack them until he is invited to cross the threshold. Much of the late-century fiction Patrick Brantlinger has described as "Imperial Gothic" revolves around the unconsciously self-destructive impulses of Britons, who persistently and inexplicably seek out exotic forces that prove to be cruel, powerful, and pitiless: Doyle's "The Ring of Thoth" (1890) and "Lot No. 249" (1892), in which mummies removed to England come alive to torment their captors; Kipling's "The Mark of the Beast" (1891), in which an arrogant Englishman who provokingly insults a temple idol is possessed by a sadistic demon; or Stoker's *Jewel of the Seven Stars* (1903), which is also about a removed mummy who comes to life, turning vindictively on her reanimators.[20]

These multivalent images of desired, self-inflicted, or otherwise cherished imperial pain could not fail to intersect attitudes toward suffering maintained elsewhere in British culture. In particular, glorified suffering had a prominent history in nineteenth-century conceptions of social class, most of all among the middle classes. Of course, a variety of British class ideologies reserved a place for the moral exaltation and social authority that might be conferred by suffering. Chivalric ideals long held by the upper class, which were appropriated by gentrified and professionalized middle-class ranks in the second half of the nineteenth century, revolved around the honor conferred by both physical and emotional trials. The ideals of stoic masculinity exalted by late-century adventure fiction were already present, in one form or another, among all Victorian social classes, including working-class cultures, whether conservative, militaristic, or

---

[20] Patrick Brantlinger, *Rule of Darkness: British Literature and Imperialism, 1830–1914* (Ithaca: Cornell University Press, 1988), pp. 227–54.

radical. The high ground of noble sacrifice was, in fact, an extremely important objective of ideological competition in nineteenth-century British culture. Harold Perkin once observed that the "struggle between the moralities was as much a part of the class conflict of the period as Parliamentary Reform or the campaign against the Corn Laws."[21] Perkin argued further (as have more recent historians, notably Dror Wahrman) that competition over moral authority was a central factor in the birth of class society itself.[22] Although cherished suffering played a role at many sites in this social transformation, it was particularly effective in helping to sustain the moral hegemony over Victorian culture that the middle classes had acquired by midcentury.

It is tempting to find the sources of this widespread valorization of suffering in British Protestantism. John Foxe's *Book of Martyrs* (1563) and John Bunyan's *Pilgrim's Progress* (1678), which, until the twentieth century, trailed only the Bible in circulation, are distinctively British texts in their emphasis on suffering and exposure to danger as signs of grace.[23] But nineteenth-century middle-class moralism far exceeded the rigors of English Puritanism in its exaltation of self-punishment. Thanks to middle-class moral despotism, Sunday in Victorian England was not simply a day of prayer but also a time for mortification. In addition, pleasurable amusements like the theater and popular sports came under increasing attack early in the nineteenth century. Middle-class self-abnegation even pervaded entrepreneurial ideals. The Congregationalist minister Robert Vaughan once declared: "In relation to the affairs of this world, no less than to the affairs of religion, the man who would be successful 'must take up his cross and deny himself.'"[24] Contemporary observers were sometimes appalled at the consequences for middle-class social power of this pervasive ethos of self-denial. In *The English Constitution* (1867), Walter Bagehot excoriated middle-class culture for what he saw as its compulsive tendency to abase itself before authority—a "hypothesis of an essentially masochistic cultural and political unconscious," as Christopher Herbert has described it.[25] While popular accounts of Victorian prudery and self-denial have often made them seem absurd or even freakish, we must not

[21] Harold Perkin, *The Origins of Modern English Society, 1780–1880* (London: Routledge and Kegan Paul, 1969), p. 279.

[22] Perkin, p. 281. Dror Wahrman, *Imagining the Middle Class: The Political Representation of Class in Britain, c. 1780–1840* (Cambridge: Cambridge University Press, 1995), p. 395, argues that evangelical conceptions of separate sphere ideology were crucial to the formation of coherent middle-class political values.

[23] Linda Colley, *Britons: Forging the Nation, 1707–1837* (New Haven: Yale University Press, 1992), pp. 27–28, makes this point.

[24] Robert Vaughan, *The Age of Great Cities* (London: Jackson & Walford, 1843), p. 312.

[25] Christopher Herbert, *Culture and Anomie: Ethnographic Imagination in the Nineteenth Century* (Chicago: University of Chicago Press, 1991), p. 137.

forget how powerful a role ideals of virtuous suffering played in the consolidation of middle-class culture.

Middle-class fiction, for example, drew on a theme placed at the heart of the British novel by Samuel Richardson: the notion that individuals are redeemed by suffering. Widely read works such as Emily Brontë's *Wuthering Heights* (1847) and Charles Dickens's *Great Expectations* (1861) defined the self-lacerating individual as the moral center of middle-class culture, an equation that inevitably gave rise to complex uncertainties and anxieties. In Brontë's novel, Heathcliff's apocalyptic wish to be annihilated follows on and parallels Cathy's enigmatic decision to frustrate her own passions by marrying a man she admits loving only superficially. These self-destructive choices, which are driven to some degree by the two characters' otherworldly idealism, are represented by Brontë as the darkest of threats to social stability—impulses that must be moderated in the more palatable forms of emotional restraint adopted by the novel's succeeding generation of lovers. Dickens, however, demonstrated how individuals could transform self-destructive tendencies directly into virtues. In the first third of *Great Expectations*, Pip's self-lacerating guilt is represented as the dangerous internalization of persecutions he suffers at the hands of hypocritical adults, a form of self-torture every reader can only hope he outgrows. But as the novel develops, it gives Pip reasons to embrace his guilt. His increasing remorse over his desire to rise out of the working classes and to enter the ranks of the gentry is precisely what defines Pip as a legitimately middle-class subject. Significantly, his moral and social purification is consummated in his penitential acceptance of colonial employment. In both novels, the struggle to define correctly the proportions, the means, and the social significance of willful self-martyrdom is represented as central to the emergence of middle-class culture.

At the fin de siècle, such struggles were aggravated by intraclass competition of several different kinds. Late-century bohemianism often posed the purity of its intellectual and fiscal askesis against the material complacency of the bourgeoisie. As Terry Eagleton has pointed out, too, late-century intellectuals who experimented with spiritualism, underworld sensationalism, or the reification of the aesthetic symbol were performing what he calls a "collective intellectual suicide" as they sought forms of experience outside of bourgeois self-interest and rationality.[26] Many of those intellectuals were performing their internal resistance to the class from which they had originated—a phenomenon we will see in more detail in Stevenson's career and to some extent in Olive Schreiner's. At the

---

[26] Terry Eagleton, "The Flight to the Real," *Cultural Politics at the Fin de Siècle*, ed. Sally Ledger and Scott McCracken (Cambridge: Cambridge University Press, 1995), p. 17.

same time, the late-Victorian lower middle class developed its own commitments to ideals of self-denial and hard work, which it saw as a means
to respectability. These and other intraclass struggles to exploit the intellectual, moral, and social authority conferred by suffering and self-denial
will be pivotal to my discussion of Victorian social hierarchies throughout
the following chapters.

Just as imperial suffering cannot be conflated with masochism, so, too,
glorifications of suffering in the realm of class ideology were overdetermined and cannot be regarded as intrinsically masochistic. It may not
even be clear in what sense the class-coded exaltations of suffering I have
been describing might be considered a discrete set of phenomena. The
grouping of these various social trends together can suggest as many differences among them as similarities. From the global cultural perspective
of Max Weber's *The Protestant Ethic and the Spirit of Capitalism* (1905),
the promotion of self-denial appeared to be a rationalized instrument
of productivity in the nineteenth century, whereas Friedrich Nietzsche
argued, in *The Genealogy of Morals* (1887), that it was a weapon wielded
by priestly elites against secular authority. As I have suggested, glorified
suffering took a variety of class-coded forms in nineteenth-century British
society as well as taking part in a cultural climate unique to British Protestantism, which was intensified by mid-Victorian evangelicalism (rather
than being wholly abstracted from religion, as Weber argued). Moreover,
class-coded forms of suffering were mediated by other elements in late-
Victorian culture, including the mythology of imperial suffering I have
already sketched out. It would be reductive to derive from multifaceted
British ideologies of glorified suffering a singular psychological or ideological determinant. Nevertheless, class-coded ideals of cherished suffering inevitably invited, encouraged, and sustained masochistic fantasy. In
the chapters that follow, I contend that the potential of these class ideologies to trigger masochistic fantasy opened up crucial channels of symbolic
exchange between discourses of class and empire in late-Victorian Britain.
Masochistic fantasy should thus be considered a switching point between
these two domains of discourse but not as their point of origin. That the
intersection was complex and variable is precisely what made it such a
contested ideological arena.

Before explaining exactly what I mean by "masochistic fantasy," I must
say a few words more about the theoretical status of social class, a concept
that has been under assault in cultural analysis for several decades. The
principal objections have often revolved around the clash between political
or economic descriptions of social stratification and claims about "class
consciousness"—perspectives that tend to produce distinctly different formulations of class identity. Cultural dynamics that do not necessarily imply
social self-consciousness—such as habits of association, antagonisms to

other social groups, patterns of consumption, common forms of speech and thought, and expectations about family life and domestic roles—are now often considered stronger factors in the organization of social class than either "class consciousness" or demonstrable economic and political affinities. The flexibility of cultural criteria for distinguishing between social groups has, of course, inevitably made the category of social class sociologically imprecise. But critics who have accepted the instability of cultural constructions of gender and race should have little difficulty understanding that such concepts remain useful even after their destabilization has been inscribed within them. The continued relevance of social class to British studies, even as a tentative social marker, should be apparent, if for no other reason than because of its obvious importance to nineteenth-century capitalism. Since it is the very nature of capitalism to distribute goods and privileges unequally and to pit social constituencies against one another, it makes little sense to object that such differentiation is never entirely clear-cut.

More powerful recent attacks have come from historians inspired by the "linguistic turn" in the social sciences. Many have pointed out that social power is more polymorphous and dispersed than is implied by conventional models of class hierarchy. The language of class also obscures other terms in which collectivity has been formulated.[27] Recent historians have been more inclined to see class as a political entity, in the sense that it has been imaginatively constructed for specific purposes and then supplied with a mystified history rather than being a stable referent grounded in the evolution of real social relationships. But the recognition that class did have an important role in political conflict, albeit a symbolic one, has compelled even a fiercely poststructuralist historian like Patrick Joyce to acknowledge that "class will not go away. It has its place, and an important one." Joyce adds, however, that "it does need from time to time to be put in it."[28] The intractability of class as an analytic tool would seem all the more important given the widespread acceptance of the tripartite model, as well as certain distinctions within each rank, among Victorian writers themselves. The increasing complexity of social stratification over the last century should not blind us to its relative clarity in the perceptions and practices of nineteenth-century social actors, whatever the sociological or economic realities to which they were responding.

In this book, I seek to put the concept of class "in its place" not by turning away from it toward other, equally problematic conceptions of

[27] See James Vernon, "Who's Afraid of the 'Linguistic Turn'? The Politics of Social History and Its Discontents," *Social History* 19 (1994), 81–97.

[28] Patrick Joyce, *Visions of the People: Industrial England and the Question of Class, 1848–1914* (Cambridge: Cambridge University Press, 1991), p. 1.

social stratification but by applying to it some of the lessons the linguistic turn has taught us. Attention to the discursive nature of class—its status as an imagined category—should make us more sensitive to the ways it was culturally shaped and revised and to the social agency assumed by writers who undertook such revisions. Although Gareth Stedman Jones, a principal architect of the linguistic turn, is often invoked as an enemy of the concept of class, his *Languages of Class* (1983) was devoted to precisely this kind of discursive rehabilitation, in which class is newly conceived as a symbolic medium relating individual actors to social structures. Attention to class as a discursive structure should also make us more sensitive to the ways in which it intersects other cultural systems, including, for example, the politics of imperialism or the fantasy structures of masochism. It should direct us, too, to study the complex intraclass tensions that any imagined community inevitably harbors. In this book, "class" designates an arena of conflict in which the constitutive effects of politics, language, culture, fantasy, and desire are all in play and where conceptions of social identity are the outcome, rather than the empirically given conditions, of these interactions.

I am thus steering a middle course between theories of linguistic agency and theories of social determination. My assumption throughout this book is that late-nineteenth-century concepts of class functioned as a constitutive rhetoric. I also assume, however, that conflicts between different social collectivities, as well as within them, were actively manipulated by writers who had the fluid social landscape of colonialism upon which to draw for leverage. Some of these writers—Schreiner and Stevenson, for example—legitimated anti-imperialist crusades by refashioning the moral and ideological foundations of middle-class culture. Others, like Kipling, broadened the social base of support for jingoism by reshaping the class interests to which it appealed. By contrast, Joseph Conrad used colonial social fluidity to align middle-class professionalism with upper-class conservatism. Masochistic fantasy played a crucial role in all these quite different projects. While these four writers and their contemporaries were compelled by masochistic fantasy structures deeply embedded in class and imperial conflict, they seized the opportunity to craft new social identities in a variety of ways at both colonial and domestic sites.

While I have been at pains to locate masochistic fantasy within a broad range of cultural contexts, which means that the emphasis in some chapters falls heavily on these writers' nonliterary work, the focus of this book remains on novelists and novels. Literary scholars are increasingly losing their nerve when it comes to defending the study of literature, sometimes, it would seem, as if turning away from literature (and from the novel in particular) had become necessary and sufficient proof of interdisciplinary rigor. But centering this study on fiction makes sense on a number of grounds. If nothing else, novels were instrumental in shaping late-century attitudes toward imperialism, a cultural fact that has long been recognized. During the last decades of the nineteenth century, as debates over imperial expansion intensified and questions about the rise or fall of the empire seemed to cut to the very heart of the national character, British readers turned increasingly to colonial fiction for coherent models of social identity. The enormous popularity of colonial fiction made Schreiner an instant celebrity when *The Story of an African Farm* was published in 1883; it compelled the *Times* to publish Stevenson's letters on Samoa and to rebuke him in print when it disagreed with his attacks on British policy; it prompted Mark Twain to call Kipling "the only living person not head of a nation, whose voice is heard around the world the moment it drops a remark."[29] It is a social phenomenon of some significance that Winston Churchill read *Kidnapped* (1886) while he was a prisoner of the Boers during the South African War; it is similarly striking that Conrad saw Captain Marryat as an "enslaver of youth," the inspiration (in translated versions) for his own early resolution to take to the sea.[30] Martin Green has claimed that "Marryat was often said to be the best recruiting officer the British Navy had."[31] For purely historical reasons, then, the ideological impact of fiction on the course of British imperialism and nationhood deserves careful study.

The same can be said of the novel's relationship to the other principal focal point of this book: social class. From the mid–eighteenth century throughout the nineteenth century, the novel played a crucial role in the formation of middle-class subjectivity. In *Desire and Domestic Fiction* (1987), Nancy Armstrong argued that "the rise of the novel and the emergence of a coherent middle-class ethos [were] one and the same"—an argument she has developed comprehensively in *How Novels Think* (2006).[32] Even among less sophisticated critics, there has been no doubt, since the time of Ian Watt's *The Rise of the Novel* (1957), that middle-class ideology and the novel were intimately related. This point becomes even more important when we consider that colonial subject matter entered the domain of "serious" literature—which meant, for the most part, middle-class literature—in the last two decades of the nineteenth century. Writers

[29] Mark Twain, *The Autobiography of Mark Twain* (London: Chatto & Windus, 1960), p. 287.
[30] Winston S. Churchill, *A Roving Commission* (New York: Scribner's, 1951), p. 290. Joseph Conrad, *Notes on Life and Letters* (Garden City, NY: Doubleday and Page, 1923), p. 53.
[31] Martin Green, *Dreams of Adventure, Deeds of Empire* (New York: Basic Books, 1979), p. 214.
[32] Nancy Armstrong, *Desire and Domestic Fiction: A Political History of the Novel* (Oxford: Oxford University Press, 1987), p. 10; *How Novels Think: The Limits of Individualism from 1719–1900* (New York: Columbia University Press, 2006).

such as Conrad, Stevenson, and Kipling published in *Blackwood's*, the *Cornhill Magazine*, and the *Illustrated London News*—journals with a predominantly middle-class readership. As Green has noted, British expansionism may always have been driven by the mercantile class; but militarism and adventure fiction had long been identified with aristocratic and working-class audiences until, at the fin de siècle, a new crop of writers identified it with middle-class culture.[33] It was through such fiction and through the cultural authority its authors acquired that masochistic narratives insisted on the relationship between imperialism and social class.

Armstrong once casually remarked, in the course of a lecture, that "the Victorian novel is more historical than history, more political than politics, and more myself than I am."[34] The allusion to Cathy's passion for Heathcliff in *Wuthering Heights*, as an instance of the novel's continuing power to produce subjectivity, points to one other important reason why fiction should be at the center of this study. No other form of writing in Victorian culture so powerfully brought together discourse about history and politics with psychological discourse. While we have recently seen a number of important studies of institutionalized nineteenth-century psychology, the narrowly rationalist, associationist tendencies of Victorian psychological science have limited the range of political perspectives that any such analysis can bring to light.[35] Novels show us that these mechanistic, physiological models were always in tension with other ways of conceiving the psyche—many retained from romantic psychology, with its emphasis on the fluidity and irrationality of psychic forces, or from the amalgamation of religious thought, epistemological priorities, gender ideology, and various other cultural practices that the novel alone was equipped to embed within narratives of desire. The Victorian novel thus observed but also exceeded the narrow limits of institutionalized psychology, and its excesses were crucial to the formation of Victorian subjectivity. Conversely, Victorian political discourse was supported by affective structures that only the novel can fully disclose, as Armstrong, Mary Poovey, Catherine Gallagher, Amanda Anderson, Elaine Hadley, and many other recent critics have demonstrated.

I should observe, finally, that my emphasis on social class has compelled me to deviate from recent "peripheralist" approaches to colonial material.

---

[33] Green, p. 37.

[34] Nancy Armstrong, "Feminism, Fiction, and the Utopian Politics of *Dracula*," Indiana University, October 18, 2003.

[35] Three excellent recent studies that investigate this relationship are Nicholas Dames, *Amnesiac Selves: Nostalgia, Forgetting, and British Fiction, 1810–1870* (Oxford: Oxford University Press, 2001); Dianne F. Sadoff, *Sciences of the Flesh: Representing Body and Subject in Psychoanalysis* (Stanford: Stanford University Press, 1998); and Sarah Winter, *Freud and the Institution of Psychoanalytic Knowledge* (Stanford: Stanford University Press, 1999).

I attend to the mediating influence of Boer, Polynesian, and native Indian cultures on British writers, but I acknowledge that these interactions have many discrete sources and consequences which it has not been my purpose to explore. I firmly believe that colonial studies needs to assess the role of "hybrid" discourses from many points of view, and that this work is profitably being conducted by a great many scholars. But the assessment of these discourses through their contributing role in the formation of British social hierarchies is the more specific task of this book.

What Is Masochistic Fantasy?

This is not primarily a psychoanalytic study, in the double sense that it makes no pretense to contribute to psychoanalytic theory and that it refrains from lengthy psychoanalytic discussion. My focal point, as I hope I have made clear, is cultural politics. Nevertheless, a central goal of the book is to demonstrate new ways in which psychoanalysis can contribute to historicism. Any historically informed study of masochism must engage with psychoanalysis in any case, if only because the cultural study of masochism has been co-opted by a particular psychoanalytic tradition that has not yet been sufficiently critiqued. This tradition—the legacy of 1890s sexology (particularly Havelock Ellis's work on the sexual origins of psychopathology)—has supported a number of rigid assumptions about masochism and the ways in which it operates in social and cultural contexts.[36] Far from having displaced psychoanalysis, as it often claims, the cultural study of masochism has thus been constructed within its dominant paradigms. For all these reasons, I will devote this section to a revisionary model of masochism, one that counters the prevailing assumptions of cultural criticism, before returning to the arenas of social analysis that this model can help us to see freshly.

Recent cultural critics tend to share the belief that masochism eroticizes subjection, which give it the potential to undermine authoritarian power either by transforming pain into pleasure or by complicating dualisms of mastery and submission through the polymorphism of sexual desire. This kind of critical thinking reflects popular assumptions that masochism is fundamentally a sexual practice and that it typically occurs within relationships modeled on the power differentials between parent

---

[36] Havelock Ellis, *Studies in the Psychology of Sex* (Philadelphia: F. A. Davis, 1900), was the first to postulate a physiological basis for masochism, describing it as a universal sexual process that he claimed to observe even in protozoa. Sigmund Freud reiterated this argument in *Beyond the Pleasure Principle, The Standard Edition of the Complete Psychological Works of Sigmund Freud*, trans. and ed. James Strachey, 24 vols. (London: Hogarth Press, 1953–73), 18:1–64. Hereafter cited as *SE*.

and child, in which the distorted expression of forbidden sexual desire is paramount. But the equation of masochism with sexuality (and with oedipal sexuality in particular) has originated within a certain tradition of psychoanalytic thought.

Freudian models of masochism always understand it in relation to drives. At one point, Freud saw masochism as the inversion of aggressive drives; later, he enshrined it as a primary drive in its own right.[37] In Laplanche's famous poststructuralist rereading, masochism becomes a fantasy *about* drives.[38] But understanding masochism as a problem of the drives, even if they are reunderstood as symbolic figurations, tends to elide masochism with oedipal sexuality. For Freud, all masochism originates in "erotogenic" masochism, and the oedipal beating fantasy is its basic form of expression.[39] For Laplanche, masochism is, quite simply, at the core of sexuality, and he locates the origins of both in oedipal conflict.[40] The Lacanian tradition also tends to model masochism on oedipal relations, since Lacan understood masochism in terms of the compulsion to repeat, which he equated with entry into the symbolic.[41] Each of these approaches views the oedipal stage as the moment when masochism is articulated erotically through conflicts with paternal authority. Each tends to see masochistic relations as triangular rather than dyadic, since the masochist appears to play out ambivalent sexual relationships with both mother and father. These approaches also emphasize oedipal themes that have come to dominate (so to speak) the cultural analytics of masochism: sexual prohibition, punishment, perversion, mastery, submission, and rivalry with the father. Popular as well as scholarly conceptions of masochism take their oedipal lexicon from this psychoanalytic tradition, which itself originated in Victorian sexology.

Gilles Deleuze's influential *Coldness and Cruelty* (1971), for example, set the terms for many cultural critics by viewing masochism as an oedipal rebellion. In his analysis of Leopold von Sacher-Masoch's novella, *Venus in Furs* (1870), Deleuze argued that the male masochist seeks to overthrow patriarchal authority in order to win the mother's love, and that,

[37] For the first position, see Sigmund Freud, "Instincts and Their Vicissitudes," *SE*, 14: 109–40; for the second, see *Beyond the Pleasure Principle*; or "The Economic Problem of Masochism," *SE*, 19:157–70.

[38] Jean Laplanche, *Life and Death in Psychoanalysis*, trans. Jeffrey Mehlman (Baltimore: The Johns Hopkins University Press, 1976), pp. 85–102.

[39] Freud consistently identified erotogenic masochism as the foundation of all other types. In "The Economic Problem of Masochism," he claimed that even moral masochism, once abstracted from its libidinal origins, becomes resexualized.

[40] Laplanche, *Life and Death in Psychoanalysis*, p. 102, proclaims "the privileged character of masochism in human sexuality."

[41] Jacques Lacan, *The Language of the Self: The Function of Language in Psychoanalysis*, trans. Anthony Wilden (Baltimore: The Johns Hopkins University Press, 1968), pp. 80–83.

in his self-punishment, a father is being beaten: "The masochist feels guilty, he asks to be beaten, he expiates, but why and for what crime? Is it not precisely the father-image in him that is thus miniaturized, beaten, ridiculed, and humiliated? . . . The masochist thus liberates himself in preparation for a rebirth in which the father will have no part."[42] Enormously influenced by this model, literary and cultural theorists of masochism tend to invoke similar oedipal battle lines and to express a similar faith in masochism's liberating subversion of oedipal power. No matter how strenuously such approaches contest the authority of the father or hypothesize libidinal alternatives to paternal sexuality, they remain bound by a post-Freudian narrative that views masochism as a sexual rebellion governed by an oedipal thematics.

Although recent cultural theorists have often tried to move away from psychoanalysis in order to give masochism a specific cultural and political history, they tend only to sustain the themes and structures of this oedipal narrative. In his introduction to the anthology *One Hundred Years of Masochism* (2000), for example, Sander Gilman claims that masochism is always modeled on the child's fascination with paternal power, and he embraces Deleuze's notion that "the formula for masochism is the humiliated father." Gilman simply emphasizes social rather than private instances of that formula—in particular, battles over what he calls "positive sexuality."[43]

Because it blurs differentials of social power with ambiguities of sexual pleasure, this conception of masochism as an oedipal drama has produced irresolvable disagreements among cultural critics about which political battle the masochist is actually fighting and which side he or she is on. Defining masochism as the destabilization of oedipal sexuality has divided feminist critics, for example, on the issue of whether that destabilization serves feminism or patriarchy, prolonging a debate central to the "sex wars" of the 1980s. Kaja Silverman has famously defended the male masochist as a rebel against oedipal norms that equate masochism with feminine submission.[44] But some have argued that masochism is a ruse by which men proclaim their own sexual marginality in order to secure moral

[42] Gilles Deleuze, *Coldness and Cruelty* in *Masochism* (New York: Zone Books, 1991), pp. 60, 66. This volume was reprinted from the work titled *Sacher-Masoch*, trans. Jean McNeil (London: Faber and Faber, 1971), originally published as "Le Froid et le Cruel," in *Présentation de Sacher-Masoch* (Paris: Editions de Minuit, 1967).

[43] Sander Gilman, "Preface," *One Hundred Years of Masochism: Literary Texts, Social and Cultural Contexts*, ed. Michael C. Finke and Carl Niekerk (Amsterdam: Rodopi, 2000), pp. vii, vi.

[44] Kaja Silverman, *Male Subjectivity at the Margins* (New York: Routledge, 1992), p. 213. Silverman's affirmative reading is echoed in various ways by Carol Siegel, *Male Masochism: Modern Revisions of the Story of Love* (Bloomington: Indiana University Press, 1995); Marianne Noble, *The Masochistic Pleasures of Sentimental Literature* (Princeton: Princeton University Press, 2000), esp. p. 9; and Eileen Gilooly, *Smile of Discontent: Humor, Gender, and*

authority.[45] Others warn that masochism's persistent association with submission makes it a dangerous weapon for women to wield against normative sexual roles.[46]

Theorists of queer sexuality have also disagreed about whether the masochist is a rebel or a collaborator. A long celebratory tradition—particularly evident in writings about lesbian sadomasochism—has seen the queer masochist as a figure who parodies the forms and techniques of political authority in order to release homoerotic energy through ungrounded roleplaying.[47] But skeptics have responded that such roleplaying can make political subjection seem palatable by infusing it with erotic pleasure.[48] Many male theorists have also suspended judgment about the dissident potentials of queer masochistic practices either because, like David Halperin, they see them as identitarian, or because, like Leo Bersani, they find them to lack gay specificity.[49]

Conceiving masochism within frameworks of eroticized mastery and submission (whether derived directly from Freud or not) limits its political legibility. It does so both by narrowing masochistic experience to real or simulated scenes of sexual domination (hence, literary and cultural critics always take S & M as the standard model) and by polarizing the masochist's oedipalized relationship (however reversible eroticization may make it) to authoritarian power. The sexualization of masochism tempts some theorists to read it as a set of infinitely ambiguous tropes for political domination and submission. In *The Mastery of Submission* (1997), for example, John Noyes concludes that "once the technologies of control become the object of erotic attachment, who is to say whether control is subverted by eroticism, or whether eroticism is reintegrated into control?"[50]

Nineteenth-Century British Fiction (Chicago: University of Chicago Press, 1999), esp. pp. 36–37.

[45] Suzanne R. Stewart, *Sublime Surrender: Male Masochism at the Fin-de-Siècle* (Ithaca: Cornell University Press, 1998).

[46] This is a central argument in Jessica Benjamin, *The Bonds of Love: Psychoanalysis, Feminism, and the Problem of Domination* (New York: Pantheon, 1988).

[47] See Pat Califia, "A Secret Side of Lesbian Sexuality," *S and M: Studies in Sadomasochism*, ed. Thomas Weinberg and G. W. Levi Kamel (Buffalo, NY: Prometheus Books, 1983), esp. p. 21; and Samois, *Coming to Power: Writings and Graphics on Lesbian S/M* (Boston: Alyson Publications, 1987). The most sophisticated recent study is Lynda Hart, *Between the Body and the Flesh: Performing Sadomasochism* (New York: Columbia University Press, 1998).

[48] Nick Mansfield, *Masochism: The Art of Power* (Westport, CT: Praeger, 1997), p. 102.

[49] David M. Halperin, *One Hundred Years of Homosexuality and Other Essays on Greek Love* (New York: Routledge, 1990), p. 2; Leo Bersani, "The Gay Daddy," *Homos* (Cambridge: Harvard University Press, 1995), pp. 77–112.

[50] John K. Noyes, *The Mastery of Submission: Inventions of Masochism* (Ithaca: Cornell University Press, 1997), p. 14.

A central contention of this book is that contemporary relational psychoanalysis can provide a better metaphorics for masochism, one less confined to an analysis of sexual domination and submission and more determinate in its decoding of masochism's ideological significance.[51] Relational theorists often argue that the sexual conflicts of the oedipal crisis characterize only one developmental phase within masochism and not necessarily the pivotal one.[52] Contemporary clinicians have claimed, in fact, that sexual practices are among the rarest forms of what they would describe as masochistic behavior.[53] By questioning masochism's supposed genesis in the sexual conflicts of the oedipal stage, relational models have the potential to displace Freudian assumptions that have long undergirded both scholarly work and popular thought.

Before going further, I should emphasize that a metaphorics derived from relational theory cannot lay claim to "the truth" about masochism. Masochism is a recently invented concept, one whose usefulness to explain or to categorize self-wounding practices will always remain a matter of debate. Relational theories of masochism must be considered heuristic, which means that they will never escape tensions with other explanatory paradigms. As we will see, writers like Stevenson, Schreiner, Kipling, and Conrad actually dramatized these tensions in various ways—sometimes by bringing what can retrospectively be described as Freudian and relational paradigms into conflict with one another, sometimes by layering the two together, sometimes by displacing one paradigm with the other. My own emphasis falls heavily on relational theory because it brings to light a long tradition of masochistic representation, flourishing with unusual persistence in the British novel, which has been entirely obscured by post-Victorian culture's identification of masochism with oedipal sexuality. A relational metaphorics can thus broaden the cultural analysis of masochism; but its assumptions about the origins and functions of masochism must necessarily remain provisional.

---

[51] I am using the term "relational" to indicate a general type of psychoanalytic theory that departs from the drive model, turning instead to intersubjective dynamics. This diverse body of work includes British object relations, self-psychology, and relational-conflict theory. Some analysts reserve the term "relational" for a particular group of object-relations theorists, including Harry Stack Sullivan, Erich Fromm, Karen Horney, and other practitioners of what is sometimes also called "interpersonal" theory. My authority for using the term in a more general sense comes from Stephen A. Mitchell, *Relational Concepts in Psychoanalysis: An Integration* (Cambridge: Harvard University Press, 1988).

[52] Jack Novick and Kerry Kelly Novick, *Fearful Symmetry: The Development and Treatment of Sadomasochism* (Northvale, NJ: Aronson, 1996), p. 47. Hereafter cited as *FS*.

[53] Robert A. Glick and Donald I. Meyers, "Introduction," *Masochism: Current Psychoanalytic Perspectives*, ed. Glick and Meyers (Hillsdale, NJ: The Analytic Press, 1988), p. 8, conclude that "sexual" and "characterological" masochism are inconsistently related to one another.

Although the relational literature on masochism is vast, a consensus has emerged on two principal deviations from the Freudian model: first, that masochism should be understood within a narcissistic problematics, not a sexual one; and second, that omnipotent fantasy is the primary narcissistic compensation that masochism provides.[54] These perspectives were first developed as long ago as 1949 by Edmund Bergler, who argued that masochism functions to preserve preoedipal fantasies of omnipotence.[55] The first conflicts the newborn must negotiate, Bergler claimed, involve threats to infantile megalomania—that benign sensation of centrality and control first theorized by Freud and Ferenczi.[56] Bergler contended that frustrations to infantile megalomania produce a sense of helplessness, which can encourage a retreat to omnipotent fantasy—defined by Bergler as the assumption that one possesses magical powers over the limitations of the real world. Omnipotent fantasy is all the more tempting, Bergler reasoned, when emotional support from caregivers (whose role is overlooked in both Freudian and Lacanian psychoanalysis) is lacking. Since Bergler's influential work, attention to the preoedipal origins of masochism in narcissistic trauma has preoccupied relational theorists with problems of individuation, separation, and self-esteem regulation. Trauma in these areas—and the feelings of abandonment, deprivation, and injustice that can result—has been theorized as the primary impetus behind masochistic versions of omnipotent fantasy (or, in shorthand, "masochistic fantasy").

Omnipotent fantasy can certainly thrive without masochism. But from a relational perspective, masochistic strategies are singularly dedicated to producing it. Jack and Kerry Kelly Novick, who have written the most comprehensive recent study, claim that "there is more to a masochistic fantasy than omnipotence but the delusion of omnipotence is a necessary part of it" (*FS*, 61). That self-inflicted pain might imply fantasies of omnipotent power may seem counterintuitive unless we remember that pain is the origin of the need for compensatory fantasies as well as the stubborn reality that omnipotence seeks magically to transform. The "omnipotent system," as it is sometimes called, creates a complex, variable set of relationships between pain and narcissistic compensation and a wide range of

[54] The psychoanalytic literature on masochism has been summarized usefully by William Grossman, "Notes on Masochism: A Discussion of the History and Development of a Psychoanalytic Concept," *Psychoanalytic Quarterly* 55 (1986), 379–413.

[55] Edmund Bergler, *The Basic Neurosis: Oral Regression and Psychic Masochism* (New York: Grune & Stratton, 1949). Deleuze's idealized figure, the "oral mother" (55), is taken directly from Bergler and constitutes his work's closest affinity with the relational paradigm.

[56] Psychoanalytic studies of omnipotent fantasy often hearken back to Sándor Ferenczi, "Stages in the Development of the Sense of Reality," *First Contributions to Psycho-analysis*, trans. Ernest Jones (London: Hogarth Press, 1952), 213–39, although this work largely follows Freud's "Formulations on the Two Principles of Mental Functioning," *SE*, 12: 215–26.

phantasmagoric strategies through which pain might be transformed into omnipotence but also inscribed within it.

Theorists often locate the source of masochistic disorders within this phantasmic economy itself rather than in specific personal traumas or psychological dispositions. The Novicks have gone so far as to claim that "this fantasy structure is 'the essence of masochism'" (FS, 47), parodying a formulation of Freud's that referred to the oedipal contents of the beating fantasy. In most relational work, omnipotent fantasy is conceived as a loosely organized, complex field that can be maintained by a great variety of masochistic practices and can, in turn, help maintain them. This assumption has tended to produce not a single, definitive model of masochistic fantasy but an evolving set of descriptions that one clinician has called a "polyphonic theory."[57] Any attempt to schematize the masochistic fantasy structure may be a futile endeavor; another theorist has described it as an "always multilayered, interdigitated, overdetermined constellation."[58] But despite this fluidity, relational theory has been consistent in viewing masochistic fantasy as a compensation for narcissistic, preoedipal pain and in regarding such fantasy as the organizing structure behind masochistic behavior.

One way to conceptualize masochistic fantasy is to connect particular preoedipal traumas with the omnipotent compensations such fantasy provides. I will describe these relationships by means of a series of clinical anecdotes and profiles, which is the most vivid way to illuminate their dynamics. It is important to remember, though, that masochistic fantasy is an integrated system of transformations that underlies and motivates behavior rather than simply a fragmented set of omnipotent wishes emerging from individual cases. I will provisionally categorize masochistic fantasies of four distinct but often overlapping types: fantasies of total control over others, fantasies about the annihilation of others, fantasies that maintain the omnipotence of others, and fantasies of solitary omnipotence. Each type of masochistic fantasy can be involved with the others, and for that reason they do not constitute a neat schema with which the four writers studied in this book can be correlated. I offer these four categories simply as a device for illustrating the great range and complexity that can be assumed by masochistic fantasy structures, which often blur such categories in practice.

Masochism can enable fantasies of total control in several different ways. Convictions that control is absolute can be derived from the masochist's occasional success in manipulating others, either by eliciting their sympathy or by provoking their punishment. Conversely, a sense of victimization can

---

[57] Margaret Brenman, "On Teasing and Being Teased and The Problem of Moral Masochism," *Psychoanalytic Study of the Child* 7 (1952), 264–85.

[58] Peter Blos, "Sadomasochism and the Defense against Recall of Painful Affect," *Journal of the American Psychoanalytic Association* 39 (1991), p. 420.

authorize the conviction that one is specially entitled to lie, cheat, or use guile to control relationships. But the sensation of omnipotent control can also bear little relation to pragmatic results and can involve purely imaginary, magical reinterpretations of events, as in the delusion of power some masochists come to believe they hold over distant, erratic, or unresponsive caregivers by assuming that their own "badness" accounts for the caregiver's neglect. Imaginary control may also take the form of a reassuring emotional connection to an absent object that has become identified as the source of pain. As one of the Novicks' patients memorably observed: "When I'm feeling good, I feel all alone; when I'm feeling bad, I'm with my mother" (*FS*, 23). In a similar way, exaggerating one's suffering may preserve lost loved ones in fantasy through the process of melancholic introjection that Freud described in "Mourning and Melancholia" (1917).

Masochism can also enable fantasies of infinite destructive power. Such fantasies can be euphoric, but they can also provoke self-punitive expiations that appear to be inextricable from that euphoria. The masochist may come to feel, possibly on the basis of observation, that self-punishment has the power to throw others into catastrophic confusion. In cases in which the masochist believes that his or her body is "owned" by an intrusive caregiver, attacks on the self may be imagined as a way to destroy the caregiver (as well as a strategy for concealing overwhelming hostility). Staging his or her victimization can also allow the masochist to fantasize about the power of annihilative wishes by projecting them onto others and exaggerating their intensity. Such staging can fulfill fantasies of reparation as well if the masochist believes that self-wounding will placate the figure against whom he or she harbors annihilative rage. Moreover, self-punishment may sustain a belief that the masochist's omnipotence is so overwhelmingly destructive that only he or she is powerful enough to control it and that such control depends on turning aggression back on the self.

Masochism may also revolve around the need to preserve fantasies about the omnipotence of others. The masochist's self-victimization may help idealize a parental figure's power in order to protect that figure, upon whom the masochist may be dependent, from his or her own annihilative rage. If the masochist's attempts to achieve autonomy are regarded as overly aggressive—a problem when caregivers feel threatened by the child's independence—then the masochist may be persuaded that parental figures need a helpless victim in order to remain in control, a conviction that can fuel grandiose delusions that the masochist keeps such figures strong by suffering. The masochist can also identify covertly with the apparent indomitability of an aggressive figure. By exaggerating his or her suffering, the masochist can provoke fantasies, too, that an unknown, infinitely sympathetic rescuer will someday appear. The projection of omnipotence onto others serves the masochist in a more general way by producing a morally simplified and thereby controllable world in which

judgments about others are always absolute and always serve the masochist's narcissistic needs. Others are seen either as lovingly authoritarian parental figures who can be safely idealized, evil sadists who can be condemned and hated, or helpless underdogs who confirm the masochist's
self-pitying worldview.

Finally, masochism may transform suffering into glory by enshrining
the masochist in the omnipotent splendor of solitude. In contrast to oedipal masochism, preoedipal masochism may thereby sustain fantasies of
control in the absence of a punitive other. Omnipotent fantasies produced
by self-wounding can sustain illusions, either conscious or unconscious,
that one "need never grow up, grow old, die, have to choose, or give
anything up" (*FS*, 89). They can make it appear that simply having a wish
makes it come true. They can generate emotional grandiosity of various
kinds, but they can also generate the belief—based on demonstrated tolerance for pain—that one can stop having feelings altogether and can live
contented within a glorified narcissistic isolation. The masochist's sense
of control may also accomplish what Janine Chasseguet-Smirgel calls "the
murder of reality" by eradicating the lines of conceptual difference that
defeat omnipotent control: differences of gender, age, temporality, the line
between wishes and satisfactions, and, of course, the difference between
pain and pleasure.[59] More simply, it may transform the feeling of being
unloved into a general sense of specialness, an existential grandeur. Conversely, attacking the self may represent efforts to cope with the dysphoric
loneliness that can be caused by omnipotent fantasy itself. It may, for example, express the wish for a strong, punitive figure who can limit the
masochist's overwhelming rage and isolation.

Because these four types of masochistic fantasy bleed into one another, I
will not maintain distinctions between them rigidly throughout this book,
although such distinctions will play important roles at times, particularly in
my discussion of Conrad. It should also be noted that conceiving masochism
as a fantasy structure that promotes delusions of omnipotence necessarily
broadens the range of behaviors that might be considered masochistic. For
those troubled by such broadening, I must point out that it sets limits on
the term, too. From a relational perspective, masochism includes any pursuit
of physical pain, suffering, or humiliation that generates phantasmic, omnipotent compensations for narcissistic trauma.[60] According to this definition, deferred gratification that facilitates achievement, sublimation for the

[59] Janine Chasseguet-Smirgel, "Sadomasochism in the Perversions: Some Thoughts on
the Destruction of Reality," *Journal of the American Psychoanalytic Association* 39 (1991),
399–415.

[60] This definition is derived from a number of sources but particularly from Jack Novick
and Kerry Kelly Novick, "Not for Barbarians: An Appreciation of Freud's 'A Child Is Being
Beaten,'" *On Freud's "A Child Is Being Beaten,"* ed. Ethel Spector Person (New Haven: Yale
University Press, 1997), p. 43.

purpose of effective functioning, self-denial mandated by moral belief, and suffering or death in the name of a cause one considers just are not inherently masochistic (even if masochistic fantasy might intrude parasitically on such behaviors). In this sense, for example, the patterns of rationalized self-denial that Weber and others have argued were fundamental to western capitalism cannot be considered essentially masochistic, even if they did furnish British culture with a set of everyday practices that could mobilize masochistic fantasy under certain conditions. The study of masochism, which can illuminate the phantasmic narcissism generated by both imperial and class ideologies, thus parallels and sometimes overlaps—without being reducible to—the pleasure-deferring, pragmatic emphasis on productivity described by the Weberian tradition.[61]

By the same token, according to this definition of masochism, such humble acts as failing to turn in homework out of a fear of tarnishing fantasies of narcissistic perfection or deferring to a spouse so as to redirect inwardly what feels like annihilative rage are grounded securely in masochistic fantasy. Recognizing masochism as a fantasy structure designed to create or protect fantasies of omnipotence makes it possible to regard it as a widespread aspect of human experience rather than a pathology or a perversion.[62] But it does not make any voluntary acceptance of pain necessarily masochistic. Conversely, not all instances of omnipotent delusion imply masochism. Only the conjunction of voluntarily chosen pain, suffering, or humiliation with omnipotent delusion—a conjunction that may bear an intermittent or partial relationship to specific physical or mental practices—signals the presence of masochistic fantasy.

Most importantly, conceiving masochistic fantasy as an instrument for transforming narcissistic trauma can help us understand how it intersects social discourses unrelated to sexual masochism or to the oedipal themes with which masochism has been commonly associated. None of the British discourses of imperialism and social class that associated self-inflicted suffering with fantasies of resurgent power simply *is* masochistic. But ideologically driven glorifications of suffering share an affinity with masochistic fantasy and offer possibilities for transforming painful experience into omnipotent delusion. The structures of masochistic fantasy can thus be abstracted from the clinical profiles I have offered and can be understood as a psychosocial system for transforming various kinds of suffering into convictions of magical power. Through masochistic fantasy, the pain of impotence and abandonment is transformed into fantasies of total control,

---

[61] A good recent example of this tradition in Victorian studies is Elaine Freedgood, *Victorian Writing about Risk: Imagining a Safe England in a Dangerous World* (Cambridge: Cambridge University Press, 2000), esp. pp. 144–45.

[62] Theodor Reik, *Masochism in Modern Man* (New York: Farrar and Rinehart, 1941), was the first to attribute masochism to universal unconscious desires for punishment, a position echoed by many contemporary theorists.

the fear of annihilation into fantasies of absolute destructive power, the agony of helplessness into fantasies of benign dependence, and the pain of solitude into fantasies of splendid isolation. By mobilizing these kinds of masochistic fantasy, particular ideologies have acquired extraordinary affective power. The burden of subsequent chapters will be to demonstrate the crucial role of such fantasy at the intersections of imperial and class discourse.

Relational theory, I repeat, cannot tell the whole story about masochism. As Jane Flax has pointed out, drive theory and relational theory often seem incomplete without each other. Relational theorists tend to overlook the erotic life of both mothers and infants (as well as risking potentially reactionary assumptions about motherhood), and the opposition between the two kinds of theory is dangerously gendered—drive theory seemingly centered on the father and relational theory on the mother.[63] These kinds of conflict between the two models should inform literary appropriations of either kind. Indeed, some relational theorists have anticipated this critique and have attempted to bridge the gap between drive-governed and intrapsychic models. Otto Kernberg, Heinz Kohut, and others have formulated developmental models of masochism that mediate between drive and relational theory.[64] These and other theorists of masochism have argued that although masochism's primary fantasy structures may arise in response to preoedipal conflicts, they can be altered dramatically in oedipal or postoedipal stages through sexualization and through sadomasochistic beating fantasies. The Novicks have argued that omnipotent fantasy binds all three developmental phases together and that none should be seen as a privileged origin or explanation (*FS*, 47).

Although I do not pretend to synthesize psychoanalytic models with the thoroughness of these ambitious projects, I have tried to avoid theoretical myopia. I have followed the relational paradigm in assuming that masochistic fantasy is most often organized around a preoedipal narcissistic problematics. Preoedipal fantasies may certainly be eroticized, but because they antedate the patterns of adult sexuality that characterize the oedipal stage, they have a more direct affinity with the problematics of narcissism. But I also assume that masochistic fantasy can be layered with oedipal elements, including sexual conflict. In this spirit, I have distanced myself from essentializing arguments about the political value of preoedipal as opposed to oedipal experience—arguments that drove many celebrations of preoedipal libido in 1980s feminist theory. While I may invoke the preoedipal to

[63] Jane Flax, *Thinking Fragments: Psychoanalysis, Feminism, and Postmodernism in the Contemporary West* (Berkeley: University of California Press, 1990).

[64] Kohut recognizes biologically given drives as well as formative intersubjective experiences. Kernberg has followed Edith Jacobson in trying to integrate drive and relational models. See, in particular, Otto Kernberg, *Borderline Conditions and Pathological Narcissism* (New York: Jason Aronson, 1975).

describe certain kinds of masochistic fantasy, I never suggest that preoedi-
pality can redeem us from the evils of socialization or that a preoedipal
emphasis alone is what makes a given writer interesting, as was the fashion
in psychoanalytic literary criticism a generation ago. I have emphasized
instead the ways in which omnipotent fantasy can wind like a common
thread through both preoedipal and oedipal modes of masochism, linking
narcissistic and sexualized gratifications to one another. On more general
grounds, I have been careful not to identify masochism with gendered or
gay-specific sexualities—elisions that have produced feeble political idealisms as well as a great deal of dangerous stereotyping.

I am aware, too, that sadism can play a role in masochistic fantasy. The
sexualization that occurs in the oedipal stage can make a means to an
end—self-inflicted pain—an end in itself, as omnipotent delusions merge
with sexual wishes and pleasures. But even in such instances, the sexualization of masochistic fantasy can harbor distinctly narcissistic elements:
compensations for abandonment, deprivation, and lack of empathy; the
imaginative projection of omnipotent nurturing figures; the simultaneous
expression of and defense against rage; delusions about self-sufficiency;
and so forth. Masochistic fantasy does not require a sadistic antagonist;
more often than not, it takes nonsexual forms. But on occasions when it
does engage sexual desires or when omnipotent rage itself becomes sadistic, the term "sadomasochism" is warranted.

Throughout the book, I have used the psychoanalytic tools at my dis-
posal rather than taking sides in debates about the origins of masochism.
Because the relational perspective on masochistic fantasy offers powerful
new instruments for cultural analysis, it will remain central. But I have
attended to the variety of different ways in which it interacts with forms
of masochism that are not reducible to a narcissistic problematics.

Multiple Masochisms

The chapters that follow use the psychoanalytic insights outlined above
to demonstrate the vital role played by masochistic fantasy at the intersection of social class and imperial politics. In the process, I am contesting
some common, intertwined assumptions of recent cultural and colonial
studies: that masochism is always about sexuality; that it always organizes
oedipal patterns of dominance and submission; and that, in colonial contexts, it is primarily about race, gender, or sexual orientation rather than
social class. I have sought instead to demonstrate a proposition about certain novelists who were writing at the very time that sexology institutionalized masochism as a sexual practice: that they were creatively inscribing
a broader range of social and cultural discourses into their representations
of masochism.

Stevenson, Schreiner, Kipling, and Conrad were the writers most instrumental in moving colonialism from the periphery of serious British culture to its center. Together, they constitute a spectrum of ideological strategies revolving around the relationships among masochistic fantasy, class, and imperial politics rather than instances of a single practice. Masochistic fantasy enabled Stevenson to resolve on colonial ground ideological contradictions that were at the heart of his own class identity. It provided both Stevenson and Schreiner with heavily revised middle-class ethical models that they used to bolster controversial anti-imperialist positions. By contrast, such fantasy was pivotal in Kipling's efforts to broaden the social base of support for jingoism by fusing the discordant values of competitive middle-class constituencies. It allowed Conrad to splice chivalric and professional ideologies together and thus to reconcile gentrified imperial detachment with middle-class ethics. By virtue of this ordering, the first half of the book demonstrates how masochistic fantasy could serve anti-imperialist causes; the second half shows how it could sustain certain collaborations between imperialist and class ideologies. In each case, I am using the evidence of masochistic fantasy structures to argue for particular, determinate political interpretations while recognizing the pliability of such fantasy in the hands of writers with distinctly different attitudes toward social and imperial conflict. I am also proposing a more important role for ideologies of social class in the shaping of these political rhetorics than has yet been recognized. Moreover, and perhaps most importantly, I seek to demonstrate how those rhetorics were animated affectively as well as how they entered into dialogue with one another by virtue of sharing a common fantasy structure.

The psychoanalytic plot of the book follows masochism's developmental stages, although this is not an evaluative mode of organization. I begin by exploring the preoedipal characteristics of masochistic fantasy in Stevenson and then the collision of preoedipal and oedipal fantasy elements that structured Schreiner's literary and feminist writings. In my discussion of Kipling, masochistic fantasy takes on fully oedipalized features, and for this reason I am more concerned with sadism and sadomasochism in his work than elsewhere. Conradian masochistic fantasy is layered with both preoedipal and oedipal elements and draws more freely than the work of any of the other writers from both registers. This ordering is not meant to suggest that one kind of writer or one kind of masochism is more mature than another. Neither is it meant to suggest that each kind of masochism corresponds to a particular ideological position.

The book is also ordered around other social systems that intersect representations of masochism, class, and imperialism. Two such systems played especially prominent roles in the late nineteenth century because of their strong affinities with masochistic fantasy: religion (particularly evangelicalism) and professionalism. If the first half of the book is more concerned with evangelicalism and the second half with professionalism, that is a fortuitous symmetry and nothing more.

One final note. A few colleagues have described this project to me as a renaming of the terms and theoretical frameworks I employed in *Repression in Victorian Fiction* (1987). I prefer to think of it as a rethinking of the relationship between self-negating practices and Victorian subjectivity, a relationship I tried to describe in that earlier book. I have come to recognize the rigidity of the libidinal model (drawn primarily from Georges Bataille) upon which my earlier work depended. I have had second thoughts, too, about the idealized form of social collectivity I endorsed—an idealization I used to critique what I described as antisocial models of desire in Victorian fiction (models that more recent criticism has elaborated in a variety of useful ways). In the work at hand, I have viewed a broader range of self-negating practices as fantasy structures. I have also emphasized the social and political instrumentality of those practices rather than either their psychological causality or their utopian (or dystopian) potentials. I have also used a highly specific definition of masochism—the production of omnipotent fantasy by means of pain-seeking behavior—in the service of a highly differentiated set of social and cultural interpretations. Those interpretations depend on distinguishing particular forms of class-coded self-victimization from more general concepts, both psychological and social, that cannot be conflated with masochism: sexual repression, the death drive, domination, submission, moral restraint, and so forth. I hope the result has been a more accurate reading of Victorian affective experience and a more nuanced analysis of the ideological conditions of Victorian subjectivity. Above all, I hope to have demonstrated that masochistic fantasy was central, not peripheral, to the psychological and social frameworks of British imperialism.

Chapter One

⸻❧❧⸻

MELANCHOLY MAGIC

ROBERT LOUIS STEVENSON'S EVANGELICAL
ANTI-IMPERIALISM

Most vain, most generous, sternly critical,
Buffoon and poet, lover and sensualist;
A deal of Ariel, just a streak of Puck,
Much Antony, of Hamlet most of all,
And something of the Shorter Catechist.
—W. E. HENLEY, "RLS"

With Christ I am nailed to the cross. It is now no
longer I that live, but Christ lives in me. And the life
that I now live in the flesh, I live in the faith of the Son
of God, who loved me and gave himself up for me.
—GALATIANS 2:19–20

ROBERT Louis Stevenson is an exemplary figure with which to begin a cultural analysis of masochism. Masochistic plots and themes abound in his fiction, whether in the stylized, fin-de-siècle mode of "The Suicide Club" (1878) and *The Dynamiter* (1885), in popular works, such as *The Strange Case of Dr. Jekyll and Mr. Hyde* (1886), or in stories drawing on Scottish folklore, such as "Thrawn Janet" (1881) and "The Body Snatcher" (1881). Masochistic impulses also played a legendary role in his life. There was the self-imposed exile in the wilderness of 1878—his whimsically morbid response when Fanny Osbourne returned to her husband.[1] There was also his nearly fatal pursuit of Fanny from France to California, in defiance of his deteriorating health and her ambivalence.[2] Stevenson once mused, with an uncharacteristic lapse of irony, that he

---

[1] The biographical account most alert to masochistic elements in this pilgrimage is Richard Holmes, *Footsteps: Adventures of a Romantic Biographer* (1985; New York: Vintage, 1996), esp. pp. 38–58.

[2] Good accounts are J. C. Furnas, *Voyage to Windward: The Life of Robert Louis Stevenson* (New York: William Sloane, 1951), pp. 151–75, and James Pope Hennessy, *Robert Louis Stevenson* (London: Jonathan Cape, 1974), pp. 120–32.

hoped one day to be buried in the Scottish hills "with the martyrs."[3] More critically, but with a similar religious metaphorics, Fanny complained, after a decade of marriage, that he was "continually offering himself up on unworthy altars" (*Letters*, 6:320).

Stevenson's immersion in masochism was not just a personal quirk, nor was it a passive manifestation of his melancholic Scottish temperament, the nightmarish religious stories he heard from his childhood nurse, or his severe illnesses. Stevenson often used representations of glorified suffering quite deliberately to renegotiate social and cultural domains in which masochism played a part. In particular, he was acutely aware of the masochistic logic—not that he would have used the term—embedded in British middle-class discourses of social and moral authority. During his last years, Stevenson experimented with a number of ways in which this psychosocial coding might be reworked. Taking advantage of fluid colonial social relations, he affiliated masochistic fantasy with both antiquated and emergent social roles as part of a coherent ideological rewriting. Most importantly, he manipulated middle-class moral masochism to legitimate his anti-imperialist activism—an eccentric but influential crusade, which made him an important figure in Samoan political debates, both locally and in London.

Stevenson's preoccupation with masochism had little to do with sexuality or with oedipal patterns of dominance and submission and more to do with preoedipal narcissistic conflicts—in particular, with difficulties negotiating problems of exclusion and inclusion, autonomy and dependence, abjection and grandiosity. His infamous avoidance of female characters and female sexuality did more than simply banish sexual material to the margins of his work. It actively emptied that material of its dangerous potentials by rewriting it in preoedipal terms—a transformation it shared with the gynophobic, homosocial conventions of much late-century adventure fiction. It is not the case that there is no oedipal or sexual content in Stevenson's writing—that, as G. K. Chesterton put it, he "barricaded himself in the nursery."[4] But the traces of this material in his work are systematically filtered through preoedipal modes of representation. In particular, Stevenson's anti-imperialist rhetoric drew on a preoedipal economy central to masochism, in which self-imposed suffering produces narcissistic fantasies of omnipotence rather than oedipal patterns of mastery and submission.

---

[3] Robert Louis Stevenson, *The Letters of Robert Louis Stevenson*, ed. Bradford A. Booth and Ernest Mehew, 8 vols. (New Haven: Yale University Press, 1994–1995), 8:153. Hereafter cited as *Letters*.

[4] G. K. Chesterton, *Robert Louis Stevenson* (New York: Dodd, Mead & Co., 1928), p. 190.

On account of the idiosyncratic associations Stevenson made with the two interdependent elements of masochism—cherished suffering and fantasies of omnipotence—I will often refer to these elements as the "melancholic" and the "magical" phases in his life and work. The melancholic phase revolves around instances of self-sacrifice or self-punishment, in which exclusion, dependence, or abjection are cherished; the magical phase, by contrast, exaggerates autonomy, inclusion, and self-esteem. In masochistic fantasy, these two phases logically reinforce one another. What is most striking in Stevenson's fiction, however, is how often it splits apart the relationship between the melancholy (or pain-seeking) and the magical (or omnipotent) phases of masochistic fantasy. A familiar device of Stevenson's, the double, proved especially effective as a way of distributing these phases of masochistic fantasy separately to characters who mirror each other in mutually destructive rivalry. Through the figure of the double, Stevenson evoked an economy of melancholic suffering and magical omnipotence in order to rupture that economy, not to reinforce it.

The central argument of this chapter is that, throughout the late 1870s and 1880s, Stevenson used disruptions in the psychological economy of masochism to articulate specific kinds of social incoherence. For most of his career, Stevenson affirmed the strong relationship between masochistic psychology and middle-class social authority, but only by revealing a breakdown in the economies of negation common to both. In his work of the 1890s, however, Stevenson overcame such psychosocial incoherence through a particular kind of anti-imperialism, whose extravagantly self-martyring moralism reconstituted the melancholic/magical economy that his earlier work tended to break apart. Rather than falling prey—like Paul Gauguin, or "coral island" novelists such as R. M. Ballantyne and W.H.G. Kingston—to the Polynesian exoticizing that one critic has called "South Seizure," Stevenson mobilized masochistic fantasy in service of a complex and progressive political engagement.[5] His preoccupation with masochism did not of itself make Stevenson an anti-imperialist. But it did provide him with the affective power and the class coordinates for his anti-imperialist critique, which he was motivated to make, in the first place, because the imperial abuses he observed in the South Seas resonated so strongly with his tragic view of Scottish history.

Crucial to this anti-imperialist reconstitution of melancholy magic was nineteenth-century evangelical discourse, whose masochistic potentials Stevenson associated with metropolitan middle-class decline while at the same time drawing on them as the basis for his own moral authority in the South Pacific. It may be a critical cliché to observe that the stern religious

[5] J. C. Furnas, "Stevenson and Exile," *Stevenson and Victorian Scotland*, ed. Jenni Calder (Edinburgh: Edinburgh University Press, 1981), p. 135.

upbringing Stevenson threw off as a young man persisted in his moralizing tone, his bouts of gloomy pessimism, his numerous essays on ethics, and his nostalgia for the seventeenth-century Scottish Covenanters he proudly claimed as his ancestors. But attention to religious elements in Stevenson's work has focused entirely on Calvinistic themes—original sin, guilt, divine punishment, and predestination—despite the fact that the Stevenson family belonged to the moderate mainstream of Scottish Presbyterianism rather than to its Calvinist branch, the independent Free Church.[6] Stevenson's nurse, Allison Cunningham, may have filled him with terrifying Calvinistic notions, which were both reinforced and tempered by his father.[7] But his mother, the daughter of a moderate Presbyterian minister, was closer to her only child than was the norm among Victorian mothers, and she shared with him an optimistic vision of spiritual redemption.[8] When Stevenson was six, he dictated to his mother his first literary work, *The History of Moses*, a biblical salvation narrative that underlay his view of the South Seas, which he regarded as his own "Pisgah sight" (*Letters*, 6:421) nearly forty years later. Because of critical overemphasis on Scottish Calvinism, the evangelical elements in Stevenson's life and work have not been properly appreciated. This chapter contends that Stevenson found in evangelical thought the materials for a coherent, politically productive masochistic subjectivity, a resolution that eluded him when he struggled with the contradictions of middle-class ideology directly.

Stevenson's allegorical fables often suggest quite strikingly his linked preoccupations with masochistic doubles, social identity, and evangelicalism. But the allegorical fiction does not usually provide stable ways of interpreting these intersections.[9] *Jekyll and Hyde*, for example, plainly revolves around masochistic doubling, but its stylized structure obscures

---

[6] This tendency in Stevenson biography is almost wholly unquestioned. Alan Sandison, *Robert Louis Stevenson and the Appearance of Modernism: A Future Feeling* (New York: St. Martin's, 1996), for example, writes: "Robert Louis Stevenson was the only child of devout Calvinist parents" (21). Claire Harman, *Robert Louis Stevenson: A Biography* (London: HarperCollins, 2005), p. 23, accepts at face-value Stevenson's ironic references to his "Covenanting childhood."

[7] On Thomas Stevenson's moderation of Allison Cunningham's religious extremism, see Ian Bell, *Dreams of Exile: Robert Louis Stevenson: A Biography* (New York: Henry Holt & Co, 1993), pp. 9, 19; or Frank McLynn, *Robert Louis Stevenson: A Biography* (New York: Random House, 1994), p. 17.

[8] See McLynn, pp. 19–20. Furnas, *Voyage to Windward*, pp. 13–14, claims that Margaret Stevenson "lightened" (13) the religious atmosphere in the household and that she "sometimes forbade [her son's] being exposed to the juiciest aspects of Calvinism" (14). But the exact nature of the competing religious influences on the young Stevenson is still in need of careful biographical analysis.

[9] Most readers have seen Stevenson's early fables as polysemous. See, for example, Peter K. Garrett, "Cries and Voices: Reading *Jekyll and Hyde*," *Dr. Jekyll and Mr. Hyde after One*

the significance of such doubling, since magical and melancholic phases of masochism constitute each of the two central figures at different times and in different ways. Throughout much of the story, Jekyll concocts magical potions that give him fantastic power over good and evil, whereas Hyde enacts the darker motivations behind omnipotent fantasy: frustrated rage and guilt. At the end of the narrative, however, Jekyll's potions produce not omnipotent control but suicide, while Hyde's deformed figure presents a series of pitiful images of human helplessness, self-pity, and humiliation that follow on the failure of magical control. Magical and melancholic polarities are thus shared between the two figures, but the relationship between these polarities is fractured across narrative time and blurred across the boundaries of character.[10] The story's class allegory also seems insistent but opaque. While a number of critics have viewed Hyde as a type of the lower orders threatening middle-class social control, others have seen him as the dangerous underside of bohemianism, the projection of Stevenson's anxiety about his own rebellion against bourgeois norms.[11] Middle-class moral and social standards are certainly under siege in the story, but it is never clear where, exactly, the threat might lie. The story also dramatizes some of the central ambitions of evangelicalism: to achieve freedom from human lusts; to experience a momentous conversion in which one is reborn to eternal goodness; to embrace suffering as a sign of such redemption. Yet the metaphysical nature of good and evil in the story makes it difficult to claim that Stevenson evoked these ambitions to comment on a specific religious tradition.

Like many of Stevenson's early fables, *Jekyll and Hyde* points to a linkage of psychological, social, and moral disordering, but without defining the nature of these relationships or the sources of disorder. However evocative such fables may be of the psychosocial intersections at the heart of Stevenson's work, I will begin this chapter by turning instead to his Scottish historical fiction. With their relatively stronger realistic perspectives and their distance from the complexities of fin-de-siècle British society, these narratives offer firmer foundations for ideological reading. In

---

Hundred Years, ed. William Veeder and Gordon Hirsch (Chicago: University of Chicago Press, 1988), pp. 59–72.

[10] I am not aware of any studies of the masochistic structure of *Jekyll and Hyde*, but Hilary J. Beattie, "Father and Son: The Origins of *Strange Case of Dr. Jekyll and Mr. Hyde*," *Psychoanalytic Study of the Child* 56 (2001), pp. 340–50, has brilliantly described the preoedipal oppositions built on the story's doubles.

[11] An example of the former, more common perspective is Patrick Brantlinger and Richard Boyle, "The Education of Edward Hyde: Stevenson's 'Gothic Gnome' and the Mass Readership of Late-Victorian England," *Dr. Jekyll and Mr. Hyde after One Hundred Years*, p. 273. An example of the latter is Stephen D. Arata's excellent "The Sedulous Ape: Atavism, Professionalism, and Stevenson's Jekyll and Hyde," *Criticism* 37 (1995), 233–59.

particular, *The Master of Ballantrae* (1889), which Stevenson wrote in 1888–89 over the course of his long emigration from Europe to Samoa (his residence for the last five years of his life), clarifies the underlying terms of his many narratives of masochistic splitting. This novel, together with some of Stevenson's other Scottish historical novels, focuses the psychosocial intersections so prominent in fables such as *Jekyll and Hyde* by defining the class markings of magical and melancholic doubles in more specific terms.

In the first section of this chapter, I will concentrate on the relationship between masochism and social class in the Scottish novels; in the second, I will discuss what evangelicalism might have had to do with masochistic doubles and, in particular, what images of psychological coherence it offered Stevenson that he could not find by confronting middle-class ideological problems straightforwardly. The remainder of the chapter is concerned with Stevenson's intermittent critique of masochistic fantasy in imperial contexts as well as his redeployment of it as an instrument of anti-imperialist activism.

Masochistic Splitting in the Scottish Novels

Three years after writing *Jekyll and Hyde*, looking back on European culture from the perspectives of the New World and the South Pacific, Stevenson was able to specify the ideological significance of masochistic splitting as he had never done before. In *The Master of Ballantrae*, the two sons of the ancient House of Durisdeer, Henry and James Durie, destroy themselves and each other fighting over inheritance of the Durisdeer title and estate and over the love of their kinswoman Alison—all of which the elder son, James, gloriously forfeits at the start of the novel by joining the doomed cause of Bonnie Prince Charlie. In their collaborative self-destruction, the two characters could not represent magical and melancholic polarities more distinctly. James is a charismatic Machiavel, a brilliant performer and manipulator. Usually called simply "the Master," he reinvents himself inexhaustibly: at various times, he is an English spy, a Scottish war hero, a pirate, a forger, a Hindu Brahmin, and, always, a "consummate actor."[12] His magical powers of self-invention are not limited by inner necessity; one character calls him "a man of pasteboard" (156). Nor are they limited by language, which he conceives as a set of

---

[12] Robert Louis Stevenson, *The Master of Ballantrae* (London: Penguin, 1996), p. 163. I have used reliable recent editions of Stevenson's fiction except in a few cases where these are unavailable. For these works and for all Stevenson's nonfictional writings, I have used the Skerryvore Edition.

empty referents, a bag of tricks: "O! there are double words for every-thing," he says: "the word that swells, the word that belittles; you cannot fight me with a word!" (167–68).[13] They are not even limited by mortality: he fakes his own death twice and improbably survives a duel in which Henry runs him through the chest with a sword. James's motives are dif-fuse, although he is clearly driven by a self-destructive megalomania: "I must have all or none," he declares, "I have a kingly nature: there is my loss!" (167). The self-destructive side of James's megalomania binds him so fatally to Henry that both die, mysteriously, at exactly the same mo-ment, after taking turns pursuing each other halfway around the world. It also places his magical capacities, which project the moral and physical limitlessness of omnipotent fantasy, squarely within the narcissistic prob-lematics of masochism.

Henry, on the other hand, is self-martyring and melancholic. An exalted sense of duty compels him to suffer stoically as James's misrepresentations convince the Durie family and the local village that Henry is a miser and expropriator. Henry is, in fact, bleeding the Durisdeer estate dry, but he does so to support his brother in luxurious exile—a self-imposed, perverse obligation that he keeps piously secret. Henry's only friend, the estate manager Ephraim Mackellar, observes that Henry "was injuring himself . . . by a silence, of which I scarce know whether to say it was the child of generosity or pride" (65). By the time his self-sacrifices are revealed and Henry is exonerated, his martyrdom has become too grotesque to be ex-changed for either love or power. A remorseful Alison accepts him as a husband but confesses: "I bring you no love, Henry; but God knows, all the pity in the world" (18). Even his unsought victories over James, in-cluding the duel to which James had provoked him, only increase Henry's guilt as the usurping son. But while Henry considers himself an innocent victim, his father suggests a more collusive relationship between the two brothers: "there are dangerous virtues," he says, "virtues that tempt the encroacher" (102). Stevenson's narratives of psychological self-division re-verberate in many different interpretive contexts—including, in this case, the collaborative nature of fraternal self-destruction, which was a familiar theme in Scottish narratives like James Hogg's *The Private Memoirs and Confessions of a Justified Sinner* (1824), a novel to which *The Master of Ballantrae* is especially indebted.[14] But one of their functions is always to

---

[13] Nels C. Pearson, "The Moment of Modernism: Schopenhauer's 'Unstable Phantom' in Conrad's *Heart of Darkness* and Stevenson's *The Master of Ballantrae*," *Studies in Scottish Literature* 31 (1999), 182–202, discusses the Derridaean implications of James Durie's con-ception of language.

[14] For an overview of the massive commentary on self-division in Stevenson's work, see Ronald Thomas, "The Strange Voices in the Strange Case: Dr. Jekyll, Mr. Hyde, and the Voices of Modern Fiction," *Dr. Jekyll and Mr. Hyde after One Hundred Years*, pp. 73–93. For a discussion of the parallels with Hogg, see Eric Massie, "Robert Louis Stevenson and

dramatize a masochistic subjectivity that has lost coherence with itself and that fails to achieve the integration of self-imposed suffering with narcissistic omnipotence that is masochism's chief goal.

The split in masochism's phantasmic economy that the two brothers embody so plainly also signals an unmistakable crisis in middle-class identity. Henry's moral masochism projects mid-Victorian middle-class codes of honesty and self-sacrifice back in time, onto the noblesse oblige of a Scottish laird.[15] James's flamboyant recklessness, in contrast, resonates doubly with the romance and gallantry of eighteenth-century Scottish aristocracy and with the glamorous aestheticism of that excrescence of late-Victorian bourgeois culture, the bohemian. The novel thus expresses a rupture between two genealogies of class legitimacy, both of which place self-negating energies at the heart of intraclass competition for cultural authority. Stevenson's fiction is often riven by a conflict between self-denying bourgeois rectitude and the flamboyantly self-destructive eccentricity (which often includes an anachronistic, genteel flair for martyrdom) that marks the bohemian artist. Conflicts between bourgeois proprietorship and impoverished but stylish rebellion thus come to revolve around competing forms of self-negation: on Henry's side, the refusal of pleasure; on James's, the refusal of conventional forms of social power (respectability, wealth, station).[16] Each of these refusals is recuperated in symmetrical ways: for Henry, as moral authority; for James, as a kind of power not limited by concrete forms of measurement—a power sometimes but not always affiliated with the aesthetic.

Stevenson's own ambivalence about middle-class identity is legendary, having been noted in everything from his love/hate relationship with his Tory father to his uneasiness about either having or flouting a mainstream readership.[17] Like many of his own contemporaries—like, indeed, Dr. Jekyll—Stevenson's cultivation of a marginalized intellectual respectability

---

The Private Memoirs and Confessions of a Justified Sinner," Studies in Hogg and His World 10 (1999), 73–77.

[15] Harold Perkin, *The Origins of Modern English Society, 1780–1880* (London: Routledge and Kegan Paul, 1969), argues that, by midcentury, self-effacing middle-class conceptions of honesty and self-denial had displaced upper-class honor—a more warrior-like virtue—as the national norm.

[16] The allegorical opposition of bourgeois to bohemian types has been noted by many critics of the novel, although this opposition has never, to my knowledge, been correlated with masochism or with other forms of self-negation.

[17] In 1886, Stevenson wrote to Edmund Gosse: "I do not write for the public; I do write for money, a nobler deity; and most of all for myself"; but he then wondered: "There must be something wrong in me, or I would not be popular"; and finally despaired: "We are whores, some of us pretty whores, some of us not, but all whores: whores of the mind, selling to the public the amusements of our fireside as the whore sells the pleasures of her bed" (*Letters*, 5:171).

signified his conflicted relationship to his position within middle-class ranks. This conflict often haunted him in the form of a closed symbolic circuit, in which bohemian acts of social or financial askesis were inevitably recuperated as forms of middle-class cultural authority. Such recuperation follows from that uniquely negative relationship between socioeconomic value and cultural capital that Pierre Bourdieu, among others, has traced in European modernism and its nineteenth-century antecedents.[18] Attempting confusedly to untangle this economy of negation, Stevenson himself often had to face the charge that he was a poseur, and that others had outdone him in the purity of bohemian askesis. When he was a young man, the view among his friends was that his cousin Bob was the real bohemian, whereas Stevenson just played at being a rebel to annoy his parents.[19] The writers and artists with whom he associated in the late 1870s at Grez-sur-Loing, near Fontainebleau, were often resentfully aware that Stevenson's decadence was subsidized by his father.[20] Many of his essays from this period also formulate a rather disingenuous argument, which he happened to be pressing on his father at the time: that middle-class youth should be a time of unremunerative, dilettantish idleness, but only because a nonproductive adolescence is actually the best preparation for more mature commitments to professionalism and marriage.[21] These problematic compromises suggest that Stevenson was plagued by a profound self-division rooted in warring ideological imperatives about the significance of self-negation. Loudon Dodd, in *The Wrecker* (1892), is Stevenson's most self-conscious portrait of a man—also subsidized by his father—who never escapes anxiety about whether or not his Parisian bohemianism, his "masquerade of living as a penniless student," is genuine.[22] Through fictional doubles like James and Henry Durie, Stevenson thus articulated a unique historical convergence of psychologically and socially productive forms of self-negation—or, to put it more accurately, a convergence of what he saw as the *failed* coherence of these psychosocial economies.

Stevenson's allegories of class, which saturate his work, are always complex and volatile. But his doubles are consistently marked both with irresolvable middle-class ideological conflicts revolving around contrary

---

[18] Pierre Bourdieu, "The Field of Cultural Production," *The Field of Cultural Production: Essays on Art and Literature*, trans. and ed. Randal Johnson (New York: Columbia University Press, 1993), pp. 29–141.

[19] See McLynn, p. 59.

[20] See McLynn, p. 74.

[21] For a useful discussion, see Liz Farr, "Stevenson's Picturesque Excursions: The Art of Youthful Vagrancy," *Nineteenth-Century Prose* 29 (2002), 197–225.

[22] Robert Louis Stevenson and Lloyd Osbourne, *The Wrecker*, *The Works of Robert Louis Stevenson*, Skerryvore Edition, 30 vols. (London: Heinemann, 1924–1926), 11:54. Hereafter cited as *Works*.

forms of principled self-negation and with the unraveling magical and melancholic psychological economy of masochism. In many nineteenth-century Scottish novels, divisions within the self were correlated to divisions in Scottish national identity, following the pattern of Walter Scott's *Waverly* (1814).[23] But Stevenson also aligned the supposed collapse of Scottish unity in the wake of the Jacobite rebellion with clashing bourgeois and bohemian sensibilities, which enabled him to root such conflicts in what appeared to be an intractable historical determinism. The ideological contradictions represented by the bohemian were, after all, the product of mid-nineteenth-century developments: the emergence of neoromantic aestheticism; the absorption of artistic production by a mass market economy; the construction of professional models of "class transvestism" by new sciences of ethnography and sociology; the masculinist backlash against effeminate, domestic middle-class males; the recolonization of exoticized urban spaces by middle-class cultural elites; the increasing rationalization and corporatization of the workplace; and a number of other historically specific occurrences. Aligning bourgeois and bohemian forms of self-denying heroism with historical traumas of Scottish national self-consciousness obscured the late-nineteenth-century origins of this intraclass competition over cultural authority. The focus of the Scottish novels on suppression of the last credible resistance to internal English hegemony in Scotland further reinforced the seeming intractability of these middle-class conflicts by eliding them with the long-term consolidation of imperial Britain.

Stevenson's Scottish fiction was, of course, concerned with eighteenth-century historical issues in their own right.[24] But, unlike even the misty-eyed Walter Scott, he flattened out the many economic and cultural tensions destabilizing Highland society from within (Europeanization of the clan chiefs, rise of a commercial tenantry, reinvestment of colonial capital by "improving" landlords, growth of an international market economy, and so forth).[25] Instead, the grand, mythologized oppositions Stevenson dramatized—between enfranchisement and disinheritance, public honor and private melancholia, shameful self-preservation and self-destructive folly—created the temporal and spatial distance he needed to focus the

---

[23] Douglas Gifford, "Stevenson and Scottish Fiction: The Importance of *The Master of Ballantrae*," *Stevenson and Victorian Scotland*, p. 69, usefully discusses this correlation between divided self and divided nation in Scottish fiction.

[24] Janet Sorensen, " 'Belts of Gold' and 'Twenty-Pounders': Robert Louis Stevenson's Textualized Economies," *Criticism* 12 (2000), 279–97, has pointed out that Stevenson saw Highlanders accurately as long-term victims of their incorporation into English capitalism rather than romanticizing them as outside of history.

[25] An excellent discussion is Eric Richards, *The Highland Clearances* (Edinburgh: Birlinn Limited, 2002), pp. 32–51.

complexities of psychosocial economies of negation. This working through was a gradual process, one that was only completed affirmatively, as we shall see, in his South Seas fiction. By contrast, his Scottish novels tend toward increasing ideological pessimism—particularly about the prospects for healing the rift between bourgeois and bohemian social identities.

In his earlier novel *Kidnapped* (1886), for example, Stevenson dramatized the same psychosocial conflicts that structure *The Master of Ballantrae*, but in less precise and less fatalistic terms. One of *Kidnapped*'s two protagonists, David Balfour, like Henry Durie, is a serial victim. David's self-esteem is sorely tried by "all those tribulations that were ripe to fall on me," which include shipwreck, suspicion of murder, and being sold into slavery.[26] As a result, he is prone to fits of despair. His companion, Alan Breck Stewart, finds him to have a "long face" (53) and to lack "a mettle spark" (142). Often yielding to "that kind of anger of despair that has sometimes stood me in stead of courage" (127) or even to the wish that he might "gladly have given up" (144), David is not above vindictive masochistic fantasies, either. At one point, surrendering to hopelessness, he "began to glory in the thought of such a death, alone in the desert, with the wild eagles besieging my last moments. Alan would repent then" (162). Yet David's melancholic bouts never result in the self-martyring morbidity that deforms Henry Durie. Nor is David's devotion to self-sacrificial duty embedded in the Puritan moral tradition or in any other specifically bourgeois social origin. Quite the contrary, David's self-denying sense of duty is inspired by the chivalrous honor modeled by Alan, which Alan is fond of attributing to his noble birth.

Despite these blurrings of the simple magical/melancholic opposition Stevenson would later develop more distinctly in *The Master of Ballantrae*, David's melancholic helplessness is plainly contrasted with Alan's superhuman power. Alan first enters the narrative when he saves himself from a rammed boat—although everyone else aboard it drowns—by leaping up, fantastically, onto the bowsprit of the brig that has rammed him. He then fights off the brig's entire crew nearly single-handedly, killing or wounding most of them. A formidable swordsman, a "dead shot" (76), and an accomplished musician who makes up songs about his own triumphs while in the course of them, Alan is meant to seem larger than life. Perhaps not quite as cultivated as James Durie, he is nevertheless, like James, a brilliant actor. Pretending to be an emissary of Highland kidnappers at the end of the novel, Alan displays considerable performative exuberance as he baits David's Scrooge-like uncle Ebenezer into a confession. Blessed with these magical talents and powers of self-invention, Alan is

---

[26] Robert Louis Stevenson, *Kidnapped, Kidnapped and Catriona* (Oxford: Oxford University Press, 1986), pp. 17, 26.

also, like James, charmingly arrogant. His only weakness, appropriately, is
his immense vanity. Yet Alan never enacts any of the destructive or vindictive aspects of omnipotent fantasy that Stevenson dramatized in James—
or in *Jekyll and Hyde*, for that matter. Indeed, the writing of *Jekyll and
Hyde*, which took place between the beginning and the completion of
Kidnapped, seems to have absorbed the darker psychological energies of
omnipotent fantasy that Stevenson declined to associate with his boyish
Scottish doubles. The two heroes may be patterned on melancholic and
magical doubles, but their polarization is neither as clear-cut nor as implosive as such doubling would become in the later Scottish novels.

   The social coding of melancholic and magical doubling is also less precisely and less fatalistically worked out in *Kidnapped*. Of course, David's
and Alan's divided national loyalties are mapped to some extent onto Stevenson's constantly reiterated opposition of bourgeois and bohemian figures. David's inherited property and social sanctuary, guaranteed by his
Whig loyalty to the English crown, contrast plainly with Alan's impoverished, idealistic flight to France. The contrast evokes underlying oppositions of property and principle, enfranchisement and disenfranchisement,
security and risk taking that inevitably come between the two friends.
Even the one momentous quarrel between them, triggered by Alan's bor-
rowing and then gambling away David's money, explicitly defines a clash
between bourgeois self-discipline and bohemian self-indulgence: "Whee-
dling my money from me while I lay half-conscious, was scarce better than
theft; and yet here he was trudging by my side, without a penny to his
name, and by what I could see, quite blithe to sponge upon [me]" (157).
But the bourgeois/bohemian opposition between the two central characters remains tenuous, if for no other reason than because their personal
loyalty seems to transcend ideological conflict. While *Kidnapped* clearly
incorporates Stevenson's characteristic linkage of magical and melancholic
doubles with middle-class ideological conflicts, it leaves the terms of this
conjunction inchoate and the prospects for resolution guardedly hopeful.
Alan and David's friendship is suspended at the end of the novel but by
no means broken.

   I am stressing the gradualness with which Stevenson came to clarify the
relationship between psychological and social economies of negation in
order to suggest a point I will later address in greater detail: the transformative impact that colonial locales had on his representations of masochism. But it is also important to recognize the trajectory of the Scottish
novels toward a more intractable sense of ideological disjunction. Stevenson's other Scottish novels, *Catriona* (1893) and *Weir of Hermiston*
(1896)—the latter not completed at his death—both use disrupted masochistic economies to express fatal middle-class ideological crises. And in
these late novels, Stevenson left as little hope for resolving such crises as

he had in *The Master of Ballantrae*. If anything, he took the collapse of psychic economies and the parallel disordering of social identity to new extremes. In each novel, the magical component of masochistic fantasy is either withdrawn to a narrative distance, leaving the protagonists mired in unproductive kinds of self-martyrdom, or it is expressed only in its most disturbing form: as vindictive, annihilative rage. At the same time, the gulf between bourgeois enfranchisement and romanticized disenfranchisement in these later novels becomes hopelessly unbridgeable except through ironic or sentimental gestures.

In *Catriona*, David Balfour is once again subjected to relentless victimization. He is coerced and swindled by the Lord of Prestongrange, nearly murdered by a hired assassin, kidnapped and imprisoned on an island haunted by the ghosts of religious martyrs, and transformed through the foul play of English authorities from a courageous hero into an apparent coward in the eyes of his Highland friends. "The whole world is clanned against me" (269), David despairs.[27] But, in contrast to his perseverance in *Kidnapped*, David becomes increasingly aware in *Catriona* that his crusade in the name of an obscurely defined sense of justice (the goal of which is the prevention of James Stewart's execution) may amount only to self-destruction: "It seemed I was come to the top of the mountain only to cast myself down; that I had clambered up, through so many and hard trials . . . all to commit mere suicide at the last end of it, and the worst kind of suicide besides, which is to get hanged at the King's charges" (232). When he learns, at the end of Part I, that despite his efforts James has been hanged, David laments: "So there was the final upshot of my politics!" (382).

In Part II, David is consoled only with his extraordinarily melancholic courtship of Catriona, which revolves around his painful obsession with the "sin" (423) of his conduct toward her. Forced by bizarre circumstances into a platonic cohabitation (she is passed off to the world as his sister), David suffers lugubriously from the moral quandaries involved: "I . . . reflected, and repented, and beat my brains in vain for any means of escape. . . . Tender and bitter feelings, love and penitence and pity, struggled in my soul" (423). The novel may end in conventional marital union, but David's courtship is conducted through elaborate rituals of guilt and self-reproach that continually disrupt progress toward romantic resolution. One of the most inept and self-lacerating courtships in all British literature, David and Catriona's love affair is constructed around the notion, as David puts it, that "there were never two poor fools made themselves more unhappy in a greater misconception" (435).

---

[27] Robert Louis Stevenson, *Catriona*, *Kidnapped and Catriona* (Oxford: Oxford University Press, 1986), p. 269.

Alan himself, David's magical counterpart in *Kidnapped*, puts in only the most peripheral appearances in *Catriona*, and the two men never form the active alliance of personal loyalties that had overcome ideological conflict in the earlier novel. Instead, omnipotent power in *Catriona* is vested in English political authority, against which David struggles in vain. In this novel, it is the English network of spies, assassins, kidnappers, and bought-off advocates that seems to be everywhere, to know everything, and to stick at nothing in reinventing its purposes, principles, and methods in order to destroy obstacles to its power. Prestongrange, in particular, exercises authority with some of the histrionic brilliance and effectiveness of James Durie. An "artful performer" who is full of "dissimulation" (359), he is "as false as a cracked bell" (365).

In ideological terms, David's fruitless martyrdom leaves him defeated on several fronts. Most importantly, his fascination with protobohemian Jacobites comes to nothing. His failure to save James Stewart is only one aspect of this anticlimax. More fundamentally, though David passionately identifies with people who are by definition his political enemies, he does so only in the compromised sense that he tries to prove in an English court that his friends are, in fact, harmless innocents. His crusade to exonerate Alan and James thus has the ironic effect of hollowing out their alluring stature as rebels. David is not the only compromised rebel in the novel. Catriona's heroic rescue of her father from prison is also revealed to be a sham. The escape is actually winked at by her father's jailers, who had previously arranged the fake rescue in exchange for his treacherous testimony against James Stewart. The novel's primary symbolic project—to bridge the political and cultural gaps between social insiders and outsiders through David's love for Catriona—is undermined by these ironies.

Weir of Hermiston is similarly centered on the psychosocial dysfunctionality of masochism. In this last, unfinished novel, the social polarities of *The Master of Ballantrae* are in one important respect inverted: in the later novel, it is the representative of the law, Adam Weir, who exercises omnipotent rage, while legendary Scottish outlaws are melancholic and inept martyrs. But this reversibility only underscores the similarity between the economies of negation Stevenson attributed to bourgeois and antibourgeois ideological systems. Archie, Adam's son—by turns melancholic and intolerant, respectable and rebellious—cannot contain the multiple, reversible forms of psychosocial division that he inherits from both his family and his nation. A student of the law aspiring to his father's profession, Archie is both embryonic revolutionary and "laird" (102) of Hermiston. Psychologically, he is, on the one hand, a "rather melancholy young gentleman" (102), whose "doleful" (130) impulses contribute to his being "parsimonious of pain to himself " (101) and to his conducting, like David Balfour, a deeply melancholic romance. On the other hand, though, Archie is a "chip of the old block" (73) in the sense that he can be as intolerant and authoritarian as his father. At its worst, this self-exalting, vindictive streak compels him to denounce an execution ordered by his father, the impulsive act for which he is banished to Hermiston. It would most likely also have played a role in the unwritten scene in which Archie murders Frank Innes, the seducer of his lover, Kirstie Elliott.[28] Hopelessly divided against himself, Archie is both the instrument through which his father and Frank destroy themselves and the agent of his own banishment.

These fatal psychological splits correspond to the novel's central ideological conflict. As was the case with David Balfour's love for Catriona, Archie's love for Kirstie holds out the promise of bridging the gulf between respectable insiders and romanticized outsiders. Archie, the laird and law student, is instinctively drawn to the rustic girl with "the poetic temper" (133), who has talents like those of a "dramatic artist" (139). If Stevenson did intend Archie and Kirstie to marry, though, we can only assume that, like the marriage of David and Catriona, their union would have been blighted by melodramatic traumas: Kirstie's spoiled honor, Archie's murder and (indirect) parricide, flight from prison, and exile. In all these ways, *Weir of Hermiston* promises no healing of the social divisions Stevenson consistently tied to masochistic splitting.

Before leaving the Scottish novels, we should note that *Weir of Hermiston* illuminates another important feature of Stevensonian masochism. In representative fashion, the novel constructs masochistic relationships exclusively in preoedipal rather than oedipal terms. Critics have often claimed that Stevenson's chronic father/son conflicts revolve around "oedipal rage."[29] But the struggle between Adam and Archie—perhaps the most fully developed of these conflicts in all of Stevenson's fiction—is structured by preoedipal failures, sorrows, and compensations. Archie may figuratively "strike his father" (81) by denouncing the execution, and he may suffer from his sense of his own "impotence" (88) in this act of "rebellion" (77) against a father who reminds him of "something very big" (93). But these superficially oedipal patterns are absorbed into the preoedipal traumas of neglect, separation, suffocation, and betrayal that the two men inflict on one another. Adam has no apparent interest in a relationship of punitive domination toward his son, or in tying punishment to erotic transgression, or in deriving from his paternal authority the kind of sadistic pleasure he takes from prosecuting criminals. Rather than playing any of these oedipal roles, Adam feels only blank indifference toward Archie. Such indifference reflects Adam's general narcissistic withdrawal: he "sufficed wholly and silently to himself " (69).

---

[28] See Sidney Colvin's "Editorial Note" to the 1896 edition, Robert Louis Stevenson, *Weir of Hermiston and Other Stories* (London: Penguin, 1979), pp. 293–94.

[29] William Veeder, "Children of the Night: Stevenson and Patriarchy," *Dr. Jekyll and Mr. Hyde after One Hundred Years*, p. 126.

On his side, Archie does not so much rebel against his father as disavow him. Far from wanting to supplant his father, to usurp his power, or to violate his father's sexual prohibitions, Archie's attitude, like Adam's toward his son, is best characterized by the absence of feeling. The result of this reciprocal self-absorption of father and son is that "there were not, perhaps, in Christendom two men more radically strangers" (74). Nevertheless, what Archie plainly misses from his father is the kind of sympathetic tenderness that he received from his mother while she was alive and that he receives from his surrogate father, Glenalmond. Fittingly, Adam punishes Archie with banishment rather than with the physical, intimate, and punitive dominance associated with oedipal conflicts. Archie responds to this banishment with a "strange instinct of obedience" (84), in which his placid submission becomes an emblem of both his sense of guilt and his apparent hope that punishment might win back his father's love.

Stevenson's father/son conflicts are routinely structured by preoedipal themes and traumas. The father in Stevenson's works, if not dead, is always absent, weak, or neglectful, and the enraged frustrations of the son can usually be read as responses to these disappointments rather than as attempts to seize or displace the father's authority. Relationships of outright rivalry in Stevenson's fiction take place not between fathers and sons but between brothers, whose competitive self-destruction can often be construed as a fruitless attempt to win the love of negligent fathers or father figures. Moreover, Stevenson's fathers do not assume the oedipal task of impeding the son's sexual access to the mother. Rather, they fail the son by not *being* the mother—that is, by not extending maternal forms of protection and love. It is difficult to imagine a more complete rewriting of oedipal content in preoedipal terms. One important result of such rewriting is the emphasis on narcissistic traumas—rather than sexual ones— that these father/son relationships dramatize. Hilary Beattie has instructively traced Stevenson's preoedipal narratives back to what she calls his "quasi-maternal, pre-oedipal father," a figure who oppresses not through authoritarian prohibitions but through refusals to accept separation and through tendencies to encourage feelings of guilt in the son about autonomy.[30] But the prospects for a psychobiographical interpretation are peripheral to my principal contention: that masochistic responses to social or psychological crises are always mediated in Stevenson's work through a narcissistic problematics rather than through the sexual conflicts that characterize oedipal rebellion.

---

[30] Beattie, p. 346. Hilary J. Beattie, "A Fairbairnian Analysis of Robert Louis Stevenson's *Strange Case of Dr. Jekyll and Mr. Hyde*," *Fairbairn, Then and Now*, ed. Neil J. Skolnick and David E. Scharff (Hillsdale, NJ: Analytic Press, 1998), pp. 197–211, points out that apparent oedipal conflicts in Stevenson's work always lack a vital element: sexual rivalry for a female object of desire.

Stevenson's Scottish fiction does not overcome patterns of masochistic splitting, nor does it promise any resolution of the conflict between bourgeois and antibourgeois factionalism. But the fatal impasses Stevenson increasingly emphasized in Scottish history and culture helped energize his search for varieties of psychosocial resolution in his South Seas fiction. At the very time that he was describing David Balfour's disillusionment with politics, he was enthusiastically embroiling himself in colonial political causes. Despite his persistent ambivalence about these causes, he seemed to believe that they promised the kind of psychosocial equilibrium his Scottish novels never achieve. "I have been wholly swallowed up in politics," he wrote in 1891, calling it "a mass of fudge and fun, which would have driven me crazy ten years ago and now makes me smile" (*Letters*, 7:163).

Stevenson's sense of psychosocial regeneration in the South Seas depended in part on shifting political landscapes. Turning away from a Scottish world that he saw as long since embedded in imperial Britain, he engaged a world in which the balance of colonial authority and resistance had not yet been settled. But this shift accompanied a more profound change in the thematic center of Stevenson's work. In the South Seas, Stevenson abandoned his earlier attempts to heal middle-class ideological conflicts between bourgeois and bohemian figures. What he sought to cultivate instead was an anti-imperialist moral authority that could be coherently grounded in masochistic fantasy. To achieve such authority, Stevenson drew on an anachronistic source of middle-class unity—its traditions of evangelical moral masochism—even as he turned away from the contemporary intraclass ideological conflicts that had absorbed and troubled all of his earlier work.

Before taking up the reorganization of masochism in Stevenson's South Seas fiction, I must first trace its evangelical cultural and historical contexts. In the next section, I will digress from Stevenson's work at some length to chart the psychological and social dimensions of evangelicalism that made it a useful instrument for Stevenson on colonial terrain. This detour will be a useful one if it helps explain Stevenson's strategic manipulation of masochistic fantasy in his South Seas writings, as well as shedding light on similar strategies adopted by other writers studied in this book.

EVANGELICALISM: PAIN IS POWER

That masochistic splitting might express a nostalgia for lost ideological and psychological coherence is not as strange an idea as it may sound, once we recognize the coherent masochistic logic at the evangelical foundations of middle-class social power. Victorian middle-class morality has always been synonymous with self-sacrifice and self-denial, but such moral masochism has not usually been understood to harbor anything resembling omnipotent fantasy. A masochistic economy, comprising both melancholic and magical phases, was nevertheless central to the evangelical tradition that fueled middle-class cultural hegemony up until the last decades of the nineteenth century. Stevenson's work can be understood only in the context of this tradition, which was deeply woven into his immediate cultural and personal past.

The term "evangelicalism" does not designate a religious sect (the movement was cross-denominational) but a moral and emotional disposition derived from principles central to the British religious revival launched in the 1730s. Of course, the evangelical tone that pervaded much of British culture from the late eighteenth century through the first half of the nineteenth influenced many who did not consciously share these principles. But most observers—then and now—agree that evangelical sensibilities, however diffuse or secularized they became, sprang from a few central tenets of the "religion of the heart" preached by John Wesley, George Whitefield, William Law, Henry Venn, and others from Wesley's "Holy Club" at Oxford. I am concerned primarily with two of these tenets. I will have little to say about the movement's biblicalism (its faith in the authority of the bible over that of priests or sacraments) or its activism (its injunction to bring the social order into conformity with its own moral codes). The latter impulse did play a role in Stevenson's anti-imperialist crusade of the 1890s, as we will see. But to uncover the masochistic elements embedded in evangelicalism, I will concentrate on two of the movement's other principles: its crucicentrism, which stressed the bloody sacrifice of Christ as the means of atonement for sin; and its conversionism, which held that moral life must be transformed through an illumination by faith and that such transformations are sudden, emotional, and momentous.[31]

Crucicentrism and conversionism implied a number of other common evangelical assumptions, some of which were central to the Puritan tradition from which evangelicalism derived: that human nature is inherently depraved, that life is an arena of moral trial, and that redemption from sin comes through suffering. But they also introduced new ideas: that Christ's crucifixion enacted a substitutive model of redemptive suffering; that moral reformation requires identification with Christ's pain and, through it, with God's grace; and that such identification is accompanied by a euphoric assurance about one's individual salvation. All of these beliefs revolved around evangelicalism's emphasis on life-changing conversion experiences, which were made possible through passionate identification with the atonement wrought by Christ on the cross.[32]

---

[31] These four defining characteristics have been theorized in an influential work by David W. Bebbington, *Evangelicalism in Modern Britain: A History from the 1730s to the 1980s* (London: Unwin Hyman, 1989), pp. 2–17.

[32] John Wesley claimed that nothing "is of greater consequence than the doctrine of Atonement. It is properly the distinguishing point between Deism and Christianity." *The Letters of the Rev. John Wesley*, ed. J. Telford, 8 vols. (London: Epworth Press, 1931), 6:297.

It has been noted before that this network of beliefs combines preoccupations with both self-punishment and megalomania. Wesley encouraged the view, for example, that human desire is naturally limitless, a point he stressed in order to require and to justify continual self-punishment.[33] But a preoccupation with states of unlimited desire was not simply the moral pretext for evangelical self-denial. Fantasies about the very existence of limitless desires—and correspondingly infinite fulfillments—can be produced by masochistic self-denial, for reasons I have outlined in the introduction. It was this masochistic fantasy structure, deeply grounded in evangelical thought, that underlay the megalomaniacal force of self-justifying middle-class authority.

Such dynamics should not be associated only with extreme, pentecostal forms of evangelicalism. Even moderate evangelical sensibilities shared the economy of melancholic and magical narcissism that characterizes masochistic fantasy.[34] In most evangelical experience, there was a persistent oscillation between melancholic pessimism and euphoric optimism, between a belief in God's eagerness to punish sinners and his certainty to reward them. The spirit of such psychological interdependence motivated William Harcourt, a friend of the influential preacher and theologian William Wilberforce, to declare that "pain and suffering are our path to the noblest excellences of our nature."[35] Boyd Hilton records that evangelical responses to personal catastrophe often drew on this conjunction in seemingly perverse ways:

> It is often recorded that victims of business crashes showed relief and even elation when the long-expected blow struck. "We shall be the better for passing through the ordeal," confided Gladstone's father in 1826, a comment which gives point to Disraeli's description of Archibald Constable as indulging in an "ecstasy of pompous passion" while on the point of his "fatal and shattering bankruptcy" the year before.[36]

Evangelicals were less despondent and gloomy than their Puritan or Calvinist forebears, and they denounced the spectacles of physical self-laceration they associated with Catholicism or with Hindu ascetics. But by associating pain with atonement, they upheld the notion that private, voluntary suffering promised salvation and vice versa.

This masochistic logic can be found plainly in Wesley's writings. His emphasis on self-denial and on the necessity of pain to spiritual rebirth is

---

[33] Christopher Herbert, *Culture and Anomie: Ethnographic Imagination in the Nineteenth Century* (Chicago: University of Chicago Press, 1991), pp. 30–32.

[34] This claim does not diminish the useful distinction made, among others, by Boyd Hilton, *The Age of Atonement: The Influence of Evangelicalism on Social and Economic Thought, 1795–1865* (Oxford: Clarendon Press, 1988), p. 16, between evangelicals who believed that intervention could improve social life and those whose fatalism argued against initiating reform.

[35] William Vernon Harcourt, *Sermons*, ed. W. F. Hook (London: [printed], 1873), p. 55.

[36] Hilton, p. 145.

always balanced by promises of "eternal pleasure," "unmerited love" from God, and eternal life as the reward for such suffering.[37] More importantly, Wesley's chief addition to the Erasmian tradition of Christian humanism was a kind of mystical piety, sustained by his lifelong emphasis on human "participation" in the divine. Wesley's sermons are suffused with the conviction that the reward for self-sacrifice is "that we may evermore dwell in [God], and he in us."[38] In such a state of fusion with the Almighty, believers "are endued with power from on high" and "every thought which arises in their heart is holiness unto the Lord" (*Works*, 1:236). Wesley's emphasis on the personal experience of God's love was a marked departure from the impersonal rationalism of the Puritan tradition or of the eighteenth-century Deism that had contested it. While it may be questionable how many of Wesley's disciples followed him in doctrinal matters, the power of an emotional identification with God's grace as an alternative to notions of self-reform based solely on moral teaching was without doubt a key to evangelicalism's popular appeal.[39]

All varieties of evangelicalism also maintained the centrality of the conversion experience, which depended similarly on masochistic economies. Evangelical rebirth produced the rapturous conviction that one had been unilaterally forgiven and saved, an experience of "justification" that could be regularly revisited through self-denial. Belief in rebirth and justification magically combined certainty in God's punitive severity with certainty about salvation in a self-exalting yet self-abasing euphoria that Henry Abelove has termed "the internalization of apocalypse."[40] Evangelical "assurance"—the unshakeable belief that one had been saved through God's love—seemed to many contemporaries the greatest novelty about early Methodism and one of its most powerful recruiting tools as well as one of the chief targets of skeptics.[41] This exalted state of assurance was at the root of Wesley's break with Calvinists and Lutherans, who condemned his doctrine of "perfection in this life," a doctrine that cannot be found in that touchstone of the Puritan tradition, John Bunyan's *The Pilgrim's Progress* (1678).

[37] John Wesley, *The Bicentennial Edition of the Works of John Wesley*, ed. Frank Baker, 23 vols. (Nashville: Abingdon Press, 1986), 2:242; 2:245; 1:208. Hereafter cited as *Works*. On constant and universal self-denial, see "Self-Denial," 2:236–50.

[38] *The Book of Common Prayer as Revised and Settled at the Savoy Conference, Anno 1662* (London: William Pickering, 1844), p. 359. This formulation is often referenced by Wesley.

[39] Herbert Schlossberg, *The Silent Revolution and the Making of Victorian England* (Columbus: Ohio State University Press, 2000), p. 31.

[40] Henry Abelove, *The Evangelist of Desire: John Wesley and the Methodists* (Stanford: Stanford University Press, 1990), p. 95.

[41] Bebbington, p. 43, notes that assurance was present in Puritanism but that Methodism made it available to all believers as well as tying it to Christ's atonement.

Evangelicalism's fusion of self-denial with spiritual self-aggrandizement played a central role in creating the moral foundations of middle-class culture. While various aspects of evangelicalism touched every corner of British society, Wesley's doctrine of worldly perfection was strongly resisted not only by strict puritanical sects but also by the Church of England. One reason for this resistance from both above and below was that Wesley's perfectionism laid great emphasis on the worth of the individual. Some historians have thus seen it as laying the foundations for political liberalism by lending individual self-control a moral justification, which could, in turn, authorize certain kinds of individual liberty. Hence, as Hilton has pointed out, the striking phraseology used by liberal middle-class economists who endorsed "the gospel of free trade" and "the sacred laws of political economy."[42]

Of course, not every segment of Victorian middle-class culture was equally suffused with evangelical masochism. Nevertheless, a highly conventionalized link was forged between evangelicalism and the respectable middle class during the first half of the nineteenth century. Appreciating the historical abruptness of evangelicalism's convergence with middle-class culture as well as the pervasiveness of this bond is crucial to understanding the evangelical nostalgia of late-century writers with conflicted relationships to their middle-class social origins—Stevenson among them.

Throughout the eighteenth century, there were two sociological strands to the evangelical revival: working-class Methodism and upper-class enclaves within the Anglican Church, such as the Clapham and Cambridge sects. The two phenomena were linked, since the missionary zeal of Anglican Evangelicals compelled them to carry the "religion of the heart" to the working-class crowd; indeed, through the early part of the nineteenth century, most Methodists considered themselves members of the Church of England (even though Methodists formally seceded in 1795).[43] Methodism swept through working-class culture in the mid-eighteenth century, where it was most concentrated among the skilled workers who formed the upper echelons of the lower social strata. By contrast, Evangelical clergymen made only small inroads into the Anglican hierarchy, although the movement began to attract upper-class converts when Hannah More, Wilberforce, and others started campaigning among their social equals in the 1780s and 1790s.

Middle-class Dissent, however, proved resistant throughout the eighteenth century. The Methodist movement, given its mass character, its emotionalism, and its antagonism to religious hierarchies, was often felt

---

[42] Hilton, p. 6.

[43] Following one of the competing conventions among religious historians, I reserve "Evangelical" with a capital "E" for members of the Church of England.

to be insurrectionary, especially in the years immediately before and after
the French Revolution.[44] Many recent historians have argued that Methodism contained working-class unrest and prevented it from boiling over
into political revolution.[45] But contemporary observers of revivalism were
often far more wary. Revolutionary politics aside, many in the middle class
believed that Methodist rapture made workers unfit for labor. Dissenters
were so embattled against the established church that they were also reluc-
tant to embrace forms of religious activism that might further increase
their political and social exclusion.

In the early nineteenth century, however, the sociological center of gravity of the evangelical movement underwent a massive shift. By midcentury,
the Church of England had become increasingly gentrified and antienthu-
siast. Meanwhile, working-class Methodism declined sharply. Anticlerical-
ism, which arose from the clergy's general indifference to working-class
social concerns; the sectarian fragmentation of Methodism (notably, the
schism between Wesleyans and "Primitive" Methodists in 1810); the
growth of organized lower-class Sunday amusements, which impacted
church attendance negatively—all took their toll. By 1845, Friedrich Engels claimed that the "workers . . . are quite free from that religious fanati-
cism which holds the bourgeoisie in its grip. If any of the workers do
possess some veneer of religion it is only a nominal attachment to some
religious body, and does not indicate any spiritual conviction."[46] Methodist ministers, it should be noted, did not respond creatively to any of these
crises. Thomas Carlyle, commenting on the stagnation of early-nineteenth-century revivalism, called it "Methodism with its eye forever
turned on its own navel."[47]

Among the middle classes, however, the upsurge in evangelical activity
in the first half of the nineteenth century was dramatic. Although evangelicalism did not begin penetrating Dissenting chapels until late in the eighteenth century, by 1832 the Baptist Union defined itself officially as a

---

[44] The classic history of this anxiety is Ford K. Brown, *Fathers of the Victorians: The Age
of Wilberforce* (Cambridge: Cambridge University Press, 1961).

[45] David Martin, *A Sociology of English Religion* (New York: Basic Books, 1967), p. 17,
noted long ago that historians often claim that Methodists dampened revolutionary fervor.
For a more sophisticated reading of these dynamics, see Mark A. Noll, "Revolution and the
Rise of Evangelical Social Influence in North Atlantic Societies," *Evangelicalism: Compara-
tive Studies of Popular Protestantism in North America, the British Isles, and Beyond, 1700–
1990*, ed. Mark A. Noll, David W. Bebbington, and George A. Rawlyk (Oxford: Oxford
University Press, 1994), pp. 113–36.

[46] Friedrich Engels, *The Condition of the Working Class in England*, trans. W. O. Hender-
son and W. H. Chaloner (1845; Stanford: Stanford University Press, 1968), p. 141.

[47] Thomas Carlyle, *Past and Present, The Works of Thomas Carlyle*, Centenary Edition, 30
vols. (New York: AMS Press, 1969), 10:117.

congregation devoted to "the sentiments usually denominated evangelical," a declaration paralleled by a similar statement from the Congregationalist Union the following year.[48] In the first decades of the nineteenth century, the steady growth of evangelical activism swept up Quakers, Presbyterians, and Unitarians—all three denominations having been in decline before this infusion of new energy. While class lines could sometimes blur within congregations, the principal evangelical denominations were almost entirely middle-class. The church census of 1851, for example, indicates a sharp correlation between middle-class social status and Sunday church attendance.[49] Herbert Schlossberg claims that by the early nineteenth century, the middle classes had become "the great engine of the religious revival."[50] The pattern was even more pronounced in Scotland, where Methodism never made more than a few brief forays into the Highlands (partly in an effort to solve the problem of a Celtic Catholic peasantry) and where the Puritan Covenanters seemed a relic of the distant past. Scottish Presbyterians, however, had become almost wholly evangelical by the 1790s, despite their sometimes uneasy alliance with traditional Calvinism.[51]

There were, of course, a great many causes for this alignment of the evangelical movement with the middle classes. For one thing, evangelical doctrines of self-control, hard work, and study all contributed to the embourgeoisement of the most earnest Methodists, especially those among the skilled workers, who were already perched on the boundary between classes.[52] For another, three of the most important arbiters of middle-class reading material—Charles Edward Mudie, founder of Mudie's Circulating Library; W. H. Smith, owner of a bookshop and railway bookstall empire; and Alexander Strahan, whose *Good Words* was by far the most popular Victorian magazine serializing new fiction—were all evangelical Dissenters. Many middle-class novelists took their obligations to religious piety with corresponding earnestness. Anthony Trollope declared that he

[48] Quoted in Schlossberg, p. 121.

[49] See Bebbington, p. 110. Philip Davis, *The Oxford English Literary History, Volume Eight: The Victorians, 1830–1880* (Oxford: Oxford University Press, 2002), p. 98, notes that although Anglicans accounted for half the churchgoers in the 1851 census, most of these were successful middle-class families who had only recently switched over from Dissenting chapels.

[50] Schlossberg, p. 232.

[51] Bebbington, pp. 34, 50, and 108. On the consolidation of evangelicalism among Scottish Presbyterians, see also C. A. Bayly, *Imperial Meridian: The British Empire and the World, 1780–1830* (London: Longman, 1989), pp. 136–37. In many evangelical circles (not just in Scotland), debates about the relative weight of Calvinist predestination and evangelical conversionism were left suspended.

[52] Perkin, p. 204, claims that by midcentury Methodism drew as much from the lower middle class as from the working classes.

considered himself primarily "a preacher of sermons," and Thomas
Hughes once confessed that "my whole object in writing at all, was to
get the chance of preaching."[53] Middle-class political orators often made
similar claims. John Bright once declared: "I consider that when I stand
upon a platform as I do now, I am engaged in as solemn a labour as
Mr. Dale" (the renowned Birmingham evangelical cleric).[54]

But perhaps no explanation for the evangelicalization of middle-class
culture is as compelling as the common perception that social "respectability" had become identified with middle-class moral seriousness.
George Stephen, a prominent evangelical abolitionist, wrote to Harriet
Beecher Stowe in 1854 that in England "respectability" was to be found
only among the "religious public."[55] Along with the theological orthodox-
ies of evangelicalism, mid-Victorian middle-class culture incorporated a
number of evangelical moral and emotional dispositions that were identified with respectability. Most important of these were the self-negating
virtues—humility, self-denial, and self-sacrifice—which were pointedly at
odds with more aggressive upper-class traditions of virtue. The virility and
chivalrous valor of Charles Kingsley's "muscular Christianity" or of public
school versions of piety ranged themselves deliberately against this evangelical ethos of self-negation, which they often ridiculed as effeminate.[56]

The elision of self-denying religious piety with respectability played an
enormous role in creating a stable conception of "middle-classness" in the
first place. Middle-class social identity was more loosely defined throughout the eighteenth century than that of the upper or lower classes, since
middle-class ranks included a greater range of social circles and career
tracks and since strains between its commercial, industrial, professional,
and intellectual factions were always acute—not to mention the long-
standing divisions between northern and southern middle-class cultures.[57]
The rallying point of respectability, grounded securely in evangelical values, thus became a crucial instrument of solidarity for a class that had
become newly aware of its common political interests in the early nineteenth century. Dror Wahrman has argued that the discordant political

[53] Anthony Trollope, *An Autobiography* (1883; Oxford: Oxford University Press, 1980),
p. 146; Thomas Hughes, *Tom Brown's Schooldays*, 6th edition (1857; New York: Harper &
Brothers, 1870), p. viii.

[54] Quoted in T. Wemyss Reid, *Politicians of Today* (1880; Richmond, England: Richmond
Publishing, 1972), pp. 87–88.

[55] George Stephen, *Anti-Slavery Recollections in a Series of Letters Addressed to Mrs. Beecher
Stowe* (1854; London: Cass, 1971), p. 161.

[56] James Eli Adams, *Dandies and Desert Saints: Styles of Victorian Manhood* (Ithaca: Cornell University Press, 1995), pp. 163–64, discusses the patrician social bias of "muscular
Christianity."

[57] Hugh McLeod, *Class and Religion in the Late Victorian City* (London: Croom Helm,
1974), p. 136.

languages of middle-classness finally converged during this period through evangelical discourses of moral virtue, including the ideology of separate spheres—a convergence that emerged only at the time of the first Reform Bill.[58] Others have pointed to the "civilizing mission" of evangelicalism as a crucial factor in the formation of middle-class social identity.[59] Anti-slavery agitation of the 1820s and '30s, which also helped galvanize middle-class political energies—and which inspired many of the tactics of the Whig reformers, from petition drives to open-air meetings—was similarly driven by evangelical standards of moral respectability.

By the 1850s, middle-class evangelicalism had become the target of many novelists who resented its cultural and political power. But the harsh fictional treatment of evangelicals—such as Brocklehurst and St. John Rivers in Charlotte Brontë's *Jane Eyre* (1848), the Murdstones and Chadband in Charles Dickens's *David Copperfield* (1850) and *Bleak House* (1853), or Bulstrode in George Eliot's *Middlemarch* (1872)—is a testament to the tremendous social achievement of the evangelical movement. The common complaint of "hypocrisy" that sustained many caricatures of evangelicals indicates how much social authority they had acquired and how powerfully their rhetorical formulas appealed to opportunists. Satire is never incompatible with sympathy, either. Brontë belonged to a devoutly Evangelical family; Dickens incorporated evangelical values into his spirit of moral reformism, his attacks on personal and institutional forms of hardheartedness, and his gospel of Christian humanism; and Eliot's "religion of humanity" owed a great deal to the strict religious upbringing she struggled to overcome.

Evangelicalism permeated middle-class Victorian culture in a great variety of ways. It fueled the sense of duty and moral circumspection that characterized middle-class earnestness, the allegorical narrative tendencies and the biblical allusiveness of mid-Victorian fiction, the zeal of the middle-class social reformers of the 1830s and '40s, the unprecedented philanthropic activism of the mid-Victorian period, and the innumerable nineteenth-century campaigns for moral reform. During the rule of the "Ten Pound Householders" between the Reform Bills of 1832 and 1867, the middle classes were also able to establish their moral practices as national norms and to achieve what Hilton has called "a moral hegemony over public life."[60] Evidence of this hegemony can be found in the gravitational pull evangelical values exercised on the faith of other social classes. The

[58] Dror Wahrman, *Imagining the Middle Class: The Political Representation of Class in Britain, c. 1780–1840* (Cambridge: Cambridge University Press, 1995), pp. 395, 405.

[59] Simon Gunn, "The Ministry, the Middle Class and the 'Civilizing Mission' in Manchester, 1850–80," *Social History* 21 (1996), 22–36.

[60] Hilton, p. 7.

enormous popularity of Charlotte Yonge's novel of Tractarian piety, *The Heir of Redclyffe* (1853), for example, owed a great deal to Yonge's reconciliation of Anglican practices with the peculiarly evangelical convergence of penitence with spiritual self-exaltation she dramatized in Philip Morville—whose moral "conversion" is inspired by the Christ-like death of his kinsman and former rival, Guy Morville.

For many late-century writers, however, evangelicalism came to represent a middle-class hegemony that now seemed belated. Evangelical allusions in fin-de-siècle culture often became shorthand for the decline of middle-class social power. One symptom of this change was the growing distaste for what I have described as evangelical masochism. Increasingly, complaints circulated that evangelicalism encouraged morbid introspection. By the 1880s and '90s, even evangelicals were looking for what Hugh McLeod has called "a more extroverted and life-loving Christianity."[61] Hilton has traced the shift away from a theology of "atonement" toward a theology of "incarnation" in late-nineteenth-century religious circles, in which notions of substitutive suffering, divine retribution, and self-punishment were replaced by a sense of the immanence of God's love and a more genteel conception of Christian compassion.[62] The theologian John Cotter MacDonnell, for example, argued in his lectures that Christianity was not "a theology of blood and wounds."[63] No doubt, anthropologists' discoveries of the centrality of sacrifice in primitive religions had something to do with this shift. There were many other reasons for the waning of evangelicalism in the second half of the nineteenth century: its anti-intellectualism, hostility to science, and unresponsiveness to the rise of secular humanism; the replacement of the church as the primary "civilizing" agency for the lower classes by improved education; and the appearance of class-specific organizations (such as labor unions) that assumed the social functions of organized religion. But the self-destructive, penitential aspects of evangelicalism—like those Stevenson evoked in the self-denial of Henry Durie, the moral fervor of Dr. Jekyll, or the "Covenanting" nostalgia of David Balfour—became widely recognized emblems of evangelical belatedness.

To claim that evangelicalism had become a signifier of middle-class cultural decline in the late nineteenth century is not the same as arguing that middle-class social or political power was, in fact, fraying. There were real threats to middle-class coherence at the fin de siècle, including the cultural ascendancy of bohemian aestheticism, which is such a central focus of Stevenson's work. The swelling ranks of the lower middle class, the increasing

---

[61] McLeod, p. 154.

[62] This is one of Hilton's central arguments, but see esp. pp. 281–82.

[63] John Cotter MacDonnell, *The Doctrine of the Atonement Deduced from Scripture, and Vindicated from Misrepresentations and Objections: Six Discourses* (London: Hodges, Smith, 1858), p. 54.

political power of labor unions, the blurrings of cultural identity created by increasingly widespread education, the class ambiguities introduced by professionalism (formerly the province only of the genteel), and the gentrification of the upper middle class that took place in the last quarter of the nineteenth century—all of these factors contributed to undermining the middle-class political and cultural solidarity of the early and mid-Victorian periods. Perry Anderson's famous diagnosis of what he saw as middle-class decay focused on its deference to and absorption by aristocratic political authority: "the bourgeoisie . . . lost its nerve and ended by losing its identity."[64] Similar views were expressed by contemporary observers, including John Morley's attacks in the *Fortnightly Review* on the "new feudalism" of the 1860s.

But the trajectory of middle-class power and stability cannot be rendered so simply. Given the victories of the Liberals over the Conservatives shortly after the turn of the century and the Liberals' ability to fend off challenges from Labour until 1924, one might easily argue that the middle class had never before been so politically ascendant. A long tradition of social analysis, beginning with Karl Marx, has contended that middle-class interests captured political institutions after midcentury even when the actual reins of power remained nominally in upper-class hands.[65] Some historians have argued that the "polymorphic ideological framework" of the nineteenth-century middle class was the reason its adaptability to new social roles and its inclusion of fragmented economic and cultural factions did not corrupt its long-standing blend of rationalism, evangelicalism, educational rigor, and economic individualism—or its sense of its historical patrimony and its unique social destiny.[66]

Late-century representations of the erosion of middle-class power must therefore be seen as calculated instruments in the hands of those with a revisionist social agenda (no matter what it might be) rather than as transparent correlatives of social decline. The thematics of middle-class decline was especially attractive to late-century intellectuals, who were often in revolt against the bourgeois values of the mid-Victorian era. In the intellectual climate of the fin de siècle, evangelicalism offered a useful

[64] Perry Anderson, "Origins of the Present Crisis," *New Left Review* 23 (1964), p. 29. Anderson's view was powerfully reinforced by Martin J. Wiener, *English Culture and the Decline of the Industrial Spirit, 1850–1980* (Cambridge: Cambridge University Press, 1981). There have been many spirited rebuttals; one of the most influential is R. J. Morris, *Class, Sect, and Party: The Making of the British Middle Class, Leeds 1820–1850* (Manchester: Manchester University Press, 1990).

[65] For a good overview, see Perkin, pp. 271–339.

[66] Simon Gunn, "The 'Failure' of the Victorian Middle Class: A Critique," *The Culture of Capital: Art, Power, and the Nineteenth-Century Middle Class*, ed. Janet Wolff and John Seed (Manchester: Manchester University Press, 1988), p. 36.

repertoire of images and allusions for writers who hoped—perhaps prematurely—to imagine Victorian bourgeois hegemony as a thing of the past and who wanted to rework the internal class conflicts that evangelicalism had seemed to resolve so successfully several decades earlier. In *Jude the Obscure* (1895), Thomas Hardy took evident pleasure in noting that the passing of Jude's relatively prosperous aunt (the owner of a bakery and Jude's last link to social respectability) symbolized also the passing of an age: "Miss Drusilla Fawley was of her date, Evangelical."[67] More poignantly, in one of the most popular "serious" novels of the nineteenth century, *Robert Elsmere* (1888), Mary Augusta Ward associated Catherine Elsmere's naively evangelical faith, which clashes tragically with her husband's more skeptical and progressive social activism, with the passing of Victorian middle-class moral consensus.

One way this socioreligious instability was expressed and reworked by late-century writers was through redeployments of the integrated masochism at the center of evangelical rapture. In Stevenson's case, traces of this reworking are fairly obvious in his absorption of evangelical themes and plots from earlier nineteenth-century fiction. To cite just one example, the dynamic of a unified evangelical masochism clearly organizes *The Private Memoirs and Confessions of a Justified Sinner*. In Hogg's novel, the antinomian Robert Colwan is persuaded by Satan that his "election" justifies any act, including murder. Colwan's numerous subsequent crimes produce a dizzying spiral of self-destructive glee and omnipotent religious exultation ending, apocalyptically, in suicide. Nevertheless, although *The Master of Ballantrae* repeats in striking ways the implosive fraternal rivalry of Hogg's novel, it reverses the trajectory of social transformation mapped onto figures of self-destructive moral extremism. In Hogg's cautionary tale, the fanatical outsider, Robert, is sufficiently empowered by his self-punishing masochism that he murders his older brother and thereby inherits the estate of the late Lord of Dalcastle. In *The Master of Ballantrae*, however, the obsessively self-mortifying Henry lacks the will either to overpower his older brother or to reign on his father's estate. The novel's moral anomie is also conveyed through the puritanical Mackellar, who finds himself ambivalently drawn to both brothers—the moral compass of his early devotion to Henry deflected by his admiration for James's vitality, which comes to seem increasingly charismatic as Henry's moralism grows increasingly harsh.

Stevenson used his characters' moral disorientation as a sign of their psychosocial confusion. But, like many late-century writers, he also saw this disorientation as an opportunity for reworking the ideological and psychological foundations of Victorian bourgeois culture. His reworking

---

[67] Thomas Hardy, *Jude the Obscure* (London: Penguin, 1998), p. 88.

of evangelical masochism in social contexts far removed from its class coding in the British metropole was, in fact, one of the central projects of his South Seas fiction.

REWRITING SOCIAL CLASS AT THE PERIPHERY: SOUTH SEAS TALES

When Stevenson traveled to the margins of the empire for his health in 1888, he suddenly found new ways of organizing his narratives. He no longer made his plots revolve consistently around magical and melancholic doubles. Instead, he was able to imagine adult protagonists who rediscover an integrated masochistic economy. These figures once again link the magical and the melancholic phases of masochistic fantasy through their evangelically inflected prosecution of the work of empire. In effect, Stevenson was observing and enacting a process that Ann Stoler has described, in *Race and the Education of Desire* (1995), as the constant making and remaking of bourgeois identity at those colonial sites where it was most destabilized.[68] Although this process took place in a great variety of ways, what fascinated Stevenson was the recovery within British imperial culture of a moral and psychological economy that had formerly been central to middle-class hegemony. Many of his South Seas characters who achieve this masochistic reintegration explicitly refer it to evangelical forms of redemptive suffering and conversion as well as to new perspectives on middle-class social standing.

Obviously, the possibility that imperial enterprise facilitated a reintegrated masochistic subjectivity closely associated both with evangelicalism and with middle-class social power was likely to have caused Stevenson great trepidation. His self-conscious representations of this process were for the most part deeply critical—of imperial enterprise, of evangelical conviction, and of bourgeois culture (no matter how thoroughly it might be renovated). It is that critique which I will examine in this section. As we will see later, though, Stevenson's critique of the colonial reformulation of social identities through masochistic fantasy was only the flip side of his own assimilation of evangelical masochism for anti-imperialist purposes.

Stevenson's critique of imperial evangelicalism revolved primarily around his demonstration that, at the margins of empire, the wrong people seemed to be profiting from a return to the traditional moral springs of middle-class social power. By focusing on problematic lower- and upper-class characters who appropriate evangelical masochism, Stevenson accentuated the factitiousness of such appropriation, although the motives of

---

[68] Ann Laura Stoler, *Race and the Education of Desire: Foucault's History of Sexuality and the Colonial Order of Things* (Durham: Duke University Press, 1995).

his evangelical opportunists are far more complex than those of evangelicals satirized in mid-Victorian fiction. In particular, Stevenson transformed conventional skepticism about evangelical hypocrisy into a moral interrogation of imperialism itself.

In "The Beach of Falesá" (1892), the vulgar working-class trader Wiltshire—whose colonial ambition is to make enough money to buy a pub back in England—undergoes a moral conversion that preposterously reworks the masochistic conventions of middle-class romance. Having tricked Uma, a native woman, into becoming his concubine, Wiltshire shocks himself by falling in love with her. He then makes her an honest woman before Mr. Tarleton, the evangelical missionary.[69] Uma's beauty and naiveté endow her in Wiltshire's eyes with the moral and social promise of the domestic angel: "It came over me she was a kind of countess really, dressed to hear great singers at a concert, and no even mate for a poor trader like myself."[70] Wiltshire pours out all his gin and blissfully cooks inedible dinners with Uma around the open fire. His reward is that Uma learns to wash dishes and assumes the domestic angel's prerogative to proclaim, in pidgin: "I think you good man" (13). Wiltshire's moral conversion thus corresponds to a transformation in his implicit class affiliation, a transformation welcomed by the missionary. "I don't set up to be a gentleman" (35), Wiltshire declares haughtily, which prompts Tarleton's thoughtful reply: "I am not quite so sure."

Wiltshire's conversion quickly incorporates both magical and melancholic energies. He discovers that he has been duped by Case, a well-educated but decadent social superior who is also Wiltshire's chief trading competitor. Setting Wiltshire up with Uma while knowing that she was tabooed, Case ruins Wiltshire's business with the native villagers. When he learns the truth, Wiltshire resolves not to do the customary thing by spurning Uma. Instead, he martyrs himself for her love: "I would rather have you than all the copra in the South Seas," he says, adding: "the strangest thing was that I meant it" (29). Wiltshire resolutely endures the ridicule of the islanders and, with Crusoe-like but downwardly mobile self-sufficiency, labors to make his own copra ("like a negro slave" [56], is Case's sneering interpretation). But all the while, Wiltshire plots a vicious revenge with

[69] Stevenson is vague about his missionary's denomination, but I infer its evangelical character from Tarleton's practice of employing native pastors (a strategy Methodist missionaries took from the East India Company), his doctrinal emphasis on individual conscience, and his biblical allusiveness (as well as the evidence of the evangelical society Bible possessed by Uma, his pupil).

[70] Robert Louis Stevenson, "The Beach of Falesá," *South Sea Tales* (Oxford: Oxford University Press, 1996), p. 12. For a fuller elaboration of the story's reworking of the domestic romance, see Roslyn Jolly, "Stevenson's 'Sterling Domestic Fiction,' 'The Beach of Falesá,' " *Review of English Studies* 50 (1999), 463–82.

the aid of Tarleton. This alliance reflects Stevenson's perception that the practices of missionaries and traders, so often at odds in the colonial world, could converge through the psychosocial logic of masochism, which underlay both moral and social standards of respectability in mid-Victorian culture. During his victorious assault against Case in the jungle, Wiltshire even lugs along a Bible (courtesy of the evangelical Foreign Bible Society), which he uses to convince Uma that no harm can come to him—a parody of the magical thinking lurking within evangelical biblicalism.

Morally and psychologically empowered through his self-righteous martyrdom, Wiltshire carries out the one-against-all omnipotent fantasy intrinsic to adventure fiction by killing Case against improbable odds.[71] Wiltshire may destroy Case's magical aura by blowing up the fake devils and the storehouse of conjuror's tricks Case had used to frighten natives. But he exercises triumphant magical talents of his own when he outwits Case by pretending to be dead and then coming murderously to life— resurrections from the dead being a standard practice among Stevenson's magical protagonists. The brutality of the killing, which is far more graphic and disturbing than anything from Stevenson's early adventure novels, also draws a problematic connection between Wiltshire's morally legitimating acts of self-sacrifice and his megalomaniacal mastery, a connection that is sustained elsewhere though his airs of superiority toward whites and his racist condescension to natives. Moreover, the villainous Case, who had himself murdered several previous competitors, turns out to have acted honorably toward exactly one person—his native wife— which establishes a parallel between private-sphere self-sacrifice and public-sphere megalomania in both hero and villain. Wiltshire, in fact, fulfills Case's murderous dreams of uncontested power, since, by killing him, Wiltshire becomes the only trader left on the island: "So there was I," he gloats, "left alone in my glory" (70).

The narrative of Case's death also dissociates Wiltshire's omnipotence from sexuality and thereby reinforces its origins in narcissistic fantasy. The feminization of Case in this scene—he "threw up his hands together, more like a frightened woman"; "I drew my knife and got it in the place" (67– 68)—evokes sadomasochistic and homosexual eroticism, but only to disavow them both by investing them in the degraded villain. In contrast, Wiltshire's love for Uma is routinely infantilized, and our last glimpse of her makes her seem an all-powerful nurturing figure rather than an object of sexual desire ("She's turned a powerful big woman now, and could throw a London bobby over her shoulder"; "she would give away the

[71] For extensive readings of this scene as a critique of adventure fiction, see Jolly, pp. 478– 79; or Rod Edmond, *Representing the South Pacific: Colonial Discourse from Cook to Gauguin* (Cambridge: Cambridge University Press, 1997), pp. 176–77.

roof off the station" [70]).[72] Wiltshire's repeated stabbing of Case also conforms more closely to the annihilative tendencies of preoedipal fantasy than to the sustained relationships of domination characteristic of oedipal sadomasochism: killing Case is for Wiltshire a matter of "good riddance" (69). Most importantly, though, Case initially pretends to be a nurturing figure. Wiltshire anticipates benefiting from his friendship and passively relies on him for something as intimate as the arrangement of his marriage. In other words, the feminization of Case during the stabbing scene suggests that he is, for Wiltshire, a bad mother—offering first care and safety but then betrayal and abandonment. The oral aspects of Wiltshire's relationship to Case (his fascination with Case's eloquence; his falling, after the stabbing scene, "with my head on the man's mouth" [68]) help sustain this maternal metaphorics.

Although recent attention to homosexual energies in Stevenson's work has been illuminating, these energies must be evaluated carefully.[73] While they are sometimes converted—as in this scene—into signs of sexual disavowal, they are more often simply rewritten in desexualized terms.[74] In Stevenson's work, male figures often turn out to be stand-ins for the absent, preoedipal mother, and anal or oral imagery often signifies regression to presexual forms of pleasure rather than to deviant sexuality. We might remember, for example, that in *Jekyll and Hyde* the relationship between the two central male figures hinges upon a magical white powder (mysteriously given, then mysteriously withdrawn), which comes from a chemist's shop named "Messrs. Maw"—a multilayered pun that includes oral, anal, and maternal displacements.[75] We might remember, too, that Alan Breck Stewart, who is just old enough to be David Balfour's father (or perhaps his mother?) "believed he was serving, helping, and protecting me" (140),

---

[72] Roslyn Jolly, "South Sea Gothic: Pierre Loti and Robert Louis Stevenson," *English Literature in Transition, 1880–1920* 47 (2004), pp. 34–35, rightly reads Stevenson's refusal to exploit conventions of "gothic" female sexuality common in Polynesian fiction as part of his refusal of exoticization. But this refusal must be placed in the context of his transformation of sexualized women into nurturing figures or into negative images of maternal failure (Uma's mother, for example).

[73] See Elaine Showalter, *Sexual Anarchy: Gender and Culture at the Fin de Siècle* (London: Bloomsbury, 1991), p. 107; and Wayne Koestenbaum, *Double Talk: The Erotics of Male Literary Collaboration* (New York: Routledge, 1989), pp. 149–51. Elaine Showalter, "Dr. Jekyll's Closet," *The Haunted Mind: The Supernatural in Victorian Literature*, ed. Elton E. Smith and Robert Haas (Lanham, MD: Scarecrow Press, 1999), pp. 67–88, seems to get the balance exactly right by reading *Jekyll and Hyde* as an instance of homosexual panic.

[74] Oliver S. Buckton, "Reanimating Stevenson's Corpus," *Nineteenth-Century Literature* 55 (2000), 22–58, insightfully analyzes the strategies of containment Stevenson used to manage homosexual desire.

[75] Robert Louis Stevenson, *The Strange Case of Dr. Jekyll and Mr. Hyde, Dr. Jekyll and Mr. Hyde and Weir of Hermiston* (Oxford: Oxford University Press, 1987), p. 44. To complete the joke, the servant Poole later refers to "the man at Maw's" (45).

as David puts it in *Kidnapped*. Beattie has noted that male passion in Stevenson is almost always "primal and pregenital."[76] In "The Beach of Falesá," the desexualization of Wiltshire's hatred of Case only reinforces the narcissistic circuits of self-sacrifice and megalomania that are deeply embedded in every aspect of his conversion experience.

Stevenson also emphasized the narcissistic character of Wiltshire's rage at Case by making clear the infantile contradictions latent in his moral conversion. Despite Stevenson's evident affection for him, Wiltshire is a deliberate parody of the integrated masochistic economy of evangelicalism. In suggesting the artificiality of Wiltshire's newfound moral rectitude, Stevenson was aided by the conventional distinction between true and false converts that was widespread in South Seas missionary writing.[77] As in most tales of false conversion, Wiltshire comically mangles moral codes, putting great stock in his word of honor, for instance, but professing his right to cheat if he has not explicitly promised to be fair; or offering up a prayer on "the off chance of a prayer being any good" (53). Moreover, the story invokes three fictional genres deeply grounded in middle-class ideology—the conversion narrative, the domestic romance, and adventure fiction—only to demonstrate the participation of all three in masochistic fantasies of omnipotence. Through Wiltshire, Stevenson exposes the subtle ways in which even seemingly innocent husks of evangelical principle could be used to legitimate dishonest mercantile exchange: Wiltshire is "half glad" to be transferred to another station, "where I was under no kind of a pledge and could look my balances in the face" (70).

But the contradictions that stigmatize Wiltshire also support a moral critique that has the potential to purify bourgeois identity—a widespread practice in colonial discourse, as Ann Stoler has pointed out. It is important to understand that Stevenson's critique of the corrupting effects of colonial life was not directed at the sensual excesses often described by nineteenth-century critics of colonialism as the principal threats to bourgeois moral order in the tropics. Instead, it was directed at the reintegrated evangelical logic of bourgeois masochism whenever that logic seemed to be appropriated by unworthy interlopers.

In his novella *The Ebb-Tide* (1894), coauthored with Lloyd Osbourne, Stevenson turned to the other end of the social scale and portrayed "a copper-bottomed aristocrat," William Attwater, who fuses evangelical zeal with ruthlessness, commanding his private island like a god.[78] A graduate

[76] Beattie, "Father and Son," p. 346.

[77] See Vanessa Smith, *Literary Culture and the Pacific: Nineteenth-Century Textual Encounters* (Cambridge: Cambridge University Press, 1998), p. 141.

[78] Robert Louis Stevenson and Lloyd Osbourne, *The Ebb-Tide: A Trio and a Quartette, South Sea Tales*, p. 197.

of Trinity Hall, Cambridge, Attwater embodies the manliness, wealth, and power of upper-class imperial authority. That authority is rooted partly in his pedigree, as is obvious to the three beachcombers who stumble on his fiefdom: the disgraced seaman, Captain Davis; the cockney clerk, Huish; and the failed Oxford graduate, Robert Herrick. As Davis says of Attwater's effortless snobbery: "that couldn't be nothing but genuine; a man got to be born to that, and notice! smart as champagne and hard as nails . . . . He's a palace at home, and powdered flunkies" (197). Davis may resent Attwater's assumption of superiority, but he remains in awe of the psychological strength class breeding engenders. When Attwater blandly acknowledges commanding a labor force of more than thirty natives single-handedly, Davis exclaims, "in a glow of admiration": "By God, but you must be a holy terror!" (216). Appropriately, of the three beachcombers, only Herrick's middle-class moral codes are outraged by Attwater's "holy" assumption of the authority to kill. Son of a successful commercial clerk who had risen to a small partnership in "a considerable London house" (125), Herrick alone is scandalized that Attwater executes his laborers for disobedience: "You monstrous being! Murderer and hypocrite—murderer and hypocrite—murderer and hypocrite—" (219).

Critics who agree with Herrick that Attwater is a monster, perhaps a precursor of Kurtz in Conrad's *Heart of Darkness* (1899)—both instances of European talent and privilege run amok—overlook the fact that responses to Attwater serve as a litmus test for class identification in Stevenson's narrative.[79] Davis and Huish, for example, find Attwater captivating precisely on account of the patrician arrogance that horrifies Herrick. Attwater's ruthless authority compels Davis to gush: "By God, you're a man, and you can say I said so" (216). For Huish, Attwater's cosmopolitan geniality (which Huish misreads as a sign of fellowship) and his trappings of luxury prove irresistible: "I like Attwater. 'E's all right; we got on like one o'clock when you were gone. And ain't his sherry in it, rather? It's like Spiers and Ponds' Amontillado! I wish I 'ad a drain of it now" (233–34). The class rage that Davis and Huish feel toward Attwater is the flip side of their admiration and envy, and it rises to the surface only when they discover that his genteel affability is a means of "guying" (221) them—behavior that the socially initiated Herrick can read more clearly. Herrick's own moments of admiration for Attwater, by contrast, revolve around an entirely different set of class values. What Herrick, the educated man, respects is Attwater's omniscient knowledge ("That man there with the cat knows all" [221], he tells Davis, impressively), and possibly his philosophical sophistication ("You wouldn't understand if I were to tell you,"

---

[79] Roslyn Jolly, "Introduction," *South Sea Tales*, p. xviii, for example, dismisses Attwater as a "monster."

he says, answering Davis's query about Attwater's beliefs [222]). Both fascinated and demoralized by Attwater's pitiless gentility, Herrick sums up his formidability in terms that reek of middle-class anxiety: "He knows all, he sees through all; we only make him laugh with our pretences—he looks at us and laughs, like God!" (222). More importantly, when Herrick throws himself at Attwater's feet at the end of the narrative, it is not because, like Davis and Huish, he idealizes Attwater's wealth, his power to command, his polished manners, or (in Davis's case) his religious fervor. Rather, as a failed middle-class son, Herrick pines for Attwater's ability to mold and cultivate character: "Can you do anything with me?" (230), he pleads. Far from taking moral responses to Attwater for granted, Stevenson anatomized such responses within a class-coded schema that makes the complex relationships among morality, class, and psychological power a central subject of the novella.

Stevenson himself marks Attwater as an unworthy social interloper not by sharing Herrick's rather conventional complaints about "hypocrisy" but by demonstrating instead how Attwater's class power is underwritten—in historically atavistic terms—by evangelical codes of self-abnegation.[80] Even from Herrick's viewpoint, "to find the whole machine thus glow with the reverberation of religious zeal, surprised him beyond words" (203). Attwater's enthusiastic religious faith, which led him into missionary work as a young man, would have been contrary to the spirit of gentrified, late-century upper-class Anglicanism, and it can hardly even be considered a throwback to the "muscular Christianity" of the 1840s and '50s. Unlike the proimperialist heroes of novels by Charles Kingsley, Arthur Hughes, G. A. Lawrence, Henry Kingsley, and other authors of the "muscular school," Attwater makes no mention of nationalism, military conquest, or social reform, nor is he concerned in any evident way with the regeneration of England's youth.[81] Attwater is more accurately understood as a throwback to—and a dislocation of—early-nineteenth-century middle-class conjunctions of evangelical piety with commercial enterprise.

Although he may seem temporally and ideologically out of place, Attwater's evangelical zeal is infused in familiar ways with the psychosocial power of masochistic omnipotence. His faith gives him the courage to accept martyrdom and even to court it deliberately. Repeatedly, Attwater

[80] Readers usually fail to take Attwater's self-denying impulses seriously. See, for example, Robert I. Hillier, *The South Seas Fiction of Robert Louis Stevenson* (New York: Peter Lang, 1989), p. 137; or Ann C. Colley, *Robert Louis Stevenson and the Colonial Imagination* (Aldershot, UK: Ashgate, 2004), p. 40.

[81] Like many readers, Guy Davidson, "Homosocial Relations, Masculine Embodiment, and Imperialism in Stevenson's *The Ebb-Tide*," *English Literature in Transition, 1880–1920* 47 (2004), p. 126, mistakenly links Attwater with "muscular Christianity."

puts himself in harm's way with delicious indifference: thoroughly out-
manned, he boards the three beachcombers' stolen schooner, the *Farallone*; knowing that the beachcombers mean to kill him, he invites them
to dinner. Hinting serenely at his knowledge of the conspiracy against
him, Attwater provokes Herrick into terrifying fantasies in which Attwater
figures as a persecuted innocent, "trussed and gagged, a helpless victim"
(211). Herrick connects his sense of imminent victimization directly with
Attwater's "holy" authority: "this building up of circumstance was like a
consecration of the man, till he seemed to walk in sacrificial fillets" (208).

Besides cultivating his indifference to suffering and death, Attwater also
maintains his authority on the island through a regimen of ascetic self-
denial. Seeking to annihilate his lust for the native girl who has survived
the island's smallpox epidemic, he marries her off to one of his laborers.
His devotion to religious self-abnegation is genuinely extremist: " 'There
is nothing here,'—striking on his bosom . . . 'but God's Grace!' " (203).
Most importantly, though, Attwater both views himself and displays himself to others as a martyr. When the scheming Davis asks him how long
he has lived on the island, Attwater replies by alluding to the Christian
martyrs in the book of Revelation who wait to be avenged: "How long,
O Lord" (195). When he proselytizes to Herrick, he "spread out his arms
like a crucifix" (206) and loses himself in a "rapture" (207) of penitential
emotion. Attwater's notions of religious conversion also revolve emphatically around penitence—his own and others'. When Davis accepts his invi-
tation to "make your peace with God" (247), Attwater spares him, declaring inwardly (in an abrupt shift of narrative point-of-view, apparently
because Stevenson wished to stress the sincerity of his faith): " 'Ah!'
thought Attwater, 'here is the true penitent' " (249).

Attwater's evangelical gestures of self-abnegation, martyrdom, and penitence are precisely what allow him to identify with the omnipotence of
God. Claiming that he "can do anything" (209) and that, as a marksman,
he never misses, Attwater compares divine grace to the insulating suit his
pearl divers wear, calling it "a dress to go down into the world in, and
come up scatheless" (202). Far from being simply a symbol of religious
salvation, the diver's suit also functions as a metaphor for indomitable
narcissistic power. Attwater explicitly contrasts his own sense of personal
impunity with Herrick's cynical estimate of the kind of conviction necessary to emerge from the world "scatheless," which Herrick calls simply
"self-conceit" (202). Attwater counters by comparing his own sanctified
arrogance disdainfully to secular self-esteem: "Ah, man, that poor diving-
dress of self-conceit is sadly tattered!" (206) Anchoring his personal fortitude in religion instead, Attwater links spiritual grace with the acquisition
of unqualified power: "religion is a savage thing, like the universe it illuminates; savage, cold, and bare, but infinitely strong" (204). Attwater is not

by any means a conventional evangelical hypocrite. Quite the contrary, he is a disturbing figure because the authenticity of his belief taps the empowering psychological dynamics of evangelical masochistic fantasy.

Attwater's masochistic evangelicalism was hardly typical of Oxbridge-trained imperial entrepreneurs in the late nineteenth century.[82] Its atypicality allowed Stevenson to critique imperial appropriations of middle-class ideology by revealing the strains and distortions they entailed. The social gap between Attwater's religious codes and his upper-class tyranny, for example, is glaring. As Herrick observes at one point: "the dark apostle had disappeared; and in his place there stood an easy, sneering gentleman" (207). And as Attwater puts it: "I was a man of the world before I was a Christian; I'm a man of the world still, and I made my mission pay" (204). Embedded in upper-class power, Attwater's evangelical masochism lies strangely beside his jarring commercial rapacity as well as his generalized sadism: "Iron cruelty, an iron insensibility to the suffering of others, the uncompromising pursuit of his own interests, cold culture, manners without humanity" (203). This disjunction represents a perversion of evangelical sensibilities rather than an authentic return. The ending of the novella also stages a distortion of evangelical paternalism as Attwater—like Wesley long before him—brings the gospel of self-denial and penitence to the lowly Davis, who happens, in this case, to have been a victim of the proselytizer's sadistic cruelty. The various moral and social dislocations Attwater embodies signify the warping of what had once been a securely middle-class evangelical ideology. Only in the fluid social world of the South Pacific, and not in the tightly stratified world of the Scottish novels, could psychosocial appropriations like Attwater's flourish.

Attwater may fuse evangelical masochism with psychological omnipotence in anachronistic, distorted forms. But the impotence of late-nineteenth-century middle-class ideology is dramatized in the novella primarily through Herrick, a hopelessly self-destructive bourgeois manqué who cannot internalize middle-class values of any kind. Although he is devoted to his father and his fiancé, he fails to live up to the domestic roles of son and husband. Indifferent to the world of trade, he is unable to attend to his duties and is repeatedly fired as incompetent. Herrick's situation aboard the *Farallone*—struggling to do his duty in the service of an enterprise he knows to be dishonest—is a metaphor for his impossible relationship to bourgeois ideology generally. Deeply attached to archaic and incapacitating middle-class codes of honesty and loyalty, Herrick cannot find

---

[82] The events of the story cannot have taken place before 1884, when Alexander George Findlay published the volume of *A Directory for the Navigation of the South Pacific Ocean*, 5th edition (London: R. H. Laurie, 1884) from which Davis quotes the description of New Island. Other references to music-hall songs and operatic performances are consistent with this dating.

his idealism mirrored by late-century capitalism. At the same time, his talent and taste, which for an earlier generation might have suggested the upward social and cultural ambitions of the bourgeois aesthete, only distract him from establishing the upper-class cultural credentials he should have achieved at Oxford: he "worked at music or at metaphysics when he should have been at Greek" (125). Unlike his namesake—the seventeenth-century poet who happens, like Attwater, to have been a graduate of Trinity Hall, and who, although an Anglican clergyman, was also a lyric celebrant of erotic innocence—Herrick resists embracing the station to which his father wished him to aspire and takes only "a paltry degree" (125). Although flattered by Attwater's respect for him as a "university man" (193), Herrick is also unable to escape outmoded middle-class moral and aesthetic reflexes despite his contempt for his own bourgeois social origins. His self-contradictions are thus a tragic expression of Stevenson's chronic preoccupation with middle-class ideological instability.

Herrick's affinity for traditional middle-class moral ideals—but his failure to uphold them—is nowhere more pronounced than in his misplaying of the masochistic relationship between voluntary suffering and psychological power. In a narrative saturated with masochistic patterns of imagery and action, Herrick is perhaps the character most intensely oriented to the pleasureableness of pain. His degradation "had stung him to that point when pain is almost pleasure" (143); he "raged against himself, as a man bites on a sore tooth, in a heady sensuality of scorn" (144). His self-contempt is so intense it is described at one point as capable of producing "orgasm" (208). Masochistically in love with his own social fall, his awareness that he is fit for better things only means that "the pain was the more exquisite" (126).

Yet Herrick is unable to recuperate his self-dramatizing masochism through penitence. Whatever positive forms of emotional exultation he derives from his suffering remain purely phantasmagoric: his parable about the magic carpet that might return him to London; his intermittent faith in the gallantry and honor of the *Farallone* adventure; even his final, capriciously hopeful submission to Attwater. His self-composed epitaph—the passages from Beethoven's Fifth Symphony and the lines of Virgil that he scrawls on the side of the Papeete calaboose—is a desperate attempt to transform his suffering into a sign of his failed cultural ambitions: "They will know that I loved music and had classical tastes" (144). But Herrick is disgusted when even this vainglorious act is interpreted in religious terms that he cannot endorse: "That's what I call Providence" (146), says Davis, contemplating Herrick's writing on the wall. Herrick's moral uncertainties may define him as a representative late-century middle class educated man, but they also indicate the inconsequentiality of traditional moral reflexes once they have become detached from the psychological power of evangelical masochism.

Nevertheless, Herrick's self-flagellations, coupled with his aspiration to affirm his social and cultural superiority, indicate his persistent yearning to convert his masochistic tendencies into moral and social authority. Davis rebukes him for sublimating ascetic virtue into class snobbery: "Don't think . . . that you'll go on doing the evangelical" (150). When Herrick dreams of a genii who will reward his virtuous behavior with a flying carpet, his fable's emphasis on good samaritanism, the honor of keeping one's word, just rewards for moral conduct, and devotion to one's family have an unmistakable evangelical resonance—as Huish points out: "[it's] like the rot there is in tracts" (130). Even Herrick's consultation of his Virgil for "*sortes*" (124) is a holdover of evangelical biblicalism. But Herrick cannot transcend his own skepticism about religious convictions and rituals. At the end of the novella, he can only view Davis's combination of devout penitence and social success cynically ("a sure thing for your wife and family" [252]). Refusing to participate in "such nonsense" (252), Herrick remains an unreclaimed middle-class prodigal son, his masochistic inclinations permanently divorced from social and moral empowerment.

We should note, finally, that the narcissistic aspects of Herrick's masochism are underscored by his obliviousness to the erotic attraction nearly every other character seems to feel for him. Attwater declares "I like you" (205) and tells Herrick that he is "attractive, very attractive" (205). Davis avows that "I love you" (149). Even the native crew aboard the *Farallone* adores Herrick and demonstrates its affection in physical ways. The cook "produced for him unexpected . . . dainties" (167), and Sally Day touches him with "a caressing hand" (168). When Herrick offers to extend his watch, "all hands clustered about their mate with expostulations and caresses" (168). As Day puts it: "Evely man he like you too much" (168). Whatever erotic component Herrick's masochism might possess in the eyes of others, the narrative emphasizes the lack of a complementary response from Herrick—yet another irony embedded in his name. Herrick's immersion in masochism, like Wiltshire's and Attwater's, is pointedly desexualized, revolving as it does around preoedipal longings: for safety and love, for the approval of authority figures, and, in particular, for a narcissistically mirroring, rescuing figure: "the unknown, kindred spirit that shall come some day and read my *memor querela*" (144). Tragically, the narcissistic forms of masochistic fantasy to which he clings simply have no place in the novella's homosocial and sadomasochistic colonial world.

In *The Wrecker*, an adventure yarn coauthored with Osbourne, Stevenson returned to his long-standing opposition of magical and melancholic doubles—a return worth exploring briefly if only to establish the contrast between his cynical views of middle-class ideology and his awareness that, in the South Seas, aspects of middle-class psychosocial power could yet be appropriated productively. As we might expect, Stevenson's return to masochistic doubling in *The Wrecker* signals a turning away from problems of evangelical moral authority and a revisiting of the ideological contradictions embodied by bourgeois and bohemian figures in his Scottish fiction. In the South Seas, as in the Scottish fiction, Stevenson saw these particular contradictions as merely disabling, in contrast to the dubious but nevertheless efficient moral authority figures like Wiltshire and Attwater have resurrected from the evangelical past of middle-class culture.

In *The Wrecker*, Loudon Dodd and James Pinkerton at first seem to represent a happier combination of melancholic and magical doubles than Stevenson had ever imagined before. Dodd, like his doleful father, continually sees himself as a "martyr" (15) when he turns his bohemian life as a Parisian art student into "misery," "misfortune," and "lamentation" (68, 79). He continues to behave "like a whipped schoolboy" (83) even when he and Pinkerton begin to prosper. Pinkerton, by contrast, is "quixotic" (41); Dodd refers to him as "The Irrepressible" (93). Constantly seeing glorious possibilities for success where Dodd sees only the prospect of failure, Pinkerton proceeds blindly (but with surprisingly good luck) on his unshakeable conviction that he will become rich.

Yet Stevenson treats the synthesis of bohemian and bourgeois figures that Dodd and Pinkerton represent farcically. While Dodd botches the role of the bohemian aesthete in Paris, Pinkerton absurdly believes he can buy an aesthetic education. Dodd tells him: "You look to the result, you want to see some profit of your endeavours: that is why you could never learn to paint, if you lived to be Methusalem" (64). And although their partnership flourishes at first, the two protagonists turn out to be the naïve prey of wealthy businessmen and corrupt lawyers. A fragile combination of bourgeois greed and bohemian adventurism, they become the laughingstock of San Francisco when their delusional pursuit of a fortune from the wrecked brig *The Flying Scud* bankrupts them.

The business partnership of these melancholic and magical doubles also raises moral questions about the particular kind of reconciliation a melancholic bohemian and a magical bourgeois might achieve through South Seas entrepreneurialism. Dodd and Pinkerton at first engage in genially fraudulent ventures: Pinkerton sells Dodd's lecture series to a gullible public by advertising him as an "Americo-Parisienne Sculptor" (95); the two organize amiably dishonest Sunday picnic excursions; they speculate serendipitously on "wild-cat" (117) stock. As the narrative develops, however, the partnership's moral decay deepens. Swept up by "the compelling spell of wizard Pinkerton" (120), Dodd finds himself engaged in predatory salvage operations, opium smuggling, and blackmail. His moral descent ends in his covering up a murder.

The novel eventually reveals the dishonesty of everyone involved in the wreck—a conclusion that seems to betray the comic tone of its opening.

But to arrive at an unqualified moral condemnation of colonial commerce seems to have been part of Stevenson's original conception. In 1889, he and Osbourne took a cruise on a trading vessel, the *Equator*, hoping to learn how to go into business themselves as traders in luxury goods (the firm was to be called "Jekyll, Hyde, & Co."). But the cruise convinced Stevenson that the business consisted of systematic "bamboozling and chicanery."[83] He and Osbourne commenced writing *The Wrecker* immediately afterwards, intending it to be an exposé disguised as an adventure tale. Nevertheless, this displacement from one kind of business enterprise to another, from trading in goods to trading in narratives, raises serious questions about the moral foundations of colonial fiction—questions that did not escape Stevenson's notice.

Although *The Wrecker* might seem to signal an abrupt break with bourgeois culture through its harsh condemnation of commerce, Stevenson was never able to allay his anxieties about middle-class ideological disjunctions and his own implication in them. As late as 1893, he lamented to Will Low, an American painter he had first met during his bohemian days at Grez (and the man who served as the model for Loudon Dodd):

> About *The Wrecker*— . . . did you not fail to appreciate the attitude of Dodd? He was a fizzle and a stick, he knew it, he knew nothing else, and there is an undercurrent of bitterness in him. And then the problem that Pinkerton laid down: why the artist can do nothing else? is one that continually exercises myself. . . . And why can't R. L. S.? . . . I think *David Balfour* a nice little book, and very artistic, and just the thing to occupy the leisure of a busy man; but for the top flower of a man's life it seems to me inadequate. Small is the word; it is a small age, and I am of it. I could have wished to be otherwise busy in this world. I ought to have been able to build lighthouses and write *David Balfour*s too. *Hinc illae lacrymae.* I take my own case as most handy; but it is as illustrative of my quarrel with the age. (*Letters*, 8:235)[84]

Stevenson played on his inability to extricate himself from this conundrum by directly addressing Low in the Epilogue of *The Wrecker*, in which he speaks of characters from the novel as if he, they, and Low all occupy the same plane of reality—a metafictional conceit that highlights his awareness that his potboiler was undertaken to finance more high-minded works, like *The Ebb-Tide*.[85]

---

[83] Quoted in McLynn, p. 359. See also Furnas, *Voyage to Windward*, p. 356.

[84] *David Balfour* was the title Stevenson gave to both the serial and the American edition of the work that his English publisher decided to rename *Catriona*, in the hope of avoiding any confusion in the minds of potential readers with *Kidnapped*.

[85] See William Gray, "Stevenson's 'Auld Alliance': France, Art Theory, and the Breath of Money in *The Wrecker*," *Scottish Studies Review* 3 (2002), 54–65, for a lively discussion of the novel's confusions of art and life, aesthetics and commerce.

The corrupt partnerships Stevenson portrayed in *The Wrecker*, together with his wary view of interloping upper- and lower-class evangelical entrepreneurs in his other South Seas stories, suggest that he evaluated imperial subjectivities in relentlessly moral terms—a frame of reference that was linked to evangelical values he both shared and disavowed. In "The Beach of Falesá" and *The Ebb-Tide*, variant forms of reintegrated masochistic self-invention appear to constitute a grammar of moral legitimacy, reinforcing or in some cases replacing more familiar hierarchies of legitimacy derived from differences of race or economic capital. This grammar provided the moral foundations for Stevenson's own idiosyncratic responses to imperialism, which reappropriated evangelical masochism in strikingly new forms.

But Stevenson's appropriations of masochistic fantasy for moral purposes had serious limitations as well as politically progressive potentials. Their deficiencies are most evident in his rigid sense of how racial differences might be inscribed in masochistic fantasy. While simple racial oppositions played an important role in the anti-imperialist moral authority he would ultimately claim for himself, the racialist potentials of a political vision deeply engaged in masochistic fantasy had serious drawbacks as well.

RACIAL PROJECTIONS

A central development of Stevenson's writing in Samoa, which complements the problematic reintegration of masochism he critiqued in British imperial opportunists, was his frequent relegation of masochistic splitting to the realm of racial otherness. In *A Footnote to History* (1892), Stevenson's account of the Samoan uprising of 1887–89, the magical/melancholic polarities represented by James and Henry Durie, Alan Breck Stewart and David Balfour, or Loudon Dodd and James Pinkerton are mapped onto warring Germans and Samoans.

Although *A Footnote to History* is an acute interpretation of events, one still cited by historians, it portrays several German consuls and German policy in general as delusionally arrogant, tyrannical, and overreaching. Twentieth-century American and Samoan historians generally agree that Germany did underestimate the complexities of Samoan politics, that its crackdown of 1888–89 was a miscalculation, and that German consuls overplayed their hand in trying to install a Samoan king friendly to their own interests—the act that precipitated rebellion. But historians also agree that Germany was forced to react to U.S. and British provocations, including an abortive American attempt to "confederate" Samoa and Hawaii, as well as to joint U.S.-British support for a native government that was plainly obstructing German interests.[86] Stevenson downplayed all these circumstances to caricature Germans as self-destructive bullies. He described German diplomacy as "the organisation [*sic*] of failure in the midst of hate"; he portrayed German settlers, "inspired with a sense of the greatness of their affairs and interests," as whip-cracking slave owners who "are naturally incensed by criticisms"; and of one German consul's omnipotent delusions, Stevenson wrote: "he continued, on the scene of his defeat and in the midst of his weakness, to bluster and menace like a conqueror."[87] Even an editorial in the *Times* complained that Stevenson's account was overfull of tyrants.[88] Such caricatures of monomaniacal ham-handedness square with British racial stereotypes of Germans, Britain's chief late-century imperial rivals. But they also project fantasies of omnipotence as the cause of German self-destruction. In an open letter to the *Times*, Stevenson claimed that "of all this bloodshed and bullying the Germans behold no profit" (*Letters*, 6:253). This analysis rested on a great deal of wishful thinking, to say the least, as German annexation of Samoa in 1900 proved.

On the other side, though the Samoan rebellion achieved some notable successes, including removal of the imposed king, Stevenson lamented, throughout *A Footnote to History*, what he saw as excessive Samoan self-sacrifice. He faulted the rebels for refusing to press their battlefield successes into resounding victory; for their deference to the Germans' declared neutral zone, which was allegedly exploited by Germany itself; and, above all, for the mutually self-sacrificing reticence of the two leading Samoan chiefs, who, after their victory, refused to confederate their opposing factions into a centralized government under a single king. "The two entered into a competition of generosity," Stevenson wrote, "for which I can recall no parallel in history, each waiving the throne for himself, each pressing it upon his rival; and they embraced at last a compromise, the terms of which seem to have been always obscure" (234). Stevenson's description of gratuitous kingly self-abnegation closely resembles his descriptions of idealistic Scottish martyrs in the historical novels (indeed, he often compared Samoans to Highlanders).[89] But his description of the kings' refusal to accept the throne disregarded what historians have since

[86] See R. P. Gilson, *Samoa 1830 to 1900: The Politics of a Multi-cultural Community* (Melbourne: Oxford University Press, 1970); and Malama Meleisea et al., *Lagaga: A Short History of Western Samoa* (Suva, Fiji: University of the South Pacific Press, 1987).

[87] Robert Louis Stevenson, *A Footnote to History: Eight Years of Trouble in Samoa, Works,* 19:175; 19:90; 19:89; 19:208.

[88] *Times*, 4 June 1892, p. 13.

[89] Roslyn Jolly, "Robert Louis Stevenson and Samoan History: Crossing the Roman Wall," *Crossing Cultures: Essays on Literature and Culture of the Asia-Pacific,* ed. Bruce Bennett et al. (London: Skoob, 1996), p. 112, traces Stevenson's identifications with those he saw as outside imperial culture.

described as the political good fortune of the Samoan factions, since native government became stronger by resisting centralization. Samoa was officially colonized much later than Tahiti, Hawaii, or Tonga partly because its factionalized internal politics were impervious to white control and inimical to the growth of commerce.[90] What Stevenson saw as a form of melancholic masochism was, whether deliberately or not, a form of resistance to the imposition of manageable secular hierarchies, an imposition that was often a crucial weapon of imperial domination.

Stevenson's interpretation of the chiefs' behavior conforms, though, to his general attribution of melancholia to Polynesians. Elsewhere, he wrote: "The Polynesian falls easily into despondency: bereavement, disappointment . . . the decay or proscription of ancient pleasure, easily incline him to be sad; and sadness detaches him from life."[91] Stevenson declared that Polynesians had a "proneness to suicide" (*ISS*, 18:31), and although he recognized that colonial exploitation was partly responsible for whatever demoralization he observed, he dismissed such causes as the dissemination of disease, alcohol, or firearms, along with the destruction of native traditions, as merely partial explanations, arguing instead that the real problem was a Polynesian "disease . . . of the will" (*ISS*, 18:31). Because life was so easy in the South Seas and desire so easily gratified, depression was a constant threat, Stevenson reasoned.[92] "It is otherwise with us, where life presents us with a daily problem, and there is a serious interest, and some of the heat of conflict, in the mere continuing to be" (*ISS*, 18:40). This familiar belief that free-ranging desire leads to anomie had its source in evangelical assumptions that Herbert has traced from Wesley to Durkheim, assumptions that play yet again on the proximity of fantasies of omnipotence to melancholia. The presence of this evangelical psychology in Stevenson's work suggests that his descriptions of Polynesian melancholy cannot be attributed narrowly to his anxieties about European cultural decay or to his deteriorating physical health—two common themes of recent criticism.[93]

Stevenson sustained this perception of native melancholia in the short stories he devoted to native characters. In "The Bottle Imp" (1890), the magic bottle acquired by the story's Hawaiian protagonist, Keawe, precipitates several different kinds of loss. Its most obvious cost, should Keawe happen to die in possession of the bottle, would be the loss of his eternal soul. But by making wishes on the bottle, Keawe also accidentally causes

---

[90] Gilson, p. 418, claims that the two chiefs reached an agreement that effectively compromised with the terms of the Berlin Treaty while also preserving harmony between Samoan factions. On the general effectiveness of Samoan resistance to colonization, see p. 189.

[91] Robert Louis Stevenson, *In the South Seas, Works*, 18:39. Hereafter cited as *ISS*.

[92] See *ISS*, 18:39–40; see also *Letters*, 6:213–14.

[93] See, for example, Edmond, pp. 160–68.

the deaths of his well-loved uncle and cousin, which the bottle magically arranges so that he might inherit land on the Kona coast—a wish he had expressed without malice. Keawe also very nearly suffers the loss of his wife's love and well-being. Such magic, he comes to believe, is better renounced than embraced, even though, fittingly, one condition of ownership is that the bottle can only be sold at a loss. Given these associations of magic with loss, it is no accident that the bottle comes to Keawe and leaves him through whites, who seem better able to manage its melancholic properties (a wealthy San Franciscan transfers ownership of the bottle to Keawe without regret); or who seem indifferent to its dangerous potentials (a drunken sailor declares he has nothing to lose by buying the bottle, since he expects to go to hell regardless). But the bottle makes every Polynesian who touches it melancholic. Keawe and his wife Kokua are so contaminated by its melancholy magic that even their escape from it is marked by dejection: "Is it not a terrible thing to save oneself by the eternal ruin of another?", Kokua laments.[94] Similarly, In "The Isle of Voices" (1892), the protagonist Keola is incapable of touching magic without losing all. Trying to benefit from the magical power exercised by his father-in-law (a man who is "more white to look upon than any foreigner" [103]), Keola is punished for this desire through near-drowning, exile, near-death at the hands of cannibals, and the loss of his wife on the Isle of Voices.[95] Sorrowful and abandoned, Keola eventually manages to escape with his life, but only by renouncing magical power and by incapacitating his father-in-law, the magician.

Stevenson's ethnographic perceptions may have been complexly motivated. But his splitting of magical and melancholic polarities between Germans and Samoans in *A Footnote to History*, together with his devotion of Polynesian characters to melancholia, confirm arguments that racial difference in the colonies was most often defined through oppositions of the normative and the deviant.[96] Most importantly, Stevenson's melancholy islanders never achieve the reintegrated masochism displayed by his successful English characters, particularly by those who revisit evangelical versions of masochism, such as Attwater and Wiltshire. Although it is true that the discourse of colonizers is never unmediated by the cultures with which they come into contact, Stevenson clearly used the clash of European and non-European cultures in Samoa to project onto natives a disrupted masochistic economy that had been transposed directly from the

[94] Robert Louis Stevenson, "The Bottle Imp," *South Sea Tales* (Oxford: Oxford University Press, 1996), p. 97.

[95] Robert Louis Stevenson, "The Isle of Voices," *South Sea Tales* (Oxford: Oxford Univ. Press, 1996), p. 103.

[96] This is Stoler's thesis. See also Robert J. C. Young, *Colonial Desire: Hybridity in Theory, Culture, and Race* (London: Routledge, 1995), p. 180.

unresolved conflicts of his earlier work.[97] This disrupted masochistic economy formed a necessary backdrop to the reinvention of a coherent evangelical masochism by European colonials—whether in the imperial opportunists Stevenson critiqued or in political terms that he endorsed.

ANTI-IMPERIALIST EUPHORIA IN THE SAMOAN CIVIL WAR

Stevenson found the colonies a place to experiment with integrated magical/melancholic projects and perhaps to reclaim their moral authority from the imperial opportunists who both fascinated and troubled him. While his fiction managed no more than a critique of masochistic reintegrations and the cannibalization of middle-class culture that characters like Wiltshire and Attwater represent, he created other texts—some imaginary or unfinished, others dispersed across the enormous range of his South Seas writings (which included history, ethnography, fables, romances, lectures, prayers, correspondence, and ballads)—that transformed the conventions of mid-Victorian fiction by rewriting evangelical forms of masochism in politically dissident terms.[98] The range and restlessness of Stevenson's South Seas writings suggest that he was attempting, in part, to fabricate a new authorial self.[99] The most important feature of this authorial self-construction was Stevenson's sublimation of melancholy magic within the evangelical moral foundations of his own uniquely masochistic anti-imperialism.

Throughout his life, Stevenson had been something of a moralist without a cause. His high-minded tendencies were often held in check by the stylistic and emotional fin-de-siècle detachment he cultivated. But in the South Pacific, for the first time, Stevenson began to find vocations he could embrace without irony. Only a few months out of San Francisco, he

[97] Critics have recently begun exploring the cross-cultural hybridity of Stevenson's South Seas writing, although not yet in terms that illuminate his representations of masochism. See Smith; or Edmond, esp. pp. 20–21. Hillier, pp. 57–82, provides the most thorough discussion of Stevenson's use of Polynesian folklore.

[98] The trajectory of Stevenson's work in the late 1880s and early 1890s has often been seen as disillusioned. See Patrick Brantlinger, *Rule of Darkness: British Literature and Imperialism, 1830–1914* (Ithaca: Cornell University Press, 1988), p. 39; or Joseph Bristow, *Empire Boys: Adventures in a Man's World* (London: Unwin Hyman, 1991), p. 123. My reading accords more closely with Edmond, Colley, or Katherine Linehan, "Taking Up with Kanakas: Stevenson's Complex Social Criticism in 'The Beach of Falesá,'" *English Literature in Transition: 1880–1920* 33 (1990), 407–22, who all regard Stevenson's South Seas writings as creatively engaging processes of social and cultural transformation.

[99] See Smith, p. 107; or Alex Clunas, "'Out of My Country and Myself I Go': Identity and Writing in Stevenson's Early Travel Books," *Nineteenth-Century Prose* 23 (1996), 54–73, esp. p. 62.

was seized with an ethnographic passion and yearned to write the definitive, encyclopedic account of the South Seas: "not many people have seen more of them than I; perhaps no one: certainly no one capable of using the material" (*Letters*, 6:335). He projected a study of history, languages, geography, customs, and climate: "if I can execute what is designed, there are few better books now extant on this globe; bar the epics, and the big tragedies, and histories, and the choice lyric poetics, and a novel or so—none." One hardly needs to observe Stevenson's ignorance of the existing ethnographic work on Polynesia, which was quite extensive at the time, to see the omnipotent thinking behind this project.[100] But nineteenth-century ethnographers always conceived their studies as, in part, a moral mission that required the extermination of the observer's ego. Herbert has documented the pervasiveness, at least since the time of Harriet Martineau's *How to Observe* (1838), of the moral and epistemological angst among Victorian ethnographers, as well as ethnography's affinity with evangelical salvation narratives, which emphasized long, painful battles to annihilate the self's desires and biases.[101] Fanny, horrified by the financial and professional disaster Stevenson's project represented, recognized the self-negating moral impulses at work when she wrote to his editor, Sidney Colvin, for help in dissuading him:

> Louis has the most enchanting material that any one ever had in the whole world . . . and I am afraid he is going to spoil it all. He has taken into his Scotch Stevenson head, that a stern duty lies before him, and that his book must be a sort of scientific and historical impersonal thing . . . . Louis says it is a stern sense of duty that is at the bottom of it, which is more alarming than anything else. (*Letters*, 6:303–304)

Stevenson's ethnographic ambitions may evoke some of the worst extremes of colonial self-aggrandizement, but they were motivated, too, by a desire for reparation and a deep revulsion from egoism and error. He once lamented: " 'tis pitiful, to come here an ignorant, elderly ass and glance at [these islands] for [a] quarter of an hour out of a ship . . . . I have found by experience that the first week in a new place is usually passed in amassing falsehoods, in the second these begin to clear off, but the globe-trotter is already homeward bound and vomiting in a stateroom" (*Letters*, 6:214).

Stevenson eventually scaled back his ethnographic project and published only a series of journalistic sketches, which were collected posthumously

---

[100] See Colley, pp. 76–77. Stevenson first mentioned George Turner's work in 1893, but although he knew of the existence of Thomas Williams, John Williams, William Ellis, and other Polynesian ethnographers, he never acknowledged having read their work, either in his letters or in his published writings.

[101] See Herbert, esp. pp. 155, 171–74.

as *In the South Seas* (1896). But there were other experiments with reintegrated masochistic economies. Although he had always been ostenta-
tiously antireligious, for example, he developed an odd affinity for South
Seas missionaries, declaring that "the missionaries are the best and the
most useful whites in the Pacific" (*ISS*, 18:81).[102] Composing a series
of prayers, each devoted to an abstract moral value shorn of any specific
religious doctrines, Stevenson even played missionary himself and conducted services for his Samoan servants on Sundays—the only white settler
to do so.

Nothing could have betrayed the evangelical within Stevenson more
clearly, perhaps, than his defense of Father Damien, a missionary martyr
and the Belgian Catholic steward of a leper colony on the island of Molo-
kai, who had recently succumbed to leprosy himself. Stevenson risked libel
by publishing a venomous attack on a Protestant cleric (named, ironically,
Dr. Hyde), who had cast aspersions on Damien's morals. Stevenson visited
the leper colony for twelve days in 1889 and transparently identified with
the lepers. He imagined the colony to be suffused with a haunting moral
climate emanating from its collective acceptance of death: a "horror of
moral beauty broods over the place: that's like bad Victor Hugo, but it is
the only way I can express the sense that lived with me all these days"
(*Letters*, 6:311). Yet this identification contributed to a kind of omnipotent euphoria as well. Stevenson's attack on Hyde was so vitriolic that he
felt certain he would be sued. After holding a family council and asking
his dependents for permission to brave the risk of publication, Stevenson
wrote: it is "*probable* I should be ruined . . . how little I care" (*Letters*,
6:377). Symptomatically, Stevenson's thirst for martyrdom in defense of
one missionary coincided with a raging desire to annihilate the other; one
of his biographers has called the Hyde essay "deliberate insult as personal
as a love letter."[103] Stevenson himself declared that he "must smash the
traducer of the dead man for whom he had conceived an ardent admiration."[104] Suffering remorse for this indulgence of self-exalting rage, Stevenson later called his own attack "brutal and cruel," "abominable," "bar-
barously harsh" (*Letters*, 6:402, 404, 420).

But Stevenson's most successful and sustained renovation of middle-
class identity—to the extent that it was grounded, during the mid-Victorian period, in both psychological and evangelical masochistic economies—took the strange form of the anti-imperialist crusade that pervaded

---

[102] For good discussions of Stevenson's relationship to South Seas missionaries and to
evangelical display in general, see Smith, pp. 127–29, 141–42.

[103] Furnas, *Voyage to Windward*, p. 338.

[104] Quoted in George MacKaness, *Robert Louis Stevenson: His Associations with Australia*
(1935; Dubbo, Australia: Review Publications, 1976), pp. 12–13.

his life and work in the early 1890s. Stevenson's anti-imperialist fervor was remarkable given his lifelong aloofness from politics. It was also remarkable given that the political positions he did take before 1890 hardly seem consistent with anti-imperialism. Stevenson's politics have often been traced to his Edinburgh Tory roots, particularly his staunch unionist views, which he expressed as late as 1888 in "Confessions of a Unionist."[105] In 1887, he had conceived an absurd scheme—only prevented by his father's death—to move his entire family to Ireland to take the place of a boycotted English family, besieged on their Tipperary farm by Parnellites. "A writer being murdered would . . . throw a bull's eye light upon this cowardly business," he wrote (*Letters*, 5:390). In addition, Stevenson's early fiction has often been read as a series of conservative allegories of class conflict. *Treasure Island* (1883), for example, can be seen as a fable of middle-class anxiety, with its squire, doctor, and their retainers attacked by a degenerate rabble and its demagogue, John Silver. *Prince Otto* (1885) was only the most virulent of Stevenson's many attacks on socialism, and his diatribes against Gladstone were slanderous. The close friends and supporters who helped him get his literary career off the ground—Charles Baxter, W. E. Henley, Sidney Colvin—were all Edinburgh Tories.[106] Moreover, Stevenson's earlier relationship to travel would not seem to predict political engagements, conservative or otherwise, in the South Seas. His European travel writings—particularly *An Inland Voyage* (1878) and *Travels with a Donkey in the Cévennes* (1879)—had aestheticized travel, making it a vehicle for the elegant detachment of the observer. His deliberately superficial, ironic contact with people and places signified the elitism of the antibourgeois traveler of the period, who, as James Buzard has demonstrated, sought to make travel a performance of personal style rather than an exercise in learning or engagement.[107]

Stevenson's ethnographic aspirations in the South Seas were already a retreat from aestheticized bohemian travel and a return to middle-class moral earnestness.[108] But his political defense of Samoan independence proved a considerably more substantial project, one which has contributed to the reluctance critics of imperialism have shown in trying to classify Stevenson's politics. His nine lengthy, devastatingly detailed

---

[105] Originally written for *Scribner's*, the essay was not published until 1921.

[106] For an informative discussion of Stevenson's place in British politics, see Christopher Harvie, "The Politics of Stevenson," *Stevenson and Victorian Scotland*, pp. 107–25.

[107] James Buzard, *The Beaten Track: European Tourism, Literature, and the Ways to Culture, 1800–1918* (Oxford: Oxford University Press, 1993).

[108] Stevenson also departed from aestheticized travel narratives on his earlier trips to the New World. In *The Silverado Squatters* (1883), he identified imaginatively with both Native Americans and Chinese immigrants to California. In *The Amateur Emigrant* (1895), he portrayed steerage passengers on the voyage across the Atlantic with great sympathy.

open letters to the *Times* about the exploitation of Samoans (in addition to a letter to the *Pall Mall Gazette*, later published as a pamphlet) as well as his fraternization with the rebel Samoan army were seen as dangerous enough to provoke new sedition regulations from the high commissioner of the western Pacific that were targeted directly at Stevenson, nearly leading to his deportation.[109] Stevenson's activism, of course, had a variety of conflicting motivations: to protect white settlers' economic interests, to preserve peace at all costs, and to correct administrative bungling and inefficiency. But they revolved as well around a deeply held conviction, which he loudly championed in the *Times*, and which, if implemented, would have cost him dearly: that the Great Powers should withdraw from Samoa and leave the native government autonomous.[110] True to form, he was willing to back his beliefs at considerable personal risk: during the uprising of 1893, he gave substantial aid and comfort to the rebels, and he declared in the *Times* that he was a "partisan" of the rebel chief (*Letters*, 8:268). One of the less immediate risks Stevenson took involved his literary reputation, which suffered because he was seen as having gone native, having lost his authorial equilibrium in the heat of a moral crusade, and having lapsed into an infelicitous realistic style. Oscar Wilde spoke for many when he remarked: "I see that romantic settings are the worst surroundings possible for a romantic writer. In Gower Street Stevenson could have written a new *Trois Mousquetaires*. In Samoa he wrote letters to the *Times* about Germans."[111]

What magical and melancholic fantasy structures can reveal about Stevenson's anti-imperialism is how deeply it drew on the regenerated evangelical masochism that colonial spaces seemed to make available for ideological reworking. They can also reveal how deeply that masochism, in turn, shaped his political perceptions. Stevenson never experienced a religious conversion, and his absorption of evangelical attitudes had something of the unorthodox homeliness of Wiltshire's. But the stringent crusade of anti-imperialist self-martyrdom to which he committed his energies in the early 1890s was deeply indebted to the moral tone of evangelical activism, particularly through its integration of the magical and melancholic phases of masochistic fantasy.

The megalomaniacal phase of Stevenson's crusade is easiest to spot. His political self-aggrandizement caused him to end *A Footnote to History* with a direct appeal to Bismarck, and he reported being disappointed by Bismarck's ensuing silence as well as by the failure of German officials in

---

[109] See Furnas, "Stevenson and Exile," pp. 400–401; or Hennessy, pp. 258–59.

[110] See *Letters*, 8:267; or Furnas, *Voyage to Windward*, p. 225.

[111] Oscar Wilde, *The Letters of Oscar Wilde*, ed. Rupert Hart-Davis (London: Hart-Davis, 1962), p. 520.

Samoa to admire the book, even after he had hand-delivered copies to each one of them it had insulted. Although Stevenson reported such disappointments tongue-in-cheek, his naïve hope that his work would have a momentous impact is nevertheless unmistakable. Repeating some of the grandiose illusions he had entertained about his ethnographic writings, he declared:

> Here is for the first time a tale of Greeks—Homeric Greeks—mingled with moderns, and all true; Odysseus alongside of Rajah Brooke, *proportion gardée*; and all true. Here is for the first time since the Greeks (that I remember) the history of a handful of men, where all know each other in the eyes and live close in a few acres, narrated at length and with the seriousness of history. Talk of the modern novel; here is a modern history. And if I had the misfortune to found a school, the legitimate historian might lie down and die, for he could never overtake his material. (*Letters*, 7:196)

With perhaps even more grandiosity, Stevenson hinted to his highly connected London friends that he would accept the British consulship of Samoa were it offered to him.[112] He also led a delegation of white settlers that absurdly petitioned the Foreign Office to make alterations to the Berlin Treaty of 1889. More disturbingly, Stevenson took advantage of native gratitude to enhance his own social power: in exchange for his interventions on behalf of political prisoners, for example, a Samoan chief had his subjects build a road to Stevenson's estate, which was itself an Abbotsford-like monument to his nostalgia for unbounded patriarchal authority. And despite his occasional successes, the giddy vanity of Stevenson's activism often lent it a puckish quality, which has given one historian "the impression of ability and energy being frittered away in petty controversy."[113] This giddiness could seem callous, as when he wrote of an impending war that was to claim hundreds of lives: "war is a huge *entraînement*; there is no other temptation to be compared to it, not one" (*Letters*, 8:122).

But Stevenson's anti-imperial megalomania, I would argue, is inextricably related to his deeply felt affinity for martyrdom—both his own and that of the Samoans, with whom he passionately identified. Stevenson's advocacy of Samoan independence, for example, began paradoxically in the conviction that it was already a lost cause. *A Footnote to History*, written before he declared for independence in the *Times*, opens with the blunt assertion that Samoan autonomy is "now no longer possible" (82). Misperceiving the plot to confederate Hawaii and Samoa as part of a "visionary [scheme] for the protection and development of the Polynesian race," Stevenson also observed that its "most obvious fault" was that "it came

---

[112] See *Letters*, 7:153; 7:310; 7:386.
[113] Gilson, p. 403.

too late" (105). And at the same time that Stevenson was agitating publicly for independence, he confessed to friends that Samoa was destined to become a Protectorate.[114] The belated quixotism of Stevenson's activism was not lost on the *Times*, which reproved him in an editorial: "It would doubtless be pleasant to wander . . . amid the verdure and flowers of Upolu with the mind so free from the carking cares of civilization as to find keen enjoyment in championing the lost causes of Samoan clans."[115]

A crucial feature of Stevenson's anti-imperialism, grounded as it was in dynamic circuits of magical and melancholic masochism, was its political fluidity. An anti-imperialist politics that depends on the psychic resonance of martyrdom is always in danger of sliding back into jingoism or into any other set of political representations that employs the logic of masochistic fantasy. The abrupt political transition Stevenson made—from unionist to defender of Samoan independence—illustrates this slippage quite clearly. Stevenson also explained the origins of his political engagements in an extraordinary way, linking his megalomaniacal fantasy of himself as Samoan rescuer to the death of that icon of imperial heroism General Gordon, the so-called Martyr of Khartoum. His friend and official biographer Thomas Graham Balfour recalls that Stevenson never ceased to reproach himself that "I did not say then in the papers what I might have said before it was too late. I might not have been able to save Gordon, but at least I should feel I had done something. It was this thought that finally induced me to write my first letter to *The Times* about Samoa. I thought, I have lost one opportunity, I will not lose another."[116] The diametrically opposed positions of Stevenson and Kipling or Haggard on British imperialism always threaten to merge through the logic of masochism, which is drawn to ideologically mobile conjunctions of the magical in the melancholic or the melancholic in the magical.

It should already be apparent, too, that one final motivation of Stevenson's defense of Samoan independence was that it promised, in rather surprising ways, to reconcile the ideological confusions of a middle-class subject torn between colorful, stylized rebellions and moral earnestness. That Stevenson found his political work in Samoa wholly consuming but also a lark suggests that only in the South Seas could he discover a political role that brought together the playful bohemian ironist and the bourgeois moralist. In a letter from which I quoted earlier, he relished the "fine elements of farce" in Samoan politics, "which repay a man in passing,

---

[114] See *Letters*, 8:125.

[115] *Times*, 2 June 1894, p. 13.

[116] Balfour, from a ms. in the National Library of Scotland, quoted in *Letters*, 6:250n. See also Graham Balfour, *The Life of Robert Louis Stevenson*, 2 vols. (New York: Scribner's, 1901), 2:26.

involving many dark and many moonlight rides, secret councils which are at once divulged, sealed letters which are read aloud in confidence to the neighbours, and a mass of fudge and fun" (*Letters*, 7:163).

Yet Stevenson's campaign for Samoan rights was often driven by a genuinely self-martyring moral passion. It was his instinctive identification with the unappreciated virtue and undeserved punishment of the Samoans' resistance that compelled him to identify wholeheartedly with their cause. As he wrote in the *Times*:

> I despair, in so short a space, to interest English readers in their wrongs; with the mass of people at home they will pass for some sort of cannibal islanders, with whom faith were superfluous, upon whom kindness might be partly thrown away. And, indeed, I recognise [*sic*] with gladness that . . . the Samoans have had throughout the honours of the game. (*Letters*, 6:252)

If Stevenson hoped to find a resolution to internal middle-class ideological conflicts in the South Seas, he looked for it, finally, in the form of a moral martyrdom—but a moral martyrdom linked to political work that engaged his sympathies unreservedly. For this reason, perhaps, he wrote to the *Times* most movingly of the exile of the rebel chief Mataafa and his followers, with whose political martyrdom and unjust treatment he identified: "Their punishment is to be sent to a coral atoll and detained there prisoners. It does not sound much; it is a great deal. Taken from a mountain island, they must inhabit a narrow strip of reef sunk to the gunwale in the ocean. . . . I remember what our present King looked like, what a phantom he was, when he returned from captivity in the same place" (*Letters*, 8:275).

The practical results of this moral identification cannot be dismissed. *A Footnote to History* is a clearsighted indictment of German economic exploitation of Samoa as well as a ferociously well-documented account of the mismanagement of the Samoan political crisis by all three imperial powers—British, German, and American. It is also a stinging critique of colonialism in general, which Stevenson called "this dance of folly and injustice and unconscious rapacity" (*Letters*, 7:153). Masochistic identifications may be transparently personal, but they can also fuel lucid historical writing as well as indignant political protest. As E. P. Thompson has shown, evangelical values inspired generations of British radicals, whatever else the social function of those values may have been.[117] Late in his life, Stevenson took up a surprising place in that radical tradition. Most importantly, his writings in Samoa help demonstrate the decisive role played by masochistic fantasy in forms of British political activism

---

[117] E. P. Thompson, *The Making of the English Working Class* (New York: Pantheon, 1964), pp. 26–54.

that were driven by class-coded, quasievangelical moral imperatives, which circumvented—rather than resolving—the ideological incoherence of his earlier work.

THE REVERSIBILITY OF MASOCHISTIC POLITICS

There are, of course, many important features of Stevenson's anti-imperialism that derive from its magical/melancholic conjunctions. One of these is its deep roots in intraclass competition and its reproduction—in strange new forms—of an evangelically inflected moral masochism that had gone underground in the late nineteenth century, becoming an often unrecognized touchstone for a variety of psychosocial colonial identities. Another is the complex grammar of identifications and disavowals that enabled Stevenson to construct a regenerated masochistic subjectivity through distinctions of class and race. Masochistic fantasy structures often blur the black-and-white political lines sometimes used to decide which Victorian writers took the most enlightened stand on questions of empire. This blurring should encourage us to see progressive political stands of any kind as, on some occasions, the product of complex class dynamics as well as the efflorescence of masochistic identifications that are complexly mediated by ideologies of class or by religious discourse. Late-Victorian masochistic fantasy is both tremendously important to political analysis and very difficult to read because it exploits a disarticulated middle-class social consciousness, which became available for drastic rewritings in colonial spaces. A central contention of this book is that such fantasy operates like a switching mechanism for rewriting social discourse rather than a political instrument with a fixed ideology of its own.

While contemporary psychoanalytic theory can interpret late-century political self-martyrdoms in ways that are precluded by conventional definitions of masochism as eroticized submission, I have done little more in this chapter than sketch some of those possible rewritings. Nevertheless, the case of Stevenson demonstrates that we can learn a great deal about political self-representations through the attentive reading of literary (and nonliterary) masochistic texts. Rather than simply manifesting a fixed psychic structure—as writers were once thought, by an older version of psychoanalytic criticism, to do—Stevenson used masochistic fantasy to rewrite his relationship to late-century middle-class culture and to extract from moral discourse a way to negotiate what had seemed in his earlier work to be hopelessly intractable ideological conflicts.

Stevenson channeled the moral and psychological authority previously identified with evangelical middle-class culture into an anti-imperialist crusade that broke with the apolitical bohemianism of his earlier writing and that enabled a dissident yet "respectable" politics—one that the *Times* as well as British authorities in London and in the South Pacific felt obliged to engage in dialogue. At the same time, the evangelical tone of Stevenson's Samoan writings was not likely to win him much of an audience among gentrified British readers, who, like Oscar Wilde, were likely to find it belated and, perhaps, vulgar—a tone more appropriate to Kipling and his readership, as we will see in chapter 3. In consequence, Stevenson's crusade may have netted only small, local victories: the dismissal of a couple of German officials, the release of a few political prisoners, the education of a few readers (and influential visitors) in the colonial realities of Samoa. His attempts to gather Polynesian ballads and folktales (following in the footsteps of Allan Ramsay, Robert Burns, Walter Scott, and others who tried to preserve oral Highland culture) were largely failures, even though they displayed a serious interest in cross-cultural translation. But, in the early 1890s, at a time when British imperial expansion was rarely contested politically, such victories are not to be dismissed, especially when we consider the improbability of Stevenson's moral and psychological conversion to anti-imperialist causes in the first place. From the rise of Disraeli's Tories in 1874 until the fiasco of the South African War (1899–1902), public criticism of imperialism was decidedly muted. Stevenson's protest against British policies stands out dramatically against this background. It made him an embarrassment to his Tory friends as well as a subtle but distinct influence on skeptics of imperialism from Joseph Conrad to George Orwell.

In regard to his attitudes toward class, many of Stevenson's critics have either lionized him for his antibourgeois gestures or generalized about his crankiness toward middle-class culture. But Stevenson was not simply a decadent aesthete, and he was not passively ambivalent about his relationship to bourgeois culture. Nor can he simply be dismissed as a colonial eccentric. His manipulation of the elements of masochistic fantasy was an aggressive, coherent intervention in the politics of middle-class subjectivity as well as in the struggles over imperial ideology that they touched—even if the results of such struggles are always inevitably mixed. Stevenson's neoevangelical approach to late-century conflicts within middle-class culture should not blind us to the vigorous displacement of those conflicts that evangelical masochism facilitated in his South Seas writings. It should also demonstrate that perversity has a vital, sometimes salutary, but often unpredictable place in the service of political radicalism.[118]

---

[118] Jacqueline Rose, *States of Fantasy* (Oxford: Clarendon Press, 1996), p. 92, has argued that we need "an account of justice" that includes its "perverse component" to counter political idealisms that deny and displace their own unconscious energies.

Chapter Two

OLIVE SCHREINER'S PREOEDIPAL DREAMS

Feminism, Class, and the South African War

As I walk'd through the wilderness of this world, I
lighted on a certain place, where was a Denn; And I laid
me down in that place to sleep: And as I slept I
dreamed a Dream.
—John Bunyan, *The Pilgrim's Progress*

OLIVE Schreiner's masochistic disposition has been obvious to anyone familiar with her self-defeating protagonists or the pathos of her own biography: the head banging; the infatuations with powerful, bullying men; the family persecutions from which, at the very least, she did little to shield herself.[1] But what makes Schreiner's masochism particularly useful to cultural analysis is the wide range of social boundaries it crossed. A native-born South African with British citizenship; a preeminent feminist who wrote instrumentally about race and empire; an obscure, bankrupt missionary's daughter who became the darling of London intellectual circles; a novelist whose tracts and speeches placed her at the center of South African politics—Schreiner illustrates like no other writer what happens to masochistic fantasy as it traverses the domains of gender, class, nation, and race.

Schreiner's masochism, however, has tended to be the exclusive concern of feminist readers. This is not simply because of the vexed theoretical relationship between masochism and feminism. Feminist readers have also been concerned about the self-punitive turn taken by certain currents in

---

[1] According to her husband, when Schreiner was a child she would bang her head against the wall until she was half stunned. See Samuel Cron Cronwright-Schreiner, *The Life of Olive Schreiner* (London: T. Fisher Unwin, 1924), p. 236. Hereafter cited as *Life*. He also records that, at a fashionable dinner party, she became so enraged with Cecil Rhodes "that she not only hammered her fists violently on her head and on the table but also banged her forehead on it with such force that the guests actually were alarmed lest she would injure herself" (208). Ruth First and Ann Scott, *Olive Schreiner* (London: Andre Deutsch, 1980), p. 115, cite unconfirmed evidence that Schreiner had a sexual relationship with a sadistic man and that she "discovered to her horror that she liked being a masochist." Both biographies have extensive discussions of the persecutions she suffered at the hands of family members.

the late-Victorian women's movement, which Schreiner seems to exemplify. While many late-century feminists continued to attack hierarchies of sexual oppression through the liberal discourse of women's rights launched by Mary Wollstonecraft and John Stuart Mill, others made women themselves their critical targets.[2] As Schreiner herself once wrote: "It is not against man we have to fight but against *ourselves* within ourselves."[3] Second-wave feminists were repelled by a number of seemingly perverse constraints some "New Woman" writers placed on themselves: a rigid code of sexual self-denial, often presented as a politicized gesture; a programmatic defeatism, which transformed disappointment with women's social prospects into postures of saintly martyrdom; and an idealization of self-sacrifice (particularly maternal self-sacrifice), which has been viewed either as a concession to eugenics or a residue of mid-Victorian gender ideology.[4]

Schreiner's masochism, in particular, has not had a good press, especially among 1970s and 1980s feminists. It has long been recognized, of course, that she was on the leading edge of New Woman feminism when she wrote *The Story of an African Farm* (1883) and that *Woman and Labor* (1911), the first part of which was published in magazine form in 1899, was "the Bible" of the suffragist movement.[5] W. T. Stead called *The Story of an African Farm* "the forerunner of all the novels of the Modern Woman," and Vera Brittain spoke for many when she remembered *Woman and Labor* as having caused "my final acceptance of feminism."[6] Yet second-wave feminists struggled to separate what they valued in Schreiner's

[2] The "New Woman" was a notoriously plural figure. For a good overview, see Ann L. Ardis, *New Women, New Novels: Feminism and Early Modernism* (New Brunswick: Rutgers University Press, 1990), pp. 10–14. For a discussion of "equal rights" feminists, who followed in the tradition of Wollstonecraft and Mill, see Sally Ledger, *The New Woman: Fiction and Feminism at the Fin de Siècle* (Manchester: Manchester University Press, 1997), pp. 15, 37.

[3] Richard Rive, ed., *Olive Schreiner Letters, Volume 1: 1871–1899*, 1 vol. (Oxford: Oxford University Press, 1988), p. 145. Hereafter cited as "*Rive*."

[4] Elaine Showalter, *A Literature of Their Own: British Women Novelists from Brontë to Lessing* (Princeton: Princeton University Press, 1977), p. 194, condemns New Woman self-punitiveness, claiming extravagantly that "in this generation [of feminists] female suicide became conspicuous for the first time." Sheila Rowbotham, *Women, Resistance and Revolution: A History of Women and Revolution in the Modern World* (New York: Pantheon, 1972), p. 94, disparages what she sees as Schreiner's mysticism of shared pain. For other second-wave feminist critiques, see Gail Cunningham, *The New Woman and the Victorian Novel* (London: Macmillan, 1978), p. 64; and Patricia Stubbs, *Women and Fiction: Feminism and the Novel, 1880–1920* (New York: Barnes and Noble, 1979), p. 126.

[5] Showalter, p. 199, describes Lyndall, in *The Story of an African Farm*, as the "first wholly serious feminist heroine." Ardis, p. 31, gives a more measured account of *The Story of an African Farm*'s place in 1880s feminist fiction.

[6] William T. Stead, "The Book of the Month: The Novel of the Modern Woman," *Review of Reviews* 10 (1894), p. 64. Vera Brittain, *Testament of Youth: An Autobiographical Study of the Years 1900–1925* (London: Victor Gollancz, 1933), p. 28.

work (her demand for women's access to intellectual professions, her protests against the inequities of marriage and the double standard, her support for suffragism) from what might generally be construed as her masochism. They disliked her harsh fictional stereotypes of women, her uncompromising destruction of her own heroines, her idealization of selfless maternity and female self-sacrifice, and her obsession with guilt and expiation. They also balked at what they saw as her self-defeating personal choices or what Elaine Showalter called her "perverse will to fail."[7] In addition, the exclusive focus of second-wave feminists on questions of gender oppression confined discussions of Schreiner's masochism to the realm of sexual politics, obscuring its connection to other social, cultural, or political phenomena and increasing the odds that it would be viewed negatively in the aftermath of the 1960s' sexual revolution.[8]

Since the 1990s, however, Schreiner has become more identified with discourses of mastery than submission. Recent critics have judged her as racist and imperialist for some of the very same gestures that troubled the preceding generation, which saw these tendencies as concessions to male power—particularly her idealizations of self-denial, sexual purity, and maternal self-sacrifice. Schreiner's exaltation of these kinds of female askesis are now often seen (sometimes rather smugly) as complicit with eugenic and evolutionary discourses that privileged white, middle-class women, whose maternal mission and sexual purity New Woman writers are reputed to have celebrated as the engine of British racial superiority.[9] Anne McClintock, for example, regrets that a "sad logic of Christian masochism" lay at the bottom of Schreiner's "tortuous logic of gender rebellion and guilt," producing "an obscure economy of feminine identity through denial." McClintock claims that the "flight into fantasy" with which

---

[7] Showalter. p. 198. The most thorough psychogenic reading is Marion V. Friedmann, *Olive Schreiner: A Study in Latent Meanings* (Johannesburg: Witwatersrand University Press, 1955), which attributes nearly everything in Schreiner's work to the negligence and cruelty of her mother.

[8] Those few literary critics who have tried to affirm Schreiner's masochism usually restrict themselves to questions of sexual freedom. See, for example, Christopher Lane, *The Burdens of Intimacy: Psychoanalysis and Victorian Masculinity* (Chicago: University of Chicago Press, 1999), pp. 93–118.

[9] Recently, there has been a flurry of work taking this critical perspective, including Ledger; Carolyn Burdett, *Olive Schreiner and the Progress of Feminism: Evolution, Gender, Empire* (New York: Palgrave, 2001); Paula Krebs, *Gender, Race, and the Writing of Empire: Public Discourse and the Boer War* (Cambridge: Cambridge University Press, 1999); and Laura Chrisman, *Rereading the Imperial Romance: British Imperialism and South African Resistance in Haggard, Schreiner, and Plaatje* (Oxford: Clarendon Press, 2000). Laura E. Franey, *Victorian Travel Writing and Imperial Violence: British Writing on Africa, 1855–1902* (New York: Palgrave, 2003), p. 79, calls Schreiner's work "an apology for paternalist (and maternalist) imperialism."

Schreiner escaped her masochistic inversion "blinded [Schreiner] to the colonial cast" of her mysticism and "concealed the very real history of colonial plunder."[10] This kind of analysis typifies the critical shift of the last decade, which has separated a narrowly sexualized view of Schreiner's masochism along with its apparent acquiescence to male power from indictments of her participation in colonialist mastery—even though what appears to be her "imperial feminism" still derives in some way from female askesis.

By shifting the political domains within which Schreiner's self-martyring tactics are said to have functioned, succeeding critical generations appear to have each been viewing one half of the dynamics of sadomasochism in her work while obscuring the other. More importantly, as I will argue at the end of this chapter, what links both generations of Schreiner's detractors is their disavowal of feminism's historical debt to the politics of masochism. This disavowal sometimes takes the form of contemporary critical fantasies of moral, political, and psychological purity, which disguise their dependence on the very same logic of masochistic victimage they proudly reject.

In this chapter, I will attempt to redress both the confinement of Schreiner's masochism to the realm of sexuality—which, I believe, has resulted in far too pessimistic a view of its function as a feminist strategy—and the recent overemphasis on imperialist discourses of mastery in her South African writings. In the first two sections, I will reread Schreiner's feminist strategies in the context of a nonsexualized model of masochism, which can help illuminate the political potency of late-Victorian gestures of feminist self-wounding. In the rest of the chapter, I will use this same model to analyze the political strategies of Schreiner's writings on South Africa. In the process, I hope to link Schreiner's feminist and anti-imperial politics by means of the political category most neglected in studies of masochism (and in studies of Schreiner): social class. My primary contention is that Schreiner conducted a visionary rewriting of middle-class identity through masochistic fantasy and that this social regeneration played a central role in her thinking about both sexual and colonial conflict. Recognizing the urgency of Schreiner's concerns with social class can thus help us understand the choices she made in other political domains. Many of Schreiner's inconsistencies on questions of race and gender spring from the peculiar relationship in her thinking between masochism and social class. But it is also through masochistic discourses of class that her feminist writings cohere with her defense—however selective—of certain victims of British imperialism.

---

[10] Anne McClintock, *Imperial Leather: Race, Gender and Sexuality in the Colonial Contest* (New York: Routledge, 1995), pp. 262, 266.

In making these arguments, I am seeking less to rescue Schreiner from her critics, past or present, than to restore the political complexities of masochism, which, like other psychological or symbolic processes, often crosses social boundaries in dynamic ways. Moreover, tracing the intersection of sexual and imperial politics with masochistic discourses of social class highlights an important theme of this book: that all forms of political idealism (right or left) are implicated in what we often think of as perversity—a recognition political radicals neglect at their peril. But my primary goal is to resituate Schreiner's political vision in a more nuanced social field than that used by critics who have seen her either as a dupe of patriarchy or a tool of imperialist domination.

I will begin by locating Schreiner's particular constellation of masochistic fantasy structures within the relational psychoanalytic model outlined in the introduction. Any understanding of Schreiner's political uses of masochism depends on recognizing their preoedipal character as well as their particular confrontations with oedipal sexuality. These aspects of Schreiner's masochism deeply conditioned the correlations between class, gender, and race in her work. The complexities of Schreiner's attempt to regenerate both British and South African culture do not emanate from postures of either submission or domination alone but from her systematic refusal of these tactics in the name of a very different kind of pleasure economy.

THE CLASH OF PLEASURE ECONOMIES IN
THE STORY OF AN AFRICAN FARM

Schreiner's masochistic imagination, like Stevenson's, was overwhelmingly preoedipal. For that reason, it has not been well served by literary and cultural criticism, which overvalues masochism's relationship to oedipal sexuality and its characteristic themes: domination and submission; sexualized sadism; rivalry within the oedipal triangle. Relational psychological approaches, by contrast, usefully explain masochism's role in the kinds of presexual difficulties with individuation and separation that have long been recognized as central to Schreiner's life and thought.[11] In particular, relational theory has charted the fantasies of omnipotence that masochism generates to resolve these narcissistic conflicts. Whatever else they might do, such fantasies can either discount the barriers keeping the

[11] See, for example, Joyce Avrech Berkman, *Olive Schreiner: Feminism on the Frontier* (St. Alban's, VT: Eden Press, 1979), pp. 49–50.

self isolated from others or glamorize self-sufficiency.[12] Conflicts between autonomy and dependence can thus be resolved by imagining either alternative as a triumphant absolute. Omnipotent fantasy can also conceive autonomy and dependence in some magical way as noncontradictory. Schreiner's masochism activates all three forms of fantasy as responses to narcissistic conflict.

Although masochism in Schreiner's work is best understood in preoedipal terms, however, it sometimes confusingly adopts oedipal forms. Psychoanalytic theorists who attempt to articulate the differences between these two paradigms for masochism have proposed various ways of accounting for their occasional convergence. Some have argued that while masochistic fantasy often begins in response to preoedipal trauma, it can be altered substantially—or even first activated—at the oedipal stage. Others have suggested that an individual's attempt to transgress the boundaries between these developmental phases may itself represent an instance of omnipotent fantasy.[13] Attempting to gratify oedipalized sexual pleasures within preoedipal patterns of relationship may constitute a form of magical thinking that "murders reality" by denying the difference between adult and infantile experience.

Schreiner's masochism revolved around this particular symbolic transgression. She often invoked forms of oedipal masochism that were sexualized, linked to aggressive or sadistic impulses, or tied to adult relationships that preclude infantile gratification. But she always then subsumed these oedipalized forms of masochism within preoedipal modes of gratification. In making this claim, I am not suggesting that Schreiner stigmatized oedipality in order to affirm some kind of "law of the mother," as a few recent critics have argued, but only that she conflated distinctly different developmental stages of experience in service of a particular kind of narcissistic omnipotence.[14] Schreiner's tendency to incorporate sadistic sexual desires within comforting, preoedipal relationships was fundamental to her reformulation of sexual love and to a number of other feminist projects in her work, including her struggle with scientific discourses of sexual difference. It was also central to her reformulation of middle-class subjectivity. In this section, I will explore exactly what it means to say that Schreiner

---

[12] See Peter Blos, "Sadomasochism and the Defense against Recall of Painful Affect," *Journal of the American Psychoanalytic Association* 39 (1991), 417–30; and Arnold Cooper, "The Narcissistic-Masochistic Character," *Masochism: Current Psychoanalytic Perspectives*, ed. Robert A. Glick and Donald I. Meyers (Hillsdale, NJ: The Analytic Press, 1988), pp. 117–38.

[13] Jack Novick and Kerry Kelly Novick, *Fearful Symmetry: The Development and Treatment of Sadomasochism* (Northvale, NJ: Jason Aronson, 1996), p. 93.

[14] For an instance of such a reading, see Simon Lewis, *White Women Writers and Their African Invention* (Gainesville: University Press of Florida, 2003), pp. 64–65.

submerged oedipal within preoedipal masochism before tracing the importance of that process to her political work in the rest of the chapter.

One of the most striking instances of Schreiner's tendency to privilege preoedipal over oedipal forms of masochism occurs in Part One of *The Story of an African Farm*. The beating of Waldo by Bonaparte Blenkins includes many of the features Freud would later identify with oedipal fantasy: punishment for sexual transgression, a wish to transform the father's sadism into love, an eroticization of punishment, and guilt over various forms of desire for both mother and father. As Blenkins ties Waldo up, he demands Waldo's "submission," and speaks of himself as a "father" who has to "check and correct" Waldo.[15] Faithful to the oedipal script, Blenkins accuses Waldo of forbidden desire for the dried fruits, stored in an inaccessible attic, that belong to the woman Blenkins himself desires sexually. The scene of paternal punishment is heavily eroticized: Blenkins calls for Waldo's "naked" (170) back, and strips him by slitting his shirt with a penknife. The beating scene is also classically triangulated by two women: Tant' Sannie, the object of Blenkins's desires, and Lyndall, the novel's feminist heroine, who identifies vicariously with Waldo's suffering while at the same time basking in her immunity from it.

Yet this scene of oedipal sadomasochism fails to come off. Waldo registers no emotional response to Blenkins, refusing to cry out or even to speak to him during the beating. Aside from "a wild fitful terror in the eyes" (108), Waldo remains strangely abstracted during this scene. The "terror" in his eyes, it turns out, derives not from forbidden sexual desire, paternal punishment, or guilt, but from the narcissistic traumas of abandonment and neglect he associates with a cruel and unresponsive deity. Praying to God after the beating, Waldo "could not feel Him. He prayed aloud, very loud, and he got no answer; when he listened it was all quite quiet" (108).

This framework of understanding is established in the novel's very first scene, in which Waldo lies awake at night, tormented by the thought of the multitudes God consigns to hell without mercy for their suffering. Soon after, he is devastated by God's apparent failure to accept the sacrifice of his mutton chop, when no fire flashes out of the heavens to consume it in response to his prayers. Waldo's disappointment with God's neglect leads him to conclude, first, in an agony of baffled dependence, that "God hates me" (25); and then, in an ecstasy of emotional independence, that "I hate God!" (26). Yet his deep-seated inability to accept divine abandonment fuels Waldo's anguished intellectual speculations throughout the first part of the novel.

---

[15] Olive Schreiner, *The Story of an African Farm* (London: Virago, 1989), pp. 106–7. For all other Schreiner texts, I have used first editions, since no recent editions are available. Dates in parenthesis refer to first publication, whether in book or magazine form.

It is this preoedipal trauma that Waldo's beating reawakens, not the oedipal crisis staged by Blenkins, who actually epitomizes, through his ineffectualness, the absence of proper paternal authority on the farm. When Waldo has the chance to reverse the polarities of mastery and submission, after Blenkins has been dismissed by Tant' Sannie for his own wayward sexual desires, he again displays no interest in this castrated father figure. He responds to Blenkins's final erotic overture ("we can both sleep in this bed: there's plenty of room. Do stay, my boy, please" [115]) by walking off without a word and sleeping in the horse wagon. In keeping with the logic of preoedipal masochism, Waldo also suppresses any anger he might feel toward Blenkins. Preoedipal masochism has often been attributed, in part, to the child's inability to direct rage outward at parental figures, against whom it would be too dangerous to rebel, or whose protective authority must itself be protected from the child's annihilative wishes.[16]

Lyndall's stark refusal to participate in Blenkins's sadomasochism parallels Waldo's. Following her earlier advice to her cousin Em not "to let Bonaparte know he is hurting you" (75), Lyndall pretends to ignore Waldo's beating and imprisonment, advising Em that to demand his release would only be to gratify Blenkins. When she finally does free Waldo, she refuses to play any part in the oedipal narrative, neither viewing Waldo as the child whose beating proves her own rivalrous possession of the father's love, nor deriving voyeuristic pleasure from his punishment, nor vicariously expiating her own sexual guilt in an identification with him.[17]

Lyndall's relationships with men in Part Two of the novel continue to privilege preoedipal over oedipal forms of masochism. But they also begin to effect the submergence of sexual sadomasochism within preoedipal fantasy that will later come to characterize Schreiner's feminist ideals for sexual love. Many critics have seen *The Story of an African Farm* as an indictment of the sadomasochism that Schreiner supposedly identified with heterosexual relations, which have sometimes been interpreted as metaphors for colonialism as well.[18] But the novel does not consistently distance sadomasochistic sexuality, as it so clearly does in the scene of Waldo's beating. Rather, it sometimes incorporates sadomasochistic sexuality into preoedipal fantasy. Lyndall's affair with a sadistic stranger, which results in her own death as well as that of her illegitimate child, has commonly been

---

[16] See Novick and Novick, p. 29.

[17] Sigmund Freud, "A Child Is Being Beaten," *The Standard Edition of the Complete Psychological Works of Sigmund Freud*, trans. and ed. James Strachey, 24 vols. (London: Hogarth Press, 1953–73), 17:175–204, locates all these impulses in the third phase of the beating fantasy.

[18] See Gerald Monsman, "Olive Schreiner: Literature and the Politics of Power," *Texas Studies in Literature and Language* 30 (1988), p. 585.

read as a warning about conventional heterosexual relations, and Lyndall has often been seen as the victim of her own contradictory desires for both feminist assertiveness and sexual submission.[19] But the preoedipal content of her sexual masochism aligns it with infantile fantasy and places it in a more complex relationship to Schreiner's feminist ideals than may be evident to those who understand masochism solely in terms of sexual mastery and submission.

Lyndall's sexual desires are, of course, unmistakably masochistic: she loves her stranger because he is "the first man I ever was afraid of" (219), and she tells him: "you love me because you cannot bear to be resisted, and want to master me." Yet her sexual masochism is oddly mixed with nonerotic desires for an omnipotent caretaker, infantile wishes that parallel Waldo's yearning for divine love. Lyndall's self-destructive plan to run off with her stranger, unmarried, is partly an attempt to transform him into a parental, rather than simply a sexual partner: "You may take me away with you, and take care of me" (220), she tells him, and as they plan their flight together, she adopts the postures of a wounded child. "She looked into his eyes," we are told, "as a little child might whom a long day's play had saddened" (221). He assumes a complementary parental role, calling her "Poor little thing!", and observing, in surprise: "You are only a child." Although his affair with her ends in abandonment, he later beseeches her to let him return as her protector: "My darling," he writes, "let me put my hand round you, and guard you from the world. As my wife they shall never touch you. I have learnt to love you more wisely, more tenderly, than of old; you shall have perfect freedom" (259).

Lyndall's affair thus submerges sexual sadomasochism within yearnings for an ideal preoedipal world: dependence on an omnipotent figure who promises to grant both full protection and "perfect freedom," the kind of freedom she had always known marriage would never provide. It was in search of such "perfect freedom," however illusory, that she had chosen an unmarried liaison in the first place. Readers sometimes forget that Lyndall fully expects to survive her flight with her lover and that she envisions their "future lives" (220). But Lyndall's lover himself points to the signs of infantile, magical thinking in her plan: "You are acting like a little child . . . . It is all very well to have ideals and theories; but you know as well as anyone can that they must not be carried into the practical world" (218).

The transformation of Lyndall's sadistic lover into an omnipotent parent who gratifies all wishes (even contradictory wishes for both autonomy

---

[19] See Lane, p. 95, or Joseph Bristow, "Introduction," *The Story of an African Farm* (Oxford: Oxford University Press, 1992), p. xix. Lyndall's sadistic potentials have also troubled critics: Monsman, p. 594, sees her as simply wishing to reverse the sadomasochistic relations that threaten to envelop her.

and dependence) was not a resolution Schreiner appeared to endorse. This conflation of oedipal and preoedipal objects of desire is, in principle, an unattainable fantasy, an instance of omnipotent thinking. But the novel does magically realize precisely such a fantasy in its concluding episodes through the figure of Gregory Rose. A would-be domineering lover, Gregory is fantastically transformed into a nurturing mother figure for Lyndall. Discovering her abandoned and terminally ill, Gregory cross-dresses and poses as her nurse. Usually understood as an exploration of androgyny, or of enlightened masculinity, or even of homosexuality, Gregory's cross-dressing should also be seen as the logical culmination of Lyndall's search for a preoedipal pleasure economy that might absorb sexual sadomasochism.[20] Lyndall's willfully chosen suffering turns Gregory into both a controlling male lover and an obedient mother who gratifies all wishes. Gregory ministers to her every need as he nurses her through her last days, refusing even to deflate the delusional, omnipotent fantasies of recovery she maintains to the bitter end: "Everything is possible if one is resolved" (262). Gregory even serves her beyond the grave when he follows her death-bed command that he should marry Em, as if it were in his interest to keep Lyndall's omnipotence alive.

Gregory's own omnipotent delusions, which had once fueled his naïve expectations of sexual mastery, are strangely realized through his chivalrous but possessive service. He finds himself "glorified" (254) by this service and rises above all human "wish for rest" (260). An important aspect of Gregory's omnipotence is the knowledge he has gained of Lyndall's situation, which gives him a power of protective control typical of preoedipal masochistic fantasy rather than of sadistic or sexual domination. Earlier in the novel, Lyndall had described Gregory explicitly as a masochist: he is like "a little tin duck floating on a dish of water, that comes after a piece of bread stuck on a needle, and the more the needle pricks it the more it comes on" (213). Although she taunts him, Lyndall recognizes the masochistic affinity they share: "I too could love so," she says, "that to lie under the foot of the thing I love would be more heaven than to lie in the breast of another" (214). Gregory and Lyndall flirt briefly with a relationship of sexual sadomasochism: taking advantage of his desire for her, Lyndall enjoys cruel pleasure in commanding him and stealing him from Em, whose melancholy identification with Lyndall triangulates this relationship. The novel's conclusion thus transforms what had earlier been a

---

[20] While many critics have seen Gregory as an androgynous figure, most have found him an unsatisfying one. Bristow, p. xxi, speaks of his incipient homosexuality, but Ledger, p. 83, finds him to be a homophobic "New Man." Carol Barash, "Virile Womanhood: Olive Schreiner's Narratives of a Master Race," *Speaking of Gender*, ed. Elaine Showalter (New York: Routledge, 1989), p. 273, while viewing Gregory more positively than most, nevertheless complains that the novel only allows men to cross gender lines.

struggle for sexual domination into a drama of mutual masochism, which dissolves gender boundaries by gratifying preoedipal wishes together with oedipal ones: Lyndall, the self-destructive child, commands and controls her nurse, while Gregory, the self-tormenting lover, possesses Lyndall physically and emotionally through his self-effacement. Whatever the asymmetries of desire that divide Gregory and Lyndall, their masochistic tableau allegorically sexualizes the relationship between nursing mother and suffering child at the same time that it desexualizes adult desire through preoedipal fantasies that entwine nurturance with pain.

The novel's engagement in omnipotent fantasy thus proceeds on several levels at once. In Gregory and Lyndall's odd coupling, self-aggravated suffering elicits loving care while still preserving the masochist's freedom and control, thus resolving conflicts between autonomy and dependence. At the same time, male and female sexual difference dissolves in a general masochistic fusion of sexual desire, suffering, and self-glorification. Given the tragedy of Lyndall's death, these scenes would appear to critique masochistic fantasy generally and, in particular, the phantasmic wish to have a dominating lover who is also an all-pleasing mother. Surely, no reader could recognize the relationship between the dying Lyndall and the cross-dressed Gregory as a positive interpersonal ideal of some kind. Up until her death, Lyndall remains an unenlightened prisoner of omnipotent fantasy. Denying all the signs of the impending end, she declares: "It is thinking and thinking of things that makes them real . . . . . When you draw your mind together, and resolve that a thing shall not be, it gives way before you; it is not." (262).

Nevertheless, as relational theory teaches us, masochists sometimes use punitive self-critique to regulate (rather than terminate) omnipotent fantasy. Schreiner's pessimism about her characters can often be understood as an attack on certain fantasies about sexual union that is designed largely to preserve and manage them. In her feminist writings, critiques of omnipotent fantasy often paradoxically sustain precisely the kind of impossible conflations of oedipal and preoedipal love that Gregory and Lyndall embody.

New Woman Feminism

Schreiner always directed her relentless authorial intelligence against characters with whose desires she clearly identified or against beliefs that she herself appears to have held. Understanding this dynamic is crucial to grasping the place of omnipotent fantasy in her feminist idealism. Schreiner's harsh treatment of her own intellectual values preserved fragile desires and beliefs in a variety of ways consistent with masochistic fantasy. It maintained their innocence and untried potential rather than actually testing their viability; it exalted their moral superiority over the cruel worldly forces that threatened to destroy them; and it implicitly attributed omnipotence to the authorial consciousness that controlled—with a harsh and capricious will—whether such wishes and beliefs were to be fulfilled. It also erased rational conceptual distinctions that are profoundly antipathetic to omnipotent fantasy.

Schreiner's criticism of what she saw as naive or childlike forms of fantasy was ruthlessly applied in a number of contexts—not just to feminist idealism. Her assaults on orthodox religious belief in *The Story of an African Farm*, through characters like Otto, were predictably severe; but she also repeatedly insisted that alternative forms of faith were delusional. She mocked such alternatives in the famous chapter "Times and Seasons," for example, when she traced the flight of the God "that we made for ourselves, that we loved . . . we see what he was made of—the shadow of our highest ideal, crowned and throned" (131). She was also harshly critical of the fantasy elements in storytelling: she parodied Otto's romances, Gregory's melodramatic epistolary narratives, and Blenkins's self-serving anecdotes. She also parodied the wishful forms of desire embedded in conventional narrative forms (the bildungsroman plot, or the Dickensian orphan plot), as well as the rhetorical devices of biblical narrative.

Schreiner also routinely satirized her favored characters for their omnipotent desires. Lyndall, in particular, is possessed at an early age by her envy of Napoleon's seemingly magical will: "When he said a thing to himself he never forgot it. He waited, and waited, and waited, and it came at last" (31). Possessed of a desire "to know everything" (29), Lyndall believes that through education "there will be nothing that I do not know," a goal that even Em realizes is "a dream of quite too transcendent a glory ever to be realized" (30). As Lyndall matures, though, she becomes the demystifier of such fantasies—her own and those of others. She mocks the futility of Waldo's tendency to "sniff after reasons" (180), and she even mocks her own early wish to know everything, calling it "my old boast" (168). Yet in her self-destructive progress toward death, Lyndall adopts an enigmatic mixture of brutally cold-eyed realism and astonishing self-delusion. This mixture points to the fundamentally masochistic dynamic of Schreiner's own imagination, in which severe critiques of omnipotent fantasy did not necessarily negate it.

In *The Story of an African Farm*, as we have seen, Schreiner seemed to reject the fantasy that a lover who causes pain might at the same time be a mother who assuages pain. Yet in her later work, the merger of masochistic heterosexual love with preoedipal fantasy occupied a central place in her ideals for sexual equality. It occurs repeatedly, for example, in the feminist allegories collected in her influential volume *Dreams* (1890). This project exemplified the utopian efforts of many 1890s feminists to reinvent the very nature of sexual love. But while Schreiner shared the late-century feminist conviction that sexuality could be reformulated rationally, it was in her dreamlike fables, which channel unconscious energies into surreal fictional forms, that she most powerfully imagined a utopian sexuality.[21] In these allegories, Schreiner erased the power differentials between men and women that haunt heroines of her realistic fiction like Lyndall. She set many of her stories instead in a future when sexual struggle has seemingly been transcended. In this mythological space, her fables conceive ideal heterosexual unions that revolve around preoedipal gratification—in particular, the fulfillment of contradictory wishes for both autonomy and dependence. Yet the masochistic nature of these gratifications persists in Schreiner's organization of heterosexual love around actively sought renunciation and loss. As she once wrote to Karl Pearson, putting the pain of self-sufficiency at the heart of sexual interdependence: "The old lover's question—Will you love me for ever?—has to be changed to—If you feel I am pressing on your individuality will you let me go?" (*Rive*, 96). Schreiner's acceptance of suffering as the psychological condition necessary for egalitarian sexual union caused her to celebrate masochistic resolutions that idealize the same conjunctions of sexuality, suffering, and omnipotence—with their incorporation of aggression and control into fantasies of nurturance—that she had seemed to critique in Lyndall and Gregory.

In her fable "The Lost Joy," for example, a couple's blissful sexual union results in a child, the eponymous Joy. After some passage of time, however, the couple loses this child only to find another, sadder child in its place—one to whom they feel even more deeply attached, although they remain haunted by a sense of loss for the first child. Their attachment is so strong that they refuse to exchange this second, melancholy child for the first one, even when a figure named "Reflection" offers them this magical choice. Reflection then explains that the first child is actually identical to the second, although its name has now been changed to "Sympathy," as they might have known from the nurturing services it renders them. Reflection declares that Sympathy, despite the chronic loss of joy inscribed into its very identity, is, in fact, "the Perfect Love."[22]

Throughout these feminist fables, sexual relations between men and women are imagined in terms of mutual sympathy. Echoing a persistent

---

[21] See Judith Walkowitz, *City of Dreadful Delight: Narratives of Sexual Danger in Late-Victorian London* (Chicago: University of Chicago Press, 1992), p. 136, on the ideal of a rational sexual utopia in the Men and Women's Club. For a broader discussion of New Woman theories of rational love, see Angelique Richardson, *Love and Eugenics in the Late Nineteenth Century: Rational Reproduction and the New Woman* (Oxford: Oxford University Press, 2003), esp. pp. 78–94.

[22] Olive Schreiner, *Dreams* (New York: H. M. Caldwell Co., 1890), p. 12.

wish of New Woman writing, such sympathy seemingly replaces the aggression and violence of sexual desire (especially male desire) with a uniformly nurturant but melancholic ideal. In another fable, Schreiner imagines that on the day when the allegorical figure of oppressed woman is finally able to rise on her own strength, her male companion will "stand close to her, and look into her eyes with sympathy" (49). In *Woman and Labor*, Schreiner explicitly celebrated what she saw as the historical evolution of sexual desire into reciprocal nurturance. She argued that in the future heterosexual relations would transcend the violence embedded in the historical experience of love: "The element of physical force and capture which dominated the most primitive sex relations, the more degrading element of seduction and purchase by means of wealth or material good offered to woman in our modern societies, would then give place to the untrammeled action of attraction and affection alone between the sexes."[23] Yet Schreiner's heterosexual fables never represent perfectly sympathetic love as free of pain. Quite the contrary, their bittersweet tone derives from their idealizing attempts to incorporate pain as the very essence of sympathetic sexual love. The persistence of such pain suggests that sexual violence has been wholly sublimated into preoedipal versions of masochistic fantasy.

The female protagonist of "In a Far-Off World," for example, wanting to give her male partner the best possible happiness, visits a shrine where it is said that if one "knelt on the steps of the stone altar, and uncovering one's breast, so wounded it that the blood fell down on the altar steps, then whatever he who knelt there wished for was granted him" (39). Thus wounding herself and wishing for whatever might be best for her lover, the woman returns from the shrine only to have a mysterious voice explain to her that "the best of all gifts for him" is "that he might leave you" (41). After a compact moment of grief, the woman responds, calmly: "I am contented" (42). Similarly, in "Life's Gifts," the allegorical figure of Life forces a woman to choose between Love and Freedom. Only after the woman renounces Love does Life then tell her that, as a reward, "the day will come" (78) when she will have both.

Schreiner's fables of sexual utopia consistently revolve around preoedipal masochistic economies, in which unqualified states of loss, intersubjective fusion, and self-sufficiency form a closed circuit of exchange. In these fables, pain is mastered by being turned into a sign of absolute self-sufficiency, while self-sufficiency becomes the necessary condition for completely fusional love, the wholeness and security of which can only be measured through its tolerance for seemingly intolerable pain. The tendency of Schreiner's fables to represent concepts like love, freedom, and joy as

[23] Olive Schreiner, *Woman and Labor* (New York: Frederick A. Stokes Co., 1911), p. 258.

monolithic abstractions and to unite them in extraordinarily stark conjunctions with loss and renunciation betrays the logic of omnipotent fantasy at work. There are no realistic compromises between emotional extremes in these fables, only an economy of profound psychological
antitheses. Schreiner's fables have always been appreciated for their ideals
of sexual equality and for their celebration of female psychological independence, which Schreiner boldly imagined to be achievable within heterosexual love. But these values, which lie at the heart of much late-century
feminist writing, need to be understood as deeply entangled in masochistic fantasy and in its potential to reimagine sexual difference as a phantasmagoric site for the fulfillment of preoedipal wishes.

The persistence of this particular fantasy despite Schreiner's apparent
critique of it in *The Story of an African Farm* would seem to be confirmed
by her own sexual experience. Like Lyndall, Schreiner often yearned after
a strong man: "When I find a man as much stronger than I am as I am
than a child [*sic*], then I will marry him" (*Rive*, 72), she once wrote to
Havelock Ellis (who, apparently, did not qualify). Infatuated with Pearson, she told him that he was "the strongest man I know" (*Rive*, 99).
She repeatedly described Samuel Cron Cronwright, her future husband,
as "exceptionally strong" (*Rive*, 244) and bragged about his supposed
love of fighting: "It's the hard fighting man that comes out in it" (*Life*,
251–52), she once remarked of a photograph of him. Before their marriage she instructed him always to pose for photographs with his sleeves
rolled up.[24] She once astonished a group of friends by announcing that
she was engaged to a fighting man, while she danced around the room
shadow-boxing.[25]

At the same time, though, Schreiner was fond of conceptualizing her
sexual relationships in mother/child terms. As she once wrote to a friend:
"My husband is unspeakably tender and good to me; sometimes I feel as
if I were a little baby and he was my mother" (*Rive*, 240). Conversely, she
was fond of referring to Cronwright as "my boy" (*Life*, 254). Although
her relationship to Edward Carpenter was never sexualized, it, too, resonated with maternal associations: "I know you and feel to you as a little
child does to its mother" (*Rive*, 148), she wrote, only then to call him, in
turn, her "Beautiful Boy" (*Rive*, 150). During her brief infatuation with
Cecil Rhodes, she wrote: "That huge hard-headed man of the world, as
you would expect to find him, is so curiously like a little child, that one
feels so tender to him" (*Life*, 210). Her intimacy with Ellis revolved
around dizzying reversals of these mother/child roles. While closing her
letters to him "Your little child, Olive" (*Rive*, 45), she was also capable of

---

[24] *Life*, p. 246.
[25] First and Scott, p. 210.

exclaiming to him: "My baby, my baby is ill! I want to take care of it. I want to love its head and put it to rest and tell it such nice little stories" (*Rive*, 54).

Some readers have complained that Schreiner wanted to escape sex and that she idealized nonsexualized, platonic relationships between men and women.[26] It seems more accurate to say that, through masochistic fantasy, she tried to relocate sexual desire (including sadistic or aggressive forms of it) within preoedipal pleasure economies. This magical fusion explains her apparent conviction that women bring to sexual union the power to teach men how to be masochistic—something Lyndall teaches Gregory Rose, for example. Before her marriage, Schreiner herself wrote to Cronwright: "It seems to me you have immense energy and will power, which is the foundation of all greatness . . . what then do you lack? It seems to me self-control, self-mastery . . . . You don't lack will. You lack the habit of putting it into action *against yourself*" (*Rive*, 222).

Preoedipal masochistic fantasies saturated Schreiner's thinking about collective feminist struggle as well, including the relationship she tried to forge between feminism and late-century scientific thought. Drawing on Herbert Spencer's social Darwinism and on Pearson's eugenic theories, Schreiner argued in *Woman and Labor* that feminist demands could be justified only in the context of women's obligations to the species as a whole. Thus, she declared: "the women of no race or class will ever rise in revolt . . . however intense their suffering and however clear their perception of it, while the welfare and persistence of their society requires their submission" (6–7). Arguing that the overdependence of women on men, which she called "sex parasitism," threatened the survival of the human species, Schreiner stressed the urgency of women's access to productive labor. But she also stressed the necessarily self-sacrificing nature of that labor, following Pearson's insistence that, for the sake of evolutionary progress, the instinctual lives of individuals must be subordinated to the needs of the social whole—which, for him, meant the devotion of women to maternity.[27]

By linking feminist demands for productive labor to this eugenic discourse, Schreiner risked aligning feminist ideals with a masculinist view of female self-sacrifice. Feminist efforts, Schreiner argued, can never be "of immediate advantage to themselves, but . . . almost of necessity and

[26] See, for example, Joyce Avrech Berkman, *The Healing Imagination of Olive Schreiner: Beyond South African Colonialism* (Amherst: University of Massachusetts Press, 1989), p. 152.

[27] Pearson insisted on women's devotion to maternity in the inaugural essay he presented to the Men and Women's Club, called "The Woman Question," July 1885, Pearson Collection, Manuscripts Library, University College, London: "if child-bearing women be intellectually handicapped then the penalty to be paid for race predominance is the subjection of women."

immediately lead to loss and renunciation, which gives to this movement its very peculiar tone" (125). Seemingly conscripted into the eugenicist's view of motherhood as the foundation of the state, *Woman and Labor* also appears to import the racist rhetoric of late-century evolutionist thought as well as a class discourse that privileged middle-class women.[28] Yet it is crucial to remember that Schreiner's arguments resonated powerfully within a feminist culture that—in the fiction of Sarah Grand, George Egerton, and other novelists, as well as in "eugenic feminist" writing—equated female sexual self-denial, along with female capacities for judicious sexual selection, with a progressive social and sexual politics.[29] This association of female sexual self-denial with social progress underlies much of the self-defeating, neurasthenic tendencies that characterize typical New Woman fictional heroines such as Thomas Hardy's Sue Bridehead, Sarah Grand's Evadne Frayling, or Grant Allen's Herminia Barton. But the affective vitality of this current of feminist masochism and its potential to fuel radical or utopian politics are still badly in need of explanation.

A long tradition in Victorian gender ideology designated middle-class women as guardians of society only by consigning them to the selfless realms of moral education and childbearing. But Schreiner's willingness to embrace the most brutally scientific versions of this tradition that emerged in the late nineteenth century unleashed elements of masochistic fantasy that account for much of the strength—and many of the problems—of her sexual politics. Understanding the unconscious fantasy structures at work in *Woman and Labor* is, therefore, as important as analyzing the intellectual contents of Schreiner's argument. While there have been tangled debates among recent critics about whether Schreiner should be read as a strategic appropriator of evolutionist and eugenic discourses or as a co-opted reactionary, the masochistic fantasy structures underlying *Woman and Labor* can better help us understand its power to energize feminist activism by offering potent preoedipal gratifications.

Most importantly, the central terminology of *Woman and Labor* derives from a preoedipal conception of women's oppression rather than a political one. Schreiner's fears about female "parasitism," the keyword in *Woman and Labor*, evoke familiar preoedipal conflicts between autonomy and dependence. Her critique of parasitism clearly began in anxieties about the psychic independence of women—anxieties that mediate much

---

[28] On the racist potentials of Schreiner's evolutionism, see, Barash, "Virile Womanhood," pp. 269–81; Ledger, p. 43; or McClintock, p. 269.

[29] This aspect of late-century feminism has been extensively documented. See Angelique Richardson and Chris Willis, "Introduction," *The New Woman in Fiction and in Fact: Fin-de-Siècle Feminisms*, ed. Angelique Richardson and Chris Willis (New York: Palgrave, 2001), pp. 9–10, 25; or Lucy Bland, *Banishing the Beast: Sexuality and the Early Feminists* (New York: New Press, 1995), pp. 230, 232–34.

of her thinking about equal wages, voting rights, or other political issues. These preoccupations also led straight to the masochistic feminist solutions she proposed. Her view of labor as a medium of self-sacrifice, not a means to advancement or self-actualization, was one of the most important of these solutions: "The Woman's Movement," she wrote, "is essentially *not* a movement on the part of civilized women in search of greater enjoyment and physical ease."[30] Instead, Schreiner idealized women as destined for suffering in their service of the evolutionary development of the species. She associated labor—seen as a fundamental condition of female self-sufficiency—not so much with political economy as with women's special, stoical capacity to accept suffering and pain. In early human history, labor "more toilsome and unending than that of man was ours; yet did we never cry out that it was too heavy for us" (28). Schreiner repeatedly mourned an earlier historical time in which "an excessive and almost crushing amount of the most important social labor generally devolved upon the female" (44–45), for in her view of human evolution women were empowered by their capacity to endure more than men, particularly in the realm of sexual reproduction: "Time was, and still is, among almost all primitive and savage folk, when the first and all-important duty of the female to her society was to bear, to bear much, and to bear unceasingly!" (52).

By linking feminist demands for labor with an idealization of suffering, Schreiner generated an omnipotent phantasmagorics. She endowed feminism with tremendous social and psychological power by representing women's assertive forms of self-denial as crucial to the survival, not just of women, but of the entire human race. "Give us labor and the training which fits for labor!" she declared, famously, in *Woman and Labor*, "We demand this, not for ourselves alone, but for the race" (27). In Schreiner's omnipotent vision, women possess the power to either destroy or save the species, and their most mundane political choices are correspondingly momentous. The grandiosity of this vision was echoed by many suffragists, who promised converts to the movement that their work would contribute to the salvation of society, not just to the emancipation of women.[31] It was echoed in a different way by many 1890s "social purity" feminists, such as Ellice Hopkins, Janet Hume Clapperton, or Henrietta Muller,

---

[30] Olive Schreiner, *Thoughts on South Africa* (London: T. Fisher Unwin, 1923), p. 205. Hereafter cited as *Thoughts*.

[31] See Jacqueline R. deVries, "Transforming the Pulpit: Preaching and Prophecy in the British Women's Suffrage Movement," *Women Preachers and Prophets through Two Millennia of Christianity*, ed. Beverly Mayne Kienzle and Pamela J. Walker (Berkeley: University of California Press, 1998), p. 322. I have followed standard usage in applying "suffragist" to any prosuffrage position, and reserving "suffragette" for militant and/or violent forms of prosuffrage activism.

who argued that the eugenic priority of women's maternal role should entitle women to dominate social policy-making—a view that was shared by some profeminist men, including Alfred Russel Wallace.[32] But while many late-century feminists used discourses of self-sacrificing motherhood to present women as "race regenerators," Schreiner's masochistic emphasis on female capacities for suffering produced a more grandiose and racially undifferentiated claim: that laboring women might redeem the entire human species. While the preeminence of the British race may have been the preoccupation of some late-century "eugenic feminists," Schreiner departed from these writers in the global reach of her phantasmic vision.

Schreiner also drew on evangelical rhetoric to exalt the feminist struggle as a glorious crusade of martyrs, placing feminism "in a line with those vast religious developments which at the interval of ages have swept across humanity" (125). Merging individual suffering with collective sanctification, Schreiner compared the work of generations of feminists to the building of Gothic cathedrals and declared "in the phraseology of old days, 'This thing is not of man, but of God' " (142).[33] Her stark juxtaposition of female suffering with feminist glory generated a rhetoric of religious fervor that at times became militaristic in tone: she referred to feminists both as saints and as a species of "warrior maid" (148). This conjunction of martyrdom with glorious heroism became a central rhetorical trope of suffragism, although it was not translated into activist tactics until Christabel Pankhurst first subjected herself to arrest in 1905.

Besides allowing her to harness the omnipotent phantasmagorics of evangelicalism, Schreiner's rhetoric of martyrdom also allowed her to root feminist grandiosity in the inevitable failure of individual agents, a crucial strategy given the long-term struggle in which turn-of-the-century feminists saw themselves engaged. Schreiner elided an omnipotent, heroic destiny with the martyrdom of individuals in a famous passage from *Dreams*, in which an aspiring young feminist is counseled by the figure of Reason:

> "Have you seen the locusts how they cross a stream? First one comes down to the water's-edge, and it is swept away, and then another comes and then another, and then another, and at last with their bodies piled up a bridge is built and the rest pass over."
>
> She said, "And, of those that come first, some are swept away, and are heard of no more; their bodies do not even build the bridge?"

---

[32] See Walkowitz, p. 151, on the furor created within the Men and Women's Club by Muller's advancement of this claim. Alfred Russel Wallace, "Human Selection," *Fortnightly Review* 54 (1890), p. 337.

[33] For an overview of the role of suffering as an instrument of spiritual growth among suffragists, see Martha Vicinus, *Independent Women: Work and Community for Single Women, 1850–1920* (Chicago: University of Chicago Press, 1985), pp. 247–80.

"And are swept away, and are heard of no more—and what of that?"
he said.

"And what of that—" she said.

"They make a track to the water's edge."

"They make a track to the water's edge—." And she said, "Over that bridge which shall be built with our bodies, who will pass?"

He said, "*The entire human race.*"

And the woman grasped her staff.

And I saw her turn down that dark path to the river. (56–57)

Constance Lytton once claimed that this particular fable "fell on our ears more like an ABC railway guide to our journey than a figurative parable."[34] Schreiner's mobilization of this kind of evangelical rhetoric was later sustained in a widespread debate about the place of martyrdom in the suffragist struggle, which saw the publication in the early twentieth century of a great many tracts advocating martyrdom, written by hunger strikers like Christabel and Emmeline Pankhurst or by extremists like Emily Wilding Davison, who, on Derby Day in 1913, threw herself in front of the oncoming pack of horses at Epsom—with the result that her funeral became a national feminist spectacle.

Equally as important as Schreiner's posture of self-martyring glory, however, was the vagueness of her masochistic grandiosity. *Woman and Labor* is not precise about the kinds of female labor it values or the social goals to which such labor should be devoted. It is not a rational argument but a mystical celebration of the power of feminist self-sacrifice. Schreiner's vagueness enabled her to circumvent troubling late-century feminist contradictions of many kinds, including the competing claims of economic independence and the sexual ideal of the couple as well as more general contradictions between feminist self-assertion and self-sacrifice. Her rhetoric solved such problems in omnipotent rather than rational terms, merging images of heroic autonomy and fusional solidarity through its exaltation of suffering. The result was a discourse whose radicalism was as nonspecific as it was seemingly boundless. *Woman and Labor* aligned feminists with martyrs to all kinds of triumphant causes: the scientific revolution, the Protestant Reformation, democratic movements, and any other social transformations Schreiner deemed progressive. And even though her work was tremendously influential among suffragettes, Schreiner promoted this more limitless conception of radical glory by declaring that the vote itself was not as important as what she called the "freedom of women," which "is something that cannot be given to her,

[34] Constance Lytton, *Prisons and Prisoners: Some Personal Experiences* (London: William Heinemann, 1914), p. 187.

that she has to work out *within herself*." As she put it, if women are "willing to dare and do and die for freedom" then "their *spirits are free now*."[35]

Above all, Schreiner's systematic blurring of conceptual differences allowed her to adopt an evolutionary defense of maternity while also affirming the province of female "labor" in expansive metaphorical terms. Unlike Pearson, Schreiner allowed the concept of female labor to float free across distinctions between economic production and sexual reproduction. While idealizing maternity, she also insisted that motherhood alone was not sufficient to guarantee women's social productivity, even though her augmented standards for such productivity were never specific. In this instance, Schreiner's collapsing of the opposition between suffering and self-assertion allowed her to dissolve ideological distinctions between different forms of female labor as well.

The vagueness of *Woman and Labor* has been one of the charges leveled against it by recent feminist criticism.[36] But the book's obliviousness of difficult conceptual and historical distinctions is a crucial source of its unconscious power. Omnipotent fantasy is by its very nature antirealistic. Schreiner's imprecision allowed her to link feminist martyrdom with a utopianism that refused to be limited by the scientific, religious, or domestic discourses of female renunciation it masochistically inhabited. Instead, Schreiner poeticized these discourses to evoke the preoedipal gratifications that, for her, lay at the heart of feminist struggle. Idealizing a magical fusion of dependence with autonomy, Schreiner exalted service to the species as the essence of feminist self-assertion. This conjunction was not a pragmatic maneuver; rather, it engaged fantasy structures central to all of Schreiner's writings on sexuality.

Schreiner's conjunctions of martyrdom and omnipotence, with all their problematic complexity as a political rhetoric, powerfully mobilized masochistic fantasy. The potency of such fantasy is not easily dismissed or separated out of her work; nor is it easily reduced to a single set of political potentials. While critics often debate whether Schreiner's use of evolutionary and eugenic discourses made her a subversive appropriator of Pearson and Spencer, or whether it signaled her self-deluded submission to their rhetoric, what they often fail to appreciate is the preoedipal potency of a feminism that fuses autonomy and service—even if only on the level of magical thinking—by mixing sexual ideals with a celebration of suffering. The political uses of omnipotent fantasy in Schreiner's feminism suggest that the "omnipotent system" cannot be conceived, as it often is in psychoanalytic circles, simply as a dysfunctional alternative to

---

[35] Samuel Cron Cronwright-Schreiner, ed., *The Letters of Olive Schreiner, 1876–1920* (London: T. Fisher Unwin, 1924). p. 291. Hereafter cited as *"Cronwright-Schreiner."*

[36] See, for example, McClintock, p. 292; or Ledger, p. 42.

normative behavior.[37] Its relationship to late-century feminist struggle was clearly a productive one, as is suggested most compellingly, perhaps, by the recollections of suffragettes who read *Dreams* aloud to one another from their prison cells.[38]

The Regeneration of Middle-Class Culture

Just as Schreiner used masochistic fantasy to envision a new political identity for women, she also used it to reinvent middle-class political subjectivity in South Africa. A great deal of her South African writings revolved around this singular project: the recreation of a notional—if not always a nominal—South African middle class, grounded in a particular relationship to masochistic fantasy. In the course of this project, Schreiner used ideological and psychological structures that resonated with traditional English middle-class ideals, particularly with evangelicalism. She did not draw on evangelical rhetoric in this way until the 1890s, when she moved beyond the preoccupation with individual women in crisis that characterized the fiction she began writing in the 1870s (including *From Man to Man* [1926] and *Undine* [1929], both published posthumously). Only when she turned to problems of political collectivity did she invoke the class-coded evangelical tradition she had so fiercely rejected in her early works. But before I discuss the relevance of masochism (evangelical or otherwise) to social class in Schreiner's work, I must explain why she needed to reinvent middle-class identity in the first place.

Given the widespread critical assumption that Schreiner despised middle-class culture, it may seem strange to suggest that she wanted to affirm it politically. But Schreiner's contempt for bourgeois culture was the flip side of her efforts to reform it, a project it was easier to imagine against the inchoate social background of South Africa, where political identities were up for grabs, than it might have been in England. When Schreiner returned to South Africa in 1889, after eight years in England and Europe, she routinely lamented the disordering of colonial class relations she found there—in particular, what she saw as a disturbance in the middle ranks. But she also used this disordering as a sociological blank slate on which to project certain revised middle-class ideological values.

Schreiner's attempts to define the source of middle-class disarray in South Africa were often obscure. At times, her attacks were directed

---

[37] The Novicks, for example, have taken the position that masochistic fantasy is always dysfunctional. See Jack Novick and Kerry Kelly Novick, "A Developmental Perspective on Omnipotence," *Journal of Clinical Psychoanalysis* 5 (1996), esp. pp. 132–35.

[38] See Lytton, p. 187; or Vicinus, p. 273.

against the vulgarity of the middle ranks. In 1890, she complained repeatedly to Ellis: "Fancy a whole nation of *lower* middle-class people" (*Rive*, 172). At times, though, what she seemed to miss was an organic society—composed of distinct, complementary classes—that might hold the social middle in its proper place. To Ellis, again, she wrote: "Fancy a whole nation of *lower* middle-class Philistines, without an aristocracy of blood or intellect or of muscular laborers to save them!" (*Rive*, 168). Similarly, to Edward Carpenter, she complained of the absence of an intellectual class, which might form a counterweight to the lower-middle-class philistine: "There are no people that think or care about social or impersonal subjects in this country, that I've found. They are all philistines. It's so funny to find a whole *nation* of philistines without the other element at all" (*Rive*, 206).

Schreiner thus wavered in defining what was missing in the South African social middle: intellectual culture, disciplined labor, or ethical refinement. More importantly, she vacillated in her conception of the underlying structure of South African class relations itself. On the one hand, she routinely stigmatized all South African whites as a monolithic body of "lower-middle-class" philistines. On the other hand, though, she conceptualized South Africa as a society comprised of a wealthy capitalist class set over against the exploited poor. In this "two nations" model of class division, a stabilizing middle class was simply and strikingly absent. In 1892, she wrote to Carpenter: "There are money-making whites, and down-trodden blacks, and nothing between" (*Rive*, 215).

The racial division in South Africa was, for Schreiner, always also a class division, and she often lumped all whites together in this way as a vast capital-obsessed class, set over against a permanent black laboring class, with "nothing between." But she sometimes conceived this polarization so as to position whites on either side of the divide between capitalist and exploited classes. This kind of oscillation permeated the essays she published in British and American journals during the 1890s, which were collected posthumously as *Thoughts on South Africa* (1923). In these essays, Schreiner consistently castigated wealthy foreign speculators, who, in her view, formed the bulk of the capitalist class. But she wavered between seeing the indigenous lower middle class as either unwittingly collaborating with the capitalists (by supporting their political and economic policies and by sharing their profits) or as passively joining the natives as their victims. On the one hand, the "South African man, whether Dutch or English," was like "those huge shaggy watch-dogs, which lie before their masters' houses" (300), serving as the mere instruments of the capitalist class. But, on the other hand, she claimed that "the bulk of the workmen being black, and any attempt to organize or combine them being at once met with the cry 'Black-men combining,' the handful of skilled English workmen and townsmen are powerless" (315). Schreiner often viewed South Africa's political fortunes as dependent on whether the indigenous British and Dutch decided to throw in their lot with the capitalists or with the natives: describing the conflict among indigenous white colonists between pronative views and "the financial attitude," she claimed: "The future of South Africa depends largely on the result of this struggle" (318).

In sum, although Schreiner believed that something had gone wrong with the middle social strata, she vacillated between seeing it either as ubiquitous but degraded ("a whole nation of *lower* middle-class Philistines") or as an absent buffer between the capitalist class and the victimized poor (whether the latter were conceived as black or both white and black). Both of these contradictory perspectives characterize the landscape of social class in *The Story of an African Farm*. South African society is dominated in the novel by "lower middle-class philistines," whether in the person of the Boer property owner, Tant' Sannie, or in the class of cynical clerks and shopkeepers Waldo encounters during his foray out of the farm. But the novel is also haunted by a mysterious evacuation of the middle ranks. No one fills the respectable middle-class position vacated, before the novel even begins, by Em's deceased father (or Lyndall's, who is never even identified). The wealthy upper class is represented briefly by two characters—Lyndall's stranger and Waldo's—but the very namelessness of these figures signifies the remoteness of this class. Aside from Gregory, who tries to deny his origins in the English yeomanry (itself a disappearing class) in favor of the delusional pretensions of his family (a "distinguished lineage . . . established . . . in their own minds" [157]), the rest of the adult characters occupy distinctly low social and economic positions.

The occlusion of middle-class identity in the novel may owe something to the contradictions of social class in Schreiner's own family background. Missionary families in South Africa tended to keep their distance from natives and whites alike and to regard themselves as culturally elevated, even though they were treated by other whites as servants.[39] The sudden bankruptcy of Schreiner's father when she was twelve and the consequent splitting up of her family must also have contributed to the sense of social dispossession haunting *The Story of an African Farm*. But such dispossession is universalized in the novel: Lyndall, Waldo, and Em all inherit diminished social prospects and endure expropriations of their possessions and fortunes (as does Waldo's father, Otto).[40] This general atmosphere of

---

[39] See First and Scott, pp. 44–45.

[40] Schreiner's insistence on the dispossession of her protagonists problematizes the claims made by Deborah L. Shapple, "Artful Tales of Origination in Olive Schreiner's *The Story of an African Farm*," *Nineteenth-Century Literature* 59 (2004), 78–114—i.e., that Schreiner

status decline, together with the absence in the novel of properly middle-class adult figures, reflects Schreiner's sense of a crisis in South Africa's defective middle social strata—not just the social fall she herself experienced. *The Story of an African Farm* thus replays in a colonial setting some of the anxieties about missing or confused middle-class social identities that mark a novel with which it is often compared, *Wuthering Heights* (1847)—another portrait of rural isolation in which unbridgeable gaps between upper and lower social strata are not mediated by any middle social stratum. In particular, through its reflections on Waldo's spiritual crisis, Schreiner's novel echoes the waning authority of middle-class evangelicalism that Brontë had conveyed through her satirical view of Nelly Dean's moralism.[41]

Schreiner saw the deformation of class in South Africa not simply as a colonial problem but also as the symptom of a general crisis in European class society. She told Carpenter that "things will have to be so much worse here before they can be better; in Europe we have almost got to the bottom already and the tide is going to turn" (*Rive*, 215). Like Carpenter, Schreiner imagined that the turning "tide" would be a socialist one, even though her ideas about socialism were extremely vague.[42] Yet, in the last decades of the nineteenth century, the absence of a moderating middle class in South Africa seemed symptomatic of a global middle-class crisis to more conservative English writers as well, which Schreiner's favoring of the term "philistine" suggests. Matthew Arnold, for example, worried that the dominance of a commercial class in South Africa, without the counterbalancing influence of a landed class, mirrored the increasing philistinization of English society, and he saw South African "philistines" as symptomatic of the global degradations wrought by a debased middle-class culture. In 1881, he wrote:

> Everywhere the attractions of this middle-class civilisation of ours, which is what we have really to offer in the way of civilisation, seem to fail of their effect. . . . Wherever we go, we put forward Murdstone and Quinion, and call their ways civilisation. . . . The English in South Africa . . . contain a wonderful proportion of attorneys, speculators, land-jobbers, and persons whose antecedents will not bear inspection. Their recent antecedents we will not meddle with, but one thing is certain: their early antecedents were those

---

uses Waldo's close bond with the land to legitimate the displacement of the San people by white settlers.

[41] Evangelicalism would have been identified with housekeepers and servants in the time of the novel's setting, but since it became the social and spiritual cement of the middle classes between the turn of the century and the 1840s, Nelly functions as an emblem of the moral belatedness of Brontë's own class.

[42] See Ledger, pp. 37–40.

of the English middle class in general, those of Murdstone and Quinion. They have almost all, we may be very sure, passed through the halls of a Salem House and the hands of a Mr. Creakle . . . . Indeed, we are so prolific, so enterprising, so world-covering, and our middle class and its civilization so entirely take the lead wherever we go, that there is now, one may say, a kind of odour of Salem House all round the globe.[43]

Although the importance of South Africa to the British colonial imagination has not received the attention it deserves, the failures of middle-class culture that it represented for writers as politically diverse as Schreiner and Arnold suggest that these failures touched deep British anxieties in the last decades of the nineteenth century. The most dramatic instance of such anxiety, perhaps, emerged in jingoist support for the South African War (1899–1902), which reveled in stereotypes of the Boers as an intractably vulgar class—stereotypes that displaced British anxieties about the degeneration of their own class structure onto colonial otherness.

For a complex set of reasons, examined in chapter 1—including the gentrification of the middle class, the waning of evangelical authority, the emergence of distinct professional and lower middle classes, and the growing interpenetration of middle-class and popular culture—the social identity of the British middle class seemed to many to have grown incoherent after midcentury. Schreiner's diagnosis of a deformation in the South African middle ranks and her attempts to do something about it can thus be viewed as one version of a widespread late-century tendency to reformulate British social identities by rewriting them at the colonial sites at which they seemed most destabilized. Schreiner was also, of course, attempting to reinvent middle-class subjectivity for political purposes unique to the South African political situation, and these twinned motivations helped give this project the special urgency conveyed in her 1890s essays.

Schreiner's conviction that colonial social problems could be corrected by a transformation of the middle ranks is most evident in *The Political Situation* (1896), a speech she cowrote with her husband, which he delivered in Kimberley in 1895 and which appeared in print under both their names a year later. *The Political Situation* proposed the rather fanciful task of creating from scratch a South African middle class—or, at least, transforming "philistine" society into one. Schreiner and her husband boldly advocated the development of a progressive political class devoted to two objectives: opposing the excesses of wealthy speculators and representing the interests of laboring natives. The first goal responded to their sense that capitalist greed was ruining the country's culture and economy; the

[43] Matthew Arnold, "The Incompatibles," *The Complete Prose Works of Matthew Arnold*, ed. R. H. Super, 22 vols. (Ann Arbor: University of Michigan Press, 1960–1977), 9: 281–82.

second to their belief that black laborers were unable to represent themselves. Resistance to the rapacious capitalist class, they argued, "lies with the necessarily small middle class section of the community . . . . These have not only to act for themselves, but for the entire labouring class, which, on account of its difference in race and colour from the rest of the community, cannot act for itself" (*Thoughts*, 314).

The Political Situation proposed accomplishing these classic goals of the eighteenth- and early nineteenth-century British middle class—opposing upper-class power while also managing the poor by serving as its political proxy—through several traditional middle-class means: progressive taxation, the enfranchisement of small property holders, and general conciliation of the (black) working classes.[44] Schreiner and her husband also proposed classic middle-class instruments for implementing these strategies: utilization of the press for political purposes (starting with purchase of a newspaper), development of political organizations, and cultivation of indigenous political leadership. They did not explicitly use the term "middle class" to define the political entity they hoped to bring into being. In fact, they followed another classic strategy of the traditional British middle class by promoting this entity as classless.[45] But the social coordinates they had in mind are notionally congruent with the middle economic strata, particularly since they excluded blacks, who made up nearly the entire unskilled labor force. They claimed to believe that

> in every town, and in every district and village, will be found (though not invariably among its most important or wealthy members) a certain body of men and women, from the bank clerk to the clergyman, from the shop assistant to the small tradesman, from the schoolmaster or mistress to the enterprising young farmer, Dutch or English, from the working man to the wholesale merchant, who are as essentially advanced in their view as any body of men or women in any country: persons wholly unaffected by the disease which seems eating the core of our national life—that fevered desire to grow wealthy without labour, as individuals by reckless speculation, and as a nation by annexations. (90–91)

The recommendations of *The Political Situation* mirrored the tactics of British middle-class politicians in the early nineteenth century, who also hoped to form the political identity of a class that had not yet recognized its common economic interests. There are no indications that any of these

[44] Dror Wahrman, *Imagining the Middle Class: The Political Representation of Class in Britain, c. 1780–1840* (Cambridge: Cambridge University Press, 1995), views political representations of the middle class as strategies of mediation between the interests of upper and lower social strata. See esp. pp. 59, 187.

[45] Olive Schreiner and S. C. Cronwright-Schreiner, *The Political Situation* (London: T. Fisher Unwin, 1896), pp. 105–6.

tactical proposals took root, and Schreiner herself was not much of a political activist. The strategies proposed in *The Political Situation* were most likely the contributions of her husband. Schreiner did devote herself to the creation of a South African middle class throughout the 1890s, but she did so in more characteristically visionary ways. A central instrument in this project was her use of masochistic fantasy to define the nature of colonial middle-class culture as well as its compatibility with British national values. Following a pattern in late-century writing that sought to redefine middle-class culture by projecting its ideals onto alien colonial objects, these masochistic elements entered Schreiner's vision through her writings about the character and culture of the Boers and the role they might play in bringing about a reformed and coherent South African political middle.

FANTASIZING ABOUT THE BOERS

During the 1890s, Schreiner valiantly campaigned to forestall the South African War by arguing that the Boers might form the core of a stable colonial middle class. In a series of essays that Paula Krebs describes as "the most important pro-Boer writings by a literary figure in a public debate that was notable for the presence of literary figures," she argued that war was unnecessary because the Boers and the small British middle class in South Africa would eventually merge.[46] This merger, she believed, would accomplish the twin objectives of traditional middle-class political culture: resistance to upper-class economic power and leadership of the lower class. Like many other pro-Boers, Schreiner believed that the conflict in South Africa was not really between the British and the Dutch but between capitalists and agrarians. She subscribed to a widely held (though since discredited) view of a conspiracy between capitalist speculators in South Africa and the British government.[47] But she extended her class-based view of the conflict further than others by taking the idiosyncratic position that the Boers were psychologically and culturally compatible with the British middle class and that, together with British colonists, they might form a stable and redemptive middle social strata. This position was the more remarkable given that most British observers regarded the Boers as a hopelessly retrograde, vulgar, uncivilized people.

[46] Krebs, p. 109.

[47] Iain R. Smith, "A Century of Controversy Over Origins," *The South African War Reappraised*, ed. Donal Lowry (Manchester: Manchester University Press, 2000), pp. 23–49, argues that the interests of capitalists in monopoly control and of the British government in expansionism were quite distinct and, moreover, that "the last thing the capitalists wanted or needed in 1899 was a war" (33).

Schreiner made her argument about the fusion of the Boers and middle-class British colonists by identifying a network of psychological and cultural ideals that she believed linked them. This network revolved around the same masochistic psychic economies—which join together martyrdom, dependence, and autonomy—and the same submergence of sadistic relations in nurturative, preoedipal ones on which she based her ideals for egalitarian sexual love and feminist struggle. The British values that Schreiner celebrated, identified with both the colonial middle class in South Africa and with what she called the "ethically developed class" (*Thoughts*, 23) in Britain, included three basic standards of conduct. The first was a stoic willingness to endure martyrdom. The second, closely allied to it, was a capacity for disciplined self-denial signifying the devotion of individuals to principles larger than themselves. The third was a somewhat paradoxical love of freedom that she shrouded in the omnipotent characteristics of an absolute. Psychologically, these three principles fuse together extremes of dependence and autonomy through the vehicle of actively sought pain. They represent Schreiner's attempt to reverse the degradation of British middle-class culture and to redefine Boer culture in politically and ethically acceptable terms by affirming the masochistic fantasy structures they both shared.

While Schreiner often complained of greed among the British in South Africa, for example, she claimed that in the British "ethically developed class" there existed a powerful counteractive to such greed. She repeatedly praised the capacity of that class for martyrdom: "If no nation has more misrepresented, neglected and persecuted its sons of light, no nation has had more of them to persecute" (*Thoughts*, 23). Rather than formulating their virtues positively, she posited them as the antithesis of self-interest: "Those very vices which most mark our national character and by which we are known throughout the earth, are the very qualities of which our greatest men and our noblest elements are the negation." She often allied this negative power with the self-denying spirit that she believed defined the national character as a whole: "There is in some corner of the best English natures a curious power for sacrificing all for humanity, a curious power of obliterating selfish interests, that is rare, rare indeed" (*Rive*, 384).

But Schreiner's self-sacrificing British martyrs were also characterized—in a paradox that lies at the heart of masochistic fantasy—by their devotion to freedom and autonomy. Britain "has not been without her tyrannies of kings and nobles, but always her people have risen up against it and in time asserted their liberty of action" (*Thoughts*, 342). Schreiner repeatedly glorified independence as the essence of the national character. She also consistently tied this love of independence back again to self-sacrifice, completing the circuit of masochistic fantasy. For Schreiner, what differentiated the British love of freedom from the aggressive South African capitalist class was the determination of the British to undermine their own world domination by extending freedom to everyone: "We love freedom not only for ourselves, but we desire with a burning passion to spread it broadcast over the earth" (*Thoughts*, 343). In effect, she maintained a paternalistic national vision by fusing omnipotent power with self-effacement:

> we believe that our desire to impart [freedom] is a more potent means of extending our true empire . . . than any mere strength of arm or valour in slaughtering. We believe that it is not impossible that the day will come when from north to south, from east to west, over the globe, our English spirit will have spread [and] in that large united people of the future every man will say: "In that I am free I am English." (*Thoughts*, 354)

In her many essays and pamphlets written in defense of the Boers' national character, Schreiner used a similar kind of masochistic economy to define Boer culture. Circumstantially, Schreiner compared the Boers to middle-class British colonials by pointing to their common victimization at the hands of foreign capital: "Is it strange that from the hearts of South Africans, English and Dutch alike, there is arising an exceedingly great and bitter cry: 'We have sold our birthright for a mess of pottage! . . . They use the gold they gain out of us to enslave us; they strike at our hearts with a sword gilded with South African gold!' "[48] But beyond this common martyrdom, she stressed the fundamentally masochistic economies of Boer psychology, which linked it, in her view, to the collective psychology of the British middle class. She established this correlation in two stages: first, by describing the Boers as child-like victims of a neglectful, abandoning, even sadistic mother-country—victims who yet desired nothing better than to have Britain recognize and welcome their filial dependence; second, by attributing to the Boers a masochistic self-sufficiency that paralleled what she saw as the Puritan tradition of the British middle class. Through their self-martyring strength, the Boers—once united with British colonists—would become a political force for the redemption of the South African nation. She argued this case strenuously at the end of her essay "The Psychology of the Boer," in which she imagined an inevitable fusion of Boers and colonists: "If during the coming century South Africa is to be preserved from that doom which we sometimes see hovering in the dim future before her . . . it will not be through the action of Dutchmen or Englishmen alone; but of brave souls irrespective of all descent—'God's-Dutchman' and 'God's-Englishman'—hand in hand" (*Thoughts*, 319–20).

---

[48] Olive Schreiner, *The South African Question* (Chicago: Charles H. Sergel Co., 1899), p. 73. Hereafter cited as *Question*.

In the first stage of this strategy, Schreiner consistently described the conflict between Britons and Boers within an extended metaphor of mother/child relations, in which Britain figured as a neglectful, unempathic mother. In *The South African Question* (1899), Schreiner repeatedly called Britain the "step-mother" of the Boers, but a step-mother incapacitated by that quintessentially British trait, "a certain shell of hard reserve" (23), which prevents empathy: "We do not readily understand wants and conditions distinct from our own" (23–24). As a result, Britain became an uncaring, or even a sadistic parent, "[putting] our foot on the weak" (21). In a gruesome image of maternal betrayal, she described British aggression against the Boers as the equivalent of "the mother's drawing a sword and planting it in the heart of the daughter" (100).

Schreiner clung to this trope of Britain as bad mother to the persecuted Boers throughout the 1890s, although she professed a hope that the tie between mother and child might be repaired, as well as a certainty that such reconciliation would be welcomed by the dependent Boers. In "The South African Nation" (1900), she cajoled Britain into becoming a kind of step-mother "not favouring those of her own blood unduly, but seeking to aid those in her power," who is then "rewarded by a love and devotion from the children not her own yet greater than that which is often given to a mother by the children of the blood" (*Thoughts*, 380). Schreiner claimed: "Such is the bond I have dreamed should permanently bind England to South Africa." She spoke warmly of the Boers' need for love and their "large and generous response to affection and sympathy" (*Question*, 25), often flying in the face of historical reality by affirming their "deep and sincere affection . . . for England" (40). She adopted a maternal, infantilizing tone toward the Boers herself, constantly referring to the Transvaal as that "gallant little Republic" (*Question*, 31) and to the Boer dialect, the Taal, as their "little language" (26).

Schreiner's propagandistic history of the Boers in South Africa reinforced this theme of national abandonment by making Britain's aggression seem the last instance in a long series of European betrayals. In an essay on the settlement of South Africa, "The Boer" (1896), she gave extraordinary prominence to historical events that foregrounded these fundamentally preoedipal themes. For example, she dwelt at length on the settlement of Huguenot refugees in South Africa in 1687, claiming that these religious martyrs reinforced the isolation of South African culture through their alienation from their "mother land" (*Thoughts*, 76). Schreiner viewed Huguenot disaffection from the "mother land" as more extreme even than that of the American Puritans, given that, in her view, the Puritans were persecuted only by an unrepresentative government: "It was not England and its people who expelled them, but a step-motherly Government. Therefore they founded 'New England' and clung to the old" (*Thoughts*, 82). Schreiner also dwelt, somewhat mystically, on the spirit of martyrdom these Huguenots infused into the Boer race, which she saw as a legacy of noble suffering. Describing the Huguenots as "winnowed by the unerring flail of religious persecution," she saw them as "the finest element that has ever been added to the population of South Africa" (*Thoughts*, 33). In "The Boer," these Huguenots represented to her "that golden minority which is so remorselessly winnowed from the dross of the conforming majority by all forms of persecution directed against intellectual and spiritual independence" (*Thoughts*, 75).

In addition to stressing the centrality of the Huguenots to Boer history and national character, Schreiner also dwelt on the orphaned girls from the Netherlands who were shipped to South Africa as potential wives, beginning in the late seventeenth century, to redress the disproportionate ratio of male to female colonists. "Alone in the world, without relatives who had cared sufficiently for them to save them from the hard mercy of a public asylum, these women must have carried away few of the warm and tender memories happier women bear to plant in the hearts of their children" (*Thoughts*, 73). These "early mothers of the Boer race" supposedly deepened the Boers' isolation from their European origins by reinforcing the sense of national abandonment. British colonists "still call Europe 'home,' " but this "bond, light as air, yet strong as iron, those early mothers of the Boer race could hardly have woven between the hearts of their children and the country they come from" (*Thoughts*, 72–73). Yet another factor Schreiner stressed in the Boers' separation from their European past was the contraction of their language, which she believed resulted from the fusion of Dutch, French, and African dialects, making a Boer speaker like "a little child, as it lisps its mother tongue" (*Thoughts*, 87).

Schreiner thus placed what she saw as contemporary British misunderstanding of the Boers as the last in a series of persecutions, beginning with the policies of the Dutch East India Co., which "crushed the people . . . under an iron heel" (*Thoughts*, 149), and including a number of incursions by British colonists that compelled the Boers into one miserable trek after another into the inhospitable interior. Identifying with Boer suffering, Schreiner was moved by fantasies of vicarious martyrdom and rescue: had she lived in those times, "I would have moved heaven and earth, I would have been a kind of Paladin redressing the wrongs of the Boer, and I almost [regret] that I had not been born in those dark times that I might have lived for, and if necessary have died for, him" (*Thoughts*, 19).

In the second stage of Schreiner's vision of the Boers as a primitive but enlightened middle-class culture, she linked their history of persecution to the self-sufficiency that masochistic fantasy often associates with martyrdom. Schreiner repeatedly affirmed the Boers' stoic acceptance of their suffering and privation as the source of their spirit of "indomitable resolution" (*Thoughts*, 19). Speaking of the Huguenots and their legacy, she affirmed "that law deep-lying in the nature of things, which has ordained that where men shall be found having the force to stand alone, and suffer for abstract conviction, there also shall be found the individuality, virility and power which founds great peoples and marks dominant races" (*Thoughts*, 75). Among these powers of "virile" self-sufficiency are what she called the Boers' "unlimited power of self-control" (*Thoughts*, 19). Arguing that the Boers would make formidable adversaries should Britain go to war with them, Schreiner also described them—with melodramatic grandiosity—as possessing the superhuman courage of victims and martyrs: "the courage of the woman robbed of her infant, who climbs where no other human foot dare tread and recovers it from the eagle's eyrie . . . the courage of the peasant woman, who, after being broken three times on the wheel, on being asked to give up the names of her confederates, already almost past speech, shook her head in refusal, is again put on the wheel, and dies" (*Thoughts*, 250).

In keeping with the dynamics of masochistic fantasy, which tend to disavow violence and rage, Schreiner insisted that, unlike the sadistic nations who had oppressed them, the Boers were nonaggressors. She distinguished their bravery, for example, from "the courage . . . of the prizefighter": "This courage is quite consistent with an extreme distaste for conflict . . . and takes its rise only in natures so constituted that impersonal passions or convictions are capable of obliterating the natural bias, and this form of courage is probably the most indomitable" (*Thoughts*, 250). Nevertheless, in Schreiner's view, the Boers' sense of their own unlimited power justified their conviction that they were the chosen people of God and that South Africa was God's personal bequest to them. As she recounted their history, Schreiner frequently merged images of the Boers as infinitely patient sufferers with images of glorious Boer triumph, thereby constructing the kind of masochistic mythology that revels in a history of martyrdom to legitimize nationalism. Schreiner presented Boer victories over the San people and the Zulus as signs of Boer worthiness and destiny or as their blameless responses to the barbaric sadism of native warriors— a mythology that ignored the complex historical alliances of the Boers with African tribes in struggles over land, alliances which Sol Plaatje's *Mhudi* (1930) makes abundantly clear. Again and again, what comes through in Schreiner's accounts of Boer history is her identification with what she imagined as Boer martyrdom and the correspondingly nonvindictive, omnipotent glory this martyrdom conferred. Speaking on behalf of those British colonists who identified with the present-day Boers, she declared: "rather than strike down one South African man fighting for freedom, we would take this right hand and hold it in the fire, till nothing was left of it but a charred and blackened bone" (*Question*, 115). This correlation of masochistic suffering with glorious destiny played a vital role in Schreiner's class-coded campaign in defense of the Boers, which has often mistakenly appeared to recent readers simply as an endorsement of white racial domination.[49]

One crucial aspect of Schreiner's reflections on Boer martyrdom and the omnipotent power inscribed within it is the peculiarly spiritualized bond she imagined to persist between the Boers and the landscape of South Africa. In the absence of a nurturing motherland, Schreiner argued, the Boer became profoundly tied to the land of South Africa, which she often represented in maternal terms, modifying a long-standing tradition of colonial fiction in which landscapes are feminized erotically. She also repeatedly described the emotional connection between Boers and the land as a surrogate for affection from the mother country. The orphaned mothers from the Netherlands, for example, arrived at "the first 'Land of Good Hope' that ever dawned on their lives; and the day in which they landed at Table Bay and first trod on African soil, was also the first in which they became individuals" (*Thoughts*, 73); thus: "On their lips, when they looked at the valley of Stellenbosch, or the slopes of Table Mountain, the words—*Ons Land*—meant all they mean on the lips of the Transvaal Boer or the Free State Burgher of to-day,—'*Our Land; the one and only land we know of, and care for, wish to know of, have any tie or connection with!*' " Celebrating the pastoral virtues of the Boers—a common theme in pro-Boer writing of the 1890s—Schreiner repeatedly emphasized the strength the Boers supposedly took from the land: "it is as necessary for the nation, as for the individual who would recuperate, to return again and again, and, lying flat on the bosom of our common mother, to suck direct from the breast of nature the milk of life" (*Thoughts*, 160–61).

Schreiner's emphasis on Boer affection for this maternal landscape was more than just a defense of their right to national independence or a justification of their displacement of native Africans (though it was certainly both these things as well). It also corresponded to a peculiarly masochistic relationship Schreiner herself had to the South African landscape and a particular omnipotent compensation which that relationship generated. Schreiner often rhapsodized the South African landscape precisely for its aridity, its barrenness, its inhospitable bleakness. This paradox is overlooked by those who follow J. M. Coetzee in seeing Schreiner's South African landscapes as antipastoral.[50] Quite the contrary, Schreiner wrote

[49] See Krebs, p. 129, for example, for this claim about Schreiner's evolutionism and her defense of Boer entitlement to the land.

[50] J. M. Coetzee, *White Writing: On the Culture of Letters in South Africa* (New Haven: Yale University Press, 1988), p. 4.

eloquently and affectionately about those aspects of the landscape that seemed to make it the epitome of deprivation. Describing South Africa as "an arid, barren country," she wrote: "Our sublime and rugged natural scenery, the joy and pride of the South African heart, is largely the result of this very aridity and rockiness" (*Question*, 67–68). Her landscape descriptions often evoke a cruel natural power, which she nevertheless portrayed with fondness and pride: "no object in inanimate nature conveys the same impression of conscious cruelty, and fierce, untamed strength," she wrote, "as a full African river" (*Thoughts*, 45). Schreiner deliberately called attention to the spectacular penury of certain parts of South Africa, such as the Great Karoo—that vast, barren plain on which there "is not a blade of grass to be seen growing anywhere" (*Thoughts*, 37)—as the essence of the country. Writing about its boundless desolation in a lengthy essay on geography, she maintained that "in describing the physical features of South Africa, we lingered longest over the Karoo, not because it was one of the largest or most important features in the country, but because it was the most characteristically South African" (*Thoughts*, 65). Yet what she saw as the "most characteristic" features of South Africa were those that could seem most terrifying because of the monumental scale of the human desolation they represented:

> Many years ago, we traveled from Port Elizabeth to Grahamstown in a post-cart with a woman who had just come from England. All day we had traveled up through the bush, and at noon came out on a height where, before us, as far as the eye could reach, over hill and dale, without sign of human habitation or break, stretched the bush. She began to sob; and, in reply to our questionings, could only reply, almost inarticulately: "Oh! It's so terrible! There's so much of it! There's so much!" (*Thoughts*, 50)

Despite this vast bleakness—or, rather, because of it—Schreiner constantly wrote about the South African landscape as an omnipotent spiritual force: "It was amid such scenes as these, amid such motionless, immeasurable silences, that the Oriental mind first framed its noblest conception of the unknown, the 'I am that I am' of the Hebrew" (*Thoughts*, 41). Schreiner often made biblical comparisons between the spiritual intensities of the landscapes of South Africa and Palestine. But she sometimes attributed an emotional plenitude to this desolate landscape in personal terms as well: alone on the Karoo at night, amid a "silence so intense you seem almost to hear the stars move . . . what you have believed of human love and fellowship—and never grasped—seems all possible to you" (*Thoughts*, 41). To her husband, she once spoke of her fondness for the South African landscape in an even plainer fusion of masochistic fantasy with omnipotent longings: "You know I have got the feeling here that I'd like to live hundreds and hundreds of years in this world, and yet also the feeling it would be a beautiful thing to die. The two feelings seem contrary, but they are really not" (*Cronwright-Schreiner*, 255). In this paradoxical way, Schreiner's influential fable, "Three Dreams in a Desert" (1890), along with many other short works from the 1890s, drew on the spiritual power she vested in barren landscapes by seeing the desert as a transformational utopian space.

Schreiner's mystical version of scientific naturalism, her belief in the underlying unity of all things, was also frequently linked in her writings with the bleak isolation of the South African landscape. In 1886, she wrote to Pearson:

> I wish you could go once to my old African world and know what it is to stand quite alone on a mountain in the still blazing sunshine . . . and the great unbroken plains stretching away as far as you can see, without a trace of the human creature, perhaps not a living creature higher in the scale than an ant within miles and miles of you! . . . That is to say, when one is in contact with that vast, dry, bright nature, one is conscious of oneself, of inanimate nature—and of something else. It is this *something-else* that has framed those religions in which there is one, sole, almighty God. (*Rive*, 83)

Predictably, though, when she returned to South Africa several years after writing this passage, she had difficulty finding God in the barren landscape, discovering that her mystical feelings were now tied to the greater pain and loneliness of her years in England. Writing to Ellis from South Africa in 1890, she complained: "I don't feel 'God' so near me as I did in England in all that agony and dark and conflict" (*Rive*, 167). The omnipotent presence she associated with nature in South Africa seemed to require, above all, the catalyst of fresh pain.

Schreiner's masochistic spirituality, which emerged consistently in her love of barren landscapes, is one that she projected—quite fantastically— onto the Boers. This strategy was yet one more effort on her part to define Boer culture in terms that would make it seem compatible with British middle-class culture. Speaking of the Huguenot immigrant, she claimed: "the South African land became from the very moment he landed the object of a direct and absorbing religious veneration, excluding all other national feelings" (*Thoughts*, 84). Schreiner generalized this natural mysticism to the Boers as a whole:

> Deep in the hearts of every old veld-schoen-wearing Boer that you may meet, side by side with an almost religious indifference to other lands and peoples, lies this deep, mystical and impersonal affection for South Africa. . . . Its only true counterpart is to be found in the attitude of the Jew towards Palestine— "When I forget thee, O Jerusalem!" His feeling towards it is a faith, not a calculation . . . his feeling for it [is] a religion. (*Thoughts*, 84–85)

Schreiner's various attempts to swaddle the Boers in collective masochistic fantasy—through her history of Boer martyrdom, her portrait of the Boers as abandoned children eager to renew their dependence on a cruel motherland, her linking together of Boer self-denial and self-sacrifice with Boer self-sufficiency, and her claim that the Boers' religious faith was grounded in a peculiarly masochistic pastoralism—all worked to construct the Boers in the image of a traditional British middle class, with strong parallels to the self-denying spiritualism and self-sufficiency of the early-nineteenth-century evangelical middle classes. But perhaps the clearest sign of this revisionism is Schreiner's willful reformulation of Boer Calvinism in evangelical terms. Schreiner insisted that the Boers were not dogmatic in their faith and that they did not depend, as Calvinists generally did, on religious authorities: "it is wonderful how very little real dogmatic theology the true primitive up-country Boer has!" (*Thoughts*, 289–90). Instead, she claimed to see the evangelical qualities of their faith: their devotion to Bible reading; the affective tone of their spirituality; their reverence for expiation; and their emphasis on personal communion with God, which she believed they forged through their mystical link with the land. This spiritual connection to the land, in particular, had the effect of transforming the Boers' Calvinist severity, in Schreiner's view, into evangelical gentleness, as the stark beauty of the land supposedly filled them with a sense of humility and atonement. Describing an encounter with a Boer woman she found surveying "the infinite beautiful land" behind her farmhouse, Schreiner claims that the woman burst into tears at the prospect of such spiritual beauty: " 'Ach,' she whispered, 'it is a beautiful land the Lord our God has given us! When I look at it so, something swells up and up in my throat—I feel I never will be angry with the servants and children again!' " (*Thoughts*, 189). In all these ways, Schreiner took pains to transform the Boers' religious heritage into something quaintly compatible with residual British middle-class values, claiming that the Boer faith "differs in no way from that still professed by the majority of Scotchmen, from the Aberdeen grocer to the Edinburgh professor" (*Thoughts*, 285).

Rather perversely, Schreiner presented the Boers not simply as compatible with traditional middle-class values but as a force for their regeneration. Imagining the Boers as an antimodern culture grounded in traditional sources of spiritual and psychological vitality, Schreiner claimed to see in them the psychological energies that might energize a new middle-class British colonial culture: "The seventeenth-century Boer has hardly less, perhaps much more, to teach us than we to teach him" (*Thoughts*, 328). These energies consisted of both the Boers' radical antimaterialism, which for Schreiner was a sign of capacities for suffering and self-sacrifice; and their devotion to individual freedom, which she believed constituted a foundational source of social power that Britain itself was in danger of losing: "This absolute freedom and independence . . . was not peculiar to those northern races who conquered and peopled England . . . . It has lived on in our brothers, the Dutch and French, and thus turns up again in their descendant, the African Boer" (*Thoughts*, 341). In her view, then, the Boers could restore middle-class British colonists to their own traditional past.

Schreiner's writings about the Boers were propagandistic and bear an uncertain relation to her actual convictions. Her idealization of the Boers in the 1890s as a vanguard anti-capitalist class sits uncomfortably with her disapproving caricatures of Boer society in *The Story of an African Farm*. Like many British observers, she retained a visceral distaste for Boer vulgarity. In 1907, she wrote to her husband: "What terrible things these young Boer girls are . . . . The lowest servant girls in England would hardly fall to such depths. The only persons who can really cope with them are people of their own class" (*Cronwright-Schreiner*, 268). Even in *The Political Situation*, she and her husband sometimes despaired of recruiting the Boers into an emergent progressive class, believing that they had already been duped by foreign speculators: "Taking advantage of that childlike simplicity which is at once the weakness and the greatest charm of the Boer, he leads him wither he would and also whither he would not" (42).

But the impracticality of Schreiner's vision of the Boers as a traditionally evangelical middle-class culture lay, most of all, in the simple fact that evangelical values had largely been relocated, in nineteenth-century Britain, within the lower middle class—as we will see in detail in chapter 3. This particular class (which was hardly the target audience for Schreiner's anti-war, anti-imperialist views) would have been the least likely political constituency in Britain to see the Boers as their ideological or spiritual kin. The domestic middle-class ranks above them would also have been unlikely to identify with the Boers on the basis of shared evangelical values; in their case, such values clashed with fin-de-siècle standards of bourgeois sophistication. Ironically, at the turn of the century, the one middle-class constituency in South Africa that did, without doubt, ground itself in evangelical values was the emergent black middle class. This elite native class benefited enormously from missionary education and came to form the core of African political leadership.[51] Schreiner's correlation of the Boers with traditional middle-class versions of evangelicalism was thus a major miscalculation, in a variety of ways. As we will see in the next chapter, Kipling was far more shrewd about negotiating this particular network

---

[51] Jean Comaroff, *Body of Power, Spirit of Resistance: The Culture and History of a South African People* (Chicago: University of Chicago Press, 1985), pp. 141–53, describes the oppressive new class divisions missionary education created within tribal society. But Leon De Kock, *Civilising Barbarians: Missionary Narrative and African Textual Response in Nineteenth-Century South Africa* (Johannesburg: Witwatersrand University Press, 1996) argues

of class ideologies. Yet Schreiner's presentation of Boer culture as middle-class in her antiwar writings can nevertheless tell us a great deal about the centrality of social class in her vision of domestic British politics and worldwide feminist struggle.

Domestic Middle-Class Identity and the War over the War

No matter to what degree Schreiner actually believed her own propagandistic arguments about the Boers, those arguments played a central role in her efforts to reform middle-class culture far beyond South Africa. Schreiner directed her essays of the 1890s principally at the middle classes in England, where most of these writings were first published and where she hoped they would influence domestic social relations as well as forestalling war. Like most pro-Boers, Schreiner mounted arguments primarily calculated to swing middle-class opinion, in large part because that was the class most divided by the war. Recent historians tend to agree that the English middle class was exclusively responsible for the pro-Boer movement, while it also seems to have been the source of the most rabid militancy. Certainly, the leadership of the violent jingo crowds was middle-class.[52] Most nonconformist clergy were also prowar. The lower middle class was probably the strongest and most unified source of support for the war, a solidarity that helped make the struggle over the sentiments of other middle-class constituencies seem all the more urgent. That divisions of opinion hit hardest in the middle ranks can be measured by the number of middle-class families that suffered serious rifts over the war—W. H. Lecky's, Arthur Conan Doyle's, or, for that matter, Olive Schreiner's (her husband and her brother Will campaigned actively against the war, but her brother Theo toured England speaking in favor of it, while her mother sent telegrams of encouragement to Cecil Rhodes, which Rhodes exhibited publicly).[53]

Although it is difficult to gauge the extent and depth of working-class support for the war, it tended to be generally patriotic but not necessarily anti-Boer. What working-class resistance did emerge to the war, however, did not revolve around the moral arguments made by middle-class pro-Boers like Schreiner. Rather, working-class resistance to the war, such as it was, centered on the distracting effects the war might have on domestic

---

that a Christian ethic of egalitarianism derived from missionary education laid the foundations for native political solidarity. See pp. 27–28.

[52] See M. D. Blanch, "British Society and the War," *The South African War: The Anglo-Boer War, 1899–1902*, ed. Peter Warwick (London: Longman, 1980), p. 220.

[53] On splits in middle-class families, see S. B. Spies, "Women and the War," in Warwick, p. 180; or Arthur Davey, *The British Pro-Boers, 1877–1902* (Cape Town, South Africa: Tafelberg, 1978), pp. 121–22.

social reform as well as its deleterious effect on prices and wages.[54] The failure of the pro-Boers (including Schreiner) to capture working-class opinion has been consistently attributed to the exclusively moral nature of pro-Boer appeals, which was determined largely by their preoccupation with middle-class spheres of debate. Some have seen this failure as a symptom of the general weakening of middle-class influence over working-class culture late in the century.[55] But the moralization of the antiwar movement, which distinguished it sharply from later British antiwar movements, was also a sign of the ferocity of the battle for middle-class opinion.[56]

One crucial weapon in this struggle was the mobilization of religious rhetoric to support the Boer cause. Schreiner may have been alone in mythologizing the Boers as an inherently middle-class culture, predisposed to unite with the colonial British middle class. But she was not unique in basing her pro-Boer arguments in Christian morality, as she did when she embedded them in a sermon delivered by the figure of Jesus Christ to a working-class infantryman in *Trooper Peter Halket of Mashonaland* (1897). Her emphasis on the moral integrity of Boer Puritanism also echoed a widespread convention in pro-Boer writing.[57] Nevertheless, by projecting onto the Boers a specifically evangelical religiosity that revolved around spiritualized suffering and by representing them as evangelical martyrs persecuted by a cruel Britain, Schreiner anticipated a public debate in which sadomasochistic imagery was widely employed by all sides.

Schreiner's writing, like pro-Boer writing in general before the summer of 1901, had little effect on public opinion in Britain.[58] But when the tide of public opinion did begin to turn against the war, sadomasochistic imagery played an instrumental role. Emily Hobhouse's campaign against the South African concentration camps, created to house Boer refugees in the wake of systematic farm burning, made effective use of sadomasochistic imagery very much like Schreiner's. Conditions in the camps were, in fact, deplorable, and by the end of the war 30,000 people, mostly women and children, had died in them—twice the number of men on both sides killed in battle. Hobhouse used the camps, along with other instances of

[54] See Richard Price, *An Imperial War and the British Working Class: Working-Class Attitudes and Reactions to the Boer War, 1899–1902* (London: Routledge and Kegan Paul, 1972), pp. 233–35. Bernard Porter, "The Pro-Boers in Britain," in Warwick, p. 244, argues that while Labour politicians spoke against the war, they never actively joined the movement against it. Blanch, p. 224, claims that unskilled workers tended to favor the war, and that it was only in the ranks of skilled laborers that muted opposition might be found.

[55] See Donal Lowry, "Introduction: Not Just a 'Teatime War,' " in Lowry, p. 13.

[56] Stephen Koss, ed., *The Pro-Boers: The Anatomy of an Antiwar Movement* (Chicago: University of Chicago Press, 1973), p. xiv, points out the difference between pro-Boer arguments and later antiwar movements.

[57] See First and Scott, p. 241.

[58] Greg Cuthbertson, "Pricking the 'Nonconformist Conscience': Religion Against the South African War," in Lowry, p. 183.

war atrocities and the injustices of martial law, to mount a campaign against British "cruelty," as she frequently called it.[59] Her incendiary reports from the field created an alarming picture of the sadism (sexual and otherwise) of British troops directed against Boer women and children. She quoted British soldiers taunting the refugees: "When you are all poor we can buy your farms for pretty well nothing, and then your husbands will be our servants and you women will serve our wives"; and she described Boer women baring their breasts to the soldiers and screaming "Shoot me, shoot me! I've nothing more to live for, now that my husband is gone, and our farm is burnt, and our cattle taken."[60] In particular, Hobhouse extolled the capacity for martyrdom displayed by the Boers in evangelical terms that paralleled Schreiner's: "The great mass have borne their unprecedented trials with a silent heroism which has astonished many who have witnessed it. . . . Often they welcomed with hymns of praise every opportunity of suffering for their country" (*Brunt*, 316). She also stressed the transgression against mother/child bonds that the camps constituted, describing "pathetic instances of children dying amid the comfortless and unfamiliar surroundings" and arguing that the camps should be turned over to philanthropic organizations because "their mother wit and womanly resolve would right many of the existing ills."[61]

Schreiner's sadomasochistic rhetoric plainly anticipated Hobhouse's much more successful campaign (which was aided, of course, by the bogging down of the British war effort in early 1901). Hobhouse's crusade against the camps, unlike Schreiner's pro-Boer writing, also took advantage of the spectre of women and children being brutalized by British men, which introduced questions about the nature of masculinity and gender relations that were missing from Schreiner's mother/child metaphorics.[62] Still, Hobhouse's success underlines how central and pervasive appeals to masochistic fantasy were in British debates about the war. Sir Henry Campbell-Bannerman, a prominent Liberal leader, for example, joined Hobhouse in the protest against British "cruelty" and "vindictiveness."[63] Campbell-Bannerman famously accused the British government of practicing the "methods of barbarism," a potent slogan that W. T. Stead used as the title of an antiwar pamphlet.[64] While these charges cannot simply be conflated with the dynamics of masochistic fantasy, they

---

[59] "Miss Hobhouse's Report," *Times*, June 19, 1901, p. 10.

[60] Emily Hobhouse, *The Brunt of the War, and Where It Fell* (London: Methuen, 1902), pp. 60, 11. Hereafter cited as *Brunt*.

[61] "Miss Hobhouse's Report," p. 10.

[62] See Krebs on this issue, p. 71.

[63] "Camps Policy: Liberal Leader's Scathing Denunciations," *Morning Leader*, November 21, 1901, p. 5.

[64] "Liberal Leaders: Trenchant Criticism of the War Policy," *Morning Leader*, June 15, 1901, p. 5. On Stead's relationship to Campbell-Bannerman, see Burdett, p. 163.

had the potential to invoke the metaphorics of masochism as a vehicle for arguments over moral authority.

The importance of the rhetoric of victimage to debates about the war is reflected, most of all, by the diverse uses to which it was put. The South African War has been called "the first propaganda war," in the sense that the telegraph enabled combatants on both sides to send dispatches from the battlefield around the world with lightening speed, accelerating the impact of distortions and exaggerations.[65] But since it was a war of attrition, these dispatches consisted largely of each side's accusations about atrocities supposedly committed by the other, making competition over the high moral ground of victimage a central front in the war effort.

Some nonconformist ministers justified the war on the grounds of the evangelical piety they ascribed to African natives, who were being victimized, they claimed, by Boer cruelty.[66] Meanwhile, jingoists accused the pro-Boers of seeking martyrdom cynically, for purposes of publicity—an accusation that was no doubt true in the case of eccentrics like Stead or even of Schreiner's husband, whose cataclysmic antiwar tour of England in the very teeth of militant pro-war crowds resulted in his becoming what the *Morning Leader* called "the most mobbed man in England."[67] Prowar propaganda also exploited images of the glorious martyrdom of the British soldier, and it made use of sentimental sadomasochistic themes: the heroism of the last stand, the gallantry of soldierly self-sacrifice, the victimizing of British troops by Boer treachery (especially devious use of the white flag). This sentimental sadomasochism can be found in government-sponsored poster art and in popular war literature.[68] The siege of Mafeking, which rallied British prowar sentiment around the melodramatic image of imperiled British civilians, was a particularly feverish instance of the role played on both sides by masochistic conjunctions of suffering and glory. Newspapers in England kept their readers enthralled for weeks by the spectacle of penned-up soldiers and civilians (including women and children, which evoked memories of Cawnpore), who were at the mercy of the encircling Boer army—a highly distorted image of the real situation.[69] Kipling was a central participant in this rabble-rousing exploitation of sadomasochistic imagery: he made whites the victims of Boer cruelty and

[65] James Morris, *Farewell the Trumpets: An Imperial Retreat* (London: Faber & Faber, 1978), p. 86.

[66] Cuthbertson, p. 180.

[67] *Morning Leader*, 15 March 1900, p. 5. On accusations about cynical uses of martyrdom among the pro-Boers, see Porter, p. 240; or Cuthbertson, p. 178.

[68] Peter Harrington, "Pictorial Journalism and the Boer War: The London Illustrated Weeklies," *The Boer War: Direction, Experience, and Image*, ed. John Gooch (London: Frank Cass, 2000), p. 229.

[69] Brian Willan, "The Siege of Mafeking," in Warwick, p. 156, reports that the relief forces were surprised by how healthy and well-fed the residents of Mafeking were and how

treachery in stories such as "A Sahib's War" (1901) and persistently reaffirmed his claim, in the absence of any evidence, that the Boers castrated black African prisoners. He wrote verses for suffering nurses and raised money for soldiers' families with his tale of pathos, "The Absent-Minded Beggar" (1900), while raging against the Boers' "primitive lust for racial domination."[70] His claims about the Boers' sadistic attacks on British troops were echoed by other popular writers, particularly Ernest Glanville, author of the influential *Max Thornton* (1901).

Schreiner's images of the Boers' voluntary suffering and martyrdom, which resonated both with traditional evangelical middle-class discourse and with the dynamics of masochistic fantasy, thus formed part of an extensive rhetorical war for British middle-class opinions and values. Such competitions over the high ground of noble suffering are hardly uncommon during military campaigns, but they were exceptionally pronounced in public debate about the South African War.[71] This rhetorical war hinged in a variety of different ways on the manipulation of masochistic economies linking martyrdom to psychological and social power—psychosocial economies that were most deeply bound up in traditional images of British middle-class identity.

Schreiner's attempt to elicit sympathy for the Boers among the middle classes in Britain was part of her more general effort to contrive a political union between the Boers and the British middle class in South Africa. This general project, however, was only an ephemeral crusade. It was motivated by two immediate objectives that both turned out to be losing battles: her opposition to the impending war and to the domination of the South African economy (and its political structure) by foreign speculation and mining wealth. Inevitably, Schreiner's attempt to reinvent a middle-class political subject in South Africa gave way, in the early twentieth century, to other causes. Nevertheless, the fancifulness and the contradictions of her vision of the Boers as the foundation for a new South African political stratum should not blind us to its far-reaching racial and ideological consequences. In addition to her contributions to the rhetoric of the anti-war movement, Schreiner set herself in opposition to virulent forms of racial as well as class prejudice through her celebratory vision of the

---

little damage there had been to the town. Mafeking actually resupplied the relieving force rather than the other way around.

[70] Rudyard Kipling, *Something of Myself and Other Autobiographical Writings*, ed. Thomas Pinney (Cambridge: Cambridge University Press, 1990), p. 97.

[71] On the use of evangelical rhetoric and values by both sides of the South African War debates, see John Wolffe, *God and Greater Britain: Religion and National Life in Britain and Ireland, 1843–1945* (London: Routledge, 1994); and D. W. Bebbington, *The Noncon-formist Conscience: Chapel and Politics, 1870–1914* (London: Allen & Unwin, 1982).

Boers.[72] This vision, of course, was itself a form of omnipotent fantasy, since it involved both willful distortions of South African social history and culture and her own willingness to martyr herself in the pro-Boer cause—one goal that she certainly did achieve. Yet its failures offer an instructive contrast to Schreiner's ideals for sexual equality and feminist struggle, which were driven by similar masochistic energies and which emanated, as I will now suggest, from the same desire to reinvent a (masochistic) middle-class subject that drove her South African writings.

FEMINIST MASOCHISM, CLASS REGENERATION, AND CRITICAL DISAVOWAL

To bring the argument of this chapter full circle, *Woman and Labor*, much of which was written during the South African War and thus at the time of Schreiner's absorption in problems of middle-class domestic and colonial identity, focused almost exclusively on Englishwomen from the middle classes. Her attempts to reimagine Boer culture as the foundation for a South African middle class thus grew out of and folded back into similar concerns in *Woman and Labor* and in her other early-twentieth-century feminist work. These writings sought, not simply to recast sexual relations in egalitarian terms, but to do so in the context of a general rehabilitation of middle-class culture. In particular, the masochistic psychological economies we have seen in Schreiner's feminist writings carry class inflections that correlate the self-sacrificial qualities of New Woman feminism with widespread fin-de-siècle efforts to renovate middle-class subjectivity. Her feminist ideals are part of a complex project of class regeneration rather than being solely an exercise in sexual politics.

Schreiner often claimed to have an antipathy toward women in general despite her feminist loyalties—a tendency she often struggled to control ("You mustn't hate us women so much," she once wrote to Carpenter, "though I do it myself!" [*Rive*, 139]). But her antipathies were most consistently directed against middle-class women. As she told Carpenter: "It's not men that trouble one, it's middle class women that are so hard to understand and reconcile with a good God" (*Rive*, 153). To her friend Betty Molteno, in 1896, Schreiner defined the difficulty in terms that would shortly merit the label "parasitism." In her view, the

> middle class married woman tends to become very selfish, and to fall into a complete state of mental and moral disease! . . . The modern middle class

---

[72] Krebs argues that Schreiner conceptualized the Boers in racial terms and native South Africans in class terms. This formula remains too neat and overlooks Schreiner's hopes for the Boers as the potential core of a South African middle class.

woman has servants and governess [*sic*] and all sorts of single women to do
her work, and then she sits and howls that she hasn't everything she wants,
and that she's so badly off, because she has to bear children etc. etc. It's this
kind of woman we want to do away with, and turn *into a working-woman*.
(*Rive*, 291–92)

She later told Carpenter: "What is so appalling is the desolating *emptiness*
and *barrenness* of the majority of middle class women's lives" (*Rive*, 311).

Schreiner's indictment of the parasitism of the middle-class woman became crucial to the historical argument of *Woman and Labor*. Transforming a familiar preoccupation in late-Victorian culture with the decline
of empire, Schreiner argued that the imperial civilizations of Greece,
Rome, Persia, Assyria, India, China, and Turkey had all been destroyed not
by the failures of ruling-class men but by the enervation of their women.[73]
Schreiner inflected commonplace Victorian anxieties about imperial degeneration by arguing that the corruption of over-privileged classes and
races always began with the female sex: "It has almost invariably been from
the woman to the man that enervation and decay have spread" (102). She
argued that "the 'fine lady,' the human female parasite—the most deadly
microbe which can make its appearance on the surface of any social organism," was the true cause of imperial decline: "Wherever in the history of
the past this type has reached its full development and has comprised the
bulk of the females belonging to any dominant class or race, it has heralded
its decay" (81–82).

But Schreiner's assessment of the decline of British society focused most
intently on the idleness of the middle-class woman. Arguing that the upper-
class English female had long since become the victim of idleness, Schreiner
claimed that an unprecedented world crisis was developing because of the
spread of parasitism into the ranks of middle-class womanhood:

> At the present day, so enormous has been the advance made in the substitu-
> tion of mechanical force for crude, physical, human exertion (mechanical
> force being employed today even in the shaping of feeding-bottles and the
> creation of artificial foods as substitutes for mother's milk!) that it is now
> possible not only for a small and wealthy section of women in each civilized
> community to be maintained without performing any of the ancient, crude,
> physical labors of their sex . . . but this condition has already been reached,
> or is tending to be reached, by that large mass of women in civilized societies
> who form the intermediate class between poor and rich. (114–15)

[73] In 1899, in an essay published in *Cosmopolitan* titled "The Woman Question," *An
Olive Schreiner Reader: Writings on Women and South Africa*, ed. Carol Barash (1980;
London: Routledge, 1987), p. 81, Schreiner made it clear that female parasitism reflected
more general conditions of exploitation: the employment of slaves, the possibilities for
living on unearned wealth, and so forth. This essay formed the basis for the first part of
Woman and Labor.

Although Schreiner was concerned with the idleness of women of all classes, the historical crisis of the moment seemed to her to be rooted in the erosion of the middle-class woman's character: "It is not uncommon in modern societies to find women of a class relatively very moderately wealthy, the wives and daughters of shopkeepers or professional men, who, if their male relations will supply them with a very limited amount of money without exertion on their part, will become as completely parasitic and useless as women with untold wealth at their command" (101). Schreiner believed that, because of the spread of parasitism to middle-class women, in a short time the conditions of idleness would begin to affect women of all ranks, at which point the fate of the entire human race, and not that of just the British Empire, would be sealed: we "stand therefore in a position the gravity and importance of which was not equaled by that of any of our forerunners in the ancient civilization" (117).

As we have seen, the evangelical resonance of Schreiner's critique of middle-class women is unmistakable. But besides supporting the conflation of suffering with omnipotent fantasy, the evangelical tone of Schreiner's feminism also indicates how deeply she wished to reinvent female subjectivity in terms consistent with the psychological principles of middle-class culture of the early nineteenth century. Schreiner's revulsion from the luxury and idleness of women's lives—especially middle-class women's lives—echoed the attitudes of earlier evangelical writers. *Woman and Labor* often reads like an evangelical tract castigating the faithful for their sinful self-indulgence and warning of the emotional emptiness that might follow; it thus conveys the fear of anomie that, as we saw in Stevenson's case, was typical of evangelical middle-class writing about the enervating consequences of fulfilled desire. As Schreiner wrote, "The debilitating effect of unlabored-for wealth lies . . . in the power it may possess of robbing the individual of all incentive to exertion, thus destroying the intellectual, the physical, and finally, the moral fiber" (101).

It is not news to say that Schreiner imposed evangelical thinking and rhetoric on feminist politics. In this maneuver, she resembled many of her time and circle, extending the tradition of George Eliot and John Stuart Mill into the era of the New Woman. While many second-wave feminists criticized the religious elements in the work and tactics of turn-of-the-century feminists, recent historians have begun to revalue this relationship, newly appreciating the ways activism was animated by spiritualization.[74] What has still been overlooked, though, is the power of omnipotent

---

[74] A representative critique of the spiritual rhetoric and tactics of suffragists is Martin Pugh, *Women and the Women's Movement in Britain, 1914–1959* (London: Macmillan, 1992), pp. 46–47. For more dynamic appreciations, see deVries, pp. 318–33, or Susan Thorne, "Missionary-Imperial Feminism," *Gendered Missions: Women and Men in Missionary Discourse and Practice*, ed. Mary Taylor Huber and Nancy C. Lutkehaus (Ann Arbor: University of Michigan Press, 1999), esp. pp. 51–53.

fantasy that feminists like Schreiner borrowed from the sadomasochistic currents of evangelical discourse, as well as the insistent middle-class coding that discourse sustained. Through this psychosocial conjunction, Schreiner proposed the reinvention of a specifically middle-class, masochistic female subject as the foundation of feminist political authority.

If Schreiner's drafting of masochistic evangelical values for feminist purposes was more effective than her attempts to use those values as props for Boer respectability or for a reformed South African middle class, one reason is that her radical feminist audience was itself eager to renovate late-century bourgeois culture. These primarily middle-class rebels were more likely to be inspired by a return to long neglected discourses of spirituality than were other feminist constituencies, for whom social or economic enfranchisement would have carried a higher priority. And we should make no mistake: the widespread feminist reversion to traditions of middle-class spirituality was a profoundly important impetus for social action at the fin de siècle. As Jacqueline deVries has put it, the evangelical rhetoric and tactics of the Salvation Army and other militant religious organizations encouraged suffragists likewise to "[move] the campaign from quiet, middle-class parlours into the nation's streets and squares."[75] The political consequences were not entirely class-bound, either, since the cross-class experiences and solidarity the movement offered middle-class feminists were pivotal to its appeal.[76] To cite only one famous instance: Constance Lytton, enraged at her preferential treatment when imprisoned for suffragette activities, successfully disguised herself as a working-class woman before an impending arrest.[77] In this regard, evangelical strains of suffragism paralleled the strong spiritual tone of the turn-of-the-century socialist movement, particularly in its efforts to recruit from ranks below the middle class.[78] Sadomasochistic strains of evangelical discourse thus underwrote feminist convictions about the universal reach of the movement while at the same time preserving its psychosocial connections to traditional discourses of middle-class psychosocial power.

Unfortunately, Schreiner's emphasis on the pivotal role of middle-class women in political change only reinforced her refusal to admit the relevance of the women's movement to working-class women. She consistently downplayed the involvement of lower-class women in feminist struggle, and she particularly singled out Boer women as irrelevant to feminism. Since Schreiner saw these women as already representing the ideals of female labor to which she believed contemporary middle-class

[75] deVries, p. 320.
[76] See Vicinus, p. 257.
[77] Vicinus, p. 274.
[78] See Stephen Yeo, "A New Life: The Religion of Socialism in Britain, 1883–1896," *History Workshop Journal* 4 (1977), p. 24; or Logie Barrow, *Independent Spirits: Spiritualism and English Plebeians, 1850–1910* (London: Routledge and Kegan Paul, 1986), pp. 148–49.

feminists should revert, any interest they might have in the advancement of women, she believed, should be discouraged:

> Tante, we, the newest of new women, stretch out our hands to you, the oldest of the old . . . we pray of you, stay where you are, and hold fast by what you have, till we come and meet you. We are coming to you in our own way. Stay where you are till we can join hands. . . . Do not force your great, free, labouring-woman's foot into the gegawed shoes of the parasite female, from which we are striving to withdraw ours. . . . Hold by your simple brave life a little longer, produce your many children, guide your household, share man's burden with him, peace or war, till in a new social condition you pass without enervation or degeneration to new labours. (*Thoughts*, 270–71)

These attitudes were certainly patronizing, although they stemmed from a critique of middle-class feminism that Schreiner naively, intermittently, and paradoxically believed to be supported by certain aspects of working-class women's culture. That she tended to see Boer women as working-class but Boer culture generally as a mirror of middle-class values is a contradiction she appears not to have recognized.

Schreiner's concerns with the dangers of middle-class self-indulgence and with women's need to return to supposedly traditional conditions of female martyrdom through labor also help explain her indifference to the oppression of native South African women in her 1890s writings. The dynamics of masochistic fantasy and the middle-class political renovation it seemed to promise led Schreiner throughout the 1890s to idealize both Boer and African women as stoic sufferers rather than to promote their civil rights, which were for her always a secondary feminist concern in any case. Infamously, she idealized the suffering of African women at the beginning of *Woman and Labor*, when she described a "Kafir" woman who expressed women's suffering "with a passion and intensity I have not known equaled," but who spoke "not one word of bitterness against the individual man, nor any will or intention to revolt; rather, there was a stern and almost majestic attitude of acceptance" (6). Schreiner took such stern majesty to represent the cross-racial essence of masochistic power. The eradication of real historical and cultural differences that resulted cannot therefore be explained simply by Schreiner's endorsement of racist eugenic or evolutionary discourses. Eugenic principles may have reinforced the racial and class inflections of her work, especially since late-century eugenics was a heavily class-based discourse, which privileged the middle-class or professional subject as its standard for racial purity.[79] But Schreiner's application of feminist ideals to white middle-class regeneration followed much more directly from the role played in all her work by masochistic psychological economies, by the preoedipal dynamics that

---

[79] A useful account of this class bias in British eugenics is Bland, pp. 224–25.

unite and energize all her political writing, and by the fluid, revisionary connections she made between masochistic fantasy and traditional discourses of middle-class subjectivity. These complex psychosocial intersections are at the heart of her attempt to revision middle-class culture, redeploying ideological materials from its moral and political past (both real and imagined) as the basis for an anticapitalist, anti-imperialist, and antipatriarchal form of subjectivity.

It is in the context of Schreiner's cross-racial, revisionary middle-class idealization of female martyrdom that we need to appreciate the complexity (as well as the limitations) of her colonial politics. Schreiner was not simply reproducing a middle-class female discourse that "othered" non-white and working-class women; she was actively *revising* middle-class subjectivity through masochism—although this project certainly did (mis) represent such women either as an ideal standard of suffering to which white middle-class feminists might aspire or as moral compatriots they might manage. Through her psychosocial revisionism, Schreiner did, in fact, channel the power of masochistic fantasy into socially transformative political tactics, even though its utopianism was inevitably entangled in the distortions and displacements of omnipotent delusion. But we must also recognize that the mobility of masochistic fantasy across lines of gender, class, and race helps explain Schreiner's quickness to identify with African women in the early twentieth century, when she vigorously championed their equality in the context of South African suffragism. In 1907, she resigned from the Women's Enfranchisement League to protest the exclusion of black women, at a time when racial politics had acquired for her a new urgency. Her abrupt alliances, after the turn of the century, with both Boer and African women against her former white middle-class allies might stand as a warning to contemporary critics who cast the Schreiner of the 1890s as a racial victimizer, and who thus follow her into sadomasochistic scripts that extract self-righteous power—in this case, for the critic—from an identification with the position of the victim.

What remains constant in Schreiner's political evolution is her logic of masochistic identification. But the conjunctions of suffering and self-sufficiency upon which its omnipotent phantasmagorics depended were extremely fluid and historically variable. They served more psychological and political purposes than can be captured by any stable alignment of her work with discourses of dominance or submission or by any confinement of that work within the boundaries of a single social or political field.

Only a recognition of the unconscious fantasy structures that link all political idealism to perversity can help us ward off the reductive tendencies of our own critical politics. As I hope I have shown, contemporary critics need to engage the full political dynamics of fin-de-siècle feminist masochism, including its attempts to renovate bourgeois culture at colonial peripheries, before hastening to indict its complicities with racism and imperialism. Among other things, to flog Schreiner for her treatment of nonwhite women is to refuse to take stock of why the victims of racism might be so central to twenty-first-century feminist critique—a refusal that runs the risk of disavowing the historical role of masochism in feminist politics while also reproducing the omnipotent phantasmagorics of the feminist tradition. When feminists flagellate themselves or their allies for being white, middle-class, or imperialistic, thus sacrificing themselves for the causes of victimized others, they sometimes perpetuate the dynamics of sadomasochistic identification in political critique—with all its mixed strategic potentials.

Such disavowals and displacements can also distract us, as I have tried to show, from the centrality of social class within British anti-imperialist writing and from the ways critical or revisionary class discourses can be organized by the logic of masochistic fantasy. Acknowledging these dynamics, in Schreiner's work and in our own, means accepting both the potentials and the difficulties of the complex, inevitable relationship between politics and the perverse. There may be no transcending this relationship. But awareness of its historical role in imperial, feminist, and class struggles can make political critique more accurate and, in the case of writers like Schreiner, more generous as well.

Chapter Three

SADOMASOCHISM AND THE MAGICAL GROUP

KIPLING'S MIDDLE-CLASS IMPERIALISM

> There we met with famous men
> Set in office o'er us;
> And they beat on us with rods—
> Faithfully with many rods—
> Daily beat us on with rods,
> For the love they bore us.
> —FROM "A SCHOOL SONG," PRELUDE TO
> *Stalky & Co.*

RECENT Kipling criticism always begins by addressing his political mul-tivalence. The most redemptive leftist readings have tried to valorize this multivalence as an instance of Kipling's "hybridity," casting him as an avatar of Homi Bhabha.[1] Sympathetic readings of another kind see Kipling as self-divided by his alienation from both metropolitan and colo-nial society.[2] More commonly, though, readers inscribe his apparent am-bivalence about the politics of empire within the inevitable contradictions of colonial experience, weighing his competing loyalties to British author-ity and to resisting colonial subjects in a great variety of ways.[3] The most

[1] Good examples are Don Randall, *Kipling's Imperial Boy: Adolescence and Cultural Hy-bridity* (New York: Palgrave, 2000); Satya P. Mohanty, "Drawing the Color Line: Kipling and the Culture of Colonial Rule," *The Bounds of Race: Perspectives on Hegemony and Resis-tance*, ed. Dominick LaCapra (Ithaca: Cornell University Press, 1991), pp. 311–43; and Abdul R. JanMohamed, "The Economy of Manichean Allegory: The Function of Racial Difference in Colonialist Literature," *Critical Inquiry* 12 (1985), 59–87. John McBratney, *Imperial Subjects, Imperial Space: Rudyard Kipling's Fiction of the Native-Born* (Columbus: Ohio State University Press, 2002), explicitly calls Kipling a precursor of Bhabha (167–69) on account of his fascination with a particular figure of Anglo-Indian hybridity, the native-born colonizer.

[2] See Ali Behdad, *Belated Travelers: Orientalism in the Age of Colonial Dissolution* (Dur-ham: Duke University Press, 1994), pp. 73–91; and Inderpal Grewal, *Home and Harem: Nation, Gender, Empire, and the Cultures of Travel* (Durham: Duke University Press, 1996).

[3] Thomas Metcalf, *Ideologies of the Raj*, The New Cambridge History of India, vol. 3, part 4 (Cambridge: Cambridge University Press, 1994), p. 161, cites Kipling as an instance of "coping with contradiction." Zohreh T. Sullivan, *Narratives of Empire: The Fictions of Rud-

critical of these readers have insisted that Kipling's imperialist fervor over-rode his occasionally mixed perceptions of Anglo/Indian relations.[4] More severely, they have argued that his contradictions and reversals were them-selves instruments of colonialist repression.[5]

However the balance is adjusted, though, debates about Kipling's politi-cal multivalence have been conducted almost exclusively in terms of race.[6] They have entirely neglected the realm of social class, where another kind of multivalence has been abandoned to conservative rehabilitators of Kip-ling's reputation. Christopher Hitchens, for example, in a recent *Atlantic Monthly* essay, lauds Kipling's "fruitful contradictions" as the source of his transcendence of class divisions: "His entire success as a bard derived from the ability to shift between Low and High Church, so to speak. He was a hit with the troops and the gallery . . . but he was also . . . the chosen poet of the royal family and the *Times*."[7] Andrew Rutherford used the phenomenon of Kipling's supposed cross-class appeal to similar effect in his "General Introduction" to the 1987 Oxford World's Classics editions, the first modern editions to appear after the lapse of copyright. Rutherford warned readers to suspend their biases against Kipling's jingoism and not to dismiss him "contemptuously" or "hysterically": "Here, after all, we have the last English author to appeal to readers of all social classes and all cultural groups, from lowbrow to highbrow, and the last poet to command a mass audience."[8]

---

yard Kipling (Cambridge: Cambridge University Press, 1993), p. 6, sees Kipling as "the quintessentially divided imperial subject."

[4] Edward Said, "Introduction," *Kim* (London: Penguin, 1987), pp. 7–46, grants Kip-ling's fondness for India but argues that he was blinded by the British view of it as a land of bucolic subjection. Other important readings of Kipling's devotion to British imperialism include Patrick Williams, "*Kim* and Orientalism," *Kipling Considered*, ed. Phillip Mallett (London: Macmillan, 1989), pp. 33–55; A. Michael Matin, " 'The Hun Is at the Gate!': Historicizing Kipling's Militaristic Rhetoric, from the Imperial Periphery to the National Center, 1: The Russian Threat to British India," *Studies in the Novel* 31 (1999), 317–56; and Sara Suleri, *The Rhetoric of English India* (Chicago: University of Chicago Press, 1992), esp. pp. 111–31.

[5] Parama Roy, *Indian Traffic: Identities in Question in Colonial and Postcolonial India* (Berkeley: University of California Press, 1998), p. 88, for example, claims that "mimicry and exchange are key to the Great Game."

[6] A few studies focused on gender and sexual orientation have also explored instabilities in Kipling's texts. Mohanty claims that gendered notions of invisibility destabilize Kipling's convictions about colonial control; Christopher Lane, *The Ruling Passion: British Colonial Allegory and the Paradox of Homosexual Desire* (Durham: Duke University Press, 1995), pp. 14–44, examines contradictions between desire and mastery in Kipling's homoerotic relationships.

[7] Christopher Hitchens, "A Man of Permanent Contradictions," *The Atlantic Monthly*, vol. 289, no. 6 (June 2002), pp. 103, 96.

[8] Andrew Rutherford, "General Preface," *The Complete Stalky & Co.*, ed. Isabel Quigly (Oxford: Oxford University Press, 1999), pp. vii–viii.

Praise for Kipling's fluid relationship to class boundaries is usually meant to deflect attention from his less palatable political tendencies. But those who simply ignore this aspect of his work miss a significant part of his ideological impact. Over forty years ago, Noel Annan famously proposed that Kipling's significance lay not in his attitudes toward imperialism but in his innovations as a sociologist. Annan regarded Kipling as "the sole analogue in England to those continental sociologists—Durkheim, Weber, and Pareto—who revolutionized the study of society at the beginning of this century." He claimed that, like the new continental sociologists, Kipling "saw society as a nexus of groups" and believed that "the patterns of behaviour which these groups unwittingly established, rather than men's wills or anything so vague as a class, cultural or national tradition, primarily determined men's actions."[9]

The thesis of this chapter is that Kipling did, indeed, locate social determination within a "nexus of groups," but that he organized such groups around a sadomasochistic psychosocial logic rather than around the more benign, informal modes of social ordering Annan claimed to find in his work. I will also argue, contrary to claims about Kipling's supposed transcendence of class, that his sadomasochistic groups underwrote a remarkably unilateral class politics, which accommodated contradictory attitudes toward imperialism within an integrated vision of middle-class authority. Rather than eroding social hierarchy, Kipling's multivalent imperialism absolutely depended upon it. If it has been difficult for critics to recognize the class politics underlying Kipling's writings about empire, his manipulation of the socially mobile characteristics of sadomasochistic groups has played an important role in camouflaging those politics.

Readers have long been aware of Kipling's sadomasochistic preoccupations: the bullyings, beatings, and cruelty that pervade his work. For several critical generations, it was around his enthusiastic treatment of brutality, more so than his jingoism, that debate pivoted.[10] But our recent

---

[9] Noel Annan, "Kipling's Place in the History of Ideas," *Victorian Studies* 3 (1960), pp. 323–24.

[10] Of his many contemporary critics, Robert Buchanan, "The Voice of the Hooligan," *Contemporary Review* 76 (1899), 774–89 (reprinted in Roger Lancelyn Green, ed., *Kipling: The Critical Heritage* [London: Routledge and Kegan Paul, 1971], pp. 233–49), famously stigmatized Kipling's indulgence in cruelty and vindictiveness. George Orwell, "Rudyard Kipling," *Dickens, Dali & Others: Studies in Popular Culture* (New York: Reynal & Hitchcock, 1946), pp. 140–60, cited Kipling's "definite strain of sadism" in arguing that it "is no use pretending that Kipling's view of life, as a whole, can be accepted or even forgiven by any civilized person" (140–41). Edmund Wilson, "The Kipling that Nobody Read," *The Wound and the Bow* (New York: Oxford University Press, 1947), pp. 105–81, claimed that "the whole of Kipling's life" was "shot through with hatred" (111), and that "a first principle of Kipling's world is revenge" (173). For an overview of critical positions taken on viciousness and cruelty in Kipling's work, see Harold Orel, "Introduction," *Critical Essays on*

absorption in questions of race has cast this subject into the shade—in part, because cross-racial sadomasochism usually signaled Kipling's retreat from the kinds of complex engagement with native otherness that have preoccupied recent criticism. Instances of cross-racial sadomasochism in Kipling often simply express his belligerent, one-sided militarism, either through his condemnations of native savagery or his glorifications of soldierly vengeance. Or, if cross-racial cruelty had a sexual dimension, it compelled stiff refusals, like the famous moral lesson drawn by the narrator of "Beyond the Pale" (1888), a story about the brutal punishments dispensed by Hindus to cross-racial lovers: "A man should, whatever happens, keep to his own caste, race, and breed. Let the White go to the White and the Black to the Black."[11] While Kipling's work may have incorporated certain kinds of racial and cultural exchange, it could only safely explore sadomasochism within the field of British class relations and the imperial order those relations sustained.[12]

My claims about the centrality of sadomasochism to Kipling's class politics are intended to reinforce the contentions of recent scholars of colonial culture: that empire was a crucial site for extending and redefining British domestic social structures by projecting those structures to the colonial periphery and back again.[13] Kipling was centrally concerned with rewriting social hierarchy on imperial terrain by merging the sadomasochistic logic of what I will call "magical groups" with both professional and evangelical values. By doing so, he synthesized the ideological languages of distinct metropolitan middle-class constituencies while also managing their ambivalence toward imperial authority. This synthesis enabled Kipling to displace conservative Tory models of power with a newly integrated

---

Rudyard Kipling (Boston: G. K. Hall, 1989), pp. 10–11; or Bernard Porter, "So Much to Hate," *London Review of Books*, vol. 24, no. 8 (25 April 2002), pp. 23–25.

[11] Rudyard Kipling, *Plain Tales from the Hills* (Oxford: Oxford University Press, 1987), p. 127. Except where noted, I have used the 1987 Oxford editions of Kipling's work where these exist—that is, for *Plain Tales from the Hills* (1888) (hereafter cited as *PT*), *Kim* (1901), and *The Complete Stalky & Co.* (1929). I have used the Uniform Edition (London: Macmillan, 1899) for stories published in *Under the Deodars* (1888) and *Wee Willie Winkie* (1888)—both of which were subsumed, in the Uniform Edition, into the volume titled *Wee Willie Winkie; Under the Deodars; the Phantom 'Rickshaw; and Other Stories* (cited as *WWW*). I have also used the Uniform Edition for stories in *Life's Handicap: Being Stories of Mine Own People* (1891), *Many Inventions* (1893), and *The Day's Work* (1898), cited as *LH*, *MI*, and *DW*. Publication dates in parentheses are to the original date of publication, whether in magazines or collections.

[12] Suvir Kaul, "*Kim*, or How to Be Young, Male, and British in Kipling's India," *Kim*, ed. Zohreh T. Sullivan, Norton Critical Edition (New York: Norton, 2002), pp. 426–36, documents the strict limits Kipling placed on cross-racial desire.

[13] See, in particular, David Cannadine, *Ornamentalism: How the British Saw Their Empire* (Oxford: Oxford University Press, 2001), and Ann Laura Stoler, *Race and the Education of Desire: Foucault's History of Sexuality and the Colonial Order of Things* (Durham: Duke University Press, 1995).

(if highly factitious) middle-class one, which helped to broaden and solidify the social base of support for British imperialism. His manipulation of several distinct fragments of middle-class culture was far more successful than Schreiner's efforts to renovate that culture, even though his affirmation of middle-class subjectivity was no less a matter of ideological rewriting than hers.

I will concentrate on Kipling's writings about India from the 1880s up to the turn of the century—particularly some of the early stories and *Kim* (1901). I will begin, however, with an extended discussion of *Stalky & Co.* (1899), a collection of stories about Kipling's schooldays that clearly articulates the sadomasochistic logic underlying his work while promoting an education in that logic as the best preparation for middle-class colonial leaders. These stories demonstrate how a particular sadomasochistic attitude toward the colonial chain of command—which posits the existence of a magical group situated halfway between official colonial authority and its dominated subjects—derived from public school education.

SADOMASOCHISM, BULLYING, AND OMNIPOTENCE IN *STALKY & CO.*

Before I address *Stalky & Co.*, I must explain how the preoedipal fantasies of omnipotence described in chapters 1 and 2 are related to oedipal sadomasochism. Stevenson's masochistic preoccupations were wholly preoedipal, and while Schreiner entertained fantasies about the blurring of oedipal and preoedipal forms of masochism, her inclination was always to submerge the former within the latter. But in Kipling's work, masochism is fully oedipalized and therefore more closely allied with sadism than is the case in either Stevenson's or Schreiner's writing.

Freud located the oedipal stage as the point at which erotic and aggressive drives condense in sadism, making it the first period at which sadism proper can be said to appear.[14] Relational theorists agree that at the oedipal stage, masochistic fantasy is for the first time embedded in relationships of mastery and submission and in the triangular configurations of the oedipal paradigm, since, at this stage, conflicts between aggression and love are complexly articulated through the subject's relationship to two distinct objects.[15] The dyadic relationships of the preoedipal phase develop

[14] Most influentially, Sigmund Freud, "A Child Is Being Beaten," *The Standard Edition of the Complete Psychological Works of Sigmund Freud*, 24 vols., trans. and ed. James Strachey (London: Hogarth Press, 1953–73), 17:175–204, asserted the centrality of the oedipus complex to the sadistic elements of beating fantasies.

[15] See, for example, Jack Novick and Kerry Kelly Novick, "Omnipotence: Pathology and Resistance," *Omnipotent Fantasies and the Vulnerable Self*, ed. Carolyn Ellman and Joseph Reppen (Northvale, NJ: Jason Aronson, 1997), p. 51; and "A Developmental Perspective on Omnipotence," *Journal of Clinical Psychoanalysis* 5 (1996), esp. pp. 150–51.

the problematics of narcissism—including conflicts over betrayal, abandonment, self-esteem, autonomy, and dependence—through relatively insular exchanges between child and caregiver. But at the oedipal stage, this dyadic drama yields to conflicts between love and aggression, dominance and submission, and activity and passivity that are negotiated in more complex triangular patterns.

Nevertheless, a central goal of this chapter is to demonstrate how oedipal sadomasochism remains linked to the problematics of narcissism. The Novicks, along with other relational theorists, have argued that oedipal sadomasochism continues to address problems of narcissistic trauma and compensation through omnipotent fantasy, even though narcissistic concerns may seem less overt than the strikingly sexual and aggressive conflicts associated with the oedipal stage: "Like a thread linking knots of fixation points at oral, anal, and phallic-oedipal phases, there is a delusion of omnipotence which infuses the [masochistic] patient's past and current functioning."[16] In the Novicks' view, the concerns of the oedipal stage with domination, aggression, and triangulation continue to invoke the narcissistic phantasmagorics inscribed within masochistic fantasy at the preoedipal stage, even if such fantasy is mediated by new conflicts and redeployed in different interpersonal configurations.[17]

I am not differentiating between oedipal and preoedipal features of masochistic fantasy for the sake of a biographical reading of Kipling.[18] I am contending only that sadomasochism—with both its triangular, oedipal patterns of domination and submission and its continued invocation of omnipotent fantasy—is fundamental to the affective organization of discourses about class and empire in his work. I do not wish to prove, either, that proimperialist thinking is inherently more oedipalized or more sadomasochistic than anti-imperialist critique, or to argue for a fixed relationship between oedipal or preoedipal structures and particular attitudes toward class. I am asserting only that the relationship in Kipling's work

---

[16] Jack Novick and Kerry Kelly Novick, "Some Comments on Masochism and the Delusion of Omnipotence from a Developmental Perspective," *Journal of the American Psychoanalytic Association* 39 (1991), p. 309.

[17] Jack Novick and Kerry Kelly Novick, "Not for Barbarians: An Appreciation of Freud's 'A Child Is Being Beaten,' " *On Freud's "A Child Is Being Beaten,"* ed. Ethel Spector Person (New Haven: Yale University Press, 1997), pp. 31–46, argue that Freud recognized the centrality of narcissistic injury and omnipotent fantasy to sadomasochism in "A Child is Being Beaten" (1919), but obscured this relationship in his later work. Margaret Ann Fitzpatrick Hanly, "Introduction," *Essential Papers on Masochism*, ed. Margaret Ann Fitzpatrick Hanly (New York: New York University Press, 1995), pp. 81–82, claims that the analytical gap between drive theory and relational theory on the subject of sadomasochism is narrowing.

[18] For such readings, see Wilson; Leonard Shengold, "An Attempt at Soul Murder: Rudyard Kipling's Early Life and Work," *Lives, Events and Other Players: Studies in Psychobiogra-*

between oedipalized sadomasochistic fantasy and class identity was ideologically productive in highly specific psychosocial terms.

In this section, I will focus on the systematic relationship *Stalky & Co.* draws between sadomasochism and omnipotent fantasy. A paradox of sadomasochism, in which the cruelty of an omnipotent figure—in Kipling's case, a bully—can be both an expression of domination and a narcissistically reparative gift of safety, love, and attachment, is the paradox that underlies Kipling's fictionalized account of his own schooldays. Later in this chapter, I will situate this link between sadistic domination and narcissistic omnipotence in Kipling's characteristically triangular group dynamics. While the sexual overtones of Kipling's bullying groups (not to mention his masculinist biases) are obvious and significant, I will focus not on issues of sexuality or gender but on the role of omnipotent fantasy in these groups and its relationship to class ideology.

Although set in a school whose mission was to train officers' sons for colonial service (modeled on the United Services College, which Kipling attended from 1878 to 1882), *Stalky & Co.* has usually been read as an exposé of the institutionalized brutality often discreetly overlooked by nineteenth-century public school fiction.[19] The three boys that comprise Stalky's gang—Stalky himself (whose given name is Corkran), M'Turk, and Beetle (the figure based on Kipling)—spend all their time avenging themselves on cruel and unjust schoolboys and housemasters. A small critical minority has cast the boys' vindictive tactics as the last resort of innocent children, tactics that "the schoolboy needs in order to keep up his end against authority and the school ethos."[20] But the majority of Kipling's critics have noted (often to their distress) that the stories revel in bullying.[21] If they expose anything, it often seems only to be "bad" bullying—that is, bullying by those deficient in intelligence or ineffective in their abuse of power.

"Bad" bullies, in other words, only pretend to have omnipotent power. In contrast, Stalky's gang, which routinely overwhelms its whining antagonists and seeks no hypocritical justifications for its power, seems to represent a kind of "good" bullying through its very indomitability. That

---

phy, ed. J. T. Coltrera (New York: Jason Aronson, 1981), pp. 243–51; or Ashis Nandy, *The Intimate Enemy, Exiled at Home* (Delhi: Oxford University Press, 1998), pp. 64–70.

[19] Wilson, p. 111, for example, called *Stalky & Co.* "a hair-raising picture of the sadism of the English public-school system." W. Somerset Maugham, "Introduction," *A Choice of Kipling's Prose* (London: Macmillan, 1952), p. vi, commented that "a more odious picture of school life can seldom have been drawn."

[20] Isabel Quigly, "Introduction," *The Complete Stalky & Co.*, p. xix.

[21] Buchanan claimed, for example, that "it is simply impossible to show by mere quotation the horrible vileness of the book describing these three small fiends in human likeness; only a perusal of the whole work would convey to the reader its truly repulsive character" (Green, 125).

Stalky & Co. might seek to affirm "good" bullying is all the more significant given that the stories originated, or so Kipling claimed, in his desire
to write a series of tracts on education.[22] He inscribed one copy: "This is
not intended to be merely a humorous book, but it is an Education, a
work of the greatest value."[23] Taken as either a treatise on education or as
a pedagogical lesson, *Stalky & Co.* could be said to celebrate the public
schools' initiation of young men into sadomasochistic practices.

Those practices can inhabit both individuals and groups in a variety of
ways. But one indication that Kipling approved the way they inhabit
Stalky's gang lies in the reverence with which the gang regards the
school's Head, who seems to be the quintessence of positive bullying
power. The story "In Ambush" (1898), for example, features an emblem-
atic encounter between Stalky's gang and the Head that glamorizes the
latter's boundless power to punish. The story begins when the gang en-
traps the most bullying of the housemasters, a man appropriately named
"King." First, the boys lure King into trying to catch them trespassing
only to maneuver him into trespassing himself—which earns him a "dres-
sin'-down" (46) from Colonel Dabney, a domineering local landowner.
Then they trick him into accusing them of both trespassing and drunkenness (they conceal the fact that Colonel Dabney had given them permission to cross his land, and they fake drunkenness before one of King's
schoolboy informants). Threatened by King with a beating for these of-
fenses, the boys formally appeal to the Head. This step is their legal right,
one they have carefully plotted to embarrass King and to flaunt their own
"injured innocence" (46). But, to their surprise, without any questioning
at all (which would have allowed them to play their various trump cards),
the Head simply "[flings] the written charge into the wastepaper basket"
and declares:

> I think we understand one another perfectly. . . . I know you went to Colo-
> nel Dabney's covers because you were invited. . . . I am convinced that, on
> this occasion, you have adhered strictly to the truth. I know, too, that you
> were not drinking. . . . There is not a flaw in any of your characters. And
> that is why I am going to perpetrate a howling injustice. . . . I am going to
> lick you. (52)

---

[22] Rudyard Kipling, *Something of Myself and Other Autobiographical Writings*, ed. Thomas
Pinney (Cambridge: Cambridge University Press, 1990), p. 79. Kipling wrote to Cormell
Price, the Head of the United Services College while he attended the school, that the stories
"will cover . . . the whole question of modern education." *The Letters of Rudyard Kipling*,
ed. Thomas Pinney, 6 vols. (Iowa City: University of Iowa Press, 1990–2004), 2:359. Hereafter cited as *Letters*.

[23] Quoted in R. E. Harbord, *The Readers' Guide to Rudyard Kipling's Work*, 8 vols. (Can-
terbury: Gibbs & Sons, 1961), 1:395.

In what sense this punishment can be called "unjust" is left open. On the one hand, the boys' mischievous pranks seem to deserve punishment of some kind; on the other hand, the Head indicates in various ways that he is more displeased by his ineffectual housemasters than by the three boys, for whom he feels both respect and affinity. But the Head's beatings end all discussion of moral complexity with authoritarian violence, which is not merely symbolic but quite real: the Head's beatings are known as "executions" (117), a term that conveys absolute authority as well as sadistic cruelty. As the boys examine their welts on one occasion, we are told: "There was not a penny to choose between any of them for thoroughness, efficiency, and a certain clarity of outline that stamps the work of the artist" (117).

Numerous times, the stories repeat this drama of "injustice" between the three boys and the Head. Technically innocent, having made their housemasters' futile attempts to punish them expose the masters' own ill temper and bad judgment, and having gotten away with acts of vengeance that cannot be proved against them (or are not even suspected), the boys appear before the Head only to reach the limit of their ability to frustrate the figure of the bully—and to assert their own bullying power. That limit is precisely the omnipotent capacity of the bully to hold himself beyond all appeals to fairness or mercy:

> what they felt most was his unfairness in stopping to talk between executions. Thus: "Among the—lower classes this would lay me open to a charge of—assault. You should be more grateful for your—privileges than you are. There is a limit—one finds it by experience, Beetle—beyond which it is never safe to pursue private vendettas, because—don't move—sooner or later one comes—into collision with the—higher authority, who has studied the animal." (117)

Stalky's boys are not the only ones to suffer the Head's "howling injustice," which he cultivates systematically. A boy named Winton is punished for a minor offense by having to write out Latin verses, even though the timing of his detention will cause him to miss football practice—the Head knowing that this unexcused absence will automatically earn him a flogging from the captain of the games. "I call it filthy unjust of the Head" (174), says one boy. On another occasion, the Head punishes the entire school with the writing out of a hundred lines of verse because the boys had stayed up most of the night listening to a soldier, an ex-student of the school, regale them with stories of military heroism. The Head had secretly orchestrated this night of imperial seduction himself, which makes chastisement the next day seem gratuitously unfair. Not even suspecting this particular injustice (to which only the reader and the soldier are privy), but because the punishment falls on the last day of term, which should be a holiday, the boys perceive it to be "monstrous, tyrannical, subversive of law, religion, and morality" (196). When they riot in protest, the Head announces that he will cane the entire upper school.

The admiration of Stalky's gang for this tyrant is evident in their responses to his beatings: "amazing man" (52), they call him after one execution. On another occasion, after being sentenced to an "an extra-special licking" (183), Stalky muses reverently: "Don't you think it rather rummy—the Head droppin' on us that way?" (184). The Head's decision to cane the upper school leaves all the schoolboys awestruck: "When this news was made public, the school, lost in wonder and admiration, gasped at the Head as he went to his house. Here was a man to be reverenced. On the rare occasions when he caned he did it very scientifically, and the execution of a hundred boys would be epic—immense" (199). Stalky's gang is sometimes perplexed by their own admiration for such tyranny. After one execution, Beetle wonders: "But look here, why aren't we wrathy with the Head? He said it was a flagrant injustice. So it is!" (118). If Beetle cannot answer his own question, though, the Head is aware that there is "a certain flagrant injustice about this that ought to appeal to—your temperament" (117).

The stories themselves make it clear that the Head's despotism satisfies the emotional needs of sadomasochistic schoolboys by sustaining omnipotent fantasy in a variety of ways. For one thing, it allows the boys to identify with omnipotent power. Conversely, it allows them to indulge their needs for dependence on an omnipotent figure. Most importantly, it enables them to construe punishment as a sign of loving collusion forged between the Head and his victims. Each of these points must be elaborated in turn, even though all are intertwined in sadomasochistic fantasy.

First, the Head allows the boys to identify themselves with omnipotence simply by demonstrating its apparent reality. The Head's autocratic authority stands in stark contrast to the weakness of the masters, whose human foibles the gang systematically exploits. The master discovered to have a fear of rats has rats shoved into his room through the chimney; the paranoiac master is diverted from cracking down on Stalky's gang by having his paranoia refocused on other boys in his house. Against this backdrop of bumbling authority, the Head demonstrates to the boys what unassailable omnipotence might look like. As Steven Marcus has put it: the Head represents "an authority which can be believed in . . . . We may think of him as a surrogate for God . . . . Whether he or anyone could ever actually embody such qualities and powers is not immediately to the point; what matters is that the boys believe he does."[24]

---

[24] Steven Marcus, "*Stalky & Co.,*" *Kipling and the Critics*, ed. Elliot L. Gilbert (New York: New York University Press, 1965), p. 157.

Modeling their bullying on the Head's, the boys share his omnipotence to the extent that they can imitate his god-like punitive power. Their willingness to use their knowledge of other people's weak points parallels the Head's manipulative skill, and their resolution to punish all injuries to themselves resembles the Head's determination to crush all challenges to his authority. The aesthetic symmetry and design of the gang's reprisals further parallel the Head's punitive "artistry." The boys are particularly expert at dispensing poetic justice: they use a dead cat to stink up a house that had accused them of being unwashed; they wreck King's study after he had evicted them from their own; they embarrass King trespassing after he had tried to catch them at it. The chaplain comments approvingly: "Observe how, in each case, the punishment fits the crime" (98).

Stalky's power, in particular, resembles that of the Head. Like the Head, his "word was law" (13). His methods are as capricious as the Head's, and similarly lacking in self-justification. Like the Head, Stalky thereby becomes an object of the other boys' dependence. "Did you ever know your Uncle Stalky forget you yet?" (30), Stalky tells them, and the boys' "experience had taught them that if they manoeuvered without [him] they fell into trouble" (13). But all three boys in Stalky's gang appropriate the methods and attitudes of bullying authority. Even King's bullying, when it comes in the context of Latin class, is an object of their emulation; in the classroom, King's bullying emanates from unimpeachable and passionate knowledge of his subject, which the boys recognize as an emblem of invincible strength. Beetle observes: "When King's really on tap he's an interestin' dog" (165). In "The Last Term" (1899), Beetle tortures a would-be persecutor "*à la* King" (270) by imitating the housemaster's rhetoric.

Kipling clearly intended us to see Stalky's gang as Heads-in-training. Like the Head's despotism, their bullying rests on unlimited punitive power and is not bound by subtle codes of justice, except for the one rule that it consistently targets weaker (and, therefore, "bad") bullies. In "The Moral Reformers" (1899), the chaplain actually commissions Stalky's gang—for the good of the whole school—to punish two older bullies, Campbell and Sefton, who had been abusing one of the younger boys. When Stalky's gang ties up the two bullies and beats them to the point of unconsciousness, their style of execution (which is carried out "swiftly and scientifically" [128]) links them to the Head, and their taunts identify them with the school as an institution: "Now we're goin' to show you what real bullyin' is. What I don't like about you, Sefton, is, you come to the Coll. with your stick-up collars an' patent-leather boots, an' you think you can teach us something about bullying. *Do* you think you can teach us anything about bullying? . . . Now this *is* bullyin' " (130). The collusion of the school authorities with Stalky's gang in "good" bullying horrified many contemporary readers and has forced recent apologists to strain at explanations.[25] Many critics have followed Marcus in trying to see the Head as a figure who models codes of honor, justice, and loyalty that could not be presented straightforwardly in an age that had "turned morality into cant," affirming them instead "by standing these terms on their heads."[26] But such tortuous attempts to moralize the Head's tyranny obscure the complex dynamics of identification and vicarious empowerment that sadomasochism makes possible through omnipotent fantasy.

Second, the Head's despotism allows the boys to indulge their needs for dependence on an omnipotent figure (no matter how hurtful such dependence might sometimes be). The Head's limitless capacity for punishment is also a sign of his potential for limitless understanding. Unlike the housemasters, the Head knows and sees all. Echoing the Head himself, the chaplain tells Stalky's gang: "He understands you perfectly" (119). After discovering the Head's previously unacknowledged acquaintance with one of his youthful peccadilloes, a visiting ex-student exclaims: "Is there one single dam' thing about us that you don't know?" (257). This omniscient comprehension—even if it guarantees inescapable, bullying punishment—also suggests that the Head might possess an omnipotent capacity for empathy. The Head responds to the returning student's exclamation by saying: "We-ell! It's a shameful confession, but, you see, I loved you all." The narrator confirms this loving paternalism by telling us that the Head "was father-confessor and agent-general to them all . . . . [Each] carried his trouble to the Head; and Chiron showed him, in language quite unfit for little boys, a quiet and safe way round, out, or under" (189–90). This potential for empathy—which, in the logic of masochistic fantasy, emanates only from genuine omnipotence, since only an omnipotent figure could know his victims thoroughly and have sufficient power to act in their interests—is essential to making certain indomitable bullies seem "good."

In sadomasochistic fantasy, the omnipotent bully is always potentially an omnipotent rescuer, in the sense that victims of abuse often wish to see in the abuser, who is usually a figure they have no choice but to depend upon, at least the possibility of limitlessly sympathetic understanding. As relational work has shown, an abusive parent's seeming omnipotence is often idealized by abused children as a potential source of redemptive love, if only as the object of a magical wish—that is, the child's omnipotent fantasy of triumphing over the abuser by transforming infinitely abusive attention into infinitely loving attention.[27] In addition, submission to abuse protects the

---

[25] H. G. Wells, *The Outline of History: Being a Plain History of Life and Mankind* (New York: Macmillan, 1920) saw this incident as "the key to the ugliest, most retrogressive, and finally fatal idea of modern imperialism: the idea of a *tacit conspiracy between the law and illegal violence.*"

[26] Marcus, p. 159.

[27] Novick and Novick, *Fearful Symmetry,* p. 56.

abuser's omnipotence from the victim's own repressed rage and aggression, thus preserving the abuser in fantasy as an omnipotent figure strong enough to offer safety and protection. The Head's despotism, precisely because of the omnipotence implicit in it, makes the possibility of nurturance and dependence seem available to the boys, who are all solitary boarders and whose parents are never represented in the stories as sources of aid or comfort. Readers have debated whether, on any given occasion, the Head is "really" kind or not to his charges. The important point, however, is that the Head's nurturing qualities, whenever he does unveil them, are deeply invested with omnipotence (including his cavalier violation of codes of propriety governing how one speaks to "little boys"), which is precisely what makes them the object of schoolboy fascination and love.

As he echoes the Head's bullying techniques, so, too, does Stalky reproduce the empathetic potentials of omnipotence. Stalky's understanding is so capacious that he can explain a wounded boy's own repressed feelings back to him. Finding Beetle wallowing in melancholic confusion, Stalky tells him: "Beetle! You're oppressed and insulted and bullied by King. Don't you feel it?" (59). Yet both Stalky and the Head resist making their emotional caretaking the object of public knowledge, since to do so would be to expose themselves to the sadomasochistic temper of the school. The logic of sadomasochistic fantasy vests omnipotent authority only in the despot, perceiving acts of kindness as signs of weakness and submission— as, in effect, the abandonment of claims to omnipotence. Unqualified kindness, if not simply irrelevant (as is the chaplain's), always risks becoming the target of sadistic aggression. When Stalky discovers that the Head has risked his life to save one of the schoolboys, he cries out: "I've got him by the short hairs!" (192). Stalky then attempts to revenge his own executions by circulating this story of the Head's compassion. Stalky spreads the story just before the Head canes the upper school, which then threatens to make a shambles of his authority by cheering as he beats them. In this remarkable scene, however, the Head resists the sentimentality of the boys (and the reader), as well as Stalky's sadistic attempts to expose his benevolence, by persevering remorselessly with the caning.

Third and perhaps most important, the Head's despotism enables the boys to construe punishment as a narcissistic sign of their specialness and as a kind of collaboration that shares omnipotence between abuser and abused. In the logic of sadomasochistic fantasy, the victim of punishment magically controls the punishment by imagining it to be designed for his or her benefit. When Stalky's gang discusses the Head's beatings with the chaplain, he tells them: "One licking once a week would do you an immense amount of good" (119). The knowledge (or the fantasy) that one's beating is done for one's own good can constitute a secret, magical bond between omnipotent authority and dependent child. Freud made this point in "A Child Is Being Beaten" (1919), when he claimed that the second stage of the beating fantasy transforms the father's punishments into a fulfillment of the wish: "My father loves only me."[28] The Head often conveys signs of special favor in the course of his abuse, with a wink or a suppressed laugh, or with enigmatic suggestions that his punishments emanate from special regard: "I am now going to pay you a tremendous compliment," he says before one beating; "I'm going to execute you without rhyme, Beetle, or reason" (52).

But the special favor the Head confers through punishment is, quite simply, the education in sadomasochistic omnipotence he provides. Although some readers have sentimentalized the Head by seeing him as a nurturing father figure hiding behind a gruff exterior, Kipling makes it clear that a training in sadomasochism and the omnipotent narcissism it engenders is the most important, most unsentimental gift that the Head bestows. One lesson the beatings teach, for example, is the value of transcending one's emotions—itself a form of omnipotent fantasy. Masochists often harbor delusions of absolute self-sufficiency through the omnipotent belief that they can stop having feelings, can transcend pain, and can maintain themselves in splendid narcissistic isolation. *Stalky & Co.* thus exposes the sadomasochistic logic beneath those British codes of masculinity that mandated displays of one's indifference to suffering.

Indeed, the success of Stalky's gang depends largely on their superhuman capacity to rise above their emotions—a skill they acquire in various ways through their beatings. On the one hand, the threat of detection and punishment induces self-control. During one of their escapades, we are told that there was "no betraying giggle, no squeak of excitement. They had learned, by stripes, the unwisdom of these things" (18). On the other, though, beating annihilates certain kinds of emotion by subsuming them in pain. Whenever one of the boys threatens to give away an enterprise by laughing, for example, the other two boys beat him. In one episode, Stalky says:

> "If you're goin' to laugh, Beetle, I shall have to kick you again."
> "But I must!" Beetle was blackening with suppressed mirth.
> "You won't do it here, then." He thrust the already limp Beetle through the cart-shed window. It sobered him; one cannot laugh on a bed of nettles. Then Corkran stepped on his prostrate carcass, and M'Turk followed, just as Beetle would have risen; so he was upset, and the nettles painted on his cheek a likeness of hideous eruptions. (21–22)

Enduring a beating without "blubbing" (117) is also an implicit test of omnipotence. While Stalky confesses after a beating that "I didn't exactly

[28] Freud, 17:187.

smile" (118), he displays his omnipotent detachment later by laughing at his punishment's injustice.[29]

Another lesson the Head imparts through his beatings is that life is, in essence, relentlessly cruel and unjust, and that one had better respond to it with narcissistic compensations rather than futile protests. As Stalky says to Beetle: "You've been here six years, and you expect fairness. Well, you *are* a dithering idiot" (75). The ability to endure an unjust beating without a trace of complaint becomes the sign of one's immunity to life's injustice, as well as a strategic device of emotional omnipotence: Stalky reproves Beetle partly because Beetle's human needs for fair treatment are what give others the power to "fetch" (75) him by teasing. Expecting injustice, by contrast, makes one omnipotently impervious to bullying. The Head's injustice can be construed, then, as a sign of his love only in the sense that it provides a number of lessons about transforming injustice into masochistic omnipotence.

The boys practice these forms of emotional transcendence in their regular beatings of one another, which are always perpetrated "dispassionately" (56). The narrator calls our attention repeatedly to this reciprocal abuse and to its enigmatic emotional neutrality: "Corkran kicked [M'Turk] as he had kicked Beetle; and even as Beetle, M'Turk took not the faintest notice" (13). The normalization of reciprocal beating within Stalky's gang signifies the immunity its members feel from either giving or receiving real injury, no matter how badly they do, in fact, abuse one another. Internalizing omnipotence by acting out dramas of despotism, submission, and injustice within its own ranks, the group performs its magical imperviousness to pain as a sign of its power and the impregnability of its internal bonds of attachment.

Beatings in *Stalky & Co.* also help to regulate omnipotent fantasy itself. One of the paradoxical functions of masochism, as Schreiner's work makes clear, is its ability to regulate omnipotent fantasy through punitive self-correction. Housemasters like King are figures of ridicule, in part because their sadistic conceit causes them to lose perspective on the reach of their own power. In contrast, the Head's beatings help the gang to establish the limits of their own megalomania and thus to preserve omnipotent fantasy by warding off its most dangerous excesses. Such excesses are exactly what the Head has in mind when he cautions Beetle that there is "a limit . . . beyond which it is never safe to pursue private vendettas" (117). In the logic of sadomasochism, submission to punishment also serves omnipotent fantasy by suggesting that only the punitive actions of an omnipotent figure are powerful enough to control narcissistic excesses; it suggests, as well, that such excesses are so dangerous that they must be carefully controlled.

---

[29] In *Something of Myself*, Kipling praised the "infernal impersonality" of Lionel Dunsterville, the model for Stalky: "He saw not only us but himself from the outside" (19).

This mechanism, by which either masochistic self-punishment or submission to a powerful figure checks omnipotent fantasy in order to sustain it, is an important feature of Kipling's own imperial posturings, one that he put to effective use in poems like "Recessional" (1897) and "The White Man's Burden" (1899). These two poems, written at the same time Kipling was composing the Stalky stories, advocate both self-humbling and submission to divine judgment as checks that help legitimate and regulate imperial power. Kipling seems to have experienced his own sadomasochistic colonial authority in precisely this reversible way. Writing to his former headmaster on his first arrival in India in 1882, he gloated: "Altogether, I find that this sort of life suits me down to the ground. I have about seventy men to bully and hector as I please and am liable to bullying if I don't do *my* share of the business properly. This is quite as it should be and I take any bullyings with a good grace" (*Letters*, 1:28).

Critics have long contended that Stalky—who eventually becomes a war hero—exemplifies the imperialist's need to have admirers of his god-like authority. But bullying omnipotence is a reversible phenomenon, as well as a social medium. Unlike the masochistic fantasies common in Stevenson's and Schreiner's work, sadistic omnipotence in Kipling always organizes reversible relationships between individuals and collectivities. It may be a commonplace to observe that the culture of schools reproduces social class—that, as John Guillory puts it, schools accomplish "the differential tracking of students according to class or the possession of cultural capital."[30] But in *Stalky & Co.*, the class culture reproduced by the public school is based not simply on cultural capital or social tracking but on psychological dynamics that construct social identity around sadomasochistic paradigms. In the next section, I will explore Kipling's use of "good" bullying to produce a particular kind of collective identity—a triangulated one—that I will later contextualize in class terms.

MAGICAL GROUPS: BULLIES, VICTIMS, AND BYSTANDERS

There has been considerable psychoanalytic work done recently on the means by which bullying binds social groups together in forms of collective intimacy, particularly in the wake of disturbing patterns of violence in middle-class American schools.[31] Some researchers have focused on the ways

---

[30] John Guillory, *Cultural Capital: The Problem of Literary Canon Formation* (Chicago: University of Chicago Press, 1993), pp. 38–39.

[31] This body of work often references W. R. Bion, *Experiences in Groups, and Other Papers* (New York: Basic Books, 1961), particularly his claim that groups submit to despotic leaders to resolve conflicts between individual and group identity. The most notable studies include Vamik Volkan, *The Need to Have Enemies and Allies: From Clinical Practice to International Relationships* (Northvale, NJ: Jason Aronson, 1988); and "Narcissistic Personality Organiza-

bullying groups repair narcissistic injuries for their members by allowing unintegrated or unstable positive aspects of identity—like those produced by omnipotent fantasy—to be projected onto and consolidated in the group.[32] Recent studies have also recognized that bullying groups depend on triangular relationships, in which bully and victim interact with a third figure, the bystander, to form a complex sadomasochistic bond.

The bystander plays a critical role within bullying groups in at least two ways. First, the bystander normalizes sadomasochistic relationships as the basis for collective identity. Second, the bystander embodies the reversible identifications that bind bully and victim together. Researchers have discovered that while individuals obviously manifest a wide range of responses to scenes of bullying, those who watch passively tend to identify with both bully and victim.[33] The passivity of the bystander acts as a defense against his or her own sadism, sublimating it into voyeurism. But the passivity of the bystander also repeats in its very helplessness the pathos of the victim. In bullying groups, bystanders are often conscripted in service of the bully, or the victim, or both. Sometimes, bystanders collaborate with bullies in complicated patterns of identification and counteridentification. They might conceal scenes of bullying from authority figures, slavishly carry out the bully's orders to bully others, or take turns submitting to the bully themselves. At the same time, bullies and victims both see in the bystander a means of aggrandizing their own narcissism by capturing the envy or the sympathy of an audience. Furthermore, all three of these positions can be transformed phantasmagorically into omnipotent "rescuer" roles, which help to distinguish "good" bullying groups from "bad" ones in the eyes of their own members. The abusive bully can become the kind of all-knowing and empathetic despot one both imitates and depends upon, like Kipling's Head. But victims can also harbor fantasies of rescuing their victimizers through their own submission. Bystanders, in turn, use

---

tion and 'Reparative' Leadership," *International Journal of Group Psychotherapy* 30 (1980), 131–52. Jerrold M. Post, "Narcissism and the Quest for Political Power," *Omnipotent Fantasies and the Vulnerable Self*, pp. 195–232, applies Volkan's work to contemporary political struggles. See also Stuart W. Twemlow, "The Roots of Violence: Converging Psychoanalytic Explanatory Models for Power Struggles and Violence in Schools," *Psychoanalytic Quarterly* 69 (2000), 741–85; "Traumatic Object Relations Configurations Seen in Victim/Victimizer Relationships," *Journal of the American Academy of Psychoanalysis and Dynamic Psychiatry* 23 (1995), 563–80; and "The Psychoanalytic Foundations of a Dialectical Approach to the Victim/Victimizer Relationship," *Journal of the American Academy of Psychoanalysis and Dynamic Psychiatry* 23 (1995), 545–61.

[32] See Volkan, *The Need to Have Enemies and Allies*, esp. pp. 30–38.

[33] See, in particular, Stuart W. Twemlow, Frank C. Sacco, and Preston Williams, "A Clinical and Interactionist Perspective on the Bully-Victim-Bystander Relationship," *Bulletin of the Menninger Clinic* 60 (1996), 296–313.

their detachment to fuel fantasies of rescue directed at either of the other two figures.[34]

Bullying in *Stalky & Co.* always revolves around the triangulation of bully, victim, and bystander; the interchangeability of these three positions; and the morphing of each of them into "rescuer" roles. In the story "Stalky" (1898), which opens the expanded volume called *The Complete Stalky & Co.* (1929), these dynamics are enacted transparently.[35] Stalky's boys are first introduced to the reader as bystanders at a scene of bullying. Another group of boys, whose ringleader is named De Vitré, has decided to take revenge on a local farmer for a string of petty insults by stealing his cows. Finding that De Vitré's scheme leaves him no opportunity to play a commanding role, Stalky refuses to participate, declaring: "We're goin' to watch" (12). From a secret hiding place inside a cart house, Stalky's gang then voyeuristically witnesses a reversal of bullying roles: a group of farmhands appears, imprisons De Vitré's boys in an empty barn, and inverts the positions of bully and victim, "De Vitré's party promising, entreating, and cajoling, while the natives laughed like Inquisitors" (18). The gloating farmhands taunt the boys with their impending flogging: "Yeou'll be wopped proper. 'Rackon yeou'll be askin' for junkets to set in this week o' Sundays to come."

At this point, Stalky's bystanding gang nearly joins the victims. The cows happen to gather around the cart house, cutting off the gang's retreat and leaving them vulnerable to exposure. Quickly assuming a bullying role, though, the gang uses slingshots to enrage the cows, which attack the two farmers who have since arrived on the scene to relieve their farmhands. In the confusion, Stalky's gang rescues De Vitré's boys and then, without being seen, locks the besieged farmers in the barn and revels sadistically in their helpless cries. To account for their own presence at the scene and to supply themselves with an alibi for being late back at school, Stalky's boys then call through an opening in the barn and offer to rescue the farmers. Merging the roles of bully and bystander, though, they first torment the farmers (one of whom owns the cows, now desperate to be milked, and the other of whom owns the lock on the barn door) by provoking an argument between them about whether the lock should be broken. Finally, when Stalky's gang returns to school, they refuse De Vitré's gratitude for being rescued and bully him instead: they force him to proclaim that Stalky is a "Great Man" and that he, De Vitré, is "a putrid

[34] Twemlow, "Traumatic Object Relations," p. 577, sees this adoption of rescuer roles as a reaction formation against identification with sadistic violence.

[35] This story, published in magazine form in 1898 and clearly intended to introduce the three central characters, was withheld from the 1899 publication of *Stalky & Co.* because of complaints that it endorsed cruelty to animals. It was restored as the introductory story to *The Complete Stalky & Co.* in 1929. See Harbord, 1:423.

ass" (27). Stalky also turns De Vitré's boys from bystanders who aspire to be fellow sadists into victimized bystanders: De Vitré's gang clamors to be told the details of Stalky's triumph over the farmers, so that they can share vicariously in it; but Stalky sadistically withholds these details, thereby aligning De Vitré with his victims. "'*Now* won't you tell us?' said De Vitré pleadingly," after submitting to the "Great Man." "Not by a heap," replies Stalky, and the story ends without compromising this sadistic refusal: "Therefore the tale has stayed untold till to-day." This withholding implicitly identifies the reader—who does know the details—with Stalky's sadism. Indeed, *Stalky & Co.* often puts the reader in the uncomfortable position of the bystander, provoking simultaneous enjoyment and discomfort. This construction and manipulation of the reader's passivity marks Kipling's persistent efforts, throughout his career, to enlist the reader within the sadomasochistic groups he describes.

In "Stalky," the triangular roles of the bullying scenario are relatively fluid. But within Stalky's gang, these three roles are maintained in stable reciprocity. Stalky is the undisputed leader, the one most likely to administer what he calls "kickings" to the others. Beetle is most often the recipient of this abuse. But there are moments when each of the boys rises in ascendancy over one of the others, with the third looking on. Sometimes, these role reversals are accomplished indirectly, so as not to disrupt the ordered hierarchy of the group. In "The Moral Reformers," for example, Stalky allows Beetle to play the most violent role in the beating of Campbell and Sefton, as a recompense for Beetle's having been bullied by older boys like them when he was young. In a similarly indirect fashion, M'Turk displaces Stalky in "In Ambush" when he outbullies Colonel Dabney, while Stalky and Beetle both look on, "quaking" (35). Toward the end of the story, when Stalky tries to make the other boys proclaim him a "Great Man," Beetle thwarts him and says: "No . . . . We've got to thank Turkey for this. Turkey is the Great Man" (39). These consensual and relatively ordered exchanges of roles distribute various kinds of narcissistic omnipotence among the three boys.

Moreover, the group is structured externally, as well as internally, by reversible sadomasochistic relationships. In its interactions with the school as a whole, Stalky's gang is by turns avenging bully, victim, or bystander. The gang takes an injury to any of its members as an injury to their collective narcissism and avenges all such attacks on its prestige and power. Yet the gang remains the permanent target of envious schoolboys and masters, and it is defenseless against the beatings of the Head. Within this stable complex of positions, the gang's vindictive bullying is fueled precisely by its presentation of itself as social victim—whether this victimization happens, at any given point, to be real or staged ("Our line is injured innocence" [69], Stalky says, on one occasion). As bystanders, the gang often flaunts its detachment from the conventional values of public school life. The boys use their detachment either to camouflage their voyeurism of the others' cruelty (as in their observation of De Vitré's boys) or to disguise their feelings of victimization (as when, in "An Unsavoury Interlude" [1899], King's house persecutes Stalky's house, but the gang refuses to join in their own house's official protest, seeing it as a futile gesture and, therefore, a sign of weakness). Most importantly, their spectatorship of the Head's violence allows them to identify with his despotism, both when they witness him reprimanding the masters and when they reminisce about their own beatings (which makes them, in a sense, retrospective spectators of their own punishment).

Stalky's gang also plays a "rescuing" role in relation to the school as a whole. In one extraordinary scene from "An Unsavoury Interlude," three of the housemasters eavesdrop on Stalky's gang, which is busy "rubbing it into" (91) the boys of another house. The masters vicariously enjoy this scene of verbal abuse—even when some of the insults begin to be directed at each one of them in turn (although their presence, as eavesdroppers, remains undetected). As consensual bystanders, the housemasters voyeuristically endorse the gang's vengeance while at the same time submitting themselves as deserving victims of it. In such scenes, the masters' tacit endorsement vindicates Stalky's gang as "good bullies"—legitimately powerful despots whose bullying unifies and orders the school, much as the Head does, by punishing weak bullies and by modeling their own bullying as a form of omnipotent power in which bystanders secretly participate (whether as vicarious sadists or appreciative victims).

The Head himself participates in this reversible phantasmagorics, built on the bully/victim/bystander relationship, through which authorized bullies can appear both to themselves and to others as aggrieved victims, and through which bystanders can identify with both roles. In "The Satisfaction of a Gentleman" (1929), the Head finds himself compelled by one of the directors of the school to administer a beating to Stalky's gang. Suppressing his misgivings about the need for punishment on this occasion, the Head beats the three boys while the director—assuming the role of bystander—listens from an adjoining room. Years later, the Head confesses to a friend that, while beating the boys, he had felt strangely like a victim himself: "I saw my face in the glass, like an ape's—a frightened, revengeful ape's ... it was all abject—paltry—time-serving—unjust" (256). This scene, in which the Head, in the act of bullying, feels himself to be bullied by an unjust bystander, and in which he becomes the helpless bystander of both himself-as-bully and himself-as-victim when he glimpses his own face in the mirror, captures an ambivalence always inscribed into the Head's authority. While ruling despotically, as the school's center of power, the Head is always profoundly alienated from its actual practices, as carried out by his own housemasters and stipulated by the directors. In this sense, his omnipotence, like the gang's, always harbors an aura of "injured innocence."

Through this sadomasochistic reversibility and precisely because he beats them, the Head is implicitly allied with Stalky's gang in a magical group that remains somewhat apart from the society of the school as a whole. By "magical group," I mean a narcissistically omnipotent bullying group that recognizes itself both as the legitimately despotic center of social order and as its permanently alienated victim. Magical groups draw their narcissistic omnipotence from both of these phantasmagoric positions, as well as from their insulation against any larger social body that might disrupt the sadomasochistic relations that structure the group both internally and externally. This sadomasochistic dynamic, I now want to suggest, profoundly organized Kipling's view of class hierarchy, in the sense that he always tended to valorize the social authority of magical groups over other political or social configurations.

What is most striking about the magical group formed by Stalky's gang, for example, is its hostility toward official social values. Stalky's gang holds in contempt all the traditionally upper-class ideals associated with the public school: the honor of the house, athleticism, honesty and fair play, the prefectoral system. These upper-class ideals serve only as targets of the gang's class resentment. As one of the boys puts it: "We aren't a public school. We're a limited liability company payin' four per cent. . . . We've got to get into the Army or—get out, haven't we? King's hired by the Council to teach us. All the rest's flumdiddle" (186–87).[36] More strikingly, the gang violently repudiates national values that one might think dear to Kipling's own heart. In "The Flag of their Country" (1899), for example, Stalky's gang is horrified by a Conservative MP, who tries to appropriate their volunteer cadet corps for patriotic purposes by bestowing a Union Jack on them during a public speech. Stalky calls the MP a "Jelly-bellied Flag-flapper" (220), and in response to M'Turk's sarcastic question "Don't you want to die for your giddy country?" (211), Stalky responds: "Not if I can jolly well avoid it." Critics have accepted at face-value the narrator's explanation for this repudiation of patriotism—that is, that the MP speaks vulgarly of matters the boys consider sacred.[37] But this interpretation ignores conflicts the story establishes between the magical group and official social values—which is to say, in this case, Tory values.

---

[36] For a good discussion of the social marginality of the United Services College, see Elizabeth Buettner, *Empire Families: Britons and Late Imperial India* (Oxford: Oxford University Press, 2004), pp. 166–68, 176–80.

[37] See, for example, Marcus, pp. 159–60; Robert F. Moss, "Kipling's Theory of Education in *Stalky & Co.*," *Kipling Journal* 200 (1976), p. 16; or Joseph Bristow, *Empire Boys: Adven-*

The story begins with Stalky's transformation of a routine form of discipline into a means of self-glorification. Drilling is the school's punishment for tardiness, a "weary game" (202) that Stalky and Beetle happen to suffer more than most. But Stalky takes over this ritualized punishment from Foxy, the school's "Sergeant," claiming he can prove that boys excel at drilling themselves and that he, in particular, "can drill as well as you, Foxy" (202). This masochistic role reversal hints at the more momentous ways in which the school trains the boys to turn inglorious suffering into heroic imperial martyrdom. The narrator tells us that Hogan "three years later [would] die in the Burmese sunlight outside Minhla Fort" (208); and that Perowne would be "shot in Equatorial Africa by his own men" (212)—the fate of a martyr in the mid-1880s, when the Sudanese infantry was composed of native troops whose reputed cowardice had become the object of national outrage. But even as a game, the student-run cadet corps brings the boys both the surprised approval of their superiors and covert opportunities for bullying; these reversible sadomasochistic dynamics structure the corps both internally and externally and thus construct it as a magical group.

Stalky "as usual [lays] down the law" (208) and becomes the corps' "generalissimo" (212). Imitating the sadism of British drill sergeants, he revels in "withering invective" (213) against his fellow schoolboys, who, on their side, extract pleasure from being "told off an' dressed down" (214) in play. Most important, Stalky insists on the radical privacy of the cadet corps, refusing to let outsiders watch the drill and postponing indefinitely any public parading. His creation of a secret, inwardly focused society through the cadet corps becomes, among other things, a means of bullying school authorities. The boys take pleasure in knowing that "this sort of secret-society biznai will drive King wild" (212), and the narrator tells us: "It troubled many more than King." The Sergeant himself feels that the whole enterprise is a way of "makin' fun o' me." These sadomasochistic dynamics are precisely what the MP's flag waving disrupts, since it shines a glaring public light on the fragile solidarity of the magical group. Before this intervention, the cadet corps had managed to contain and express contradictory attitudes toward imperialism through the structural ambivalence magical groups entertain toward social authority of any kind.

Stalky's identification with the sadomasochistic bonding of the magical group, rather than with the social order of the school or with nationalist solidarity, is dramatized explicitly in "Slaves of the Lamp, Part II" (1897). In this story, Stalky's peculiar relationship toward British authority in

---

tures in a Man's World (London: Unwin Hyman, 1991), p. 79. Kipling himself wrote from the school, in 1882: "I'm afraid we are scarcely loyal and patriotic enough" (Letters, 1:18).

India suggests that his primary allegiance is to a certain mode of domination rather than to his superiors or their values. A maverick commander, Stalky's magical qualities as a military tactician derive directly from his schoolboy bullying. When his band of soldiers is hopelessly outnumbered by two Afghan tribes, Stalky employs sadomasochistic triangulation. As a schoolboy, in "Slaves of the Lamp, Part I" (1897), he had taken revenge against one bully (a master) by turning him into the victim of a second bully (a peasant)—a maneuver that required making the second bully feel himself to be the victim of the first. The result had been that Stalky and his gang emerged from the fray as triumphant bystanders, when master and peasant attacked each other. In "Part II," Stalky uses the same trick with the Afghan tribes, making each feel itself to be the victim of the other's bullying tactics, which allows Stalky's band to prevail from the sidelines when the two tribes attack one another. "Practically he duplicated the trick over again" (296), one of the grownup schoolboys gushes.

What is more important than the military success of this trick, though, is the sadomasochistic structure that Stalky's unorthodox methods establish for him generally vis-à-vis colonial authority. Stalky's heroic stature in the field brings him omnipotent authority of many kinds, including the ability to rule over large numbers of Afghan natives, much in the style of Peachy Carnehan and Daniel Dravot in "The Man Who Would Be King" (1888) but with more success (which indicates, among other things, how much more proimperialist Kipling had become in the decade intervening between these two stories). Stalky makes his own treaties, carries out his own military maneuvers and road-building schemes, corresponds with the British government with "the manner of a king," and generally does everything "except strikin' coins in his own image and superscription" (294). Besides bullying Afghan fighters, though, he also bullies his own government, writing insulting letters to his commanding officers as if he were "one fat brigadier slangin' another" (282). This defiance is not tolerated by the military chain of command, and Stalky is rebuked by the Viceroy himself, in terms that suggest sadomasochistic reversal: he is "offered up on the horns of the altar" and "sent up for his wiggin' like a bad little boy" (295). Yet, in Stalky's view, he—rather than the Viceroy—represents most accurately the nature of British mastery in India: "If I thought that . . . basket-hanger governed India, I swear I'd become a naturalised Muscovite tomorrow."[38] His former schoolmates agree that "India's full of Stalkies—Cheltenham and Haileybury and Marlborough chaps—that we

---

[38] "Basket-hanger" is a reference to the housemaster who had been Stalky's nemesis in "Part I." The allusion links the Viceroy to the housemaster, both of whom are bullies bullied.

don't know anything about" (296). As a supremely effective agent of empire, Stalky thus becomes both an embodiment of official British military authority and its defiant whipping boy. In the view of his old schoolmates, he is thereby linked to others like himself—and like them—in a magical group of middle-level military officers, whose omnipotent power is signaled by their simultaneous defiance of and abjection before official authority, as well as by both their merciless military triumphs and their willingness to die in the name of that authority.

The psychological dynamics of magical groups have no essential affinity with any particular segment of the social order. For historical reasons, however, they resonated most strongly with the nineteenth-century British middle class's uncertainty about its social centrality and power. That Kipling called his magical group "Stalky & Co.," a tag that echoes his description of the College as "a limited liability company" (186), underlines the school's precarious status on the middle-class fringes of public school education. In keeping with the school's marginalized status, Kipling's magical group consistently critiques upper-class values. In particular, *Stalky & Co.* deliberately opposes itself to the upper-class imperial ideology promoted by Thomas Hughes's *Tom Brown's Schooldays* (1857), which set the pattern for schoolboy fiction during the second half of the nineteenth century. Repudiating the swaggering bully figure that typified aristocratic Regency schoolboy fiction (represented by the villainous Flashman), *Tom Brown's Schooldays* incarnated a new kind of upper-class schoolboy hero whose social authority derived from his manly honor on the playing field and at war. Hughes's novel thus exemplified the Tory patriotism of midcentury, which, as Joseph Bristow has pointed out, "was designed to challenge the individualism of the liberal-minded middle classes who were to be viewed as traitors to their country by putting their hands in their pockets and vouching for peace" (58). In the wake of the Crimean War (1853–56), the notion that the public schools produced a chivalric warrior class promoted the identification of upper-class interests with imperialism. Hugh Cunningham has demonstrated that Tory imperialism outflanked middle-class politicians for much of the second half of the nineteenth century by cultivating this warrior ideal:

> The measuring rod of patriotism was one erected by the Conservatives in the 1870s; the patriot was above class, loyal to institutions of the country, and resolute in defence and honour of its interests. Liberals, radicals and socialists who protested their own patriotism were singularly unsuccessful in wresting the initiative from the right. Patriotism was firmly identified with conservatism, militarism, royalism and racialism.[39]

[39] Hugh Cunningham, "The Language of Patriotism, 1750–1914," *History Workshop Journal* 12 (1981), p. 24.

Kipling's assault on upper-class schoolboy ideals was an attempt to steal imperial ideology away from the Tory upper class and to identify it instead with a middle-class conception of imperial subjectivity.[40] Ironically, *Stalky & Co.* rehabilitated the bullying figure that upper-class schoolboy fiction rejected, relocating it in Kipling's newly glamorized middle-class bullies and, more importantly, in the magical groups whose sadomasochistic energies were central to his conception of social hierarchy. The performatively private, aggrieved jingoism implicit in the Stalky stories thus represents a victory of specifically middle-class patriotism over the Tory Conservatism that had monopolized the banner of imperialism since mid-century. By affirming magical groups that were both marginalized and central, victimized and omnipotent, Kipling managed middle-class ambivalence toward imperialism while displacing upper-class imperial ideals. In the process, he reorganized patriotism around a recognizably middle-class intersubjective dynamic that fused class resentment with class pride.

In two subsequent sections of this chapter, I will discuss Kipling's affiliation of magical groups with ideological discourses that played important roles in late-nineteenth-century middle-class power: professionalism and evangelicalism. I will spend more time on the former than the latter simply because I have already established the affinities between evangelicalism and masochistic fantasy in previous chapters. In the next section, however, I will first explore Kipling's affirmation of magical groups in *Kim*. In this novel more clearly than anywhere else, Kipling promoted magical groups as the foundation for British imperial rule in India and, therefore, as the fulfillment of the dreams of middle-class authority he entertained in *Stalky & Co.*

KIM: THE MAGICAL GROUP AS IMPERIAL AGENT

Kipling's most acclaimed novel, *Kim*—written shortly after the principal Stalky stories were published—idealizes magical groups as the most effective imperial organizational structure. Kim's initiation into the British Secret Service, in particular, reveals the fundamentally sadomasochistic dynamics holding together the small-scale administrative, military, and professional units Kipling regarded as the backbone of the empire. In this sense, the novel is not a work of social realism but an expression of Kipling's wish to promote on colonial terrain a form of psychosocial power

---

[40] Bristow, p. 75, views Stalky's gang as a "gentleman's club" representing a "minority Conservative belief" about the authority of colonial officials over politicians. But this interpretation ignores the drift of his own argument—that the gang affirms a radical form of individualism over against the values of the public school.

that, when exploited by schoolboys, had strained against the moral limits of British metropolitan culture, as the mixed responses of readers to *Stalky & Co.* attest.[41]

Kim's ascension to manhood—the novel's central theme—charts the incorporation of his extraordinary personal talents into a secret brotherhood of imperial espionage. The novel's project could thus be described as the relocation of fantasies of individual omnipotence within a collective social body. It is crucial to recognize first, though, that sadomasochistic omnipotence is always implicit in Kim's remarkable personal abilities. Its presence can be felt, for example, in the novel's famous opening, in which Kim overwhelms several Indian children in a game of king-of-the-castle as they fight for control of an old artillery gun. In this scene, Kim seems an unproblematic paragon of British triumphalism—partly because his triumph is the work of a child and partly because he is poor and Irish.[42] Nevertheless, his victory suggests his indomitable destiny, which depends not on his physical strength but on his seemingly magical powers: his talents for acting and disguise; his unlimited resourcefulness; his command of verbal invective; his ability to summon up, genie-like, the protection of powerful others; and his irrepressible will. Kim's abilities are meant to seem superhuman. They cause villagers to wonder about his "supernatural origin" (39), and the lama doubts whether he is "woman-born" (70). At one point, the lama exclaims proudly: "Said I not he was from the other world?" (48). When he resists Lurgan Sahib's telepathic power, the astonished Lurgan tells him: "You are the first that ever saved himself. I wish I knew what it was that . . . . But you are right. You should not tell that—not even to me" (155). Shortly afterwards, Kim himself brags about what he calls his "magical gifts" (186).

Kipling does his best to make these omnipotent personal qualities seem innocent of aggression. After this first scene, Kim's talents obviate the need for physical assault. Early in the novel, too, his skills are exercised simply to win food, shelter, or immunity from the dangers inherent in being a young vagrant in India. They appear most unobjectionable when he exercises them to protect the seemingly helpless lama. Often, when Kim bullies others for food or justice, he is simply playing the role of rescuing, good father to his dependent friend. But Kim's superhuman talents plainly serve narcissistic ends as well. Among other things, they help him win the adulation of everyone he meets. He is the "Little Friend of all the World"

---

[41] Critical commentary on *Kim* often tries to adjudicate the novel's accuracy as social realism. See, in particular, Roy, pp. 75–91; Suleri, pp. 111–31; and Tim Watson, "Indian and Irish Unrest in Kipling's *Kim*," *Postcolonial Theory and Criticism*, ed. Laura Chrisman and Benita Parry (Cambridge, UK: D. S. Brewer, 2000), pp. 95–113.

[42] For discussions of the role of Kim's Irishness, see Bristow, p. 195; Watson, pp. 97, 106–107; or Matin, p. 364.

(3), the epithet itself expressing a wish for universal, unqualified love.[43] His talents also help him to fulfill the fantasies of infinite mobility that Edward Said has identified with the imperial imagination: the wish that one might "do everything, be anything, go anywhere with impunity."[44] By making Kim's power seem benign, however, Kipling camouflages its affinity with sadomasochistic energies that always lie just beneath the surface of both narcissistic and imperial grandiosity.[45]

It is Kim's capacity for cruelty, for example, that enables him always to remain king-of-the-castle. When a policeman harasses the lama, Kim bullies him with unjust accusations and a threat to unleash the power of his gang:

> "Huh! Owl!" was Kim's retort on the lama's behalf. "Sit under that gun if it please thee. When didst thou steal the milk-woman's slippers, Dunnoo?"
> That was an utterly unfounded charge sprung on the spur of the moment, but it silenced Dunnoo, who knew that Kim's clear yell could call up legions of bad bazar boys if need arose. (12–13)

Moreover, like Stalky's gang, Kim omnisciently detects the weaknesses of others, which he then uses to dominate and control them. Intuiting the miserliness of a farmer and his wife, for example, he shames them into providing food by insulting their stinginess: "The shot told: they were notoriously the closest-fisted couple in the village" (49). Like Stalky's gang, too, Kim always gets the best of others in repartee. Stalky's frustrated fellow schoolboys complain: "You chaps always behave as if you were jawin' us when we come to jaw you" (106). Similarly, Kim never meets with the insult he cannot top, and he brags that his "curses have the knack of biting home" (66). Most tellingly, like the members of Stalky's gang, Kim models himself on a seemingly omnipotent authority figure, Colonel Creighton. At one point, he mimics Creighton so convincingly that his native audience exclaims: "It is He. Past all doubt it is He" (48).

Kim's "magical gifts," like those of Stalky's gang, also make his triumphs seem effortless, the efflorescence of his very being rather than the result of malicious conquest or ordinary labor—an important characteristic of omnipotent fantasy. Stalky defeats both housemasters and Afghans by simply turning others against themselves. Likewise, Kim puts others in the position to carry out against themselves his own destructive wishes

---

[43] Kipling shared the fantasy by applying this epithet to himself. Alice MacDonald Fleming, "My Brother, Rudyard Kipling," *Kipling: Interviews and Recollections*, ed. Harold Orel, 2 vols. (Totowa, NJ: Barnes & Noble, 1983), 1:10.

[44] Said, p. 42. See also McClure, p. 78; Parry, p. 54; or Sullivan, p. 447, who explicitly calls this kind of ambition a "fantasy of omnipotence."

[45] Said, p. 12, describes Kim as "wonderfully attractive," claiming that he "remains a boy, with a boy's passion for tricks, pranks, clever word-play, resourcefulness."

toward them. The downfall of two foreign spies, for example, "had come about through no craft of Hurree's or contrivance of Kim's, but simply, beautifully, and inevitably" (248). For the most part, Kim's vengeance is enacted for him by others: Hurree Chunder Mookerjee torments the two spies all the way out of India while posing as their helpful guide; Mahbub Ali beats the drummer boy who had beaten Kim. But while the novel distances Kim from its most direct reprisals against his tormentors, it often reveals his unmistakable enthusiasm for such revenge. Vanquishing the policeman, Kim "hooted at him all down the road" (60); assaulting the Russian spy who had struck the lama, Kim "[bangs] his breathless foe's head against a boulder" (242).

Like Stalky, M'Turk, and Beetle, too, Kim transcends emotion through his tolerance for pain. Hectored by Father Victor, he "betrayed no emotion"; kicked by the drummer boy, he did not "complain" (117). When insulted by the servants of the royal widow, he responds in a voice that "was sweeter than ever": "In *my* country we call that the beginning of love-talk" (66). This magical immunity to pain is what allows Kim to regard the entire world buoyantly and to see what the lama regards as a "great and terrible world" (35) as instead a "great good-tempered world" (34). It also enables him to endure the ambiguity of others' feelings about him—particularly the ambiguity of father figures like Creighton and Mahbub, who, like the Head, are alternately either protective and affectionate or threatening, unjust, and cold. It enables him, too, to experience his wanderings throughout India, with all their deprivations and hardships, as unmitigated pleasure. Moreover, as we have seen, capacities for submission allow masochists to internalize checks to their own pride that can help preserve omnipotence. The lama tells Kim frequently that his pride must be humbled, and at the end of the novel their journey of penitence through the Himalayas serves both of them as a form of expiation. But this humbling also legitimates omnipotent authority. Mahbub and the lama agree that, after his ordeal of penitence, Kim is ready to "go forth as a teacher" (285).

Kim also takes up all three positions in the bully/victim/bystander triangle. Bullying and begging are often the same activity for him; one character captures the duality concisely by calling him a "master-beggar" (49). Occasionally, Kim plays the role of voyeur to the bullying of others, as when he overhears the royal widow abusing her servants and thinks to himself "his hostess would rather heighten the enjoyment of the road" (73). She does not disappoint him; on one occasion she unleashes a "volley of invective": "It did not last long, but in kind and quality, in blistering, biting appropriateness, it was beyond anything that even Kim had heard. . . . 'Oh, *shabash*!' murmured Kim, unable to contain himself" (74).

Kim's enthusiastic participation in contests of intimidation, one-ups-
manship, and bullying is, in one sense, simply a mirroring response to his
environment. For all the supposed fondness critics have found in Kipling's
portrayal of bucolic India, *Kim* represents native life as profoundly sadomasochistic.[46] The "Grand Trunk Road is a wonderful spectacle" (57),
gushes the narrator when Kim first sets foot on it. But by way of illustra-
tion, we are immediately treated to a torrent of abuse, as "a venomous
whip-cracking came out of a pillar of dust fifty yards away, where a cart
had broken down" (58). A horse rider "rockets" out of the dust "in chase
of a shouting man . . . scientifically lashing his victim between plunges."
Rural India in *Kim* is full of such scenes: floggings, harassments, threats
of violence, extortion, money-lenders who extract "cruel interest" (62),
and unrelieved "rudeness" (120). It is also a carnival of verbal humilia-
tions, in which Sikhs insult Dogras, sepoys taunt Sikhs, railway traveling
companions provoke one another, old soldiers "curse" their men and are
reviled in turn as "toothless old [apes]" (54). If these scenes have been
rhapsodized as instances of local color, even by left-leaning readings of
Kim (including, most notably, Said's pleasure in Kipling's "affectionate
descriptions of Indian life on the Grand Trunk Road"), it may be because,
as Lionel Trilling once observed, reading *Kim* always returns us to perspectives "fixed deep in childhood feeling."[47] But childhood feeling is seldom as innocent as it appears. Through the eyes of Kim the child, the
reader is encouraged to transform verbal or physical violence into the detached pleasures of voyeurism. In many of the novel's supposedly pastoral
scenes, some other child of India is being beaten.

Kipling clearly sought to recuperate Kim's child-like indulgence in
domination, submission, and voyeurism within some larger social ideal.
He did so by incorporating these pleasures within the magical group constituted by the British Secret Service. Internally, the Secret Service is structured around the interchangeability of sadomasochistic roles. Mahbub,
the "bullying, red-bearded horse-dealer" (21), is also Kim's rescuer and
protector, whether directly—as when he beats the drummer boy who had
beaten Kim—or indirectly, when he plays the role of "rescuing" bystander
("I have turned aside the Colonel's whip from thy skin" [132]). For the
most part, Kim responds submissively to this despotic kindness, rendering
Mahbub "service" (21). But the two often exchange insults, and on one
occasion Kim provokes Mahbub so bitingly with racial slurs that the latter

---

[46] Despite the prevalence of Indian sadomasochism in *Kim*, many critics continue to regard it as a celebration of cultural difference. See esp. JanMohamed, pp. 68, 78; Randall, pp.
110–59; or McClure.

[47] Said, p. 12. Lionel Trilling, "Kipling," *Kipling and the Critics*, p. 89, applies this phrase
to all of Kipling's work, but particularly to *Kim* on p. 92.

draws his knife. Playing the role of rescuer, though, Kim also saves Mahbub from two assassins. Correspondingly, Mahbub's protective attitude toward Kim is sometimes self-martyring: "No harm comes to thee, my son. I am thy sacrifice!" (178). These sentimental moments of gruff paternalism and protective submission veil a darker intersubjective logic, for the two frequently acknowledge that their love is sealed by the power of life and death they hold over one another—what Kim describes, during one particularly tense moment, as "a very sure tie between us" (132). Similarly, Creighton treats Kim with both benevolent and authoritarian solicitude, while Kim, always seeking his mentor's love, commits frequent acts of "insolence" (128), which Creighton is helpless to punish and can only endure passively.

As is the case in Stalky's gang, these reversible relationships are often triangulated by spectatorship, which can mix sadism with empathy. Thus, Mahbub rails at Kim while Creighton looks on: "Here was deadly insult on deadlier injury—and the Sahib to whom he had so craftily given that war-waking letter heard it all" (109). Yet in this particular scene, Creighton's gaze is one of critical appreciation. Likewise, the reading of Creighton's "war-waking letter," which declares that the Colonel will "punish" (38) rebellious Afghans, is a spectacle that Kim observes approvingly through a window. Early in his introduction to the Great Game, Kim is also thrilled by watching one British agent pretend to bully another. The two enact this charade to throw off pursuit, but, at a deeper level, their performance expresses the triangular sadomasochistic energies that animate and unify the spy ring: "E.23, not moving a muscle of his countenance, answered with a stream of the filthiest abuse, at which Kim naturally rejoiced. It reminded him of the drummer-boys and the barrack-sweepers at Umballa in the terrible time of his first schooling" (207). These memories underline the pedagogical role that sadomasochistic abuse plays in Kim's training for imperial service. Such abuse is redeemed, ultimately, in Lurgan's school for spies, in which Kim is subjected to various forms of magic meant to terrorize him, against which he proves his omnipotent immunity. In general, the reversible roles within the spy ring constitute it as a sadomasochistic group, in which domination, submission, and voyeurism are sustained within a stable intersubjective economy.

Kim's relationship to the lama also mixes pain with love, but in preoedipal terms, which complement the oedipalized, sadomasochistic dynamics of the spy ring without seeming to contradict them.[48] Kim's alternating submission to and protection of the lama wins him comfort, security, and

---

[48] Without observing the masochistic patterns linking Kim's relationships to both the lama and the spy ring, many critics have noted the novel's efforts to portray Indian spiritualism and British imperialism as non-contradictory. See Said, p. 23.

affection in return. Such pleasures are often expressed in preoedipal masochism through self-sacrifice and the acceptance of loss. Kim's adoption
of these roles culminates in his self-martyring care for the lama during
their trek into the mountains. Burdened "like a mule" (227) and "beaten
down" (235), Kim tells the lama: "May I be thy sacrifice!" (260). On his
side, the lama declares that he will relinquish Kim's companionship if the
boy's interests would best be served at boarding school: Father Victor,
"wise in the confessional, heard the pain in every sentence" (92).

This relationship of reciprocal nurturing and sacrifice avoids some of
the instability and aggression latent in triangular oedipal relationships.
The spy ring, however, generates a form of omnipotence that exceeds
anything the lama can provide. The sadomasochistic omnipotence imma-
nent in the spy ring is defined explicitly through Lurgan, who terroris-
tically initiates Kim into gifts more advanced than any he already possesses; Mahbub warns Kim: "Men say he does magic" (147). But the spy
ring exudes a general aura of omnipotence, which attaches to each of its
members, and which they all mirror back to one another. Lurgan, while
pitying himself as an uncelebrated hero, models a self-satisfaction greater
than mere fame: "honour and credit in the mouths of a chosen few"
(175). Kim learns to aspire after this "clean pride" (219): "Earth has
nothing on the same plane to compare with it." The Great Game thus
answers Kim's questions about his own identity by folding him into the
magic of British national omnipotence:

> Well is the Game called great! I was four days a scullion at Quetta, waiting on
> the wife of the man whose book I stole. And that was part of the Great Game!
> From the South—God knows how far—came up the Mahratta, playing the
> Great Game in fear of his life. Now I shall go far and far into the North playing
> the Great Game. Truly, it runs like a shuttle throughout all Hind. . . . and I
> am Kim—Kim—Kim—alone—one person—in the middle of it all. (224)

If the spy ring is structured internally by sadomasochistic forms of omnipotence, it is also structured externally through its sadomasochistic relationship with official authority. On the one hand, the spy ring mobilizes
the sadistic energies of British power. When Creighton unleashes British
troops, he declares: "It's punishment—not war" (37). Not only does the
spy ring model the despotic and sadistic aspects of British rule, but its
lawless techniques prove it to be more effective than are the government's
official agents. During E.23's escape, a police officer—a "hot and perspir-
ing young Englishman" (206)—unwittingly does the work of the coun-
terspies who have misled him. Only Kipling's stock character Strickland,
himself a member of the spy ring, prevents this government agent from
carrying out the will of his enemies.

On the other hand, though, Kipling represents the Secret Service as an abused or even persecuted group within the imperial order rather than a duly appreciated extension of it. The near-death of E.23 through the loutish ignorance of the British police highlights a deep structural antagonism between the spy ring and the government, which often seems to have abandoned its own operatives, like a cruelly negligent parent: "We of the Game are beyond protection," says E.23; "If we die, we die. Our names are blotted from the book. That is all" (200). This antagonism sometimes erupts in the spy ring's open resentment of centralized British authority. Mookerjee abuses government inaction in private to Kim, adding: "Of course, I tell you this unoffeecially to elucidate political situation, Mister O'Hara. Offeecially, I am debarred from criticizing any action of superior" (221). Kipling shared this kind of resentment and expressed it more openly. During the South African War, he liked to say that England is "our only enemy."[49] But because he saw himself as the betrayed victim of a cruel government and of the vicious conspiracies he loved to imagine within it—that is, precisely because he saw himself, narcissistically, as the special target of imperial omnipotence—Kipling could reverse this relationship when it suited him and identify fully with such omnipotence.

What have often been regarded as ambivalently pro- and anti-imperialist impulses within Kipling's work can only be coherently understood within the intersubjective dynamics of sadomasochistic solidarity. Kim's acceptance of his double life suggests that his deepest emotional commitments are to the magical group and to the sadomasochistic tensions it creates—between himself and the British government or between himself and Indian society and culture. Kim's loyal membership in the magical group comes long before he has any knowledge of nations, or imperialism, or patriotic service. Before he has even heard of the Great Game, he is recruited as a spy through the sadomasochistic structure of his personal relations with Mahbub and Creighton.

Kipling's work is full of small, insular, sadomasochistic groups—the soldiers three, Stalky's gang, the professional enclaves at Indian hill stations, Mowgli's animal alliances. The stability of these magical groups depends on sadomasochistic relations that structure each group both externally and internally. This formula proved very effective in other British spy novels of the early twentieth century, particularly works by John Buchan such as *The Thirty-Nine Steps* (1915) and *Mr. Standfast* (1919), which incorporate Kiplingesque features of the magical group into imperial espionage. Conversely, magical groups are the specific object of George Orwell's critique of colonialism in *Burmese Days* (1934), a novel in which jagged class conflicts tear apart a remote outpost of British agents and civilians, who

---

[49] See, for example, *Letters*, 3:82.

are nevertheless bound to one another through their own internal sado-masochistic tensions. Buchan's sympathies clearly lay with the professional middle class, as much as Orwell's did not. In Kim's case, emotional commitment to the magical group, in the form of the spy ring, may precede ideological self-awareness, but Kipling was intent on using the psychodynamics of the magical group to anchor a broad but nevertheless highly specific class identity. In the next two sections, I will demonstrate how Kipling used magical groups to overcome a particular gap between middle-class ideological constituencies.

Magical Professionals in the Short Fiction

Like his other fantasy of childhood omnipotence in India—the *Jungle Book* (1894), which features a powerful but embattled alliance between Mowgli, his wolf brothers, Kaa the python, and Bagheera the panther—*Kim* exemplifies Kipling's wish to regard magical groups as the ideal form of social organization. The sadomasochistic group dynamics central to these two works and to *Stalky & Co.* repeat those found throughout Kipling's Indian short fiction of the late 1880s and early 1890s. But in his Indian fiction, Kipling also fused the psychological dynamics of magical groups with two disjunctive middle-class ideological systems.

One of Kipling's most important ideological interventions, in fact, was his alignment of magical groups with both professional expertise and evangelical values. This conjunction consolidated and revitalized middle-class ideological languages in two complementary ways: on the one hand, by infusing evangelical codes of self-denial and self-sacrifice with the social cachet enjoyed by late-century professionals; and, on the other, by injecting a moral center and a messianic spirit into professional practices, which Kipling and others felt were degenerating in late-nineteenth-century India, due to the deadliness of procedural routines and the absence of the culture of conquest that had galvanized Anglo-Indian society earlier in the century.[50] This conjunction also had the potential to broaden middle-class ideological unity by linking an emergent upper-middle-class professional discourse to archaic spiritual values that had largely been relocated in the lower middle class at the fin-de-siècle. It thus helped produce the expansive popularity Kipling enjoyed, both in India and in Britain, as well as synthesizing distinctly different kinds of social support for the jingoism he inspired. Although this convergence of two distinct languages

---

[50] Many historians and literary critics have noted that late-century Anglo-Indian observers worried over the loss of a conquest mentality and the enervations of bureaucratic routine. For an excellent discussion, see Lewis D. Wurgaft, *The Imperial Imagination: Magic and Myth in Kipling's India* (Middletown, CT: Wesleyan University Press, 1983), pp. 32–41.

of class took place on intellectual as well as affective grounds, the role played by magical groups was crucial in sustaining it.

In this section, I will focus on the rigorous association Kipling made between professionalism and sadomasochism in the formation of magical groups. Readers have long recognized that Kipling held figures at the top of the political, military, or administrative hierarchy in contempt, but that he had a special regard for the middle-level professional. This figure often plays a heroic role in the stories, especially those written during the 1890s, when—after having left India in 1889—Kipling's occasionally satiric attitudes toward administrators gave way to consistent reverence. In "The Head of the District" (1890), for example, Kipling lionized the dying Deputy Commissioner Yardley-Orde, who is loved by British subordinates and natives alike, and whose love for them is as strong as his love for his wife. "It isn't that I mind dying," Yardley-Orde laments on his deathbed, "It's leaving Polly and the district" (*LH*, 104). Similarly, "In the Rukh" (1893) idealizes the Forest Officer Gisborne, who "learns to grow wise in more than wood-lore alone; to know the people and the polity of the jungle" (*MI*, 201–202). The first of Kipling's Mowgli stories, "In the Rukh" shows how Mowgli's magical abilities could be integrated into human society only by his joining the Civil Service as a midlevel forestry official.

Kipling's admiration for these professional figures rested on his adulation of technical knowledge, which was driven by a number of his characteristic concerns (his love of secrecy and cultish groups, his fascination with masculine self-sufficiency, and his attraction to seemingly magical forms of power). But, among its many functions, Kipling's admiration for technical knowledge reflected the ascension of scientific and professional discourses to social authority in the second half of the nineteenth century, as well as the importance of knowledge-gathering as an instrument of colonial domination. Contemporary historians have long been aware, as Bernard Cohn puts it, that "the conquest of India was a conquest of knowledge."[51] This was especially true after the events of 1857, when British authority came to depend on increased surveillance and on the categorizing potentials of ethnography, sociology, and other social sciences.[52] Kipling's fiction dramatized the power wielded by professionals who possess specialized knowledge

[51] Bernard S. Cohn, *Colonialism and Its Forms of Knowledge: The British in India* (Princeton: Princeton University Press, 1996), p. 16.

[52] Good discussions of the role of colonial knowledge as a form of social control in India include Susan Bayly, *Caste, Society, and Politics in India From the Eighteenth Century to the Modern Age*, The New Cambridge History of India, vol. 4, part 3 (Cambridge: Cambridge University Press, 1999); C. A. Bayly, *Empire and Information: Intelligence Gathering and Social Communication in India, 1780–1870* (Cambridge: Cambridge University Press, 1996); and Gauri Viswanathan, *Masks of Conquest: Literary Study and British Rule in India* (New York: Columbia University Press, 1989), esp. pp. 27–30.

about departmental politics, administrative procedures, engineering, ethnography, and colonial argot (native, military, and technical).[53] Even military expertise, whether possessed by officers or infantrymen, was especially honored when it seemed to rest on or at least to resemble scientific knowledge. A subaltern in "A Conference of the Powers" (1890), for example, claims: "There's nothing nicer than a satisfactory little expedition, when you find your plans fit together, and your conformation's *teek*—correct, you know, and the whole *sub-chiz*—I mean, when everything works out like formulæ on a blackboard" (*MI*, 35).

Of course, Kipling admired knowledge of all sorts, not simply the kinds of knowledge officially associated with professionals or even with specifically middle-class occupations. His admiration extended to working-class expertise, to the stereotypically "feminine" social arts, and even to the frontiersmanship skills of "savages." Yet Kipling construed all these various forms of knowledge in unmistakably professional terms. Such knowledge, for Kipling, always required strict, impersonal detachment and judicious neutrality; devotion to a craft or cognitive base that could be formalized and reproduced; and membership in a guild that guarded, regulated, and distributed training.[54] These features of Kiplingesque knowledge no doubt prompted Trilling to attribute his own boyhood fascination with Kipling's infamous air of "knowingness" to the fact that it "suggested the virtue of disinterested professional commitment."[55]

Kipling consistently stressed the congruity of non-middle-class forms of expertise with professionalism. Kim's many raw talents, for example, are recognized and refined in Lurgan's school for spies: what initially seem to be Kim's uniquely personal skills for cross-cultural shape shifting turn out to be arts that are the domain of the British Secret Service, which Kim can only perfect by submitting to its professional training. In addition to honing his perceptual skills through Lurgan's training, Kim must also be introduced to the newest, most modern forms of surveillance available to the professional spy ring, including the processing and classification of information in reports, memoranda, and academic papers. Similarly, Peachy Carnehan and Daniel Dravot, in "The Man Who Would Be King,"

---

[53] Recent cultural critics have questioned the unidirectionality of the power/knowledge axis described by Said, Cohn, and others. Peter Burroughs, "Imperial Institutions and the Government of Empire," *The Oxford History of the British Empire*, Vol. 3: *The Nineteenth Century*, ed. Andrew Porter (Oxford: Oxford University Press, 1999), p. 184, claims that effective intelligence gathering was a hybrid construction, the result of a dialogue between westerners and native informants.

[54] These are the principal features of professionalism identified by Magali Sarfatti Larson, *The Rise of Professionalism: A Sociological Analysis* (Berkeley: University of California Press, 1977), pp. 35, 40–41.

[55] Trilling, p. 87.

recognize that colonial conquest depends on imitating the methods of professional soldiers, administrators, and judges. Even the romantic manipulations of Mrs. Hauksbee depend on her clubby alliances with women like Mrs. Mallowe, with whom she discusses objectives and techniques, and on the disinterested, intellectualized character of her seductions. They also reflect her belief in the value of information and instruction. Mrs. Hauksbee's "rescue" of Pluffles is also the "education of Pluffles" (*PT*, 44). "The Education of Otis Yeere" (1888) begins: "This is the history of a failure: but the woman who failed said that it might be an instructive tale to put into print for the benefit of the younger generation" (*WWW*, 3).

Kipling's eagerness to construe knowledge that emanated from a variety of social locations in professional terms served several middle-class ideological goals. For one thing, it reinforced the late-century notion that middle-class authority depended on its ability to appropriate the knowledge domains of other social groups. Thus, Kipling's narrator presents himself as a kind of expert on experts. Kipling's own ability as a writer to mimic the skills and the slang of lower-class types is a sign of the social prerogatives of the expert, not of his populism.[56] Late-century critics who bridled at the vulgarity of Stalky and other Kipling characters—as well as contemporary critics who read such vulgarity as a sign of Kipling's freedom from bourgeois constraints—miss the ways Kiplingesque vulgarity signified the expertise of cultural appropriation. It is a sign of Stalky's protoprofessional skill that he can mimic both Devonshire and cockney accents or manipulate Afghan superstitions by using a corpse to conceal a secret tunnel. Similarly, it is a sign of the journalist-narrator's professional skill that he can reproduce an Irish brogue, the slang of troopers, or the hybridized speech of a babu.

Kipling also participated in a widespread late-century effort to train working-class and lower-middle-class youths as servants of empire by teaching them how to model themselves on the professional middle class. One of the chief goals of the Boy Scouts, for example, was to train proletarian youths by disciplining them to middle-class intellectual standards, chief of which were perceptual and classificatory skills like those taught to Kim by Lurgan.[57] As a number of historians have suggested, interest in the training of young men to middle-class intellectual standards often arose in the late nineteenth century as a response to worries about working-class degeneration.[58] In this context, it is worth noting that it was not so much

[56] Bristow makes this point, p. 79.

[57] Bristow, pp. 188–95, 205–6, describes the standards that Baden-Powell's *Scouting for Boys* (1908) sought to disseminate. See also Mohanty, pp. 329–31.

[58] See, for example, Richard A. Soloway, *Demography and Degeneration: Eugenics and the Declining Birthrate in Twentieth-Century Britain* (Chapel Hill: University of North Carolina Press, 1990), pp. 38–59.

their vulgarity or their rebelliousness that Kipling admired in his working-class privates (on the contrary, his favored infantrymen are deferential to authority) but their professional competence.

In some cases, Kipling's extension of professional codes of conduct beyond the official professional class also reflected (and compensated for) a general late-century anxiety over middle-class social enfranchisement. Harold Perkin has described the spread of professional pretensions through a number of late-nineteenth-century trades, and the resultant confusion over who might legitimately lay claim to the social authority of professionalism.[59] One particularly poignant instance of this struggle is the gratuitous classical education received by Stalky's gang. Lovingly described in "Regulus" (1917), this classical training both initiated the schoolboys into the common body of knowledge shared by all professional British men in the late nineteenth century and reminded them of their likely exclusion from professional ranks—the danger that their education might simply be "flumdiddle" (187). In this sense, Kipling's fluidity with the exact social location of professionals or aspirant-professionals tapped into one of the masochistic dynamics of magical groups: the bittersweet glory that comes from seeing oneself and one's peers as being both at the center of social power and the victim of its injustice.

Moreover, Kipling's extension of professional forms of knowledge across lines of class, gender, and race dramatized the magical omnipotence he wished to find in those bodies of knowledge. By using their knowledge to cross social boundaries, Kipling's experts often demonstrate the limitlessness of their epistemological power. Strickland, for example, "hates being mystified by natives, because his business in life is to overmatch them with their own weapons" (*LH*, 211–12). Like Kim's, Strickland's knowledge of native cultures is so comprehensive that he can "pass" for someone of a different race (as he does in "Miss Youghal's *Sais*" [1887]) or put himself into the mind of others (as he does in "The Return of Imray" [1891] or "The Mark of the Beast" [1890]). Kipling's affirmation of socially unorthodox kinds of knowledge thus exalted the expert's omnipotent freedom from his own social environment.

Of course, as many readers have noted, Kipling constantly satirized his experts' tendencies to exaggerate their own social and epistemological power—to engage, in other words, in fantasies of omnipotence. "The Man Who Would Be King," for example, plainly satirizes the omnipotent delusions of Carnehan and Dravot. The story turns on Dravot's blindness to the limits of his power, limits that the more professionally minded Carnehan (the man who honors contracts) sees clearly. The story could be said to drive a wedge between delusional amateurs and more cautious and

---

[59] Harold Perkin, *The Rise of Professional Society: England since 1880* (London: Routledge, 1989), pp. vii–viii.

realistic professionals (including the skeptical journalist-narrator) except that the ambivalent fascination the narrator feels for both Carnehan and Dravot reveals that professionals are deeply and dangerously drawn to omnipotent ambitions.

Kipling also understood that knowledge could be inflated or faked in the service of imperial delusions. In "The Education of Otis Yeere," when people notice that Yeere has gained in personal self-confidence, they conclude that he must have resources of expertise they had not previously suspected. On no evidence other than Yeere's newfound self-assurance, they begin to call him the "greatest authority on the aboriginal *Gullals*" and see in him "a vast knowledge of the aboriginal tribes" (*WWW*, 27). Like H. Rider Haggard, Stevenson, and many other late-century authors of colonial fiction, Kipling also knew that Western authorities deliberately cultivated illusions about the magical qualities of their power. He often celebrated characters who make use of the appearance of omnipotent power while remaining free from any real belief in it themselves. John Chinn, in "The Tomb of His Ancestors" (1897), for example, finds the hill people's belief in his supernatural powers amusing but uses it only to make vaccinations against smallpox acceptable to them.

Because Kipling could satirize omnipotent delusions, however, does not mean that he was immune to their allure. He sometimes dramatized this ambiguity directly in his stories. The narrator of "Wressley of the Foreign Office" (1887), for example, emphasizes that Wressley's knowledge was a "delusion" (*PT*, 224). Nevertheless, the narrator cannot fully dismiss his lingering belief in Wressley's uncanny abilities. Reading through his finished work, the narrator calls it "the best book of Indian history ever written" (228). Wressley himself, trapped in an oscillation between continued omnipotent delusion and bouts of melancholic demystification, speaks dismissively of his failure while at the same time marveling "how in the world" he came "to write such damned good stuff as that" (228).[60] Kipling's delight at the superhuman magic of Mowgli, Kim, George Cottar of "The Brushwood Boy" (1895), and many other magical protagonists often indulged a belief in the reality of omnipotence. As he once wrote to his cousin: "A man who has the confidence of the natives can do *anything*" (*Letters*, 1:100). This simultaneous belief and disbelief in the magic of British omnipotence was widely shared. Lord Curzon's private secretary, for example, expressed it in his memoirs:

Our life in India . . . rests on illusion. I had the illusion, wherever I was, that I was infallible and invulnerable in my dealing with Indians. How else could

---

[60] Purnima Bose, *Organizing Empire: Individualism, Collective Agency, and India* (Durham: Duke University Press, 2003), pp. 173–79, discusses the seriousness with which Kipling took Wressley's endeavors.

I have dealt with angry mobs, with cholera-stricken masses, and with proces-
sions of religious fanatics? It was not conceit, Heaven knows: it was not the
prestige of the British Raj, but it was the illusion which is in the very air of
India. . . . They, the millions, made us believe we had a divine mission. We
made them believe they were right.[61]

Kipling's professionals, by virtue of the social fluidity their expertise
implied, also acquired a freedom from archaic bourgeois moral codes of
conduct. Indeed, one of the most important consequences of Kipling's
belief in the power of professional knowledge was his granting of moral
license to colonial experts. Superior knowledge is what enables Kipling's
subalterns and military veterans to justify their unorthodox and sometimes morally dubious tactics. Their god-like defiance of ethical conventions may have disturbed some of Kipling's contemporary readers. But the
moral license of his military men reflected a widespread fact of British
imperial history, which is full of instances of local commanders who exceeded their authority with impunity.[62]

It was not simply the moral license of soldiers, however, that Kipling
celebrated. Many of his experts take morality into their own hands with
his narratives' evident approval. By affirming the moral license of experts
of all kinds, Kipling participated in a widespread late-Victorian ideological
maneuver, through which middle-class professionals asserted their cultural
superiority by means of transgressive, unorthodox, or explicitly antibourgeois forms of moral sophistication.[63] Late-Victorian professionals often
laid claim to the freedom to violate traditional ethical standards on the
basis of their superior knowledge and as a badge of their social sophistication. Many of Kipling's "knowing" characters take pride in their authority
to deviate from standards of truthtelling and candor or to adopt tactics
not condoned by their superiors—simply because, as professionals, they
know best.[64] Reggie Burke, for example, in "A Bank Fraud" (1887), earns
the narrator's sympathy for perpetrating an elaborate personal and commercial deception when he discovers that his tormentor, a conceited young
accountant named Riley, is dying of consumption. Reggie intercepts correspondence from the directors of the bank and keeps the dying man from
knowing he has been fired. Reggie continues to pay Riley's salary out of
his own pocket, and he even forges complimentary letters to Riley from

---

[61] Walter R. Lawrence, *The India We Served* (London: Cassell and Company, 1929), pp. 42–43.

[62] Burroughs, p. 177, claims that "weary acquiescence" was the most common response
of the authorities in London, who usually felt "a reluctance to reject the advice or counter-
mand the actions of forceful men on the spot."

[63] I have written about this phenomenon extensively in *The Power of Lies: Transgression in
Victorian Fiction* (Ithaca: Cornell University Press, 1994).

[64] Without associating it with professionalism, many readers have commented on the prevalence of lying in Kipling. See Ambreen Hai, "On Truth and Lie in a Colonial Sense: Kipling's Tales of Tale-Telling," *ELH* 64 (1997), 599–625.

the directors. In such cases, the professional's privileged relationship to knowledge authorizes a self-martyring moral despotism, like that exercised by the Head in the Stalky stories.

To further ground moral license in professional authority, Kipling explicitly contrasted the effective lying of professionals with the clumsy lies of less competent characters. The evangelical missionaries who adopt a native girl in "Lispeth" (1886), but who encourage the young Englishman with whom she is infatuated to lie to her about his plans to return, miscalculate tragically. "You have killed Lispeth . . . . You are all liars, you English" (*PT*, 11), she tells them, before returning to her own people and renouncing Christianity. The shabby lies of adulterous middle-class men and women in Kipling's early stories are also disastrous, as when the multiple lies of "A Wayside Comedy" (1888) turn a lonely hill station into a social hell, or when the narrator of "Bitters Neat" (1887) remarks that the "lies" of inept lovers "result [in] a heart-rending muddle that half-a-dozen open words would put straight" (*PT*, 243).

Kipling associated the various features of professionalism I have outlined—its appropriation of the knowledge domains of other classes and races; its troubled relationship to status anxiety; its potential to fuel omnipotent fantasy, even in the teeth of disconfirmation; and its usurpation of unorthodox moral authority—with the magical groups that his stories represent as the only effective ruling class of British India. Readers have long been aware of Kipling's fascination with the superhuman powers of his favored characters, but that fascination has often been tied to imperialist and racialist ideology, not to the class discourse of professionalism. A long tradition of colonial studies—often rooted in the power/knowledge theories of Michel Foucault and including the work of Said, Cohn, and many others—has studied the imperial quest for knowledge in terms of national and racial power.[65] What has not received its share of attention is the class dynamic this quest for knowledge often underwrote.

A crucial component of Kipling's class discourse was the sadomasochistic interpersonal structures that organize magical groups. While Kipling's general admiration for professionals has, of course, been widely recognized, the affinities between professionalism and sadomasochism in his work have not.[66] As a result, critics have overlooked the reversible power relations generated by sadomasochistic forms of knowledge (including the

[65] The most influential theoretical work is Michel Foucault, *Discipline and Punish: The Birth of the Prison*, trans. Alan Sheridan (New York: Pantheon, 1977). Said's many relevant works include *Orientalism* (New York: Pantheon, 1978), and *Culture and Imperialism* (New York: Knopf, 1993). See also Bernard S. Cohn, *India: The Social Anthropology of a Civilization* (Englewood Cliffs, NJ: Prentice-Hall, 1971).

[66] Wurgaft, for example, has written usefully on British colonial omnipotence, but he explains it only as a consequence of British convictions of superior self-control. See pp. 64–65, 144–46.

role of the "knowing" bystander in professional networks, a role often played by Kipling's narrator).

Sometimes, Kipling made expert knowledge the vehicle for sadistic revenge, creating unexpected sources of group intimacy rather than solitary triumph. In "Pig" (1887), for example, a government official named Nafferton takes revenge against another official, Pinecoffin, who had sold him a bad horse, by sending Pinecoffin on a bureaucratic wild-goose chase. Nafferton exploits Pinecoffin's enthusiasm for knowledge by maneuvering him into an exhausting campaign to supply the government with information on a scheme to feed the Army with pork. Once Pinecoffin has fallen into the trap, Nafferton badgers him with endless requests for information. At first compliant, then dazed by all the work, Pinecoffin finally protests—which enables Nafferton to represent him to the government as a shirker and to the newspapers as a gaseous pedant, wasting government resources on frivolous schemes. Pinecoffin is shocked when he discovers how Nafferton has abused him, but this bureaucratic sadism actually repairs an emotional rift between the two characters: "Pinecoffin found nothing to say save bad words; and Nafferton smiled ever so sweetly, and asked him to dinner" (*PT*, 168).

Occasionally, Kipling associated this kind of sadism with the expertise required to run the empire, especially when it seemed to create intimate alliances within professional imperial groups. When Private Otheris, an expert marksman, shoots a deserter turned sniper in "On Greenhow Hill" (1890), for example, he is portrayed as viciously, coldly triumphant: he gazes at the corpse "with the smile of the artist who looks on the completed work" (*LH*, 83). But this professional "artistry" forges an intimate sadomasochistic bond between Otheris and the three men (including the narrator) who play the part of voyeuristic bystanders, passively watching his murderous skill. One of these bystanders, Private Learoyd, actually identifies with the slain sniper. Having just recounted a tale of his own suffering over a woman he had loved, Learoyd reflects mournfully: "Happen there was a lass tewed up wi' him, too" (*LH*, 83).

Sometimes, Kipling's experts use their knowledge to exclude the objects of their abuse from magical groups, as when the subalterns in "A Conference of the Powers" lord it over an ignorant civil servant. At other times, though, intimate bullying through superior knowledge is a sign of the sadomasochistic affection that binds magical groups together, as when Private Mulvaney occasionally rebukes the narrator: "An' you thinkin' you know things!" (*PT*, 151). The narrator himself often teases readers in this fashion, taunting them with his superior knowledge. Breaking off a digression, he tells us: "That is quite enough for you to know" (*PT*, 78); anticipating the reader's skepticism, he scoffs that "a little bit of sober fact is more than you can stand" (*PT*, 126). These instances of bullying, in which differentials in knowledge facilitate affectionate teasing, activate the sadomasochistic dynamics of omnipotence and dependence that bind magical groups.

Conversely, professional knowledge offered Kipling's characters opportunities to indulge masochistic self-glorification. Reggie Burke, for example, responds to his knowledge of Riley's fatal disease not simply by faking his good standing with the bank and paying his salary, but also by playing the role of penitent, absorbing Riley's persistent criticism and vowing to reform himself to the dying man's absurd standards. Sometimes, Kipling represented knowledge as the basis for fantasies of emotional transcendence, fantasies that underlie the self-pitying masculine toughness readers have often criticized in his work. Kipling also emphasized the tremendous suffering and deprivation that must be endured to gain knowledge. Wressley, for example, subjects himself to isolation, the deferral of his romantic desires, and the disruption of his promising career in order to gain his "special and laboriously acquired knowledge" (*PT*, 226–27). At times, Kipling saw suffering as itself the stimulus to knowledge: as he explained in *Something of Myself* (1937), his own childhood beatings enabled him to cultivate techniques of "knowingness" that later served him well as a professional writer: "constant wariness, the habit of observation, and attendance on moods and tempers; the noting of discrepancies between speech and action; a certain reserve of demeanour; and automatic suspicion of sudden favors."[67] Kipling also frequently suggested that the most profound knowledge of all is precisely the knowledge *of* cruelty and suffering. Many of his characters are gripped by melancholic convictions about the inevitability of suffering, which is the principal yield of their hard-won knowledge. In "Baa Baa, Black Sheep" (1888), when Punch is restored to his mother's love, the narrator stresses the permanence of his knowledge of pain: "When young lips have drunk deep of the bitter waters of Hate, Suspicion, and Despair, all the Love in the world will not wholly take away that knowledge" (*WWW*, 310).

To some extent, this correlation of knowledge with suffering came out of Kipling's identification of life itself with cruelty—one of the lessons taught by the Head in *Stalky & Co*. Kipling's stories often document the seeming unfairness of their characters' suffering and helplessness at the hands of the impersonal forces of everyday life. His insistent portrayal of the cruelty of life includes a large number of characters obsessed with suicide: Love-o'-Women in the story of the same name, Hummil in "At the End of the Passage" (1890), the subaltern of "Thrown Away" (1888), and Dick Heldar of *The Light that Failed* (1890). Sometimes, naturalized cruelty is associated with conditions in India, a place where "men die with great swiftness, and those who live suffer many and curious things" (*LH*,

---

[67] *Something of Myself*, p. 11.

2). But specifically Indian cruelty is also embedded in Kipling's broader preoccupation with what he represented as life's fundamental unfairness.

Kipling also repeatedly insisted that those who possess specialized knowledge are distinguished by their heroic sufferance of the neglect, mis-understanding, and abuse of others. So it is that Strickland, perhaps the most knowledgeable policeman in all India, finds that his knowledge "has done him no good in the eyes of the Indian Government" (*PT*, 24). Some-times, this neglect is benign: in "Only a Subaltern" (1888), Mr. Wick, a successful administrator in India, retires to an English village where "no-body knew anything about this" (*WWW*, 101). Scott, in "William the Conqueror" (1895), is untroubled by the irony, "not rare in India, of knowing that another man was reaping where he had sown" (*DW*, 216). Sometimes, though, neglect is deeply embittering, and experts must tran-scend the emotional pain that is also the badge of their merit. Tallantire, in "The Head of the District," assumes all the responsibility for running his district but none of the credit, which goes to the Bengali installed over him by a Liberal government. "I know what I've got to do," Tallantire says, "and I'm going to do it. But it's hard" (*LH*, 111). Most often, though, Kipling's experts suffer injustice dispassionately, their acceptance signaling a masochistic triumph of emotional omnipotence much like Stalky's. Mulvaney, in "Love-o'-Women" (1893), puts the case: "Betune you an' me an' Bobbs I was commandin' the Company, an' that was what Crook had thransferred me for; an' the little orf'cer bhoy knew ut, and I knew ut, but the Comp'ny did not. And *there*, mark you, is the vartue that no money an' no dhrill can buy—the vartue av the ould soldier that knows his orf'cer's work an' does ut for him at the salute!" (*MI*, 273–74).

Most importantly, the martyrdom of the expert is always witnessed in Kipling's work by onlooking, sympathetic professional colleagues. Tal-lantire's acceptance of his martyrdom wins him the respect and love of his fellow-official Bullows, the policeman Curbur, and the garrison com-mander Tommy Dodd. In "At the End of the Passage," knowledge of loneliness and terror binds together the four professionals Mottram, Lowndes, Spurstow, and Hummil.[68] In "The Bridge-Builders" (1893), Findlayson and Hitchcock "trusted each other" (*DW*, 4) and desire to "go up the service together" because of the bond formed by their shared suffering: "They had been tried many times in sudden crises." Scott, in "William the Conqueror," realizes that "there were men in the North who would know what he had done" (*DW*, 218–19). Although critics have often seen Kipling's colonial administrators as lonely, marginalized figures,

---

[68] Daniel Bivona, *British Imperial Literature, 1870–1940: Writing and the Administration of Empire* (Cambridge: Cambridge University Press, 1998), pp. 73–80, notes Kipling's awareness of the costs implicit in this story's self-sacrificial professional ethos.

their melancholy is always witnessed by a fraternity of professional bystanders who identify fully with the victimization of experts and with the glorification such victimage confers.[69]

As a professional witness, Kipling's journalist-narrator also performs a crucial role in the construction of magical groups. The narrator's privileged knowledge of characters and events allows him to be either a voyeuristic or a sympathetic bystander to brutality and vindictiveness, thus modeling contradictory identifications with both bully and victim for the reader. Fittingly, Kipling's bystanding narrator is often conscripted to enter the action on the side of either bully or victim. In "False Dawn" (1888), for example, the narrator is drawn into the action as a kind of "good" bully. Knowing that Saumarez has proposed to the wrong sister in a blinding dust storm, the narrator chases the disappointed, fleeing sister on horseback, which puts him in the position of a bullying "rescuer": "Why can't you let me alone?" (*PT*, 41), the poor girl laments as the narrator rides her down over rough country, leaving her "bare headed, plastered with dust, and crying bitterly." But the narrator's fierce pursuit is intended kindly: "The guidance of this misguided world seemed to lie in my hands." When the narrator returns successfully with the "right" girl, he is greeted with applause from the audience of bystanders that had earlier engaged in gossipy voyeurism over Saumarez's unintentional tormenting of the two sisters. In other stories, the narrator's potential for cruelty sometimes takes the form of stinging commentary, which an early reviewer referred to as Kipling's "gay malice."[70] In the original version of "The Bisara of Pooree" (1887), the story's troublemaker is sent off to Madras "where there is a fine hope of his drinking himself to death. He is no good alive any way."[71] The narrator of "Wressley of the Foreign Office" remarks that Wressley "was immensely struck with Miss Venner's intelligence. He would have been more impressed had he heard her private and confidential accounts of his calls" (*PT*, 226). This cruel commentary is more than simply a sign of detachment, for the narrator is often amused by the cruelty of life he records.

But the journalist-narrator is also sometimes pulled into the action on behalf of victimized characters. In "The Other Man" (1886), the narrator protects the victimized Mrs. Schreiderling ("The first thing was to take Mrs. Schreiderling home, and the second was to prevent her name from

---

[69] For comments on the supposed isolation of Kipling's administrators, see Wurgaft, p. 78; or McClure, p. 31. Sullivan, p. 88, typifies readings of "Thrown Away" in her focus on the loneliness of the suicidal subaltern.

[70] William Hunter, from a signed review in the *Academy* 852 (1 September 1888), p. 129; reprinted in Green, p. 40.

[71] These lines were deleted from later editions. See Rudyard Kipling, *Plain Tales from the Hills* (London: Penguin, 1987), p. 291.

being mixed up with the affair" [*PT*, 73]). Sometimes, however, the narrator becomes so identified with the victim that he becomes paralyzed, as at the conclusion of "In the House of Suddhoo" (1886), when he cannot speak out about the seal cutter's crime without provoking the seal cutter to murder Janoo, even though his silence guarantees that Janoo will murder the seal cutter. Knowledge thus implicates Kipling's journalist-narrator in either bullying or victimage, or else in a kind of passive spectatorship that can incorporate both.

The story "Thrown Away" displays concisely many of these relationships between professionalism, sadomasochism, bully/victim/bystander triangles, narratorial and readerly voyeurism, and magical groups. The story begins as a parable about the tragic consequences of ignorance. A young subaltern, whose parents sheltered him from worldly knowledge, fails to manage worldly pleasures—alcohol, gambling, women—and is ruined. Taking his failures far too seriously (again, because he lacks knowledge of the world), the subaltern asks leave to go on a hunting trip, retires to a deserted Canal Engineer's Rest House, and shoots himself. After the subaltern has left for the Rest House, one of the majors in the regiment guesses his intentions, thus demonstrating the major's own worldly knowledge. The major does some expert detective work and finds that the subaltern had taken only a revolver and writing case on his trip. The major then enlists the aid of the narrator-journalist, whose own knowingness establishes an instantaneous bond between the two men ("I saw what was in his mind" [*PT*, 19]; "I saw exactly what that help would be" [20]). Besides the bond of worldly knowledge, the military man and the journalist also share the professional's moral license to finesse the truth. "Can you lie?" the major asks the narrator, who responds: "It's my profession" (19). After rushing to the Rest House but arriving—as they had feared—too late, the two men conspire to bury the subaltern and conceal all evidence of his suicide, including his suicide notes. They spare his parents pain by writing a letter full of lies about their son's successful career and noble death and report to their superiors that the subaltern died of cholera.

In their conspiracy, the major and the narrator enact a reversible sadomasochistic relationship. The major, a "masterful man" (19), draws the narrator out of his detached, voyeuristic observation of the subaltern's decline to enlist him in a plot that both men feel to be cruel as well as rescuing and redemptive. The narrator comes to know "exactly how a murderer feels" (22), and, in fact, both men are said to feel "like murderers" (23). The narrator's sense of cruelty is particularly acute when he imagines the recipients of his deceitful letter: "I choked while I was putting down these things and thinking of the poor people who would read them" (21). The sadism latent in the writing of this letter bubbles up in the next sentence: "Then I laughed at the grotesqueness of the affair, and the laughter mixed itself up with the choke" (21–22). As they bury the subaltern, the major and the narrator share a bizarre "laughing-fit" (22), and even if the laughter can be attributed to the tension of the situation, it mixes uncomfortably with the sarcasm the narrator had indulged toward the subaltern early in the story. The narrator satirizes the subaltern's vulnerability to events that "hurt his feelings" (18), compares him repeatedly to a puppy, and condescends to what he calls "The Boy's follies" (21). The two men's coverup also thwarts the final wishes of the subaltern, adding another twist to his victimization by frustrating his last attempts to revenge himself on people and circumstances he believed had victimized him. The narrator's tendency toward heartless mockery—he refers to the subaltern condescendingly throughout the story as "The Boy"—is complemented, however, by both his and the major's identification with the subaltern's pain. Toward the end of the story, the major tells "awful stories of suicide or nearly-carried-out suicide . . . . He said that he himself had once gone into the same Valley of the Shadow as The Boy . . . so he understood how things fought together in The Boy's poor jumbled head" (23). This masochistic identification is completed when the two men send a lock of the major's hair back to the subaltern's parents, presenting it as their son's (the subaltern's own hair being too bloodied for this purpose).

Finally, the major and the narrator share the ambivalence toward social authority characteristic of magical groups. The two men clearly act in defense of national codes of honor ("Nice sort of thing to spring on an English family!" [21], the Major says, after reading the subaltern's suicide notes). But they also violate conventional procedures, bringing official dishonor on themselves, which they accept stoically: "Many people . . . found time to say that the Major had behaved scandalously in not bringing in the body for a regimental funeral" (23). The narrator also displays a trace of self-pity at the lack of recognition of their heroism. When the subaltern's mother writes to them about "the obligation she would be under to us as long as she lived," the narrator observes: "she was under an obligation, but not exactly as she meant" (23). The major and the narrator thus constitute a misunderstood community of two, which is triangulated through their sadomasochistic relationship to the subaltern, especially through the sense of unrewarded virtue and injury shared by all three men. Having been let in on the secret of the coverup, the bystanding reader is also implicitly engaged as a member of this knowing but misunderstood, magical group—the narrator's movement across the threshold between observation and involvement modeling our own ambiguous affective positioning.

Through sadomasochistic bonding of this kind, facilitated by professional styles of knowledge, Kipling harnessed an emergent, late-century, upper-middle-class ideological system to the psychological dynamics of magical groups. Specialized knowledge would not have galvanized his magical groups nearly so effectively if it did not collaborate in the sadomasochistic tendencies of such groups to forge strong internal bonds through the intimacies of bully, victim, and bystander relationships. Kipling glamorized such knowledge sadomasochistically by representing it as the badge of honor uniting small groups of men, who are set over against a British colonial government that seems both congruent with their own omnipotent power and the persecutor of those whose glorious expertise never receives the recognition or rewards it deserves.

EVANGELICALISM AND MIDDLE-CLASS UNILATERALISM

Kipling's association of professional knowledge with magical groups harnessed an emergent late-century middle-class ideological system to the intersubjective dynamics of sadomasochism. Kipling also made use of a historically discordant, atavistic middle-class discourse, one that previous chapters have already shown to possess an affinity with sadomasochism: evangelicalism. Of course, Kipling had contempt for religious zealots, and he portrayed evangelicalism as a hellish source of childhood torment in the semiautobiographical "Baa Baa, Black Sheep." This story dramatizes evangelicalism's dangerously sadomasochistic potentials: its image of God as a punitive and enraged omnipotent figure, its convictions about innate human sinfulness, and its belief in the salutary nature of corporal punishment. But despite his dislike of organized religion, and despite his own ambivalent agnosticism (he once called himself "a godfearing Christian Atheist"), Kipling was deeply drawn to these sadomasochistic potentials, which underlay his endorsement of the spiritualized tone that pervaded the nineteenth-century Raj.[72]

Although evangelicalism influenced Kipling in various ways—prompting his frequent allusions to the Bible and the hymnal, for example—its specifically sadomasochistic elements are most evident in his idealization of imperial suffering and self-sacrifice. In a famous letter to his cousin Margaret in 1885, Kipling claimed that "if ever a foreign country was made better through 'the blood of the martyrs' India is that country" (*Letters*, 1:98). In his poetry and fiction, Kipling celebrated a variety of self-sacrificing imperial martyrs, such as Mrs. McKenna in "The Daughter of the Regiment" (1887) and Bobby Wick of "Only a Subaltern," who

---

[72] Quoted in David Gilmour, *The Long Recessional: The Imperial Life of Rudyard Kipling* (New York: Farrar, Straus and Giroux, 2002), p. 5. See also Kipling's 1889 declaration of his religious beliefs to Caroline Taylor, *Letters*, 1:378–79.

sacrifice their lives tending the victims of cholera epidemics. In journalistic essays, he honored a variety of administrative, military, and technocratic imperial martyrs.[73] He also idealized the work-oriented asceticism that inspires a character like Hummil to stay at his post even though his nerves are shot in order to spare another, weaker man with a sick wife: "I thought all that sort of thing was dead and done with" (*LH*, 178), Dr. Spurstow tells him; Hummil responds: "Bosh! You'd do the same yourself." In "William the Conqueror," the eponymous William Martyn willingly submits to pain, suffering, and sexual renunciation in the relief of famine victims: "Life with men who had a great deal of work to do, and very little time to do it in, had taught her the wisdom of effacing as well as of fending for herself" (*DW*, 194). The actual mismanagement of colonial conditions by British officials was lost on a domestic audience that thrilled to the mythology of spiritualized martyrdom such images of self-sacrifice promoted.[74]

Occasionally, Kipling announced the relationship between evangelicalism and these images of imperial self-sacrifice explicitly. In "On Greenhow Hill," Learoyd recounts the story of his conversion by Yorkshire Methodists. Although the conversion is at first inspired by his infatuation with 'Liza Roantree, the daughter of a Methodist miner, Learoyd claims that love led him to real spiritual regeneration: "I meaned it . . . I become what they called a changed character" (*LH*, 72). He is eventually drummed out of the sect for his violent and self-destructive response to his discovery that 'Liza is terminally ill, but his enlistment in the Army is represented as an act of expiation that ritualizes his pain, making enlistment a continuation rather than a contradiction of his religious conversion.[75] Learoyd's intense emotional bond with an evangelical preacher, Amos Barraclough, who had been his rival for 'Liza's love, further reinforces this parallel between evangelical and military forms of self-martyrdom. The two men identify deeply with one another through their self-punishing responses to the pain of losing 'Liza, however different the form these responses

---

[73] In "A Free Gift," *The Pioneer* (Allahabad), 19 March 1888, p. 3, for example, Kipling portrayed a representative English bureaucrat, who responds to the slanders of a Bengali newspaper editor by saying: "Keep on slanging me. I'm paid for it, you know, and I can't hit back. Look here, we'll make a bargain. You can call me a thief, a bureaucrat, a ravisher, an unsympathetic alien, and anything else that you like, every day except Sundays, and I won't say a word if . . . you'll only help me to clean up a few sewers now and again."

[74] Mike Davis, *Late Victorian Holocausts: El Niño Famines and the Making of the Third World* (London: Verso, 2001), pp. 156–57, discusses Kipling's mythologizing in the context of western responsibility for late-century subtropical famines.

[75] Most readers of "On Greenhow Hill" assume that Kipling disavowed the evangelical notions about suffering and expiation Learoyd adopts. See, for example, William B. Dillingham, "Sorrow and the Redemptive Role of Fate: Kipling's 'On Greenhow Hill,' " *Papers on Language and Literature* 39 (2003), 3–21.

take; as he resolves to enlist, Learoyd says: "I were cut as deep for him as I were for mysen" (81).

Kipling also routinely idealized evangelical forms of expiation. One of the most striking instances occurs in *Kim*: the lama's quest to be washed in the waters that will cleanse him of sin and thereby free him of human desire is more expressive of evangelical values than Buddhist beliefs. Following in the footsteps of Sir James Fraser and Max Muller, Kipling greatly exaggerated Indian mysticism, particularly its supposed belief in the illusionary nature of the material world.[76] Exploiting this misunderstanding, he used the lama to express an anti-materialistic spiritualism with distinctly evangelical overtones of repentance. "The sin is mine and the punishment is mine" (92), the lama declares when he recognizes he must relinquish Kim's services. Kipling's choice of a Tibetan Buddhist rather than a Hindu to represent Indian spirituality also reflected British abhorrence for the "Romish" excesses of Hindu abstinence and corporal punishment, as opposed to modes of self-denying piety that could be squared with evangelical beliefs and attitudes. The apparent complementarity of Kim's expert spying and the lama's quest to free himself from sin and desire—a combination that emblematizes Kipling's fusion of professional and evangelical values—absorbs both characters in an elaborate pilgrimage of expiation at the end of the novel.

Kipling also imported evangelical narrative patterns through his plots' dependence on conversion, which he often mixed with sadomasochistic gestures of penitence and humility. In "Miss Youghal's *Sais*," a lecherous general, when confronted by Strickland, admits he "deserved a thrashing" (*PT*, 28) and atones for his misbehavior by interceding with the girl's father to enable her to marry the man she loves. In "The Rescue of Pluffles" (1886), Mrs. Hauksbee draws on her better nature and converts Pluffles to fidelity: after she brutalizes him verbally, he feels "limp and repentant—as if he had been in some superior kind of church" (*PT*, 46). In "The Bronckhorst Divorce-Case" (1888), Bronckhorst is chastened by a beating into behaving responsibly toward his wife.

In sum, the sadomasochism inherent in Kipling's evangelical borrowings helped reinforce magical groups in familiar ways: by legitimating relationships of authority and submission, by extending sadomasochistic social bonds through the shared witnessing of suffering, and by incorporating the omnipotent qualities of masochistic suffering into a collective sense of legitimacy and power. But Kipling's evangelical impulses also had important atavistic qualities, which were implicated in both imperial and

---

[76] On Fraser's and Muller's distortions, see Joanne Punzo Waghorne, *The Raja's Magic Clothes: Re-Visioning Kingship and Divinity in England's India* (University Park: Pennsylvania State University Press, 1994), p. 255. To my knowledge, no one has described Kipling's lama in evangelical terms.

class ideologies. Their imperial implications are, perhaps, better known. Evangelicalism exercised an enormous, widely recognized influence on British policy in India during much of the first half of the nineteenth century.[77] Charles Grant and John Shore, for example—the former a director of the East India Company, the latter advisor to Cornwallis—became founding members of the Clapham Sect after returning to England, and they made the evangelical reform of India one of the chief goals of the Clapham movement. After the 1813 Charter Act opened up India to missionaries, evangelicals helped liberalize Indian education, government policy, and the Indian Civil Service. Organized evangelical activity may have waned after midcentury, both in India and in England. But evangelical attitudes continued to sustain Anglo-Indian culture, especially in the wake of the Mutiny, by portraying the defense of colonialism as a spiritual crusade. Military leaders who suppressed the Mutiny were dubbed with titles that made them, as John MacKenzie puts it, "evangelical knights, defenders of the faith as well as the Empire."[78] Sir James Outram was known as the "Bayard of India," and Herbert Edwardes was referred to as a "military bishop" by John Ruskin.[79] Eric Stokes has gone so far as to claim that "the key" to British rule during the latter half of the nineteenth century was its "transposition of evangelicalism to wholly secular objects, or alternatively the translation of secular objectives to a religious level."[80] He adds that this idea took its "final shape in the teaching of Kipling."

Kipling's particular evocation of evangelical values coincided with what some have called the "Punjab spirit": a mixture of messianic frontiersmanship that was both moralistic and despotic.[81] This frontier spirit was already largely nostalgic in the 1880s, since the era of conquest in the Punjab had been completed by the 1850s. Kipling explicitly affirmed the "Punjab spirit" through William, Scott, Tallantire, and other characters from the northwestern frontier, whose heroism contrasts starkly with the passivity of the non-Punjab characters with whom they have to work. Kipling's affirmation of the "Punjab spirit" attempted to reinvigorate what he saw as a debilitated colonial system by reviving its earlier messianic qualities. Through this and other celebrations of evangelical values, Kipling could be said to have participated in a general British effort to shore

[77] Eric Stokes, *The English Utilitarians and India* (Oxford: Clarendon Press, 1959), documents the various ways evangelicalism provided the Raj with "its programme of social reform, its force of character, and its missionary zeal" (xiv).

[78] John M. MacKenzie, "Empire and Metropolitan Cultures," *The Oxford History of the British Empire*, Vol. 3: *The Nineteenth Century*, pp. 281–82.

[79] John M. MacKenzie, "Heroic Myths of Empire," *Popular Imperialism and the Military, 1850–1950*, ed. John M. MacKenzie (Manchester: Manchester University Press, 1992), pp. 109–38.

[80] Stokes, p. 308.

[81] See Wurgaft, pp. 35–37.

up and revitalize the late-nineteenth-century Raj by infusing the imperial project with the emotional and spiritual resonance of its evangelical past.

Kipling's evangelical borrowings had another kind of atavistic resonance that intersected domestic British class relations for quite different purposes. By combining emergent professional ideals with evangelical values—both drawing their psychological and emotional urgency from the logic of sadomasochism—Kipling linked the ideological languages of two fractured elements of middle-class culture in domestic society. In the last decades of the nineteenth century, as I suggested in chapter 2, the class in Britain most drawn to evangelical values was the lower middle class. This class had grown substantially due to the widening of elementary education, the bureaucratization of commerce, and the internationalization of the financial industry (which required an army of clerks). Yet membership in the lower middle class was increasingly insecure after 1870 as a result of increasing unionization of the working class and competition from women and educated immigrants. The lower-middle-class clerk was also embattled culturally in the face of working-class disdain for his effeminacy and bourgeois contempt for his vulgarity. In these circumstances, lower-middle-class Britons propped up both their embattled dignity and their economic vulnerability by resurrecting archaic middle-class discourses of social respectability, especially moral ones (at a time, ironically, when the gentrified ranks immediately above them were increasingly scorning those values).[82] Charles Booth, writing in 1902, described the lower middle class as forming "the bulk of most religious assemblies," and added that "many of the Nonconformist churches are entirely filled" from lower-middle-class ranks.[83] The widespread jingoism among the lower middle class at this time has been understood as, in part, a way of clinging to traditional moral codes of service and self-sacrifice that had historically been identified with middle-class respectability.[84]

It was to the lower middle class and not to the working-class crowd that Kipling's evangelicalism addressed itself. As Orwell put it:

> Can one imagine any private soldier, in the 'nineties or now, reading *Barrack-Room Ballads* and feeling that here was a writer who spoke for him? It is very hard to do so. . . . "What have I done for thee, England, my England?" is

[82] Hugh McLeod, "White Collar Values and the Role of Religion," *The Lower Middle Class in Britain, 1870–1914*, ed. Geoffrey Crossick (London: Croom Helm, 1977), pp. 61–88. See also Hugh McLeod, *Class and Religion in the Late Victorian City* (London: Croom Helm, 1974), p. 144.

[83] Quoted in David Martin, *A Sociology of English Religion* (New York: Basic Books, 1967), p. 32.

[84] Richard N. Price, "Society, Status and Jingoism: The Social Roots of Lower Middle Class Patriotism, 1870–1900," *The Lower Middle Class in Britain, 1870–1914*, pp. 89–112.

essentially a middle-class query. Almost any working man would follow it up immediately with "What has England done for me?"[85]

Although the significance of the British spiritualization of self-sacrifice has long been recognized in colonial society, the sociological underpinnings of the evangelical attitude are less commonly acknowledged. Whatever its other functions, Kipling's fusion of professional and evangelical values blended upper- and lower-middle-class ideological systems. This imaginative fusion was absolutely central to the broadened middle-class appeal of his work that some have misconstrued as "classlessness."

Kipling's imaginative projection of synthesized middle-class values, it should be noted, constituted a rewriting of his colonial—as well as his metropolitan—ideological inheritance. By fusing professional and evangelical ideals, Kipling replayed, in a sense, the union of utilitarian and evangelical reform movements in 1820s and '30s India. Kipling repeated an emphasis on rational individualism, the value of knowledge and education, the inherent depravity of animal nature, and the prospect of self-transformation through devotion to duty that had characterized both of these earlier movements.[86] Yet there are some striking differences. For one thing, Kipling's affirmation of professional expertise expressed a narrower middle-class ideal than the faith in rationality and abstract principles of social good that was central to utilitarianism. More importantly, perhaps, Kipling's fusion of professional authority with evangelical spirit had none of the utopian optimism of these earlier movements.[87] Kipling did not believe his magical groups would radically transform political structures, as utilitarians and evangelicals had hoped; it is not clear he believed they could even make existing institutions more efficient, which was the moderate goal of most late-century Anglo-Indian reforms. Rather, his magical groups were entrenched in a sadomasochistic defensiveness that deepened the insularity of their aggrieved claims to imperial authority. Kipling also had no interest in native assimilation, which was a hallmark of both evangelical and utilitarian reform earlier in the century; likewise, he distanced himself from the socially leveling tendencies that had been central to these movements. The middle-class ideological fusion for which he stood depended on the permanence of social hierarchy rather than its elimination,

---

[85] Orwell, p. 149.

[86] Viswanathan, p. 77, explores the tensions between evangelical and utilitarian views of education; and Stokes, pp. 55–56, stresses the conflict between utilitarian faith in government and evangelical belief in divine law. Nevertheless, Stokes, pp. 54–55, elaborates on the basic similarities I have described.

[87] For an account of Kipling's resistance to reform movements in India, see Andrew Hagiioannu, *The Man Who Would Be Kipling: The Colonial Fiction and the Frontiers of Exile* (New York: Palgrave, 2003), pp. 6–18.

and on the promotion of a particular social class he saw as cruelly disen-
franchised—but also, for that very reason, as magically powerful.

Kipling's fusion of professional expertise with evangelicalism sought to
bind together two ideological sources of middle-class identity that had
taken opposite social trajectories in the late-nineteenth century. It did so,
in part, by fiercely opposing itself to upper or lower-class social identities,
as I will argue in the next section. In that sense, it served to perpetuate a
view of intractable social hierarchy—and to privilege a broadened conception of middle-class authority—by grounding both in a vision of the fundamentally sadomasochistic character of social relations. Defenses of Kipling's "classlessness," like those with which I began this chapter, obscure
the virulent class politics underlying his consolidation of middle-class
ideological systems. They also obscure the ways in which reversible attitudes toward social hierarchy—in particular, the adulation of British imperial authority and the self-righteous contempt for it that Kipling mixed
together so well—could collaborate within a sadomasochistic social subject whose primary allegiances were not necessarily to the empire but to
class-coded modes of solidarity and domination.

Class Hostility, Classlessness, and the Magical Middle Class

If one attends to the psychosocial fantasy structures anchoring Kipling's
work rather than to the shifting field of public figures and political causes
he championed, his promotion of a generalized middle class and its interests is unmistakable. An astute observer like Orwell was quite certain
about Kipling's ideological base:

> Kipling's "message" was one that the big public did not want, and, indeed,
> has never accepted. The mass of the people, in the 'nineties as now, were anti-
> militarist, bored by the Empire, and only unconsciously patriotic. Kipling's
> official admirers are and were the "service" middle class, the people who read
> *Blackwood's.* . . . As a rule it is the British working class that he is attacking,
> but not always. That phrase about "the flannelled fools at the wicket and the
> muddied oafs at the goal" sticks like an arrow to this day, and it is aimed at
> the Eton and Harrow match as well as the Cup-Tie Final.[88]

Some of Orwell's generalizations may be overly simplified, and he may
have been too eager to disavow Kipling's appeal to the ranks immediately
above the "service" middle class (which include the professional classes of
which Orwell himself was a member). But there is good reason to believe

[88] Orwell, p. 147.

that Orwell was correct about Kipling's social exclusions. Recent historians have confirmed that working-class readers bypassed Kipling. Jonathan Rose includes Kipling among a number of writers who were installed by the late-Victorian middle classes in school curricula but who went unread by working-class readers making their selections from lending libraries when, as Rose puts it, they were "uncontaminated by middle-class cultural hegemony."[89] Robert Buchanan may have tried to tar Kipling by associating him with working-class "hooligans," but Kipling's more rabid admirers were likely to be those from higher social stations, who could afford to sentimentalize working-class life. Conversely, although Kipling may have allied himself with upper-class conservative politicians on various issues, as Trilling once put it: "His toryism often had in it a lower-middle-class snarl of defeated gentility."[90] The persistent accusations of vulgarity leveled against Kipling also suggest that there were limits to his acceptability by upper-class readers.

Kipling's work was driven by an unusually intense animosity toward both the social top and bottom. On the one hand, he routinely denigrated top-tier Anglo-Indian administrators for their self-serving ambitions and their obtuseness (as in "The Enlightenments of Pagett, M.P." [1890]). Oxbridge graduates, in particular, are not treated kindly: McIntosh Jellaludin, "an Oxford Man," is "a prig" (*PT*, 239); and *Stalky & Co.*, as we have seen, savagely repudiates the values of upper-class public school education. Kipling's distaste for the Oxbridge elite was no doubt aggravated by the general condescension with which he appears to have been received by the officer class of the British Army, one of whom reported that he was "looked upon with great disfavour by Staff officers as being bumptious and above his station."[91]

On the other hand, though, Kipling's sentimental portraits of infantrymen were often felt by soldiers themselves to be patronizing, especially because of their refusal to grant that working-class men might be educated.[92] In "The Islanders" (1902), the source of the infamous "flanneled fools" line, Kipling abused the social top and bottom equally for what he saw as their collective responsibility for the South African War debacle.

---

[89] Jonathan Rose, *The Intellectual Life of the British Working Classes* (New Haven: Yale University Press, 2001), pp. 244–45.

[90] Trilling, p. 95. Orwell, p. 160, observes that Kipling "sold out" to the governing class, but was never fully accepted by them.

[91] Harold Orel, ed., *Kipling: Interviews and Recollections*, 2 vols. (London: Macmillan, 1983), 1:110.

[92] Orwell, p. 148, observes that Kipling's private soldier, while "loveable and romantic, has to be a comic," and that Kipling's real affections lay with the officer class. Gilmour, p. 49, records the widespread resentment among working-class infantrymen of Kipling's portrayal of them.

After sarcastically ridiculing "the People" for their arrogance ("No doubt but ye are the People—your throne is above the King's"), he taunted them:

> Will ye rise and dethrone your rulers? (Because ye were idle both?
> Pride by Insolence chastened? Indolence purged by Sloth?)[93]

Kipling's legendary hostility to the Bengali babu is yet another instance of his middle-class defensiveness. His satirical treatment of the "hybrid, University-trained mule" (*PT*, 149) has often been analyzed in terms of racial prejudice.[94] But Kipling's condescending portraits of figures like Mookerjee in *Kim* are also a sign of class anxiety. Lewis Wurgaft argues that frontier fiction as a whole furnished Anglo-Indian readers with an escapist retreat to a social world far removed from the indigenous urban middle class that was rising elsewhere in India.[95] During the 1880s and '90s, colonial society closed its ranks against the Indian middle class, which was largely based in Bengal, and which had been growing exponentially with the expansion of elementary and university education after 1860.[96] Support among reformers for the development of an Indian middle class largely evaporated with the founding of the Indian National Congress in 1885 (with the significant exception of those who, like Annie Besant, played a role in creating it), but it had been waning since the Mutiny. And in the debate over the Ilbert Bill, which would have given Indian judges the power to try British subjects (a debate that Wurgaft calls Kipling's "journalistic baptism of fire"), as well as in colonial resistance to opening the Civil Service to Indians, racial difference was often exploited to protect the class privileges of the British.[97] Like many Anglo-Indians, Kipling stigmatized the Bengali babu for being upwardly mobile (even Mookerjee satirizes the educated babu: "All we Babus talk English to show off" [183]), in contrast to Punjabi natives, who were often falsely mythologized by Anglo-Indian writers—including Kipling—as casteless.[98] Kim's condescension to the schoolboys at St. Xavier's can also be read as a subtle form of class rather than racial snobbery (particularly since only a few of the boys at St. Xavier's are Eurasians). In this case, it is the

---

[93] Rudyard Kipling, "The Islanders," *Complete Verse*, Definitive Edition (New York: Doubleday, 1940), p. 302.

[94] Representative accounts are Metcalf, pp. 166–67; and Nandy, pp. 37–38, 69–70.

[95] Wurgaft, p. 14, points out that roughly ninety per cent of late-century Anglo-Indian fiction was set in the Punjab frontier.

[96] Susan Bayly, p. 309.

[97] Wurgaft, p. 32. Harry Ricketts, *Rudyard Kipling: A Life* (New York: Carroll & Graf, 1999), pp. 57–60, discusses Kipling's involvement in the Ilbert Bill controversy.

[98] This was the thesis of Denzil Ibbetson's influential 1883 report, *Punjab Castes* (Lahore, India: Superintendent of Government Printing, 1916).

social stagnation of the schoolboys—their tendency to fall out of middle-class social trajectories—that triggers Kim's contempt: "At St. Xavier's they know the first rush of minds developed by sun and surroundings, as they know the half-collapse that sets in at twenty-two or twenty-three" (124).[99] A generation later, E. M. Forster's *A Passage to India* (1924) registered many of these same attitudes (evident in the Anglo-Indian community's eagerness to prosecute Dr. Aziz) as symptoms of the imminent end of British imperial authority.

Yet the supposed "classlessness" of Kipling's work is hardly just a figment of critical imaginations. Kipling systematically exploited a very particular representation of "classlessness," one which still seduces many contemporary readers, in order to present middle-class values as universal. As Harold Perkin once reminded us: "The whole purpose of a [class] ideal was to sublimate the interest of a class and present it in a form acceptable to men of other classes."[100] Historically, claims about classlessness were a particularly prominent aspect of middle-class ideology, given its democratic pretensions.

Sadomasochism played a vital role in this universalizing process. The sadomasochistic dynamics that structure Kipling's magical groups, because of their power to forge intimate bonds across the boundaries of social hierarchy, gave these groups the appearance of extraordinary social fluidity—even as, in Kipling's case, such groups held fast to upper-middle-class professional and lower-middle-class moral values. This apparent social fluidity made magical groups a particularly effective means for celebrating the apparent universality of what was, in fact, a generalized middle-class ideological program with multiple synthesized constituencies.

The sadomasochistic paradox that made Kipling's magical groups seem classless and yet profoundly middle-class at the same time is demonstrated succinctly in "His Private Honour" (1891). In this story, class hierarchy appears to collapse when a subaltern named Ouless settles a difference between himself and Private Otheris by proposing that the two beat each other up. The initial difficulty arises when Ouless loses his temper with a crop of new recruits, lashes out with a riding cane, and strikes Otheris by mistake, tearing the coat of his uniform. The offense is a complex one: Ouless has overstepped the authority of his rank by striking an enlisted man, a veteran and a volunteer; Otheris, by army regulations, is not permitted to strike back, but he cannot exercise his right to report the offense

---

[99] Priya Joshi, *In Another Country: Colonialism, Culture, and the English Novel in India* (New York: Columbia University Press, 2002), p. 35, notes that Kipling, like most British novelists, completely effaced the literacy of Indians.

[100] Harold Perkin, *The Origins of Modern English Society, 1780–1880* (London: Routledge and Kegan Paul, 1969), p. 322.

to his superiors, either, without losing caste: "My right! I ain't a recruity to go whinin' about my rights to this an' my rights to that, just as if I couldn't look after myself" (*MI*, 162). Ouless, for his part, realizes he is in the wrong but cannot make the offense up to Otheris, either with an apology or with money for the torn coat, without insulting the infantry-man's social pride. The impasse—which is observed passively but with great interest by several bystanding characters of various social classes—signals a failure of official hierarchical structures to resolve a simple, accidental transgression.

Ouless overcomes this crisis of rank by proposing that he and Otheris fight each other, well off army grounds. In effect, he substitutes a ritual of reversible sadomasochism for the moral and social crisis he has inadvertently perpetrated. In the fight, the two men bloody one another dispassionately, much as the members of Stalky's gang often do—without rancor, personal animosity, or sensitivity to pain. Otheris "painted 'is little aristocratic white shirt for 'im" (160); but Ouless knocks out one of Otheris's teeth before finally mastering his man. Mulvaney recognizes that the mutual beating has restored a certain kind of equality between the two men: "You're a pair, you two. An', begad, I don't know which was the better man" (161). The two men's equality derives from the sadomasochistic intimacy they achieve, an intimacy that binds them in mutual acceptance of several things: the pervasiveness of social injustice, the magical reversibility of bully/victim relations, the empathetic omnipotence "good" bullying can signify, the sense of specialness and narcissistic collusion bullying creates, and the omnipotent transcendence of emotion that sadomasochistic rituals performatively enact. The sadomasochistic intimacy of Ouless and Otheris is also collectivized through the story's bystanders. This gallery of witnesses constitutes a magical group, a group that repeats the two men's apparent transcendence of class difference by bringing the journalist-narrator, Privates Mulvaney and Learoyd, and several officers into a cross-class conspiracy of approving silence. The story's magical group reveals men of all ranks to be equally concerned in notions of honor, which participate in omnipotent fantasy to the extent that they suggest indifference to fear or pain, self-sufficiency, and invulnerability to criticism. The story generalizes honor so widely, in fact, that it is impossible to say it is any single individual's "private honour" that is at stake. As some readers have noted, Kipling's beating scenes always imply a democratic ethos; the dynamics of sadomasochistic identification help explain why.[101]

Yet, at the same time, the act of one man's beating another defines the fixity of social hierarchies. Before the Ouless/Otheris crisis develops, we

---

[101] See Bivona, for example, pp. 81–82.

are told that veteran infantrymen routinely beat recruits while their officers look the other way. Otheris himself takes out his frustrations with
Ouless on a recruit named Samuelson, whom he "bullied disgracefully"
(153). These unquestioned relationships of hierarchical bullying and submission are normalized, finally, by Ouless's physical mastery of Otheris.
Ouless's decision to propose a fistfight in the first place also evokes both
the professional and the evangelical ideals that were specific to Kipling's
vision of middle-class ideological authority. Ouless "studies" (159) the
crisis between himself and Otheris until knowledge, rational calculation,
and self-reliance suggest a solution. He takes on himself the professional's
prerogative to violate official codes of conduct and to propose an unorthodox resolution. But the subaltern's proposal also manifests a heartfelt desire to repent and to expiate his transgression. After the beating has established Ouless as a "good," omnipotent bully rather than a "bad," weak
one, he can freely expiate his crime without giving social offence: he both
apologizes to Otheris and gives him money to repair the coat. The result
of this bullying blend of professional resourcefulness and spiritual reparation is Otheris's acknowledgment: "'E's a gentleman, 'e is" (156). The
story thus restores hierarchical order while reinforcing the particular authority of the evangelically inspired professional. At the same time, it paradoxically universalizes a model of reversible sadomasochistic equality
across the boundaries of social class.

Throughout Kipling's fiction, the logic of this social illogic is persistently repeated. Representations of class hierarchy that affirm middle-class
ideological principles are both legitimated and camouflaged as "classless"
through the fluid dynamics of sadomasochism. Carnehan and Dravot, in
"The Man Who Would Be King," for example, may be cautionary examples of how omnipotent power can be abused when it is assumed by bullying riff-raff; but at the same time, the two loafers demonstrate the universal capacity of British nationals to embrace both disciplined suffering
and disciplined cruelty when military or administrative objectives require
it. They also demonstrate the magical social power that such suffering (and
such bullying) can confer when riff-raff emulate their professional betters
and bully natives to "improve" them. It is through the inherent sadomasochistic paradox of the magical group—its status as permanent victim of
unjust social hierarchies and as authorized social despot—that Kipling
fashioned a myth of collective British omnipotence. Such collectivity was
ideologically affiliated with his broadened, mythically fused middle-class
values; but, in affective terms, it appeared to incorporate all British social
identities in the seemingly classless transcendence facilitated by sadomasochistic fantasy.

Sadomasochistic dynamics fueled appearances of classlessness in Kipling's work in yet one more way: they enabled him to identify ephemerally with the political causes of either social elites or the working classes by casting their political opponents in the role of the "bad" bully. Kipling's hatred of the Labour movement, of unions, of social welfare, and of democracy itself usually vented itself in accusations of working-class bullying. He once wrote that supporters of the working classes made "the People" into "gods above the law of wrong doing," resurrecting "nothing more than the old bunkum about the Divine right of kings transferred to an ungetatable Fetish which isn't responsible for its own actions" (*Letters*, 2:116). Portraying himself as an opponent of this arrogant populace and its bullying demagogues, Kipling identified with upper-class Tory politicians in their opposition to Lloyd George's "People's Budget" of 1909—Lloyd George himself was, for Kipling, simply a "brute."[102] In "The City of Brass" (1909), Kipling stigmatized the lower-class supporters of the People's Budget as bullies:

> They said: "Who has hate in his soul? Who has envied his neighbour?
> Let him arise and control both that man and his labour."[103]

By the same token, Kipling's popular sympathies depended on his turning accusations of bullying against upper-class figures—an act of bullying on Kipling's part. Many of his Indian stories glory in reversing the relationship between bullying gentlemen and bullied infantrymen: in "The Three Musketeers" (1887), Lord Benira Trig, who acts "like a Cossack in evening-dress" (*PT*, 53), is made a fool by the soldiers three; in "The Rout of the White Hussars" (1888), the freshly arrived, arrogant new colonel, "a mean man and a bully" (*PT*, 171), is victimized by his cavalrymen's practical jokes. In these ways, the fluidity of Kipling's political affiliations was facilitated by his projection of bullying dramas everywhere, with their multivalent potentials for identification.

The saturation of Kipling's work and thought with sadomasochistic fantasy, which enabled him to play the role of "rescuing" bully—defending the victims of various social classes against the supposedly despotic aggression of their opponents—allowed him to claim an extraordinary right to "classless" moral authority. Yet the underlying ideological values that informed Kipling's magical groups demonstrate a far more partisan reality. Kipling's engagement with the sadomasochistic logic of magical groups was the means by which he rewrote a broadened conception of middle-class social authority and defended it against the encroachments of social

---

[102] From the Strachey Papers; quoted in Gilmour, p. 217.
[103] Rudyard Kipling, *Complete Verse*, p. 314.

others. His preoccupations with middle-class social privilege thus formed a constant, stabilizing subtext to his sometimes ambivalent imperial narratives. His affirmation of middle-class authority through sadomasochistic omnipotence did not succumb to the contradictions of the colonial experience it negotiated. It was, rather, the most coherent ideological project in his work.

Chapter Four

―◦૯৩৩৩৯◦―

THE MASOCHISM OF THE CRAFT

CONRAD'S IMPERIAL PROFESSIONALISM

> The next moment he gave me a very special impression
> beyond the range of commonplace definitions. It was as
> though he had stabbed himself outside and had come
> in there to show it; and more than that—as though he
> were turning the knife in the wound and watching
> the effect. That was the impression, rendered
> in physical terms.
> —JOSEPH CONRAD, *Under Western Eyes*

> I admit that almost anything, anything in the world,
> would serve as a good reason for not writing at all.
> —JOSEPH CONRAD, "A Familiar Preface"

SPECTACLES of self-destruction dominate Joseph Conrad's novels. The psychic wounds Kaspar Almayer, Peter Willems, Tom Lingard, Lord Jim, and other early protagonists inflict on themselves anticipate dramatic self-immolations such as Martin Decoud's suicide in *Nostromo* (1904), the implosion of the Verloc family in *The Secret Agent* (1907), and Kirylo Razumov's fatal surrender to his persecutors in *Under Western Eyes* (1910). In *Heart of Darkness* (1899), the pattern is upheld by the unlikely Kurtz— that icon of imperial brutality—who embraces death by refusing to leave his outpost despite his failing health (after laying waste to his career, his moral character, and perhaps his sanity). Conrad's fiction offers us fifteen suicides, as well as many near-suicides and other self-injurers.[1] Narcissistic excess routinely implicates these figures in masochistic fantasy. Yet critics tend to regard Conradian self-destructiveness as the endpoint of interpretation, a signifier of irresolvable problems whose causes lie elsewhere, not

---

[1] This is the count of Bernard C. Meyer, *Joseph Conrad: A Psychoanalytic Biography* (Princeton: Princeton University Press, 1967), p. 5.

a site of interpretive possibility in itself.[2] Even psychoanalytic studies consider it a symptomatic effect—usually, of oedipal guilt triggered by the early deaths of Conrad's parents.[3]

Despite its shadowy critical status, masochistic fantasy is a primary organizing structure in Conrad's work. It cannot be understood wholly in psychological terms, however, since it engages political content as well. But its political meanings are especially difficult to decode, entangled as they are with Conrad's well-known ambivalence about imperialism, which has made coherent interpretation of his work difficult. As one might expect, extremist views—that Conrad was fundamentally proimperialist or anti-imperialist—have only made either perspective alone seem reductive. But arguments for a controlling principle of some kind behind these political ambiguities (modernist aesthetics? Polish history? existential ethics?) often falsify his work's irreducible opacity.[4] Even reasonable attempts to balance Conrad's critique of some aspects of imperialism against his idealization of others can seem oblivious to the unreasonable, self-canceling force of his writing.[5] As one of his biographers put it: "At the root of almost all Conrad's important works we find a struggle against the views toward which he himself was drawn."[6]

[2] Two of the most interesting studies of self-destructiveness that nevertheless see it only as symptomatic are Daniel Cottom, "*Lord Jim*: Destruction through Time," *Centennial Review* 27 (1983), 10–29; and Suresh Raval, "Narrative and Authority in *Lord Jim*: Conrad's Art of Failure," *ELH* 48 (1981), 387–410.

[3] An orthodox Freudian, Meyer resorts to this explanation, while also reserving the term "masochism" for erotic fantasies of domination and submission. Other psychoanalytic studies focused on oedipal conflicts and sexual masochism include Catherine Rising, *Darkness at Heart: Fathers and Sons in Conrad* (New York: Greenwood, 1990); and Joseph Dobrinsky, *The Artist in Conrad's Fiction: A Psychocritical Study* (Ann Arbor: UMI Research Press, 1989).

[4] Fredric Jameson, *The Political Unconscious: Narrative as a Socially Symbolic Act* (Ithaca: Cornell University Press, 1981), argues that modernist aestheticization in Conrad both expresses and compensates for the reifications of industrial capitalism. Geoffrey Galt Harpham, *One of Us: The Mastery of Joseph Conrad* (Chicago: University of Chicago Press, 1996), contends that Conrad's experience of Polish politics resulted in his having "no settled attitude" (46) toward imperialism. The most influential study of Conrad's existential ethics is Roy Roussel, *The Metaphysics of Darkness: A Study in the Unity and Development of Conrad's Fiction* (Baltimore: Johns Hopkins University Press, 1971).

[5] Benita Parry, *Conrad and Imperialism: Ideological Boundaries and Visionary Frontiers* (London: Macmillan, 1983), for example, finds in Conrad an estranging perspective that undercut imperialist ideology, although she claims that this perspective was in turn undercut by "fantasy representations of the colonial universe" (2) that reconfirmed western superiority. Another influential compromise position is Patrick Brantlinger, *Rule of Darkness: British Literature and Imperialism, 1830–1914* (Ithaca: Cornell University Press, 1988), pp. 255–74, who argues that Conrad critiqued imperialism without escaping late-Victorian racism.

[6] Zdzislaw Najder, *Joseph Conrad: A Chronicle* (Cambridge: Cambridge University Press, 1983), pp. 166–67.

Self-destructive energy, it would seem, is not simply at the core of Conradian thematics. It also underlies his self-consuming practices as a writer. These two kinds of implosive energy need to be distinguished from one another carefully, since they often spawn contrary political interpretations. On the level of characterization, masochistic tendencies among Conrad's characters can mark the colonial psyche as grotesque. Masochism has thus seemed to offer stable grounds for an anti-imperialist critique, anchored in a pathologizing of the imperial subject. As Daniel Cottom has written, apropos of Lord Jim's narcissism: "The parable of modern imperialism is written in this paradox: in the self-destructiveness of self-adoration."[7] But on the level of implied authorship, masochistic fantasy can also be said to fuel Conrad's disingenuous attacks on his own political values, attacks that sometimes glorify those values. This strategy, although never named as masochism, has infuriated critics such as Edward Said and Chinua Achebe, who complain that Conrad's and his critics' breast-beating over imperialism reaffirms the exalted nobility of the self-flagellating imperial subject.[8]

Conrad's deployment of masochistic fantasy for complex political ends requires a patient delineation. But first we must recognize both the comprehensiveness and the variability of masochistic fantasy in his work. On the one hand, Conrad's colonial world is a psychological prisonhouse, in which no one escapes omnipotent delusion and, in most cases, the masochistic dispositions that sustain it. Precisely because of its pervasiveness, masochistic fantasy saturates the divergent ideological positions his texts circulate. Beth Sharon Ash speaks for many readers when she claims that Conrad saw imperialism as "a cult of narcissism."[9] But Conrad distributed fantasies of omnipotence (masochistic or otherwise) promiscuously to his European characters—those who resist imperialism as well as those who serve it. He also disseminated such fantasies among native characters, whether they rebel against or collaborate with colonial rule.

On the other hand, Conradian masochistic fantasy draws on a number of disparate psychic energies. As I noted in the introduction, such fantasy can support omnipotent delusions that express wishes for control, annihilative rage, excessive idealization, or solipsistic self-love. In Conrad's work, masochistic fantasy also varies by freely engaging both oedipal and preoedipal dynamics rather than assuming a singular relationship to either of them, as it does in the work of Stevenson, Schreiner, and Kipling. This

---

[7] Cottom, p. 29.

[8] Edward Said, *Culture and Imperialism* (New York: Knopf, 1993), p. 24; Chinua Achebe, "An Image of Africa: Racism in Conrad's *Heart of Darkness*," *Heart of Darkness*, by Joseph Conrad, ed. Robert Kimbrough, Norton Critical Edition (New York: Norton, 1988), p. 257.

[9] Beth Sharon Ash, *Writing In Between: Modernity and Psychosocial Dilemma in the Novels of Joseph Conrad* (New York: St. Martin's, 1999), p. 94.

complex capaciousness makes masochistic fantasy a more useful instrument for linking the Conradian psyche to politics than the fragmentary personal and social ideals usually referenced by his critics—in particular, fidelity, work, and service. Recognizing masochistic fantasy's pervasiveness illuminates the general psychosocial structures that organize Conrad's world, whereas tracing its variability enables us to articulate important distinctions among the ideological megalomanias it supports.

Both a universal condition and a highly variegated one, masochistic fantasy intersects Conradian imperial subjectivity without being identical to it. Conrad politicized such fantasy, however, precisely through its variability. The distinctions between different forms of omnipotence as well as between different masochistic vehicles for sustaining it provided him with crucial leverage for ideological rewritings. In particular, Conrad mythologized professional seamen, who often stand in for the broader class of British imperial agents and officials, by expelling the most dangerous kinds of masochistic fantasy from their ranks and endowing them with benign, sublimated forms of it instead. He also conferred on this class a redemptive self-consciousness about the delusional nature of its own imperial idealism. In effect, Conrad legitimated the social authority of certain imperial actors by affirming their lucidity about their own failures. The melancholia saturating his work is thus no ancillary stylization; rather, it articulates the imperial politics he constructed around status hierarchy.

The privileged relationship Conrad maintained between professionalism and masochistic fantasy organized his thinking about imperialism clearly and coherently. Many of his apparent political ambiguities can be resolved by recognizing that his attitudes toward imperialism are class-coded and that this ordering depends, in turn, on his careful management of masochistic fantasy's multiple forms. The central argument of this chapter is that Conrad affirmed a class-bound conception of imperialism, while discrediting the competing imperial ideals he associated with adversarial social groups. His selective endorsements of imperialism fused the mariner's code of conduct with gentrified moral and social values, resurrecting a residual upper-class form of professional ideology—in stark contrast to the class coordinates of imperial professionalism in Kipling's work. This class-specific imperial ethos wholly depended on professionals' capacity to negotiate masochistic fantasy and to mark their own imperial melancholia in redemptive ideological terms.

In the first half of this chapter, I will survey the principal forms of omnipotent delusion in Conrad's work and their implication in masochistic fantasy in order to lay the groundwork for an analysis of his ideological rewritings. Readers familiar with this kind of typology from previous chapters, or impatient with the relatively decontextualized psychological schema I offer here, might want to skip to the last three sections. These

final sections demonstrate how Conrad distributed various forms of masochistic fantasy strategically across a spectrum of class-coded subjectivities.

I will focus primarily on fiction from Conrad's early career, including
his four novels set in the Malayan archipelago: *Almayer's Folly* (1895), *An
Outcast of the Islands* (1896), *Lord Jim* (1900), and *The Rescue* (1920)—
the latter begun in 1896, although not completed for another twenty-two
years. These novels, which maintain a continuity of characters, settings,
and social backgrounds, map a panoramic colonial social order that brings
the professional values of Lingard, Jim, Marlow, and other mariners into
relief. Recent critics have salvaged some of these novels from neglect because they mediate between the imperial romance tradition Conrad inherited and his overt interrogation of that tradition in later novels, such as
Heart of Darkness and *Nostromo*.[10] But these early novels, together with
The Nigger of the "Narcissus" (1897) and a few shorter works from this
period, are also significant because they affirm the "fellowship of the craft"
over against the colonial social order as a whole—an affirmation Conrad's
later novels mute by focusing on relatively abstract tensions between political pragmatism and ideals of honor.[11]

VARIETIES OF COLONIAL OMNIPOTENCE

Although critics have long recognized the excessive "egoism" of Conrad's
protagonists, most have assumed it to be a homogeneous condition—usually an ethically negative one.[12] Some have attempted to distinguish between healthy and unhealthy forms of egoism as a way to acknowledge his
characters' pervasive narcissism without eroding moral distinctions between them.[13] These approaches assume that Conrad resolved the problematics of narcissism by positing normative psychological standards that
counter the narcissistic monstrosity of figures like Kurtz as well as the

---

[10] The most influential of these studies is Andrea White, *Joseph Conrad and the Adventure
Tradition: Constructing and Deconstructing the Imperial Subject* (Cambridge: Cambridge
University Press, 1993).

[11] Joseph Conrad, "Youth: A Narrative," *Youth, Heart of Darkness, The End of the Tether*
(London: Penguin, 1995), p. 9. Hereafter cited as *Y*. I have used reliable recent editions of
Conrad's fiction, except in a few cases where these are unavailable. For these works and for
all his non-fictional writings, I have used original sources or standard editions.

[12] For a good summary, see Marshall W. Alcorn, Jr., *Narcissism and the Literary Libido:
Rhetoric, Text, and Subjectivity* (New York: New York University Press, 1994), p. 163. Classic
accounts are Ian Watt, *Conrad in the Nineteenth Century* (Berkeley: University of California
Press, 1979), p. 149; and Albert J. Guérard, *Conrad the Novelist* (Cambridge: Harvard University Press, 1958), pp. 104–5.

[13] Alcorn, for example, differentiates narcissistic "illusions," which he finds to be "devel-
opmentally enabling" (173), from narcissistic "delusions." Robert Hampson, *Joseph Conrad:*

frustrated vanity of, say, Lingard or Lord Jim. But Conrad exempted no characters from disturbing entanglements in omnipotent fantasy, nor did he differentiate those entanglements in clear-cut moral or psychological terms. Lingard's "absurd faith in himself," Willems's "ferociously conceited" view of his own success, Jim's "exalted egoism," and Gentleman Brown's "mad self-love" are not reducible to one another.[14] Neither are their differences fixable in positive or negative terms. Rather, each character embodies a unique constellation of omnipotent fantasies. Comprehending this diversity is a necessary first step toward understanding how Conrad put it to work ideologically.

On the simplest level, Conrad's characters routinely cultivate solipsistic illusions of grandiosity. This self-absorbed form of omnipotent fantasy resembles the child-like, preoedipal megalomania common in Stevenson's work and in much imperial adventure fiction.[15] Immediately after testifying to his desertion of the crippled *Patna*, for example, Jim declares his fearlessness to Marlow, as if his public confession had never happened:

> By Jove! He was amazing. There he sat telling me that just as I saw him before my eyes he wouldn't be afraid to face anything—and believing in it, too. I tell you it was fabulously innocent and it was enormous, enormous! I watched him covertly, just as though I had suspected him of an intention to take a jolly good rise out of me. He was confident that, on the square, "on the square, mind!" there was nothing he couldn't meet. (*LJ*, 70)

Jim's stubborn convictions about his courage derive from an inward world of fantasy, impervious to external disconfirmation, which he has nursed from his youth:

> Ever since he had been "so high"—"quite a little chap," he had been preparing himself for all the difficulties that can beset one on land and water. He confessed proudly to this kind of foresight. He had been elaborating dangers and defences, expecting the worst, rehearsing his best. He must have led a most exalted existence. Can you fancy it? A succession of adventures, so much glory, such a victorious progress! and the deep sense of his sagacity crowning every day of his inner life. He forgot himself; his eyes shone. (*LJ*, 70)

Jim's fantasies may demonstrate his youthful innocence, but if this kind of omnipotent fantasy has an immature (or even infantile) cast, it can haunt

---

Betrayal and Identity (New York: St. Martin's, 1992) argues that Conrad's characters seek authentic rather than inauthentic self-esteem.

[14] Joseph Conrad, *An Outcast of the Islands* (Oxford: Oxford University Press, 1992), pp. 14, 9. Hereafter cited as *OI*. Joseph Conrad, *Lord Jim: A Tale* (Oxford: Oxford University Press, 1983), pp. 304, 280. Hereafter cited as *LJ*.

[15] For good discussions of preoedipal longing in Conrad's work, see Meyer, p. 182; and Ash, pp. 48–50.

Conrad's characters at any stage of life. Walking "in the radiance of some light of his own that was invisible to other eyes" (*OI*, 57), Willems has similar delusions about his power over people and things: at one point, he has "a confused notion that with one sweep of his hand he could tumble all these trees into the stream" (*OI*, 57). Even a grizzled veteran of the tropics like Lingard is a "man of infinite illusions," susceptible to a "state of exaltation in which he saw himself in some incomprehensible way always victorious, whatever might befall."[16]

Delighted by this inward world of omnipotent illusions, many of Conrad's characters become self-absorbed dreamers, lost in reverie—like Jim, who "loved [his] dreams" (*LJ*, 15), finding them "the best parts of life, its secret truth, its hidden reality." Almayer lives "with his head in the clouds," delighted by an "enchanting vision" of future happiness that is so regularly undermined by actual events he requires opium, finally, to sustain it.[17] The gap between fantasy and the real for these characters often results in fatal blunders, like those Lingard makes pursuing gold upriver— a dream as fragile as the house of cards he builds for Nina, which collapses "before the child's light breath" (*OI*, 151).

Among Conrad's "heroic" characters, solipsistic dreaming encourages a refusal to compromise with banal or vulgar realities. Waving off Marlow's suggestion that he has "had [his] opportunity" (*LJ*, 243), Jim refuses to leave Patusan for the more prosaic world beyond it, claiming that "nothing less will do." Although many recent critics have seen Conrad's protagonists as deliberate caricatures of adventure fiction heroes, contemporary readers were more likely to have admired their uncompromising determination.[18] Conrad himself wrote that James Brooke had been "one of my boyish admirations, a feeling I have kept to this day strengthened by the better understanding of the greatness of his character and the unstained rectitude of his purpose."[19] Despite his occasionally satirical use of adventure conventions, Conrad clearly exploited them to make his protagonists'

---

[16] Joseph Conrad, *The Rescue: A Romance of the Shallows* (Garden City, NY: Doubleday, 1920), pp. 466, 219. Hereafter cited as *R*.

[17] Joseph Conrad, *Almayer's Folly: A Story of an Eastern River* (New York: Modern Library, 2002), pp. 34, 14. Hereafter cited as *AF*.

[18] Recent studies tend to exaggerate the extent to which Conrad's revisions of the adventure tradition amount to an anti-imperialist critique. Linda Dryden, *Joseph Conrad and the Imperial Romance* (New York: St. Martin's, 2000), praises Conrad for "subverting" (14) the romance tradition, finding Lingard to be an unqualified satire on heroic types (60). But James Payne, reviewer for the *Illustrated London News*, was not alone among contemporary readers in describing Lingard as "a noble character." *Conrad: The Critical Heritage*, ed. Norman Sherry (London: Routledge & Kegan Paul, 1973), p. 67.

[19] Joseph Conrad, *The Collected Letters of Joseph Conrad*, ed. Frederick R. Karl and Laurence Davies, 7 vols. (Cambridge: Cambridge University Press, 1983–2005), 7:137. Hereafter cited as *Letters*.

idealism a sign of exalted (if unrealizable) potentials.[20] Nevertheless, he recognized that such idealism depended on solipsistic dreams of invulnerability that deny reality. "Nothing can touch me" (*LJ*, 302), Jim declares, in a "last flicker of superb egoism," before he goes to face what he knows will be certain death.

In his final moments, Jim may begin to apprehend the tension between heroic dreams and realistic limitations. But many of Conrad's characters maintain omnipotent fantasies through unrelenting powers of denial. Almayer wipes Nina's footprints off the sand, pitiably enacting a wish that he might obliterate her existence. Willems, who "lied to himself every minute of his life" (*OI*, 62), blinds himself to the widely known fact that his wife is his master's daughter: "But did you really think that Hudig was marrying you off and giving you a house and I don't know what, out of love for you?" (*OI*, 29), an astonished Lingard asks him. Denial sometimes inspires belief in the magical power of thought to alter reality. Outraged by Willems's betrayal, Lingard tells him: "To me you are not Willems, the man I befriended and helped through thick and thin, and thought much of. . . . You are not a human being that may be destroyed or forgiven. You are a bitter thought, a something without a body and that must be hidden" (*OI*, 212).

Besides their dreams of future success, or their denial of present distress, Conrad's characters employ omnipotent fantasy to erase important conceptual boundaries. A few act on the magical belief that time can be transcended. Almayer's love for Nina deludes him into thinking that through her youth and beauty he will become ageless: "Witnessing her triumphs he would grow young again" (*AF*, 4). Others believe they can transcend racial differences. The great cross-racial friendships of Lingard and Hassim, Stein and Doramin, Jim and Dain Waris—each sealed by token rings of "eternal friendship" (*LJ*, 170)—are all destroyed by these characters' naïveté about racial barriers. Similarly deluded, Almayer believes that once he marries Nina to a rich white man, no one "would think of her mixed blood" (*AF*, 4), despite Captain Ford's warning that Almayer "can't make her white" (*AF*, 25) and in stark contrast to Nina's own complicated negotiation of the difference between her white and nonwhite heritages. Conrad's thoughts about racial difference were notoriously

---

[20] Parry makes this point, p. 43. Martin Green, *Dreams of Adventure, Deeds of Empire* (New York: Basic Books, 1979), p. 310, claims that *The Rescue* describes "possibilities for heroism, romantic friendship, greatness, out on the seas, which are ruined by the intrusion of representatives of London and civilization." Ian Watt, "The Ending of *Lord Jim*," *Critical Essays on Joseph Conrad*, ed. Theodore Billy (Boston: G. K. Hall, 1987), p. 92, argued influentially that the failure of Conrad's heroes made them "a symbol of the romantic world-view."

complex.[21] But his characters often proceed as if these complexities can simply be willed away. As Babalatchi tells Lingard bluntly: "You do not understand the difference between yourselves and us" (*OI*, 175).

In addition to transgressing boundaries of temporality and race, some of Conrad's characters imagine themselves to be beyond class difference. After his fall, Willems remains "yet aware of his superiority" (*OI*, 22) to his fellow clerks. Marlow is astonished by Jim's "insolence" (*LJ*, 172), the "exaltation in a man appointed to be a trading-clerk." As we will see later, Conrad explored the malleability of colonial social hierarchy in strategic ways. But if some of his characters pragmatically exploit opportunities for upward mobility, others simply deceive themselves about their social status.

Besides maintaining solipsistic control by transgressing limits of time, race, and class, Conrad's characters sometimes delude themselves about the permeability of intersubjective boundaries. Such delusions often support an aspect of omnipotent fantasy common in Schreiner's work: transgression of the threshold between preoedipal and oedipal forms of desire. The Conradian romance between fathers and daughters suggests this confusion of preoedipal and oedipal love quite clearly. Almayer's love for Nina, Lingard's for his adopted daughter, and Lingard's for Nina all suggest a magical conflation of different kinds of desire.[22] Lingard's love for his ship conveys this kind of omnipotent conflation metaphorically: "To him she was always precious—like old love; always desirable—like a strange woman; always tender—like a mother; always faithful—like the favourite daughter of a man's heart" (*R*, 10). Conrad tended to be silent about his characters' sexual desires—in part, because their ecstatic experience usually takes narcissistic rather than sexual forms. But his father/daughter romances suggest a wish to triumph over the realities of sexual difference as well as to amalgamate distinctly different libidinal impulses.

Attempts to preserve illusions of safety further elide solipsistic dreaming with preoedipal wishes. Willems complacently imagines that he "had won

---

[21] While recent critics have revised Watt's view that Conrad's nonwhites are "flat" (*Conrad in the Nineteenth Century*, 62), they have disagreed sharply on how to describe them. Harpham claims Conrad depicted nonwhites as "rounded" (47). Robert Hampson, *Cross-Cultural Encounters in Joseph Conrad's Malay Fiction* (New York: Palgrave, 2000), goes further, claiming that his novels not only assume readers with broad cross-cultural knowledge but "work to construct such readers" (103). Christopher GoGwilt, *The Invention of the West: Joseph Conrad and the Double-Mapping of Europe and Empire* (Stanford: Stanford University Press, 1995), however, argues that Conrad never grasped the cultural and historical implications for native peoples of his material.

[22] Conrad denied any incestuous impulses in Almayer's love for Nina. But for critical arguments to the contrary, see H. R. Lenormand, "Note on a Sojourn of Conrad in Corsica," trans. Charles Owen, *The Art of Joseph Conrad: A Critical Symposium*, ed. Robert W. Stallman (1960; Athens: Ohio University Press, 1982), pp. 6–7.

the game of life" (*OI*, 10) and sees himself as "quite safe; solid as the hills" (*OI*, 13). Jim, after establishing himself in Patusan, confesses that "I must go on, go on for ever holding up my end, to feel sure that nothing can touch me. I must stick to their belief in me to feel safe" (*LJ*, 243). But the tremendous risks these characters undertake to preserve their dreams of safety help expose them as delusional. Willems's convictions of security come at the very time he steps out of the "safe stride of virtue" (*OI*, 7), which results in his dismissal for embezzlement. Jim's safe haven is, in fact, immensely fragile; it also compels him to risk death constantly—every time he drinks Rajah Allang's coffee, for instance. Occasionally, Conrad compared the loss of safety to the loss of protective maternal care, which highlights its tie to preoedipal desire. Just before the *Patna*'s collision with a submerged wreck, Jim contemplates the "everlasting security," the "scheme of a safe universe," and the "great certitude of unbounded safety and peace that could be read on the silent aspect of nature like the certitude of fostering love upon the placid tenderness of a mother's face" (*LJ*, 13). Afterwards, he sees only "the suspended menace discovered in the midst of the most perfect security" (*LJ*, 71).

The solipsistic forms of omnipotence I have described are relatively non-aggressive, usually causing more suffering to the characters who entertain them than to others. Most of them can be described as forms of idealism: belief in the unity of one's desire with that of another; in the purity of heroism; or in the transcendability of time, race, class, and sexuality. Because Conrad viewed these child-like, preoedipal forms of omnipotent fantasy as idealistic, he represented them as characteristically European rather than Malayan. The realism of Babalatchi, the "barbarous politician" (*OI*, 166), for example, stands in stark contrast to the infantile delusions of the white characters he manipulates. Babalatchi's "pliability to circumstances and adaptiveness to momentary surroundings" (*OI*, 45) compel him to give up childish dreams of violent reprisal and inspire him to become a manipulative realist, a "true statesman." None of Conrad's white characters achieves the mature freedom from delusion such pragmatism requires. Ascribing the pitiable, ineffective, preoedipal versions of omnipotent fantasy to whites rather than to Malayans was one of the subtle ways Conrad suggested the fundamental innocence of imperial heroism.

Conrad often combined the preoedipal forms of omnipotent fantasy I have so far described, however, with more aggressive delusions. Although his white characters may appear foolish because of their infantile dreams, they sometimes blend fantasies of glory, love, and safety with masterful desires for control. Jim vows early in life to be "better than anybody" (*LJ*, 6) and often loses himself in "contemplating his own superiority" (*LJ*, 17). In his case, competitiveness remains largely phantasmagoric. But for other characters, the aggression latent in delusions of superiority erupts as sadism, invoking oedipal rather than preoedipal themes: domination and submission, sexualization, and triangular patterns of relationship.

Like solipsistic dreams of glory, the assumption of a right to dominate others takes a number of discrete forms in Conrad's work. Sometimes, his characters exercise vindictive fantasies by trying to live through others. Almayer wants to see "white men bowing low" (*AF*, 80) before Nina. Similarly, Lingard's identification with victims of colonialism betrays his own vindictive desires. Others idealize loved ones or supporters who are imagined as protective and whose magical strength seems to extend the power of the self. Almayer's view of Lingard as a "god" (*AF*, 7), Willems's view of Aïssa as "the very spirit of that land" (*OI*, 55), or Lingard's view of his ship as "the most perfect of its kind" (*R*, 11)—all involve regarding other people (or things) as omnipotent saviors, possessing protective power that can also support vindictive fantasies. Mrs. Almayer indulges this form of fantasy through her daughter's marriage to Dain Maroola: "I was a slave, and you shall be a queen" (*AF*, 118), she tells Nina. Aïssa hopes Willems will carry out her bitter dreams of vengeance against whites: "The fragments she understood she made up for herself into a story of a man great amongst his own people, valorous and unfortunate; an undaunted fugitive dreaming of vengeance against his enemies" (*OI*, 59).[23] These women's vicarious identifications with avengers have not pleased critics who claim that Conrad's Malayan women exercise no agency of their own.[24] But they also suggest, contrary to some readers' claims, that he did not represent narcissistic trauma and compensation as exclusively male.[25]

Although Conrad assigned preoedipal, solipsistic omnipotent fantasy exclusively to Europeans, his Malayans regularly enact more aggressive, vengeful, or sadistic forms of omnipotence. Like other western observers, Conrad believed that Malayans were inherently more cruel than whites. As Alfred Russel Wallace once observed: "A reckless cruelty and contempt of human life . . . is the dark side of their character."[26] In "Karain: A Memory" (1897), the delusional fantasies of Karain, who dreams obsessively about a runaway Malayan woman he imagines as his destined "companion," are embedded in his "Odyssey of revenge" against her, which is triangulated by his ambivalently loving and murderous attitude toward her

[23] Anne Tagge, " 'A Glimpse of Paradise': Feminine Impulse and Ego in Conrad's Malay World," *Conradiana* 29 (1997), 101–112, documents Conrad's emphasis on vindictiveness among Malayan women as a reflection of typical British views.

[24] See, for example, Padmini Mongia, " 'Ghosts of the Gothic': Spectral Women and Colonized Spaces in *Lord Jim*," *Conrad and Gender*, ed. Andrew Michael Roberts (Amsterdam: Rodopi, 1993), pp. 1–15; or Heliéna Krenn, *Conrad's Lingard Trilogy: Empire, Race, and Women in the Malay Novels* (New York: Garland, 1990), esp. p. xix.

[25] Scott McCracken, " 'A Hard and Absolute Condition of Existence': Reading Masculinity in *Lord Jim*," *Conrad and Gender*, p. 31, for example, claims that Conradian narcissism is inherently masculine.

[26] Alfred Russel Wallace, *The Malay Archipelago* (New York: Harper & Brothers, 1869), p. 587.

brother.[27] Likewise, Abdulla, who believes omnipotently that "all his attempts always succeeded" (*OI*, 86), becomes wholly absorbed by his commercial rival, Lingard: "the wish to get the best of him in every way, became Abdulla's mania, the paramount interest of his life, the salt of his existence" (*OI*, 86). Nina's passion for revenge against the whites who snubbed her in Singapore offers explicit proof that she has thrown off civilized values: "Listening to the recital of those savage glories . . . where men of her mother's race shone far above the Orang Blanda, she felt herself irresistibly fascinated, and saw with vague surprise the narrow mantle of civilised morality . . . fall away and leave her shivering and helpless as if on the edge of some deep and unknown abyss" (*AF*, 33). In "Youth," Conrad identified the East itself with "a stealthy Nemesis" (*Y*, 42). As we have seen, his whites sometimes share these vindictive fantasies. But vindictiveness is precisely what signals his Europeans' reversion to barbarism, in contrast to the preoedipal, solipsistic omnipotence that defines, in some cases, their tragic innocence.

Omnipotent fantasies of revenge in Conrad's novels are all-consuming, as if his characters (both white and nonwhite) feel their very existence to be threatened by injuries they must avenge. Lingard rages against Willems because he fears annihilation: "It seemed to him that he would have to confront the very devil himself, and he had a kind of a glimmer of consciousness within him that he might prove unequal to the task. . . . For the first time in his life he ceased to be himself" (*OI*, 182). Similarly endangered, Maroola "had lost faith in himself, and there was nothing else in him of what makes a man" (*AF*, 133). Dreaming of retaliation, he fantasizes vindictively that some day he "would be in the midst of them, kriss in hand, killing, killing, killing, and would die with the shouts of his enemies in his ears, their warm blood spurting before his eyes" (*AF*, 132).

Their apocalyptically self-righteous character also distinguishes omnipotent fantasies of revenge from ordinary vindictiveness. As Marlow observes about Gentleman Brown's revenge against Jim: "Notice that even in this awful outbreak there is a superiority as of a man who carries right—the abstract thing—within the envelope of his common desires. It was not a vulgar and treacherous massacre; it was a lesson, a retribution—a demonstration of some obscure and awful attribute of our nature which, I am afraid, is not so very far under the surface as we like to think" (*LJ*, 296). A great many of Conrad's characters enact this phantasmic conviction of righteousness and the annihilating violence it appears to legitimate. Lingard's retribution against Willems, for example, certifies and authorizes his desire "to execute the verdict of justice. Justice only! Nothing was further from his thoughts than such a useless thing as revenge.

[27] Joseph Conrad, "Karain: A Memory," *Tales of Unrest* (London: Everyman, 2000), pp. 30, 32. Hereafter cited as *TU*.

Justice only. It was his duty that justice should be done—and by his own hand" (*OI*, 172). In the logic of omnipotent fantasy, the desire to annihilate others is the reverse side of the phantasmic belief that others have the power to annihilate the self.

Some of Conrad's protagonists sublimate their omnipotent narcissism into seemingly benevolent fantasies about rescuing others, although such fantasies remain linked to aggression. Almayer's love for Nina makes her little more than a prop for "his dream of wealth and power" (*AF*, 3). Lingard's yearning to save others is presented as an amalgamation of omnipotent impulses: to assert his god-like powers; to vindicate himself against his enemies, and even to annihilate them (which Jörgenson, his agent, accomplishes for him by blowing up the ship on which Lingard's antagonists gather); and to live vicariously through others by identifying with their suffering. More generally, Conrad exposed the linkage of sadistic and paternalistic motivations in imperial authority. When Babalatchi hears Lingard defend his actions as altruistic, he declares: "This is a white man's talk . . . . That is how you all talk while you load your guns and sharpen your swords; and when you are ready, then to those who are weak you say: 'Obey me and be happy, or die!' " (*OI*, 174–75).

Conrad worried tirelessly about the damage to self and others caused by omnipotent fantasy, as well as the impossibility of disentangling moral or imperial ideals from it. His fears about the ineradicability of narcissistic delusion conditioned his general wariness about political action: "I have not been revolutionary in my writings," he once wrote. "All claim to special righteousness awakens in me that scorn and anger from which a philosophical mind should be free."[28] Nevertheless, his attitude toward omnipotent fantasy harbored a certain leniency, which should not be confused with endorsement—a leniency rooted in his sense of narcissistic delusion's inescapability. Although quick to expose the solipsism of characters in his own narratives, for example, Marlow affirms the impossibility of distinguishing their illusions from "truth": "there is so little difference . . . and the difference means so little" (*LJ*, 162). Apologizing for the necessity of illusion in less metaphysical terms, Marlow claims that it sustains essential ideals, like courage:

> Nothing easier than to say, Have no fear! Nothing more difficult. How does one kill fear, I wonder? How do you shoot a spectre through the heart, slash off its spectral head, take it by its spectral throat? It is an enterprise you rush into while you dream . . . . You require for such a desperate encounter an enchanted and poisoned shaft dipped in a lie too subtle to be found on earth. An enterprise for a dream, my masters! (*LJ*, 231)

---

[28] Joseph Conrad, "A Familiar Preface," *A Personal Record: Some Reminiscences*, Concord Edition (1912; New York: Doubleday, 1923), p. xxii. Hereafter cited as *PR*.

As Conrad himself once wrote: "Egoism saves everything—absolutely everything—all that we abhor and all that we love" (*Letters*, 2:159).[29]

Conrad's own writing practices often suggest the presence of omnipotent fantasy. Delusional forms of denial subtend his famous capacity for distortion, exaggeration, and erasure—what Said has called his "willful inaccuracy" and what others describe as an ongoing project of auto-mythology.[30] Biographers recount many occasions on which Conrad claimed a special right to distort the truth, as when he challenged his wife about the beginnings of his career: "On one of his naughty days he said that 'The Black Mate' was his first work, and when I said, 'No, *Almayer's Folly* was the first thing you ever did,' he burst out: 'If I like to say "The Black Mate" was my first work, I shall say so!' "[31] Conrad also displayed a telling pride in his self-consciousness about narcissistic delusion. Many of his prefaces apologize for what he saw as the professional writer's inevitably outsized narcissism. In his "Author's Note" to *The Shadow-Line* (1917), he confessed the "natural" fact that "when we begin to meditate on the meaning of our own past it seems to fill all the world in its profundity and its magnitude."[32] Excusing an earlier edition's dedication, he then claimed: it "strikes me now as a most disproportionate thing—as another instance of the overwhelming greatness of our own emotion to ourselves."

Conrad's sense of the inextricability of omnipotent fantasy from human desire underlay his refusal to condemn imperialism on the grounds that it was simply a "cult of narcissism." Nevertheless, he did valorize some forms of omnipotent delusion over others: the distinctions between solipsistic and sadistic forms of it that mark his conception of racial difference are one important instance. But such distinctions could become considerably more complicated. They could incorporate his characters' self-conscious display of their own delusions, for example. They could also either organize or undermine forms of collective solidarity, including imperialist solidarity.

To propose that imperialism and omnipotent fantasy have much in common is not news. I hope I have indicated, however, that surveying different forms of omnipotent fantasy produces a more comprehensive perspective on colonial mentalities than assuming that "egoism" is all of one kind in Conrad's work, that it characterizes his imperial subjectivity in a monolithic way, or that he believed in alternative psychological or moral norms.

---

[29] My translation.

[30] Edward W. Said, *Joseph Conrad and the Fiction of Autobiography* (Cambridge: Harvard University Press, 1966), p. 11.

[31] Quoted in Frederick R. Karl, *Joseph Conrad: The Three Lives* (New York: Farrar, Straus and Giroux, 1979), p. 235.

[32] Joseph Conrad, *The Shadow-Line: A Confession* (Oxford: Oxford University Press, 1985), p. xxxix. Hereafter cited as *SL*.

Before exploring his ideological deployment of omnipotence in greater detail, however, we must first recognize the variable forms of masochistic fantasy that enabled his characters to sustain their omnipotent dreams.

"In the Destructive Element Immerse"

With the death of Dain Waris, Jim's power over Patusan, along with his most exalted narcissistic delusions, comes to an abrupt end. Urged by his lover Jewel to fight, Jim resolves instead to appear unarmed before Waris's enraged father Doramin; Marlow claims: "He was going to prove his power in another way" (*LJ*, 300). Throughout Conrad's fiction, self-destructive strategies always offer "another way" to sustain omnipotent fantasy, whether such fantasy is solipsistic or sadistic, preoedipal or oedipal, paternalistic or vindictive. The necessity of finding a circuitous route to omnipotence follows from the inevitable narcissistic demystifications his characters suffer. The resulting network of relationships between self-destructiveness and omnipotence—which I have proposed as the definition of masochistic fantasy—thus played a critical role in Conrad's construction of colonial subjectivity.

Jim's case illustrates a characteristic paradox of masochistic fantasy: embracing death conveys his despair at narcissistic deflation while simultaneously recuperating his delusions. On the one hand, his fatalism acknowledges that his social power is irretrievably gone. On the other hand, it converts frustrated omnipotence into an alternative, phantasmagoric glory. After Doramin shoots him, but before he falls to the ground, Jim "sent right and left at all those faces a proud and unflinching glance" (*LJ*, 304), enacting even in death the omnipotent fantasy that he can always convert failure into distinction. Jim's search for "another way" to omnipotent power thus fulfills Stein's gnomic parable: "A man that is born falls into a dream like a man who falls into the sea" (*LJ*, 155). The way to avoid drowning, Stein claims, is: "In the destructive element immerse .... To follow the dream, and again to follow the dream—and so—*ewig—usque ad finem*" (155–56). This famous conundrum expresses concisely the proximity of masochistic fantasy to omnipotence. Although the parable signifies in many different ways, it distinctly elides "destructive element" with "dream."[33] It proposes that dreaming sustains individuals only if they surrender to its destructive power rather than trying to extricate themselves from it.

---

[33] Early critics, such as Guérard, pp. 165–66, and Dorothy Van Ghent, *The English Novel: Form and Function* (New York: Holt, Rinehart and Winston, 1953), p. 230, chastised readers who overlooked this equivalence of "dream" and "destructive element" in Stein's parable.

Even more explicitly, through Captain Brierly in *Lord Jim*, Conrad dramatized the double valence of an immersion in dreaming: its production of both despair and self-exaltation, self-destruction and omnipotent fantasy. Brierly's suicide follows his antiomnipotent realization that "one of us" (*LJ*, 32) might be imperfect, when the exposure of Jim's cowardice shatters Brierly's illusions about professional honor. At Jim's trial, according to Marlow, Brierly "was probably holding silent inquiry into his own case," arriving at "some thought with which a man unused to such a companionship finds it impossible to live" (*LJ*, 44). Yet it remains unclear whether Brierly kills himself out of narcissistic deflation or whether his suicide restores "that belief in his own splendour which had almost cheated his life of its legitimate terrors" (*LJ*, 48). "Almost! Perhaps wholly," Marlow reflects. "Who can tell what flattering view he had induced himself to take of his own suicide?" From this perspective, Brierly's immersion in the destructive element reasserts once and for all his invulnerability to the flaws that taint others.

The Nigger of the "Narcissus" is perhaps Conrad's most thorough exploration of the paradoxes linking masochistic fantasy to omnipotence. The crew of the *Narcissus* may be preoccupied with one persistent question about James Wait: is he dying or shamming? But Wait also poses for them—and for readers—another question even more difficult to answer: does his histrionic suffering enhance his grandiosity and power, or does it dramatize his despair at imminent annihilation? On the one hand, Wait uses his performative suffering to bully others and glorify himself. His impending death is "thrust at them many times a day like a boast and like a menace . . . he was overbearing about it, as if no one else in the world had ever been intimate with such a companion; he paraded it unceasingly before us."[34] The reward Wait reaps is despotism: "Had we been a miserable gang of wretched immortals, unhallowed alike by hope and fear, he could not have lorded it over us with a more pitiless assertion of his sublime privilege" (*NN*, 29). If nothing else, puzzling out the riddle of Wait's performative suffering paralyzes the crew: "He would never let doubt die. He overshadowed the ship" (*NN*, 29).

On the other hand, though, Wait's suffering signals despair over his inner emptiness. Captain Allistoun claims that Wait has "no grit to face what's coming to us all" (*NN*, 78). Yet the question whether Wait enriches his narcissism or declares its poverty through histrionic suffering defeats resolution, since even his seemingly genuine moments of despair may harbor self-aggrandizement. As Donkin puts it: "Who's yer ter be afeard

---

[34] Joseph Conrad, *The Nigger of the "Narcissus,"* ed. Robert Kimbrough, Norton Critical Edition (New York: W. W. Norton, 1979), p. 22. Hereafter cited as *NN*.

more'n any one?" (*NN*, 93). Together, Donkin and Wait, who both control others through self-martyrdom, exemplify the paradoxical trajectories of masochistic fantasy. At the end of the novel, Wait dissolves at last into what the narrator calls his "undying fear" (*NN*, 99) while Donkin lives on, more tyrannical than ever, scorning the crew's frailty: "I am a man. . . . Not one of yer 'as the sperrit of a bug" (*NN*, 105).

Conrad's work is full of characters who deploy masochistic fantasy in these bivalent ways, although they usually exemplify either grandiosity or despair more emphatically than its twin. The resulting shifts in narrative tonality should not obscure masochistic fantasy's consistent doubleness. Almayer, for instance, indulges in overwhelming despair when he burns down his own house, forcing himself to occupy his "folly"—his uncompleted new house. His desolation is unmistakable, although this self-immolating spectacle also serves as a last-ditch attempt to go out, literally, in a blaze of glory. Similarly, his histrionic agonies over what he takes to be the corpse of Dain Maroola, whose death would undo him, foreground his despair even if they are tinged with perverse self-aggrandizement: "pompously" (99), he detains the investigating Dutch officers before theatrically unveiling the body. Willems also taps into omnipotence in the midst of his despair by using self-inflicted pain to claim control over his own emotions: " 'Look!' and he bared an arm covered with fresh scars. 'I have been biting myself to forget in that pain the fire that hurts me there!' He struck his breast violently with his fist, reeled under his own blow, fell into a chair that stood near and closed his eyes slowly" (*OI*, 71). For Almayer and Willems, self-destructive impulses betray the shattering dysphoria of frustrated omnipotence even as they still seek feebly to glorify abjection. Far more common in Conrad's works, however, are self-destructive performances like Jim's or Brierly's, which transform suffering into grandiosity much more efficiently.

Although Conrad's plots often revolve around cataclysmic suffering, his characters' self-destructiveness often invokes omnipotent fantasy in more pragmatic ways. Some assume, for example, that they can control others through self-sacrifice. Almayer hopes to coerce Lingard's generosity by obediently marrying his adopted Malayan daughter—even though, since Lingard takes this acquiescence for granted, Almayer turns out merely to have "sold [his] soul for a few guilders" (*OI*, 71). Willems plays a similar game equally badly, marrying a Malayan girl in the expectation he will win Hudig's favor. In return for "the greatness of his sacrifice" (*OI*, 23), he also expects his wife's unquestioning submission—only to be disappointed on both counts. Similarly, Mrs. Almayer unsuccessfully offers her "calm submission" (*AF*, 18) to Lingard, hoping to become his wife. That these scheming self-sacrifices fail to be honored exposes the magical thinking that underlies and often undoes masochistic fantasies of control.

Delusions of victimization can also invoke omnipotence pragmatically. They enable some characters to explain away the failures of omnipotent fantasy, thus preserving narcissistic dreams from retrospective disconfirmation. Almayer retains belief in the sanctity of his dreams by lamenting: "They all got on but I. Why? I am better than any of them" (*OI*, 277). Others cherish injustice to sustain fantasies of self-righteous revenge. In *The Rescue*, Lingard's exalted self-esteem depends on his campaign to restore Hassim's throne: d'Alcacer views Lingard as "naively engaged in a contest with heaven's injustice" (*R*, 346). Taminah, likewise, feels that "the injustice of the suffering inflicted upon her without cause" (*AF*, 93) entitles her to betray Maroola. Moreover, seeing oneself as a victim contributes to phantasmagoric disavowals of reality. Informed of rumors—which are quite accurate—that he has been unfaithful, Willems's cherished self-pity inspires him to deny the facts: " 'It's a damned lie!' shouted Willems, waking up for a moment into righteous indignation" (*OI*, 267). Conrad's fascination with those who falsely view themselves as victims earned him Fredric Jameson's epithet: "the epic poet of *ressentiment*."[35]

Through their self-sacrificial acts, Conrad's characters often identify with victimized others, enlarging their sense of rectitude and passion for revenge. Jim initially remains in Patusan, for example, to stop Cornelius's abuse of Jewel. Marlow reports: "He told me further that he didn't know what made him hang on—but of course we may guess. He sympathizes deeply with the defenceless girl, at the mercy of that 'mean, cowardly scoundrel'" (*LJ*, 210). Conrad routinely emphasized the self-serving, narcissistic aspects of such identification. As Almayer points out, Lingard's tendency to shelter victims often selfishly incorporates others into his self-destructive grandiosity:

> What about that half-starved dog you brought on board in Bankok in your arms. . . . It went mad next day and bit the serang. . . . The best serang you ever had! You said so yourself while you were helping us to lash him down to the chain-cable, just before he died in his fits. Now, didn't you? Two wives and ever so many children the man left. That was your doing. . . . And when you went out of your way and risked your ship to rescue some Chinamen from a water-logged junk in Formosa Straits, that was also a clever piece of business. Wasn't it? Those damned Chinamen rose on you before forty-eight hours. . . . I might have been ruined for the sake of those murderous scoundrels that, after all, had to be driven overboard after killing ever so many of your crew—of your beloved crew! (*OI*, 125–26)

Masochistic expiation can also fuel pragmatic forms of omnipotent fantasy. On some occasions, it camouflages the masochist's destructive power.

---

[35] Jameson, p. 268.

Lingard's perverse tendency to shield his enemies is, in part, an attempt to rescue victims of his own aggression, as when he adopts the daughter of a Malayan he has killed, believing that he had thereby "done his duty by the girl" (*AF*, 19). Less directly, the splendor of Lingard's success strikes him as a cause for guilt, requiring self-punitive restitution. Remembering his boyhood Sunday-school lessons, Lingard makes recompense for his good fortune (which he omnipotently exaggerates) by rescuing others: "amazed and awed by his fate, that seemed to his ill-informed mind the most wondrous known in the annals of men" (*OI*, 153), he devotes himself to repairing the "stray lives he found here and there under his busy hand" (*OI*, 152). Lingard also senses that any mistrust he entertains toward others must be expiated, as if thought itself constitutes aggression. Turning the command of his ship over to Carter, whom he had once doubted, is "distasteful and bitter as an expiation should be" (*R*, 195). Having mistrusted Edith Travers, he kneels before her and confesses: "It seems as if I had sinned" (*R*, 342).

Conrad's representations of masochistic fantasy share the leniency he extended to narcissistic excess, since he viewed both as ineradicable from human desire. He plainly criticized the most selfish and futile forms of masochistic fantasy: Almayer's wallowing in failure, Willems's megalomaniacal self-destructiveness. Through other characters, he exposed the arrogance of expiatory paternalism, the deluded vanity of self-abasement, and the vindictiveness fueled by identification with victims. But his work also betrays considerable sympathy with masochistic fantasy, if only by implicitly adopting many of the self-destructive tendencies to which his characters are drawn.

Like his characters, for example, Conrad's narratives are obsessed with injustice and betrayal, assuming a masochistic perspective on what he portrayed as the world's inherent cruelty. Occasionally, his references to the "brutal and unnecessary violence" (*AF*, 4) of nature and "the villainy of circumstances" (*LJ*, 89) stigmatize his characters' self-pity through indirect discourse, which distances their belief in natural spitefulness.[36] But more often these references establish a sadomasochistic authorial worldview, much as similar rhetorical patterns do in Kipling's work. Descriptions of the cruelty of nature, unaffiliated with any particular character, often locate a sadomasochistic ontology within the narrative consciousness:

> On three sides of the clearing, appearing very far away in the deceptive light, the big trees of the forest, lashed together with manifold bonds by a mass of

---

[36] On Conrad's attitudes toward the cruelty of the natural world, see C. F. Burgess, *The Fellowship of the Craft: Conrad on Ships and Seamen and the Sea* (Port Washington, NY: Kennikat Press, 1976), pp. 36–51.

tangled creepers, looked down at the growing young life at their feet with the sombre resignation of giants that had lost faith in their strength. And in the midst of them the merciless creepers clung to the big trunks in cable-like coils, leaped from tree to tree, hung in thorny festoons from the lower boughs, and, sending slender tendrils on high to seek out the smallest branches, carried death to their victims in an exulting riot of silent destruction. (*AF*, 130)

To Marguerite Poradowska, Conrad spoke without qualification of his "indignation against . . . the cruelty of things and the brutality of the inevitable" (*Letters*, 1:85).[37]

Conrad's celebrated pessimism also perversely undermined some of his cherished ideals, reinforcing his masochistic relationship toward his own work. Aware that pessimism often implies narcissistic grandiosity, he once declared: "What one feels so hopelessly barren in declared pessimism is just its arrogance. It seems as if the discovery made by many men at various times that there is much evil in the world were a source of proud and unholy joy unto some of the modern writers."[38] In this spirit, Conrad often satirically blurred his characters' pessimism with their self-exalting sense of cosmic injustice. At the end of *An Outcast of the Islands*, he put both metaphysical gloom and masochistic self-pity into Almayer's mouth: "Where's the sense of all this? Where's your Providence? Where's the good for anybody in all this? The world's a swindle! A swindle! Why should I suffer? What have I done to be treated so?" (*OI*, 279). At the same time, though, it is difficult to decode many Conradian descriptions of cosmic malevolence as either genuine or sham—an ambivalence that echoes the narcissistic paradoxes of Wait's self-dramatizations. The indeterminacies of Conrad's texts often derive from a characteristic strategy—one we have also seen in Schreiner's writing—of attacking his own most cherished assumptions: through Kurtz, the principle that work and efficiency are ennobling; through the crew of the *Narcissus*, that fidelity is the highest of human values; through Jim, that honor is a coherent ideal; and, through his critique of pessimistic grandiosity, his own relentless pessimism.

While critiquing both omnipotent fantasy and masochistic strategies for producing it, Conrad's narratives embrace both. His work's involvement in masochistic fantasy had serious consequences for his affirmation of specific class ideals, as we will see. Most importantly, his ideological affirmations depend on both the inevitability of narcissistic delusion and the interminable self-critique it compels. But Conrad's social marking of masochistic fantasy also relied on another critical psychological framework. Besides playing an important role in the dynamics of masochistic

<hr />

[37] My translation.
[38] Joseph Conrad, "Books," *Notes on Life and Letters* (London: Dent, 1949), p. 8.

fantasy, ideals of interpersonal recognition mediate the particular psychosocial strategies for managing masochistic fantasy that, in the end, Conrad endorsed.

EMPATHY AS A NARCISSISTIC DISORDER

Interpersonal recognition—or its absence—plays a vital role in Conrad's narratives. Its importance suggests, among other things, the strong presence of preoedipal fantasy in his work, since dramas of interpersonal recognition always imply conflicts over emotional nurturance, individuation, and separation. More importantly, the ambivalent structure of these dramas highlights the masochistic elements in his characters' laments that they have been misunderstood, betrayed, abandoned, or unloved. On the one hand, despair over real failures of empathy drives his characters into masochistic abjection. On the other hand, though, their delusional self-victimization generates purely imaginary convictions about empathetic failure.

Many of Conrad's characters complain suspiciously loudly of being misunderstood. When Almayer confesses to Nina his failed dreams of triumphing through her beauty and wealth, for example, he believes that "he had laid clear before his daughter the inner meaning of his life" (*AF*, 80). This moment of self-disclosure—which elicits her scornful indifference—prompts a series of enraged demands on Almayer's part, all revolving around the question: "have you no sympathy?" (*AF*, 80). He may be right when he tells her: "You never cared; you saw me struggle, and work, and strive, unmoved; and my suffering you could never see" (*AF*, 79–80). But the "inner meaning of his life," as he represents it, consists entirely of his ambition to incorporate her into his self-aggrandizing vengeance, which makes his appeal for her empathy disingenuous, to say the least. More importantly, the fact that Nina may understand Almayer quite well but not sympathize with him—or that others might use such understanding to manipulate him, as do Babalatchi and Abdulla—suggests that his self-aggrandizing complaints about being misunderstood emanate from his own misapprehensions.

Many of Conrad's protagonists stubbornly overlook or even refuse interpersonal understanding while at the same time complaining about their desire for it. When Marlow discovers Jewel's melancholic mistrust of Jim's love, he declares: "Why couldn't she believe? Wherefore this craving for incertitude, this clinging to fear, as if incertitude and fear had been the safeguards of her love. It was monstrous" (*LJ*, 229). Jewel's behavior suggests that masochistic mistrust can, in fact, safeguard love, by inflating the injured self-image of the lover or by preserving an aggrieved attachment to the love object. For these purposes, Conrad's characters often withhold critical information about themselves from those who love them. In "The End of the Tether" (1902), Captain Whalley declines to tell his daughter of his impoverishment or his increasing blindness despite his belief that they share a "perfect understanding" (*Y*, 161). Perversely, Jim refuses to seek forgiveness from his father, a man who "seemed to fancy his sailor son not a little" (*LJ*, 58), and whose last letter had "nothing in it except just affection" (*LJ*, 249). Jim believes grandiosely that his father's sympathy cannot withstand the enormity of his guilt: "I could never explain . . . . He wouldn't understand" (*LJ*, 59). This refusal to gratify what Jim often claims as his deepest desire—to be understood—permeates his flight from the *Patna* scandal, in which he repeatedly banishes himself from sympathetic employers. Proudly, too, Jim declares that his subjects in Patusan "had trusted him with their lives . . . and yet they could never, as he had said, never be made to understand him" (*LJ*, 299). Jim's intransigence thus comments ironically on the novel's epigraph, from Novalis: "It is certain my Conviction gains infinitely, the moment another soul will believe in it" (*LJ*, 1).

Astute as they are, Marlow's attempts to understand Jim do fall short in his own estimation. Marlow famously sprinkles his narrative with regrets that his subject's inner life remains "veiled," a "vast enigma" (*LJ*, 245). These regrets resonate suggestively with Jim's masochistic despair about interpersonal recognition, especially because Marlow actually manages to convey his subject's emotional complexity quite well. Many critics have been puzzled by what, exactly, Marlow does not think he understands about Jim.[39] To some degree, Marlow's bewilderment betrays the sense of inadequate empathy Jim rigorously imposes on others as the mark of his wounded self-love.

Whether interpersonal understanding is impossible to achieve or impossible to accept because it diminishes grandiosity, its absence often becomes the source of great suffering among Conrad's protagonists. The protracted breakdowns of Almayer, Willems, and others dramatize Conrad's own horrified fascination with failures of empathy. The extravagance of his prose suggests the enormity of the pain he associated, for example, with Aïssa's disappointed hopes for human connection:

> Her hands slipped slowly off Lingard's shoulders and her arms fell by her side, listless, discouraged, as if to her—to her, the savage, violent, and ignorant creature—had been revealed clearly in that moment the tremendous fact of our isolation, of the loneliness impenetrable and transparent, elusive

---

[39] See, for example, Van Ghent's comments, p. 68; or Najder, *Conrad in Perspective*, p. 82.

and everlasting; of the indestructible loneliness that surrounds, envelops, clothes every human soul from the cradle to the grave, and, perhaps, beyond. (*OI*, 192)

Tellingly, Conrad's novels dwell with considerable empathy on characters who fail to attain it in their own lives.

Conrad regarded the absence of empathy as a generalized colonial crisis, not just a private one. His strongest objections to imperialism often targeted the unempathic detachment of colonizers from the communities they controlled. His criticism of Dutch imperialism in Borneo returned repeatedly to his charge that the Dutch had no ties to local affairs, and his revulsion from the dehumanization of Africans in the Belgian Congo is legendary.[40] As some readers have pointed out, too, the misogyny of Conrad's male characters often emanates from their sense of exclusion from the emotional solidarity of women.[41] Failures of interpersonal recognition thus shape Conrad's diagnosis of social dysfunction in both sexual and imperial terms.

Conversely, as many have noted, the most prized values in Conrad's world include trust, fidelity, and understanding. In "A Familiar Preface" (1912), he famously claimed: "Those who read me know my conviction that the world, the temporal world, rests on a few very simple ideas; so simple that they must be as old as the hills. It rests notably, amongst others, on the idea of Fidelity" (*PR*, xxi). Not surprisingly, then, Jim's redemption hinges on winning the faith of his people. His sense that in all the houses of Patusan "there's not one where I am not trusted" (*LJ*, 180) allows him to say: "Well, I am all right anyhow." By contrast, Conrad's deepest feelings of shame and disappointment often revolved around his own failures to achieve interpersonal connection: "There can be nothing more humiliating than to see the shaft of one's emotion miss the mark of either laughter or tears. Nothing more humiliating!" (*PR*, xviii). His prefaces consistently stressed his desire to make himself understood and his horror of failing to do so.

No matter how much he valued it, however, Conrad saw interpersonal recognition as a hopelessly compromised ideal. He expressed this conviction obliquely in *The Rescue* through Lingard's dependence on a personified object—his ship: "He was aware that his little vessel could give him something not to be had from anybody or anything in the world; something specially his own. . . . His will was its will, his thought was its impulse, his breath was the breath of its existence" (*R*, 11). These ideals

---

[40] See Avrom Fleishman, *Conrad's Politics: Community and Anarchy in the Fiction of Joseph Conrad* (Baltimore: Johns Hopkins University Press, 1967), pp. 84, 89.

[41] Paul Armstrong, "Misogyny and the Ethics of Reading: The Problem of Conrad's *Chance*," *Contexts for Conrad*, ed. Keith Carabine et al. (New York: Columbia University Press, 1993), pp. 167–68.

of perfect reciprocity, of course, announce the narcissism that naggingly contaminates desires for sympathetic understanding. For Lingard, as for many of Conrad's characters, the quest for interpersonal recognition is often indistinguishable from desires for omnipotent control. Still, Conrad believed, like Lingard, that the desire for recognition could only be gratified in nonhuman or impersonal relationships. He had an especially powerful fondness for the kind of bond Lingard affirms between seamen and their ships. He presented some of these ideals parodically—in particular, his frequently expressed conviction that ships are "faithful."[42] But in *The Mirror of the Sea* (1906), he idealized the relationship of seamen to ships by unself-critically repeating Lingard's narcissistic identification: "There are ships that, for the right man, will do anything but speak" (*MS*, 92). In contrast to Lingard's self-aggrandizing delusions, however, Conrad most often idealized his relationship to ships by emphasizing his self-abnegating submission. In particular, self-sacrifice pervades his elision of seamanship with artistry: "To forget one's self, to surrender all personal feeling in the service of that fine art, is the only way for a seaman to accomplish the faithful discharge of his trust" (*MS*, 46).

Conrad's difficulties prying interpersonal recognition free from the problematics of narcissism compelled him to idealize it in the nonhuman relationships of seamen to their ships and artists to their craft. He distanced these idealizations further by embedding them in his more exoticizing representations of Malayan culture. One of the starkest contrasts between Malayans and Europeans, in Conrad's early work, involves the greater availability of understanding, trust, and loyalty among the former. Lingard, troubled by his dealings with dishonest Europeans, adopts Hassim's cause because he admires the extraordinary trustfulness of Malayans: "What appealed to him most was the silent, the complete, unquestioning, and apparently uncurious, trust of these people. They came away from death straight into his arms as it were, and remained in them passive as though there had been no such thing as doubt or hope or desire" (*R*, 88). Jaffir, Hassim's messenger, strikes him particularly as "faithful above all others" (*R*, 87). Similarly, Whalley's deception in "The End of the Tether" depends on his trust in his "faithful Serang" (*Y*, 152), a Malayan. Of course, Conrad's Malayans are no strangers to intrigue and betrayal. These exaggerated images of Malayan trust also point to the ways white characters incorporate natives into their own narcissistic needs. Nevertheless, Conrad strikingly banished the achievement of interpersonal recognition from his European characters, relegating it instead either to the realm of impersonal craftsmanship or to racial otherness.

---

[42] Joseph Conrad, *The Mirror of the Sea* (New York: Harper & Bros., 1906), p. 111. Hereafter cited as *MS*.

Symptomatically, the most exemplary romance in Conrad's early fiction joins the half-caste Nina with the Bali-born Dain Maroola. Although critics have sometimes doubted the genuineness of their love, Conrad took pains to dramatize "the subtle breath of mutual understanding" (*AF*, 51) between the two characters.[43] Nina senses "her identity with [Maroola's] being" (*AF*, 51), and Maroola surrenders himself wholly to "their world, filled with their intense and all-absorbing love" (*AF*, 55). He declares: "I breathe with your breath, I see with your eyes, I think with your mind, and I take you into my heart for ever" (*AF*, 140). No other romance in Conrad's fiction rivals the mutual empathy of these characters. Despite Mrs. Almayer's cynical (and unconfirmed) prediction that this reciprocity will eventually fade, Maroola's and Nina's mutual trust transcends the stereotypes of imperial romance by enabling them to become active agents of their own fates—even if their agency consists chiefly in their departure from the world of the novel.

Alone among Conrad's lovers, Maroola and Nina accept their differences from one another—those of personal temperament and those inscribed in sexuality and culture. Nina's love survives her estrangement when Maroola compares her (prisoner of sexual stereotypes that he partially remains) to the treacherousness of the sea: "No two beings could be closer to each other, yet she guessed rather than understood the meaning of his last words that came out after a slight hesitation in a faint murmur, dying out imperceptibly into a profound and significant silence: 'The sea, O Nina, is like a woman's heart'" (*AF*, 137). Maroola's and Nina's love tolerates the potential discord contrary perceptions such as these imply. Similarly, when Nina cries over her parting from Almayer, we are told:

> These tears and this sorrow were for him a profound and disquieting mystery. Now, when the danger was past, why should she grieve? He doubted her love no more than he would have doubted the fact of his own existence, but as he lay looking ardently in her face, watching her tears, her parted lips, her very breath, he was uneasily conscious of something in her he could not understand. . . . No desire, no longing, no effort of will or length of life could destroy this vague feeling of their difference. With awe but also with great pride he concluded that it was her own incomparable perfection. She was his, and yet she was like a woman from another world. (*AF*, 148)

Poised between comprehension and incomprehension, Nina's and Maroola's love tolerantly absorbs such moments of imperfect understanding.

---

[43] Many critics have claimed that cross-cultural fantasies distort the lovers' perceptions of each other. See, for example, Jacques Berthoud, *Joseph Conrad: The Major Phase* (Cambridge: Cambridge University Press, 1978), p. xxiii. Those who disagree include Roussel, pp. 39–42; and Hampson, *Cross-Cultural*, pp. 106–7.

This Malayan romance contrasts starkly with cross-racial passions like that of Willems and Aïssa, which is undone by failures of reciprocal understanding. The racial gulf between these two characters, as well as Willems's tendency to view Aïssa as the incarnation of dangerous eastern sexuality, deepen their more general failures of mutual comprehension.[44] Aïssa "looked at him with her big sombre eyes, in which there was no responsive light. His thought was so remote from her understanding" (*OI*, 109). Likewise, Willems complains to Lingard: "You can't believe her. You can't believe any woman. Who can tell what's inside their heads? No one. You can know nothing" (*OI*, 207). The cross-racial romance of Jim and Jewel also ends in Jim's remaining "even for her who loved him best a cruel and insoluble mystery" (*LJ*, 288).

Similarly, the two white lovers Lingard and Edith Travers fail to negotiate problems of mutual recognition, even though at times they achieve euphoric intimacy. When challenged by Carter that she does not really know Lingard, Edith answers: "I do know him. . . . There is not, I verily believe, a single thought or act of his life that I don't know" (*R*, 236); Lingard murmurs in response: "It's true—it's true." Nevertheless, the novel's catastrophic climax results from several profound failures of trust between the two lovers, the most important being Edith's refusal to deliver Hassim's ring, which prevents Lingard from answering his friend's appeal for help. Throughout the novel, Lingard and Edith oscillate between faith in one another and utter lack of sympathy. Trying to communicate his past to her, Lingard laments: "And now I've told you, and you don't know. That's how it is between us. You talk to me—I talk to you—and we don't know" (*R*, 218–19). Or again, he tells her: "What is all this to you? I believe that you don't care anything about what I feel, about what I do and how I end" (*R*, 324–25).

In Conrad's early fiction, only the Malayan love of Nina and Maroola preserves emotional reciprocity. But while the greater trust Conrad patronizingly imagined to prevail among Malayans points up the emotional poverty of white culture, even these nonwhite figures mix intersubjective recognition with the inevitabilities of narcissistic excess. Maroola and Nina hardly lack omnipotent delusions. Nina sees in him "the ideal Malay chief of her mother's tradition" (*AF*, 51), and she embraces her mother's fantasy that Maroola will avenge their race. She also derives a sense of power from her desire to mold "a god from the clay at her feet," a desire the narrator attributes to "the sublime vanity of her kind" (*AF*, 136). On his side, Maroola feels himself "to be the equal of the gods" (*AF*, 58) because he idealizes Nina's love, imagining her to possess "the wisdom of

---

[44] On Conrad's exoticization of Aïssa, see Rebecca Stott, *The Fabrication of the Late-Victorian Femme Fatale: The Kiss of Death* (London: Macmillan, 1992), p. 128.

perfect beings" (*AF*, 148). These elements of omnipotent fantasy sustain the sadomasochistic overtones pervading their relationship. Maroola is "carried away helpless" (*AF*, 55) by a love "far more tormenting than the sharpest pain" (*AF*, 66), and Nina feels that the "man was her slave" (*AF*, 135–36). Yet Maroola also displays a "quiet masterfulness it was [Nina's] delight to obey" (*AF*, 52). At one point Nina offers herself up to be killed for Maroola's sake, appealing to him as "your slave" (*AF*, 143). These power differentials between the two lovers help explain Nina's declaration: "No two human beings understand each other. They can understand but their own voices" (*AF*, 141). Yet bitter comments like these do not dispel the reciprocity of their love. They point instead to Conrad's unwillingness to conceive interpersonal recognition as ever completely beyond the problematics of empathy—except, as we will see later, in the collectivized professional culture of mariners and artists.

With more destructive results, Lingard's excessive narcissism undermines his reverence for trust. Self-righteously arrogant, he blandly expects others to trust him so that he can manipulate them. After soliciting Edith's faith in his good intentions, he asks her to trick her husband: "What Machiavellism!" (*R*, 160), she exclaims. He also expects others to trust him so perfectly that he need never explain his actions. His assumption that others will fuse their thoughts and wills with his own (like the fusion he believes he has with his ship) is precisely what causes his fatal mistakes. Failing to explain the political conflicts at the Shore of Refuge results in Carter's untimely attack on the Malayan pirates; failing to explain their danger to the gentry aboard the yacht results in their kidnapping; and failing to explain his relationship to Jörgenson causes Edith mistrustfully to conceal Hassim's ring, the token of his cryptic message for help.

Ironically, when Lingard does achieve unqualified trust, it swamps his capacity to act. His exalted sense of the "indestructible—and, perhaps, immortal!" (*R*, 432) bond between himself and Edith immobilizes him: "He tried to regain possession of himself, his old self which had things to do, words to speak as well as to hear. But it was too difficult." That interpersonal recognition, when it does come, should be disempowering, suggests the omnipotent qualities with which Lingard invests it. Only an omnipotent idealization of love could make it so devastating a threat to self-sufficiency—the reverse side of the annihilating power Lingard associates with the hatred of his enemies.

Conrad's sense of the inextricability of masochistic omnipotence from empathy was more than an insight about human psychology. It had profound consequences for his political vision. The ideals of trust, honor, and fidelity that anchored his belief in certain forms of social authority—especially professional authority—remained complexly implicated in the logic of masochistic fantasy. In particular, his conviction that interpersonal recognition could never free itself of narcissistic excess—a greater problem among his European characters than among his Malayans but an inescapable difficulty for all—energized his affirmation of professional solidarity, which promised collective solutions to this dilemma. Nevertheless, the close ties between interpersonal empathy and masochistic fantasy demanded that Conrad's professionals manage the problematics of masochistic fantasy rather than simply try to escape them. This project lay behind Conrad's rewriting of professional ideology. The differentiated networks of masochistic fantasy and omnipotent narcissism I have traced in the first half of this chapter enabled Conrad to legitimate the authority of imperial professionals by contrasting their ability to manage these psychosocial energies with the failure of discredited imperial classes to do likewise.

Class Magic and Class Melancholia

Until the last two decades of the twentieth century, critics routinely claimed that Conrad minimized social identity, stripping his characters of ideological markings in order to explore problems of pure being, ethics, or aesthetic form. While recent criticism has rightly insisted on his work's social embeddedness, Conrad did explore the abridgement of social identity in one important sense. Like most late-century novelists of empire, he found the fluidity of colonial life an opportunity for radically reconceiving the terms of social hierarchy.[45] Masochistic fantasy facilitated his efforts both to articulate and to control that transformation.

Conrad's ideological rewritings tapped into masochistic fantasy in two diametrically opposed ways. On the one hand, he indulged the fantasy—shared by many of his characters—that social identities could be willfully remade on colonial terrain. Such remaking was often a matter of private self-fashioning, but it could also involve symbolic processes, such as the resurrection of antiquated class ideals or the grafting of unlikely social ideologies onto one another. In addition, it could shore up Conrad's interpersonal ideals—recognition, empathy, trust, and fidelity—through mechanisms of collective identity formation. On the other hand, though, Conrad portrayed radical transformations of social identity (personal or collective) as illusions that must be strenuously critiqued. He redeemed this ambivalent view of social metamorphosis, finally, only in the masochistic self-consciousness of imperial professionals.

---

[45] A useful account is Scott A. Cohen, " 'Get Out!': Empire Migration and Human Traffic in *Lord Jim*," *Novel* 36 (2003), 374–97.

To grasp these relationships among masochistic fantasy, self-fashioning, and class ideology, we must first return to the omnipotent fantasy, indulged by some of Conrad's protagonists, that social boundaries can be wholly dissolved. Conrad's imperial dreamers often aspire not just to social mobility but to a conquest over the limitations of social classification itself. Lingard rises out of the confused crowd of "pedlars," "gentlemen," and "seamen" in Macassar to become "the acknowledged king of them all" (*AF*, 6). As the Rajah Laut, the King of the Sea, he holds a semimythical royal status. As if this were not enough, he is also, by turns, an explorer, a trader, a mariner with working-class origins, and a colonial adventurer one step removed from a pirate. Edith testifies to the profound disruption of social categories Lingard represents, dismissing d'Alcacer's suggestion that she ought to understand him because he "is *your* countryman after all" (*R*, 149); Edith counters: "I can not—what shall I say?—imagine him at all. He has nothing in common with the mankind I know." D'Alcacer himself comes to view Lingard as having "the distinction of being nothing of a type" (*R*, 309), since Lingard's judgment appears "altogether independent of class feeling." Lingard's boundary-breaking abilities evaporate when Europe swallows him up on his return there, as if to emphasize their availability only at the imperial periphery: "Fancy a man like Captain Lingard disappearing as though he had been a common coolie" (*OI*, 277), Almayer muses.

Jim, an English gentleman by birth, similarly explodes social categories when he becomes, first, a water-clerk and shipping agent, and then the virtual king of Patusan. Not simply a businessman, Stein is by turns a gentleman-scientist, a soldier of fortune, an explorer, and an adventurer. Even less resourceful colonists like Almayer and Willems dream of bursting the bounds of social classification. Almayer imagines a future that "gleamed like a fairy palace" (*AF*, 9), in which he "would pass the evening of his days in inexpressible splendour." Although Almayer's dreams may seem the generic stuff of colonial romance, Conrad authenticated the wish to transcend social classification by extending the social base of those characters to whom such a wish appealed. His traders and clerks predictably dream of the magical transformation of their social identities, but so does a former "fisher-boy" (*OI*, 196) like Lingard or, at the other end of the social scale, "gentlemen for whom that kind of life had a charm" (*AF*, 6). Not entirely a masculine preserve, either, social boundary breaking sometimes engages Conrad's colonial women. Martin Travers, scandalized by his wife's behavior, tells her: "It's my belief, Edith, that if you had been a man you would have led a most irregular life. You would have been a frank adventurer" (*R*, 268).

Conrad's willingness to portray Malayan as well as white self-fashioning in fantastic terms also indicates how deeply he shared the omnipotent dream of annihilating social classification. Although recent scholars have tried to avoid critical Eurocentrism by attending to the cross-cultural voices in his texts, Conrad always filtered his native characters' social identities through European class categories and concerns. None of his class-coded perspectives on Malayan society find the slightest resonance, for example, in either Wallace's *The Malay Archipelago* (1869) or John Frederick McNair's *Perak and the Malays* (1878)—the two most important of the "dull, wise books" (*Letters*, 2:130) Conrad consulted about native culture.[46] They reflect instead his preoccupation with western conceptions of status hierarchy as well as his own fantasies about social fluidity. A vital sign of Conrad's own imperial phantasmagorics is that his Malayans—like his Europeans—remake themselves spectacularly in unfamiliar colonial locales.

Babalatchi, the former Sulu pirate; Abdulla, the Arab trader from Penang; Dain Maroola, the Bali-born Hindu Brahmin; Mrs. Almayer, the daughter of Sulu pirates; Mrs. Willems, an immigrant from Sirani; Doramin, a Bugis immigrant from Celebes; Hassim and Immada, refugees from the Wajo states; Karain, "an outcast, a ruler" of a "wandering Bugis" (*TU*, 9) tribe—all reinvent themselves in new and open-ended social circumstances. The real fluidity of Malayan social relations—an effect of nineteenth-century colonial disruptions—underlie, to some extent, these images of native self-fashioning. But Conrad's narratives dwell on the outlandish successes of characters whose ascendancy surpasses all reasonable expectation rather than the more modest, scrupulously observed processes of social hybridization documented, for example, in Stevenson's South Seas fiction. Lakamba and Babalatchi, both former pirates and "Bohemians of their race" (*OI*, 41), make themselves over with astonishing agility: Babalatchi develops into a "statesman" (*OI*, 166), while Lakamba becomes a "half-cultivator, half-trader" and even "declared himself to be . . . of a princely family" (*OI*, 41). The trader Doramin rises to such power he dreams of a royal lineage for his son. Nina, contemptuous of both the white world where she was educated and the native village of her birth, becomes the consort of a would-be Malayan Rajah. For these characters, social self-reinvention seems magically wide open.

Conrad's most provocative explorations of colonial social fluidity extend beyond the fates of individuals, however, and encompass ideological transformations. The hybridized gentleman-trader figure, for example, represents one of his most important ideological grafts, since such figures play

---

[46] On some of Conrad's distortions of figures described in Wallace and McNair, see Norman Sherry, *Conrad's Eastern World* (London: Cambridge University Press, 1966), pp. 139–63.

a dominant role throughout his Malayan fiction. Both a successful trades-
man and a would-be gentleman, Lingard splices traditional aristocratic
codes of honor with non-class-specific ideals of trust, loyalty, and fidelity.
Similarly, Marlow's faithful friend Stein is a "wealthy and respected merchant" (*LJ*, 146) as well as the knightly ally of a Malayan chief: "They
both became the heroes of innumerable exploits; they had wonderful adventures" (*LJ*, 149).

The gentleman-trader figure was a common one in British adventure
fiction.[47] But Conrad celebrated this figure as a class ideal rather than a
strictly imperial one—so much so that he deployed it even among his favored Malayan protagonists. The narrator of *The Rescue*, describing the
Wajo tribe, tells us that "with those people trading, which means also
traveling afar, is a romantic and an honourable occupation" (*R*, 67). Thus,
Hassim is both a noble-born warrior and a great trader. Maroola, too, is
both a trader and a "great Rajah" (*AF*, 53), one of "the better class Malays" (*AF*, 42). A Hindu Brahmin, Maroola seems "so unlike in appearance
to the rare specimens of traders [Nina] had seen before" (*AF*, 44). Karain
is the son of a Bugis queen and a "rich trader" (*TU*, 13). Doramin combines the power of trade with social majesty: while "only of the *nakhoda*
or merchant class" (*LJ*, 187), he becomes the "chief of the second power
in Patusan," as well as being personally "imposing, monumental" (*LJ*,
189), and "majestic" (*LJ*, 190). In contrast to his trading competitor,
Rajah Allang, whose "idea of trading was indistinguishable from the com-
monest forms of robbery" (*LJ*, 187), Doramin represents the fusion of
commercial prosperity with noblesse oblige.

Although he recognized the mythical character of the hybrid gentleman-trader figure, Conrad promoted its ubiquity to highlight the liabili-
ties of more fixed and unitary social identities. In European and Malayan
cultures alike, he opposed the gentleman-trader both to rising commercial
classes and to established upper-class elites. He did so by systematically
upholding differences between the forms of omnipotent fantasy he affiliated with these social classes. The gentleman-trader mobilizes relatively
benign forms of omnipotence, in which individuals sublimate narcissistic
excess by imagining themselves as rescuers or idealizing their own and
others' faithfulness. But vilified social classes routinely draw on aggressive
or malevolent forms of omnipotent fantasy.

Conrad identified commercial classes, for example, with sadistic, oedipalized fantasy. Abdulla's megalomania revolves around his lust to destroy
Lingard's business; Willems and Almayer dream of wealth in hopes of
avenging themselves on their masters and their enemies; most notably,

---

[47] See Dryden's discussion of the imperial romance tradition's tendency to identify both
naval and merchant heroes as gentlemen, pp. 16–34.

Kurtz makes sadism and commercial efficiency indistinguishable. Significantly, Conrad represented commercial forms of sadistic omnipotence as threats to interpersonal ideals, particularly fidelity and trust. Almayer has outright contempt for what he calls "scruples" (*AF*, 109) and tells insidious lies, like his deceitful pledge that he will reunite Mrs. Willems with her husband, a pledge he makes on "my word of honour" (*OI*, 239). Willems's embezzlement proceeds from a systematic philosophy of commercial dishonesty: "He disapproved of the elementary dishonesty that dips the hand in the cash-box, but one could evade the laws and push the principles of trade to their furthest consequences. Some call that cheating. Those are the fools, the weak, the contemptible. The wise, the strong, the respected, have no scruples" (*OI*, 10). Willems learns this philosophy from Hudig, his employer, who engages in "the quiet deal in opium; the illegal traffic in gunpowder; the great affair of smuggled firearms, the difficult business of the Rajah of Goa." Conrad's bitter contempt for commercial dishonesty—indeed, for dishonesty of any kind—departed dramatically from Kipling's middle-class ethics, which celebrated the benevolent deceit of sophisticated experts.

The gentleman-trader Lingard abuses all tradesmen as cheats and liars: in trade, Lingard claims, a "man sees so much falsehood that he begins to lie to himself" (*OI*, 35). Similarly, Marlow disdains "the usual respectable thief of commerce you fellows ask to sit at your table" (*LJ*, 31). *Heart of Darkness* does not critique Belgian imperialism so much as bourgeois commerce, which values profit over the principled beliefs about labor, efficiency, and progress Marlow idealizes, and which encourages social climbers like Kurtz to rise to his Intended's rank by abrogating moral principles. In contrast to commercial ruthlessness, Lingard's imperialist prescriptions for Sambir, however paternalistic and vain, are "after all, not so very far wrong" (*OI*, 154). Readers eager to celebrate Conrad's selective critiques of imperialism often miss their class-bound character, not to mention the correlations they impose between specific social actors and variant forms of omnipotent fantasy. Conrad's contempt for the commercial lust of Almayer or Willems (or that of Marlow's employers in *Heart of Darkness*) must not blind us to his admiration for colonial gentleman-traders like Lingard or Stein.[48] Even the tawdry despair of characters like Almayer and Willems owes something to the petty-bourgeois hysteria—as well as the faithless dreams of narcissistic grandeur—that Conrad associated with the class of Flaubert's Emma Bovary, a figure they resemble both morally and emotionally. Such despair does not constitute a general

---

[48] White, for example, pp. 116–33, equates Almayer's and Lingard's failed promise, indecisiveness, greediness, vague expectations, and blindness to others. She claims that these parallels undermine the conventions of adventure fiction.

warning about the psychological costs of imperialism; it functions as a marker of social class.

At the other end of the social scale, Conrad affirmed the gentleman-trader over against what he portrayed as the solipsistic, preoedipal dreaming of the late-Victorian upper class.[49] Martin Travers most plainly exemplifies the self-absorbed careerism of this class, which is "devoted to extracting the greatest possible amount of personal advantage from human institutions" (*R*, 123). Lingard's resourcefulness points up, by contrast, how badly this self-adoring careerism can lose touch with reality. Ironically, Travers's blindness to political exigencies on the Shore of Refuge overwhelms even Lingard's abilities to ward off the novel's tragic ending.

Conrad's critique of Travers remains exceptional, however, since he usually gendered upper-class solipsistic dreaming as female. Ian Glenn has pointed out the class-specific anger characters like Lingard or Marlow direct against women, which targets the complacent illusions of upper-class figures while affirming the pragmatism and sagacity of other feminine types.[50] Lingard rebukes Edith, for example, while praising the Malayan princess Immada: "She knows war. Do you know anything about it? And hunger, too, and thirst, and unhappiness; things you have only heard about. She has been as near death as I am to you—and what is all that to any of you here?" (*R*, 141). Marlow's famous diatribes against women who are "out of touch with truth," and who live in "a world of their own" that is "too beautiful altogether" (*Y*, 59), as well as his refusal to shatter the self-flattering illusions of Kurtz's Intended, originate in his conviction that upper-class women never question their dreams of safety, control, and worthiness of love.[51] He even vents his generalized misogyny in *Chance* (1912) against women who have snubbed him. This misogyny contrasts with Conrad's respect, however condescending, for practical nonwhite women like Jewel and Nina, or for capable lower-class women like Lena in *Victory* (1915).

Conrad draped Malayan aristocratic ranks, too, in solipsistic narcissism. Belarub wishes "to preserve the mystery and the power of his melancholy hesitations" (*R*, 433). The Sultan of Batu Beru is "a restless and melancholy old ruler who had done with love and war" (*Y*, 246). These demoralized, older elites often make themselves dependent on powerful outsiders to shore up their authority. The Rajah Allang joins with the leader of the

---

[49] These dispositions are well known, apart from their relationship to masochistic fantasy. Fleishman, p. 157, for example, claims that Conrad felt an "inveterate hostility" toward two groups: "the old ruling class [and] the new, the bourgeoisie."

[50] Ian Glenn, "Conrad's *Heart of Darkness*: A Sociological Reading," *Literature and History* 13 (1987), 238–56. See esp. pp. 247–48.

[51] Joseph Conrad, *Heart of Darkness*, ed. Robert Kimbrough, p. 16.

Patusan tribesfolk Sherif Ali in a classic political alliance between a decadent old order and a discontented rabble; both the Rajah Patalolo and
Belarub maintain their tenuous grip on power only with Lingard's support. The next generation of Malayan aristocrats promises to deepen this
decadence: Syed Reshid vainly contemplates his "aristocratically small
hands" (*AF*, 35) while his uncle buys him a bride. In contrast, the beloved,
young, heroic Malayan ruler featured in "Karain" tragically evokes "by-
gone" (*TU*, 5) times.

The trajectory of colonial social change in Conrad's world reflects his
own phantasmagoric associations between social class and omnipotent fantasy. Conrad reduced the social landscape of Malaya largely to a sadomasochistic vision, in which bourgeois commercial figures cruelly prey upon
the wounded, self-effacing authority of gentleman-traders—a perspective
that would have been contradicted by his reading of Wallace, who repeatedly cited the stabilization and enrichment of native chiefs by trade.[52] Even
among Conrad's Malayans, an older order of idealistic patriarchs pros-
trates itself before a new class of native tradesmen who follow on the heels
of rapacious colonial commerce. Abdulla, Tengga, and Daman, greedy
traffickers in goods, imitate the pitilessness of the colonial traders who
have preceded them, which earns them Conrad's contempt. Tengga is "a
mere shopkeeper smitten by a desire to be a chief" (*R*, 294). "There is
nothing [Abdulla] would not buy, and there is nothing he would not sell"
(*AF*, 41), Almayer claims. Nina sees in white and native commercialism
alike "only the same manifestations . . . of sordid greed chasing the uncertain dollar in all its multifarious and vanishing shapes" (*AF*, 34).

In Conrad's mythologized view of colonial social relations, the gentleman-trader of all races fights a losing, dream-befogged battle against the
cruel rise of bourgeois imperialism. A consortium of Malayan and Arab
commercial forces, in temporary alliance with the white clerk Willems,
maliciously ruins Lingard; Stein, perhaps more prescient, withdraws into
his butterfly collection, having failed to sponsor Jim—a would-be gentleman-trader—as he had been sponsored by the patriarchal Scotsman who
first set him up in Celebes. Lingard's belatedness induces Edith's "vivid
dream," in which he appears "in chain-mail armour and vaguely recalling
a Crusader" (*R*, 458). D'Alcacer calls Lingard a "knight," a "descendant
of the immortal hidalgo errant upon the sea" (*R*, 142).

Nevertheless, the desire to graft archaic upper-class values onto more
viable social types continued to engage Conrad, for reasons that were overdetermined by the hybridized qualities of his own social identity. The Polish class from which Conrad emerged—a class in which gentleman-traders

---

[52] Wallace, pp. 263, 444. Wallace noted the disruptions caused by the English system of
trade (as opposed to the Dutch), but he consistently saw it as a civilizing force, an instrument
of peace and stability.

flourished—constituted one source of this engagement. As biographers have pointed out, the Polish nobility of Conrad's youth was exceptionally numerous and porous.[53] More than ten percent of the population, including professionals and wealthy businessmen, considered themselves equals of the nobility, forming a class called the *szlachta*. Adhering in principle to the nobility's chivalric values, the *szlachta* also espoused democratic ideals consistent with its insurrectionary goals—an unusual combination among European elites of the period. In addition, Conrad absorbed the chivalric codes of the high literary traditions with which he was familiar, through his reading of Homer, Shakespeare, Tasso, Mickiewicz, Cervantes, and de Vigny.[54] But these chivalric traditions also resonated with the "organicist" tendencies of the middle-class British writers he admired: Thomas Carlyle, Charles Dickens, and George Eliot, in particular. Most importantly, Conrad's idealization of chivalric codes of honor owed something to the gentrification of the late-nineteenth-century English middle class, which reached unprecedented heights during the two decades before World War I.[55] Conrad's attempts to live as an old-fashioned English country gentleman reflected a widespread social phenomenon at the fin de siècle; Peter Laslett claims that during this period "a third of the population was trying to live in a way that only a seventeenth of the population could live."[56]

These ideological concerns mediated Conrad's efforts to affirm a particular form of masochistic fantasy and to manage its dangers by identifying it with stable political values. Seeking to distance both sadism and preoedipal solipsism, Conrad exalted a chivalric spirit of self-sacrificing paternalism, which sublimated omnipotent mastery into "rescuer" roles—satirized yet affirmed through figures like Lingard, Marlow, Stein, Allistoun, and others. In addition, the warrior virtues central to Conrad's chivalric code drew on self-endangering or self-destructive forms of omnipotent fantasy that disavow sadism and vindictiveness. Chivalric codes routinely mask aggressive impulses in Conrad's work, for example, by representing "pure" adventure as a heroic, death-driven quest rather than an attempt to control others. Conrad sanctified these chivalrous sentiments in "Geography and Some Explorers" (1926) by emphasizing the heroic acceptance of death, suffering, and abuse they entailed:

[53] See Najder, *Joseph Conrad*, p. 3; or Harpham, pp. 25–27.

[54] Najder, *Conrad in Perspective*, p. 159, makes this point.

[55] Mark Girouard, *The Return to Camelot: Chivalry and the English Gentleman* (New Haven: Yale University Press, 1981), pp. 261–69. See also Robin Gilmour, *The Idea of the Gentleman in the Victorian Novel* (London: Allen & Unwin, 1981).

[56] Ford Madox Ford, *Joseph Conrad: A Personal Remembrance* (London: Duckworth, 1924), p. 57, wrote that Conrad's "ambition was to be taken for—to be!—an English country gentleman of the time of Lord Palmerston." Laslett's comments are quoted in Najder, *Joseph Conrad*, p. 314.

geography is the most blameless of sciences. Its fabulous phase never aimed at cheating simple mortals (who are a multitude) out of their peace of mind or their money. At the most it has enticed some of them away from their homes; to death may be, now and then to a little disputed glory, not seldom to contumely, never to high fortune.[57]

Similarly, according to the narrator of *The Rescue*, Lingard "recognized chivalrously the claims of the conquered"; like James Brooke, he is "a disinterested adventurer" (*R*, 4). Conrad portrayed Lingard as "visiting out-of-the-way places of that part of the world . . . not so much for profit as for the pleasure of finding them" (*OI*, 15).

Honor, the most combative virtue among Conrad's chivalric ideals, also required that its violent phantasmagoric potentials be sublimated, as we will see later in detail. Conradian honor did not entirely exclude the private, interpersonal standards of honesty that were a hallmark of nineteenth-century middle-class culture. But it called more directly on traditional upper-class warrior virtues, which emphasized the identity of public and private self-presentation, the value of one's public reputation, the willingness and ability to defend one's honor aggressively, the impractical prioritization of principles over results, and the identification of honor with masculinity.[58]

Conrad controlled the narcissistic and aggressive excesses of chivalric values by merging them with acceptable forms of masochistic fantasy. Chivalric valorizations of service, self-sacrifice, duty, indifference to suffering, and willingness to die for a just cause furnished Conrad with masochistic instruments for dissociating such values from both solipsism and vindictiveness. The long-standing affinities between chivalry and masochism could not have failed to strike someone with Conrad's Polish past. The poem his father composed to honor his birth, "To My Son Born in the 85th Year of Muscovite Oppression," suggests how indelibly this conjunction must have been impressed on him:

> Bless you, my little son:
> Be a *Pole*! Though foes
> May spread before you
> A web of happiness,
> Renounce it—love your poverty.
>
> . . .
>
> Baby son, tell yourself

---

[57] Joseph Conrad, "Geography and Some Explorers," *Last Essays* (Garden City, NY: Doubleday, Page, & Co., 1926), p. 3.

[58] Zdzislaw Najder, *Conrad in Perspective*, pp. 153–57, notes that although Conrad identified honor with nobility, he also saw it as a code of conduct transcending boundaries of birth or station.

> You are without land, without love,
> Without country, without people,
> While *Poland—your Mother* is entombed.[59]

Not surprisingly, Conrad's gentleman-traders maintain the omnipotent idealism of chivalry in unmistakably masochistic terms. Lingard's craze for exploration causes him to spend "all the profits of the legitimate trade on his mysterious journeys" (*AF*, 20). As we have seen, his notions of honor also compel him to serve or to rescue even those who would destroy him. Similarly, Jim's unquestioning faith in the pledge of Gentleman Brown results in the massacre that then causes his own death.

Jameson, among others, has disdained the "feudal" character of Conrad's chivalric values.[60] But Conrad's efforts to distinguish chivalric from other varieties of masochistic fantasy played a key role in his attempt to graft archaic upper-class social values onto viable contemporary discourses of social class. He sometimes went so far as to fuse chivalric principles with a gentrified version of colonial evangelicalism. Edith, for example, yearns for a self-sacrificing vocation with genteel evangelical overtones. The "romantic ideas" she entertained as a young girl compel her to imagine "a lifelong devotion to some unselfish ideal" (*R*, 151). She marries Martin Travers for some of the same reasons that Dorothea Brooke marries Edward Casaubon in George Eliot's *Middlemarch* (1872), hoping to realize her selfless ideals by supporting his work. Conrad established Lingard's would-be gentility, too, by blending his desire to be "pure in heart" (*OI*, 153) with his defense of manly honor. Not simply a distraction from *The Rescue*'s political concerns, as most critics have claimed, the spiritualized romance of Edith and Lingard attempts to graft chivalric ideals onto a union that transcends and rewrites class difference.

Conrad's interest in evangelical idealism, however, was faint, episodic, and semiparodic. He grafted masochistic chivalric ideals much more consistently onto his mariners' professional codes of conduct. This jointure depended on the radical form of social fluidity he imagined to exist on sailing ships, although his idealization of maritime egalitarianism exaggerated historical realities.[61] Conrad may have portrayed disorder on the *Narcissus* as a dangerous consequence of social equality: "Discipline is not ceremonious in merchant ships, where the sense of hierarchy is weak, and

---

[59] Najder, *Joseph Conrad*, pp. 11–12.

[60] Jameson, p. 217, declares that the feudal ideology of honor is irrelevant to capitalism, and that its appearance in Conrad "must mean *something else.*" Jameson's indifference to honor stems from his Lukácsean reading of reification, which minimizes class analysis.

[61] Conrad's aestheticized, moralistic vision of sailing ships has long been demystified. For a good critique, see Robert Foulke, "Life in the Dying World of Sail, 1870–1910," *Journal of British Studies* 3 (1963), 105–36.

where all feel themselves equal before the unconcerned immensity of the sea and the exacting appeal of the work" (*NN*, 9). But he also fancied that this weakened sense of hierarchy could facilitate dramatic refashionings of social identity. Noting Singleton's absorption in Edward Bulwer-Lytton's *Pelham* (1828)—a common craze among nineteenth-century seamen— the narrator puzzles over this "wonderful and bizarre phenomenon":

> What ideas do his polished and so curiously insincere sentences awaken in the simple minds of the big children who people those dark and wandering places of the earth? What meaning can their rough, inexperienced souls find in the elegant verbiage of his pages? What excitement?—what forgetfulness?—what appeasement? Mystery! (*NN*, 3)

This passage, as well as repeated discussions among the crew about what, precisely, defines a gentleman, suggests strange affinities between upper- and lower-class codes of conduct that only emerge on these "dark and wandering places of the earth." Indeed, at their best—both before being infected by the omnipotent narcissism of Donkin and Wait and after having outlasted it—the crew identifies with chivalric ideals modeled for them by their officers, particularly their "austere servitude of the sea" (*NN*, 6).

These conjunctions of lower- and upper-class codes of conduct cannot be dismissed simply as imperial propaganda (though they were certainly that). They also sustain Conrad's efforts to rewrite professional ideology through chivalric versions of masochistic fantasy. His nonfictional writings sometimes explicitly invoke the concept of honorable labor to melt distinctions between masters and laboring seamen. In *The Mirror of the Sea*, he described yacht racing as both the pastime of the "wealthy" and "for a great number of people . . . a means of livelihood . . . an industry" (*MS*, 36). This conjunction, he maintained, points to a "moral side of [the] industry" (*MS*, 36), which he located in the craftsman-like skills that all seamen share:

> Such skill, the skill of technique, is more than honesty; it is something wider, embracing honesty and grace and rule in an elevated and clear sentiment, not altogether utilitarian, which may be called the honor of labor. It is made up of accumulated tradition, kept alive by individual pride, rendered exact by professional opinion, and, like the higher arts, it is spurred on and sustained by discriminating praise. (*MS*, 37)

Conrad idealized the work ethic, in part, to affiliate officers and men in the cross-class "brotherhood of the sea" (*NN*, 18). Largely through their commitment to chivalric ideals of service, fidelity, and "the honor of labor," the crewmen of the *Narcissus* heal social disorder by yoking lower- class solidarity to upper-class ideals.

In *The Nigger of the "Narcissus,"* Conrad candidly displayed this ideological graft's tenuousness. His laments about steam's eclipse of sailing ships also recognize that seamen's labor had become increasingly organized around industrial rather than paternalistic relations in the late nineteenth century. But Conrad drew on the magical social fluidities he imagined at sea to affirm a particular version of professionalism—one very different from Kipling's, with its fusion of lower-middle-class evangelical and upper-middle-class technocratic ideologies. This divergence suggests how contentious struggles over professional ideology could be during the late nineteenth century and how central a role masochistic fantasy played in competing evangelical, clerical, chivalric, and working-class appropriations of the professional ethos.

Of course, Conrad frequently acknowledged the belated character of chivalric values, including those held by seamen. Singleton complains that the "men who could understand his silence were gone . . . they had been men who knew toil, privation, violence, debauchery—but knew not fear . . . . It was a fate unique and their own; the capacity to bear it appeared to them the privilege of the chosen!" (*NN*, 15). Conrad's tragic descriptions of Malayan culture must be understood as part of this masochistic pathos. Maroola can only dream of overthrowing his white masters and reasserting his people's glorious past, whereas Nina passively imbibes her mother's "tales of the departed glories of the Rajahs" (*AF*, 35). Hassim is a "ruler without a country" (*R*, 445), and Babalatchi's diplomatic manipulations attenuate his own warfaring youth. Significantly, Lingard links himself to Malayan culture's fading nobility by supporting its aging rulers. Conrad's mythologized parallels between European and Malayan chivalric traditions reinforced his sense that upper-class ideals, to survive at all, must be fused with a more coherent class ideology, one that could preserve upper-class values against commercial imperialism while at the same time negotiating the psychosocial problems of masochistic omnipotence.

Conrad activated the redemptive potentials of masochistic fantasy most consistently through an antimodern rewriting of professionalism. In doing so, he articulated chivalric ideals together with forms of imperial and class ideology he unproblematically endorsed. Significantly, Conrad's nonwhite seamen do not exhibit professionalism as a privileged class marker, for they never elicit the respect and adulation he showered on their European counterparts. Conrad represented their moments of honorable behavior—like the steadfastness of the Malayan helmsmen aboard the *Patna* or the dutifulness of Marlow's African fireman in *Heart of Darkness*—as the effect of mechanical obedience, not inspired idealism. Only among white (and for the most part British) seamen did he hope to consolidate and sustain belated chivalric ideals and to escape his compulsively idealistic attacks on imperial idealism.

Professional Redemption

As Jameson has pointed out, professionals constituted the ruling class of British imperialism, or what he calls the "heroic bureaucracy of imperial capitalism which takes that lesser, but sometimes even more heroic, bureaucracy of the officers of the merchant fleet as a figure for itself."[62] When Conrad spoke glowingly of the confraternity of the sea, he thus affirmed a class ideology he regarded as identical with the best features of British imperialism. This class-coded endorsement of imperialism depended, however, on organizing professional ideology around honorific forms of masochistic fantasy, particularly those that sustained ideals of interpersonal recognition. By contrast, Conrad remained an unforgiving critic of class ideologies that he believed degraded the imperial project by disrupting its fragile psychosocial dynamics. The coherence of Conrad's political views can be fully appreciated only by analyzing these intersections among class, imperial ideology, and fantasy.

Conrad celebrated his mariners' chivalric professionalism by dramatizing how well they manage narcissistic omnipotence. He legitimated professional authority primarily by favoring benevolent forms of omnipotence among his mariners and distancing aggressive or sadistic ones. But these professional figures manage narcissistic excess in more subtle ways as well. For one thing, they sublimate solipsistic fantasies of omnipotent invulnerability into conventionalized professional courage. They also redeem masochistic suffering by transforming it into professional distinction. In addition, they check the potential excesses of omnipotent fantasy in several discrete ways: they displace omnipotent delusion into collective narcissism; they use suffering to regulate and correct their own grandiosity; and they embrace the illusoriness of professional ideals, proving their magical, indomitable resolution by surviving such demystification. In this section, I will take up in succession each of these psychosocial strategies for rewriting and affirming professional ideology.

Conradian professionalism manages omnipotent fantasy most plainly through its valorous conception of honor, in which courage, rather than technocratic skill or intellectual principle, provides the foundation for vocational self-esteem. As "one of us," Jim stands for "all the parentage of his kind" (*LJ*, 32), exemplifying an "inborn" and "unintellectual" virtue—"the instinct of courage." Marlow explains:

> I don't mean military courage, or civil courage, or any special kind of courage. I mean just that inborn ability to look temptations straight in the face—a readiness unintellectual enough, goodness knows, but without pose—a

[62] Jameson, p. 265.

power of resistance . . . to the strength of facts, to the contagion of example, to the solicitation of ideas. Hang ideas! They are tramps, vagabonds, knocking at the back-door of your mind, each taking a little of your substance, each carrying away some crumb of that belief in a few simple notions you must cling to if you want to live decently and would like to die easy! (*LJ*, 32)

Marlow's association of "ideas" with "vagabonds" and "tramps," and his reverence for "inborn" virtues, suggest the aristocratic lineage of courage. Conrad reinforced this chivalrous resonance by rooting courage in quixotic, potentially self-destructive illusions—"a power of resistance . . . to the strength of facts."

Nevertheless, Conradian professionalism always conventionalizes the chivalric code of courage. It never affiliates such courage with romantic individualism or with the desires for reciprocal intimacy his characters inevitably fail to gratify in any case. Thus, Jim escapes the solipsistic tendencies of his valorous dreams by submitting to social demands that render them impersonal. His declaration to Jewel—that "I should not be worth having" (*LJ*, 302) without honor—repeats the formula of the novel's unnamed French lieutenant, who declares private belief in one's courage illusory but public belief in it indispensable: "The honour . . . that is real— that is! And what life may be worth when . . . the honour is gone—*ah ça! par exemple*—I can offer no opinion" (*LJ*, 108). In effect, Jim transcends his grandiose private illusions by conforming to the terms of a grandiose public illusion, even if that choice literally results in his self-extinction.

Besides channeling chivalric illusions about courage into conventionalized honor, Conradian professionalism converts the suffering of sailors directly into masochistic glory. Conrad's penchant for regarding the sea as sadistic, for example, sanctified professional mariners by infusing their suffering with the sea's indomitability, which he elided with their own potentials for resistance, resurgence, or even resurrection. One particularly horrific storm plasters the crew of the *Narcissus* to the ship's masts "in attitudes of crucifixion" (*NN*, 34) before they answer the sea's ravages with a reemergent fortitude of their own. When he celebrated the virtues of sailing, in particular, Conrad portrayed it as noble service achieved through suffering, unlike steam's risk-free commercial vulgarity. Through this opposition, Conrad protested the tendency of steamship labor to undermine traditional hierarchical relations by creating a skilled laboring class that earned higher pay than its nominal "masters."[63] But he also used it to glorify the professional sailor's abjection before nature. In *An Outcast*

---

[63] See Lillian Nayder, "Sailing Ships and Steamers, Angels and Whores: History and Gender in Conrad's Maritime Fiction," *Iron Men, Wooden Women: Gender and Seafaring in the Atlantic World, 1700–1920*, ed. Margaret S. Creighton and Lisa Norling (Baltimore: Johns Hopkins University Press, 1996), pp. 189–203.

of the Islands, the narrator refers to the chivalrous "servants" and "devoted slaves" of sailing ships, who give their lives to that "beautiful and unscrupulous woman, the sea," a mistress "with cruel and promising eyes" who rewards them with a "boundless faith" (*OI*, 14) but also kills them capriciously. By contrast, modern steamships reverse this sadomasochistic script, tearing "down the veil of the terrible beauty in order that greedy and faithless landlubbers might pocket dividends," turning their sailors into "a calculating crowd of cold and exacting masters."

In "A Familiar Preface," Conrad wrote of sailors that "it is the capacity for suffering which makes men august in the eyes of men" (*PR*, 14). In " 'Well Done' " (1918), modulating the ideal of suffering into one of faithful service, he claimed that "the main characteristic of the British men spread all over the world, is not the spirit of adventure so much as the spirit of service."[64] Conrad often personified this masochistic indomitability through his descriptions of ships themselves. Although "devastated, battered and wounded," the *Narcissus* "drove foaming to the northward, as though inspired by the courage of a high endeavour" (*NN*, 57–58). In *The Mirror of the Sea*, he asserted that

> No seaman can look without compassion upon a disabled ship, but to look at a sailing-vessel with her lofty spars gone is to look upon a defeated but indomitable warrior. There is defiance in the remaining stumps of her masts, raised up like maimed limbs against the menacing scowl of a stormy sky; there is high courage in the upward sweep of her lines towards the bow; and as soon as, on a hastily rigged spar, a strip of canvas is shown to the wind to keep her head to sea, she faces the waves again with an unsubdued courage. (*MS*, 104–5)

Testimonials like these implicate Conrad unmistakably in the masochistic professional stoicism that haunted the British imperial adventure tradition.

In addition to these strategies for conventionalizing professional courage and suffering, Conrad represented chivalric professionalism as the deindividuation of heroism, which it fuses with fraternal solidarity. Marlow speaks of seamen as "an obscure body of men held together by a community of inglorious toil and by fidelity to a certain standard of conduct"; Jim's crime thus constitutes a "breach of faith with the community" (*LJ*, 37, 114). Marlow attends Jim's trial, in fact, to witness a restorative, communal spectacle of suffering, in which Jim will "squirm for the honour of the craft" (*LJ*, 34). Appropriately, Jim redeems himself from the scandal of his youth by enduring imprisonment, persecution, and ritualized

---

[64] Joseph Conrad, " 'Well Done,' " *Notes on Life and Letters* (1921; London: J. M. Dent, 1949), p. 189.

threats of death to reorder the native community in Patusan; Marlow argues that Jim attains the moral equivalent of professional solidarity by stabilizing this social order through suffering.[65] Although the "privileged man" (*LJ*, 246) who receives Marlow's written account protests that self-sacrifice is only honorable when offered "in the ranks" (*LJ*, 247), Marlow declares that Patusan's faith in Jim "made him in his own eyes the equal of the impeccable men who never fall out of the ranks" (*LJ*, 288). In more orthodox terms, Captain Allistoun restores social order on the *Narcissus* by modeling chivalrous self-denial for his crew: the value "of courage, of endurance, and of the unexpressed faith, of the unspoken loyalty that knits together a ship's company" (*NN*, 6). In contrast, Conrad posed the spectacular failures of gentleman-traders—such as Lingard or Stein, who both fail to hold communities together—against professional figures (whether in fact or in their own eyes) such as Allistoun and Jim.

A mutually masochistic relationship to the sea also binds Conrad's merchant seamen in solidarity with one another. Seamen on sailing vessels, in particular, form a tight-knit community because the "close dependence upon the very forces that, friendly to-day, without changing their nature, by the mere putting forth of their might, become dangerous to-morrow, make for that sense of fellowship which modern seamen, good men as they are, cannot hope to know" (*MS*, 119). For this reason, Wait's performative suffering is a poisonous aberration; even Donkin reprimands him: "Yer all for yerself" (*NN*, 68). Bonding with each other through shared suffering and victimization also facilitates a transhistorical sense of community among seamen, since, "brought into sympathy with the caravels of ancient time," they look upon ancient sailors as their "professional ancestors" (*MS*, 120).

Idealizing a similar fraternalism forged among sea captains through suffering, Conrad subtly reinforced organic hierarchies of authority within his supposedly egalitarian professional ranks. After taking command of his first ship, the narrator of *The Shadow-Line* stares into the captain's mirror, recognizing that the pain all sea captains must endure initiates him into that "composite soul, the soul of command" (*SL*, 53). Such fraternity deliriously mixes abjection with power: "'You, too!' it seemed to say, 'you, too, shall taste of that peace and that unrest in a searching intimacy with your own self—obscure as we were and as supreme in the face of all the winds and all the seas, in an immensity that receives no impress, preserves no memories, and keeps no reckoning of lives.'" This glorious composite

---

[65] Andrew Mozina, *Joseph Conrad and the Art of Sacrifice: The Evolution of the Scapegoat Theme in Joseph Conrad's Fiction* (New York: Routledge, 2001), regards Conradian martyrdom as a ritual of social formation but thereby overvalues the social stability achieved by the deaths of characters like Jim or Kurtz.

suffering convinces the narrator that he is "not exactly a lonely figure." The sadomasochistic bond forged between the beleaguered narrator of "The Secret Sharer" (1910) and his persecuted but murderous double, Leggatt, both of whom served on the same officer's training ship, also conjoins suffering with sea-captainly solidarity.

The volatility of the relationship between individual and collective dynamics of masochistic fantasy, which professionalism helps regulate, is nowhere more clear than in Brierly's suicide. As if following the steps of an official procedure, Brierly plots the ship's course, gives instructions to the ship's mate, writes to the owners, puts a drop of oil in the log, confines his dog to the chart room, and hangs his gold chronometer watch carefully from the taffrail before jumping over it. Besides the parodic code of professional conduct Brierly inaugurates, his suicide betrays his personal failure to ward off traumas to professional self-esteem and solidarity. Conrad thus dramatized the power of masochistic rituals either to bind groups together or to wrench individuals out of sympathy with them. In *The Nigger of the "Narcissus,"* Wait's histrionic suffering does both at the same time. Such ambivalence emphasized the necessity of harnessing these psychosocial energies in ritualized collective forms.

Within the community of seamen, suffering corrects professional conceit and therefore prevents perilous and abrupt demystifications, such as Brierly's. The crew of the *Narcissus*, for example, endures pain and suffering that successfully chastens its "conceited folly" (*NN*, 61). At one point, the narrator ascribes this corrective intentionality to the omnipotent sea itself:

> Through the perfect wisdom of its grace they are not permitted to meditate at ease upon the complicated and acrid savour of existence. They must without pause justify their life to the eternal pity that commands toil to be hard and unceasing, from sunrise to sunset, from sunset to sunrise; till the weary succession of nights and days . . . is redeemed at last by the vast silence of pain and labour. (*NN*, 55)

Conrad constantly emphasized the sea's salutary power to undo narcissistic illusion through its implacable cruelty. In *The Mirror of the Sea*, viewing a wreck provides "an extraordinarily destructive effect upon the illusion of tragic dignity our self-esteem had thrown over the contests of mankind with the sea." This spectacular shipwreck reinforces Conrad's horror of nature's sadistic power: "The cynical indifference of the sea to the merits of human suffering and courage, laid bare . . . revolted me." Yet, at the same time, the blow to his self-conceit admits him to the glamour of a shared professional identity: his "illusions were gone . . . . I had become a seaman at last" (*MS*, 238). When he drives his men despotically, Allistoun thus imitates the sea's "perfect wisdom," knowing that pain alone will deflate their dangerous narcissism: "Don't give the men time to feel themselves" (*NN*, 55), he urges his mate; "Mustn't stand. Won't do" (*NN*, 56). Choosing to "wait" invites narcissistic self-contemplation, a lesson Allistoun has internalized: when offered water, he refuses it "impatiently" (*NN*, 38); when tempted to rest, he "tore himself away from the delight of leaning against the binnacle" (*NN*, 56).

Conrad recognized full well that chivalric professional ideals evoked omnipotent delusion. Marlow proudly bares the illusions underlying his professional pride in his outbursts against Jim: "I was aggrieved against him, as though he had cheated me—me!—of a splendid opportunity to keep up the illusion of my beginnings, as though he had robbed our common life of the last spark of its glamour" (*LJ*, 96). Following the logic of masochistic fantasy, however, demystification often only deepens the glory of these mariners' perpetually wounded narcissism. Brierly's suicide, for example, dramatizes how chivalric professionalism can transform narcissistic disillusion into self-glorification. Brierly destroys himself because both personal and professional fantasies of omnipotence fail him. As he tells Marlow:

> Hang it, we must preserve professional decency or we become no better than so many tinkers going about loose. We are trusted. Do you understand?— trusted! . . . We aren't an organised body of men, and the only thing that holds us together is just the name for that kind of decency. Such an affair destroys one's confidence. A man may go pretty near through his whole sea-life without any call to show a stiff upper lip. But when the call comes . . . Aha! . . . If I . . . (*LJ*, 50)

Brierly's anxieties echo Allistoun's charge that his crew's dereliction of duty deprofessionalizes them, making them a "crazy crowd of tinkers! Yes, tinkers!" (*NN*, 78). But through the extraordinary excess of professional self-criticism it exemplifies, Brierly's suicide proves the fact that "there was not such another commander" (*LJ*, 43).

Nevertheless, Conrad exposed all professional ideals—including even that of freeing oneself from illusion—as illusory. He frankly declared the "common bond" (*NN*, 96) that the crew of the *Narcissus* constructs through the "latent egoism of tenderness to suffering" (*NN*, 85) to be "the strong, effective and respectable bond of a sentimental lie" (*NN*, 96). The crew's evaporation into the streets of London at the end of the novel poignantly dramatizes his recognition of this sentimental lie's insubstantiality. The solidarity of officers at sea also proves deceptive. After his reassuring meditations before the captain's mirror, the narrator of *The Shadow-Line* discovers that his predecessor, a sociopathic self-tormentor, had perpetrated the "betrayal of a tradition" (*SL*, 62) by trying to kill his entire crew, along with himself. As *The Nigger of the "Narcissus"* demonstrates, however, the "sentimental lie" of professional solidarity can fuel very different kinds of social action, depending on whether it is appropriated by antisocial narcissists like Wait and Donkin or professionals like Allistoun.

Conradian professionalism revolves around the clear-eyed acceptance of disillusionment, recuperating narcissistic wounding through its own omnipotent stoicism. Marlow, for example, does not imitate Brierly's suicidal response to narcissistic wounding. Nor does he follow Jim's elaborate quest to deny his weaknesses and remain in "a dream" (*LJ*, 154). Instead, he safely incorporates such trauma by mercilessly rubbing his listeners' noses in the universal human flaws Jim embodies: "Not one of us is safe," Marlow tells them, from "weakness unknown . . . weakness that may lie hidden, watched or unwatched, prayed against or manfully scorned, repressed or maybe ignored more than half a lifetime" (*LJ*, 32). In this way, Marlow incorporates the knowledge of human weakness into professional self-consciousness as yet one more salutary aspect of masochistic pain. At one point, he admits having "paraded [Jim] before you" (*LJ*, 163), acknowledging the self-serving function of his angst-ridden narrative. But Marlow's ritualistic incantation—that Jim is "one of us"—suggests, among other things, that the "fellowship of the craft" treasures the wound to its own narcissistic illusions Jim represents. Wearing his professional wounds on his body—his scarred hands and face—the French lieutenant models this combination of unqualified professional pride and courageous disillusionment. His "professional opinion on the case" (*LJ*, 107) recognizes that even if human frailty is universal, "you have got to live with that truth" because "the trade demands it" (*LJ*, 107). The masochistic paradox of professionalism ensures that only by embracing the painful knowledge of human weakness, while concealing such knowledge in yet another stoical act of solitary suffering, can professionals maintain omnipotent ideals of honor. By thus revealing the illusory qualities of his own most important professional ideals, Conrad inscribed masochistic fantasy directly into class identity.

In contrast to open-eyed professional self-wounding, Conrad represented the commercial middle class as systematically concealing its human frailties in the name of "efficiency" (*LJ*, 126). Speculating on how preferable Jim's dying might have been to the shameful ordeal of his trial, Marlow observes:

> To bury him would have been such an easy kindness! It would have been so much in accordance with the wisdom of life, which consists in putting out of sight all the reminders of our folly, of our weakness, of our mortality; all that makes against our efficiency—the memory of our failures, the hints of our undying fears, the bodies of our dead friends. (*LJ*, 126–27)

For this reason, commerce requires that one refrain from the excesses of omnipotent fantasy altogether: "I could be eloquent," Marlow declares, "were I not afraid you fellows had starved your imaginations to feed your bodies. I do not mean to be offensive; it is respectable to have no illusions—and safe—and profitable—and dull" (*LJ*, 164). Entrepreneurs who make the mistake of indulging their illusions suffer extermination in Conrad's work—Chester in *Lord Jim*, a foolhardy fortune hunter, whose guano island is ravaged by a hurricane; or Kurtz, who embodies commercial enterprise run amok.

On another social front, Conrad's work increasingly criticized the intellectual class's unmanaged masochistic omnipotence, a critique reflecting what Glenn describes as his "fairly typical conservative fear of deracinated intellectuals."[66] Stein, for example, fails to manage his narcissistic delusions through suffering. Motivated, in part, by the inassimilable pain of having lost his wife and child, Stein gratifies his solipsistic idealism through the nonhuman beauty of his butterflies: "On the bronze sheen of these frail wings, in the white tracings, in the gorgeous markings, he could see other things, an image of something as perishable and defying destruction as these delicate and lifeless tissues displaying a splendour unmarred by death" (*LJ*, 150). His fascination with both fragility and immortality suggests that, like Marlow, Stein relishes the tension between omnipotent fantasy and mortal weakness. But his withdrawal from life constitutes an enervated renunciation, a solitary retreat into a world of illusion meant to obliterate rather than to manage pain. This detachment renders him complicit in Jim's catastrophic end and reduces him to helpless befuddlement about its causes and meaning.

Stein anticipates a number of Conradian figures who exemplify the narcissistic dysfunctions of the intellectual class in a variety of sadomasochistic forms. An artist, a musician, a journalist, a political orator, and a writer of philosophical treatises, Kurtz incorporates all branches of intellectual life as targets of Conrad's critique. The Professor of *The Secret Agent* and the émigré intellectuals who persecute Razumov in *Under Western Eyes* share Kurtz's unmanaged sadomasochistic energies, as does the murderous captain of *The Shadow-Line*. A would-be "artist" (*SL*, 58), who serenades himself on the violin, the captain desires only to "cut adrift from everything" (*SL*, 62)—a masochistic recklessness that parallels the narrator's own rash endangering of his professional status at the novel's opening. This sociopathic figure stands in marked contrast to the novel's other, more protective captains, Giles and Ellis, a contrast that eventually induces the narrator to channel his youthful narcissism into paternalistic, self-effacing service.

---

[66] Glenn, p. 239.

Self-destructive grandiosity drives all of Conrad's intellectuals, yet none sublimates such grandiosity into a collective ethos or a masochistically ordered social community. Rather, these figures amplify the antisocial forms of masochistic omnipotence that, in Conrad's earlier work, characterize alienated figures like Almayer, Willems, Wait, and Donkin.

If not grotesquely malignant like Kurtz or the deceased captain of *The Shadow-Line*, Conrad's intellectuals manifest their unsublimated sadomasochism passively, like Stein. Van Wyk, in "The End of the Tether," who reads periodicals in three languages, plays the piano in the jungle, and practices a sophisticated skepticism, has "thrown away the promise of a brilliant career" (*Y*, 245) as a seaman for a genteel but embittered retirement. His self-wounding "retreat from his profession" (248), motivated by his narcissistic denial of the "many sorts of heartaches and troubles" that can "find a man out" (278), underlies his "seclusion from his kind" (246). This antisocial retreat—triggered, like Stein's, by the unendurable pain of losing a loved one—inevitably impairs his capacity for "sympathy," which he represses through "a sort of haughty, arbitrary indifference of manner" (248). Although Van Wyk does act "impulsively" (278) to silence Sterne, the *Sofala*'s chief mate, who threatens to betray Captain Whalley's blindness, this strategy protects Whalley insufficiently. Ironically, silencing Sterne only makes it easier for the *Sofala*'s owner to sabotage it, which costs Whalley his life. Like Stein, Van Wyk thus presides over the tragic demise of a story's protagonist, even helping indirectly to arrange it, like a negligent god. Stressing the point at which "Van Wyk's thought abandoned the *Sofala*" (279), the narrator highlights the limits of intellectual empathy.

Although he often vilified intellectuals, Conrad deployed among professional artists some of the same strategies his seamen use to manage masochistic fantasy. In the "Preface" to *The Nigger of the "Narcissus,"* Conrad allied masochistic solidarity at sea with the artist's dedication to craftsmanship. When the artist "descends within himself," into "that lonely region of stress and strife" (*NN*, 145), he returns with the "subtle but invincible conviction of solidarity that knits together the loneliness of innumerable hearts" (*NN*, 145–46). Conrad consistently suggested that dedication to craftsmanship, whether artistic or maritime, activates a professional masochism that checks narcissistic excess. Captain Whalley, who vows to "die in harness" (*Y*, 168) by sacrificing himself for his daughter, frees himself of egoism, for example, through dedication to his craft: "He talked well, without egotism, professionally" (253). Akin to "the special call of an art," sailing generates an agonized confrontation with "the incertitude which attends closely every artistic endeavour," an instability that provides "the artistic quality of a single-handed struggle with something much greater than yourself" (*MS*, 47–48). Conjoining artistry with the negotiation of omnipotent delusion, Conrad endowed the modern artist with a carefully ordered form of chivalrous masochism.[67]

Most of all, Conrad's intellectuals fail to recognize what artists presumably know too well: the inevitability of illusion in human life and the necessity of managing it.[68] "Ideas" in Conrad's fiction often lead only to grandiose fantasies—a formulation that encompasses Kurtz's sadistic idealism, on the one hand, and Stein's bittersweet butterfly collection, on the other.[69] Deeply convinced of the inescapability of omnipotent fantasy, Conrad placed his faith in carefully managed dreams rather than ideas— Marlow's "tramps" and "vagabonds." As he once wrote to Cunninghame Graham: "It is impossible to know anything tho' it is possible to believe a thing or two" (*Letters*, 1:370). Conradian professionalism therefore revolved not around intellectual systems but the preservation and management of narcissistic illusion. Indeed, his critiques of professional idealism maintain what Marlow calls "the fellowship of these illusions" (*LJ*, 94).

Of course, Conrad was himself a member of the intellectual class. His critique of intellectualism included, perversely, his own literary identity, as many readers have recognized, for example, in his exposure of Kurtz's powerful but deadly linguistic skills. Yet, in Conrad's work, there can be no more chivalric intellectual system than one prepared to parade before us its own susceptibility to delusion. Ultimately, the ideological work performed by this masochistic strategy promoted a conservative rather than an individualist vision of cultural authority, one that exalted a chivalrously detached form of professional and aesthetic class solidarity.

MASOCHISTIC IMPERIALISM

Conrad's attitudes toward empire tended consistently toward a conservative critique. He abhorred the middle-class commercialism driving late-nineteenth-century imperialism as well as the intellectual justifications of expansion that threatened his own cultural authority. But he retained a

[67] For an excellent discussion of Conrad's legitimation of the novelist's social authority relative to that of professionals, see Byron Caminero-Santangelo, "Story-Teller in the Body of a Seaman: Joseph Conrad and the Rise of the Professions," *Conradiana* 29 (1997), 193–204.

[68] The complexity of Conrad's faith in "illusion" has received extensive commentary. See, in particular, Martin Price, *Forms of Life: Character and Moral Imagination in the Novel* (New Haven: Yale University Press, 1983), pp. 327–28.

[69] Brian Artese, "'Speech Was of No Use': Conrad, a New Journalism, and the Critical Abjection of Testimony," *Novel* 36 (2003), 176–97, contends that Conrad's modernist narrative techniques challenged the epistemological hegemony of journalism and law, and that his convoluted perspectivism affirmed seaman-like knowledge instead.

deep nostalgia for the genteel professional values he believed the empire, as then constituted, jeopardized—psychological and social values he regarded as traditionally embedded in the imperial project.

Nevertheless, Conrad envisioned professionalism as crucially, self-consciously mythical. By associating it with loss, mourning, and nostalgia, he entwined it inextricably with masochistic fantasy. Alone among his fraternal auditors in fidelity to the fellowship of the craft, Marlow sometimes mocks his friends' opportunism. But this mockery also suggests Marlow's own belatedness, as well as Conrad's fear that late-nineteenth-century capitalism had irrevocably eroded professional moral and social authority. Yet Conrad did not simply blame the arrival of steam, the unionization of labor, the vulgarity of commerce, the emergence of corporate capitalism, or the ascendancy of new forms of intellectual authority for dooming the older codes of maritime honor Marlow eulogizes. The psychosocial distinctions that he insistently maintained—opposing sadism and solipsism; fraternal and solitary masochism; chivalric, commercial, and intellectual castes; unregulated narcissism and self-critical illusion—actively shored up professionalism's heroic aura of belatedness. They also provide the means of tracing its ideological work. Conrad celebrated a form of imperialism whose extravagantly idealized features could not possibly have been matched by colonial realities or by the complex transformations of social identity taking place in turn-of-the-century Britain. No matter. He affirmed this imperial ideal by glorifying the flaws at the heart of its psychosocial logic and the courage of a privileged community able to confront its own illusions without illusion.

Such a project could have had no appeal for the broad, middle-class, mostly jingoistic readership at the turn of the century that idolized middlebrow writers of adventure fiction like Kipling, H. Rider Haggard, or Arthur Conan Doyle. But it did capture the sentiments of a gentrified cultural elite that longed to see itself as both the traditional and the redemptive social force sustaining the empire. Professionalism, particularly when conceived as a discourse about imperialism, had not entirely shed its ideological roots in upper-class culture, even at the turn of the century. Critical studies of what Lauren Goodlad, echoing Matthew Arnold, has called a Victorian middle class "cut in two" by conflicts between its entrepreneurial and professional ideals need to recognize professionalism's residual affinities with upper-class values.[70] Conrad was instrumental in making this conservative version of professional ideology palatable to the

---

[70] Lauren Goodlad, "'A Middle Class Cut into Two': Historiography and Victorian National Character," *ELH* 67 (2000), 143–78.

patrician artistic and intellectual classes that formed the core of his reader-ship early in his career. Of course, he did not represent to them a psychoso-cial reality but a self-consciously mythologized fantasy, since there is no reason to believe professionals actually manage masochistic fantasy more effectively than do members of any other social group.

In this chapter, I have not proposed a radically new set of conclusions about Conrad's ideological loyalties. Other critics have diagnosed his legit-imation of imperial professionalism, even if that diagnosis has not com-manded universal assent. I have tried to bolster and particularize that po-litical interpretation by embedding it in Conradian psychosocial dynamics. I also hope to have clarified the psychological and affective power his myths of imperial professionalism mobilized through masochistic fantasy. In the process, I hope to have demonstrated how his class loyalties an-chored a coherent, multifaceted attitude toward imperial power. Conrad's ideological sympathies appear ambiguous only if we overlook these rela-tionships among imperialism, social class, and fantasy. I also hope to have shed some light on Conrad's famous inconsistencies and self-contradic-tions—aesthetic, ethical, and political. The convolutions of his work—whatever else their function may have been—sustained a class-specific en-dorsement of imperial ideals as well as a model of genteel professionalism that he identified closely with them.

CONCLUSION

IMPERIAL MASOCHISM emerged out of a nested set of ambitions: to demonstrate the continued relevance of psychoanalysis to historicism; to elucidate the role masochistic fantasy plays in identity formation well beyond the field of sexuality; to illuminate the social function of such fantasy in British culture, especially its organization of imperial and class ideology; and to provide an accurate understanding of the relationship between the psyche and the social in several influential writers of colonial fiction.

Crucial to these ambitions has been a conception of masochism derived from relational psychoanalysis, which emphasizes the role—both as origin and goal—of narcissistic fantasies of omnipotence. The relational paradigm assumes that any form of voluntary pain, suffering, or humiliation that sustains omnipotence may activate the transformational symbolic potentials of masochistic fantasy. This conception has made it possible to reexamine a form of experience generally regarded as a private sexual oddity and to construe it much more broadly as a vehicle for social action. I also hope it demonstrates that psychoanalytic theory did not abruptly end a half century ago, as one might conclude on reading much contemporary psychoanalytic literary criticism.

A critical tradition that might be called "masochism studies" has long been engaged in analyzing the politics of masochism. As I have suggested, though, the Freudian terms that tradition uses to define masochism, which it sees as a drama of sexualized domination and submission, obscure the more extensive political significance of fantasy structures that can mediate a great variety of social pressures. Such mediation links psychological dynamics to ideological processes of many different kinds, not just to those that represent the social order as a binary opposition of power and subjection.

I hope to have shown how this broadened conception of masochistic fantasy sheds new light on a host of seemingly unrelated or contradictory tendencies in British colonial texts. It explains, for example, how the disparate patterns of psychological obsession in Conrad's work—solipsistic self-love, vindictive rage, idealization of others, and megalomaniacal control—collaborate in a class-coded affirmation of imperial culture. It explains why

Schreiner's ethos of labor and self-sacrifice inspired a generation of militant suffragettes, how Stevenson's anti-imperialist activism redeemed his frustrations with middle-class culture, and by what means the virulent class warfare of Kipling's "magical groups" masqueraded as classlessness. It also explains the sadomasochistic dynamics that made magical groups paradigmatic of British imperial hierarchies of command.

As this synopsis indicates, the book also participates in efforts to recuperate for historicist studies both the category of social class (viewed as a symbolic medium rather than an economic or political category) and the domain of the psychological—two astonishingly undervalued objects of study in recent literary and cultural criticism. Perhaps because class is the most neglected social reference point in masochism studies, my focus on class generates the book's most polemical claims. None of these claims will compel universal assent, but they might suggest, in the aggregate, that attending to specific class codings of masochistic fantasy can dissolve perplexities that have bedeviled criticism: uncertainties about Conrad's stance on imperialism, the nature of Kipling's ambivalence toward social authority, the relationship between politics and aestheticism in Stevenson's work, or the relevance of Schreiner's self-martyring politics to postmodern feminism. They might also suggest that masochistic fantasy facilitated numerous discursive intersections in late-Victorian culture—not just those between ideologies of class and empire but also between those two ideological spheres and discourses about religion (particularly evangelicalism) and institutionalized knowledge (particularly professionalism).

Above all, attention to masochistic fantasy makes it clear that social class played a far more important role in the political rhetoric of colonial fiction than has yet been recognized. In many cases, I have not presented unfamiliar views of each writer's positions on either class or imperialism taken separately. Those positions have been described in so many different ways that the judicious critic is well advised not to strain at idiosyncratic interpretation. What I do hope to have formulated freshly, however, is the unique relationship each writer developed *between* the politics of class and that of imperialism. To this end, I have followed traces of masochistic fantasy to argue for particular, determinate interpretations of the ways thinking about empire drew on and revised thinking about social class, and vice versa.

While specifying the political work enabled by masochistic fantasy, I have also recognized its pliability in the hands of writers with distinctly different political agendas. The four writers studied in this book represent a spectrum of ideological strategies rather than a unified masochistic politics. Even the topical questions that preoccupied them—how to reconcile entrepreneurialism with bohemianism, spiritual fervor with technocratic enthusiasm, feminism with middle-class culture, and so forth—offered very different entry points into the tangled relationship between imperialism and social class. It should be no surprise that masochistic fantasy enabled Stevenson and Schreiner to yoke middle-class ideals to anti-imperialist crusades, while providing Kipling and Conrad with a contrary set of class-coded filters for colonial experience—jingoistic in Kipling's case, patrician and nostalgic in Conrad's. Stark as these writers' differences on imperialism may have been, their uses of colonial material to manipulate ideologies of class were even more divergent. Such dissimilarities help indicate that middle-class culture, although internally fractious throughout the nineteenth century, was riven by extremely sharp tensions and subgroup alliances during the period of late-Victorian imperial expansion. That social complexity makes the analysis of fantasy, viewed as a medium of collective identity formation, an important and intricate kind of work. Only by rejecting facile assumptions about class identity, not to mention peremptory disavowals of the concept itself, can that work proceed.

Masochistic fantasy is not specific to colonial fiction or to the intersection of imperial and class rhetoric. Neither does it have a special affinity for late-nineteenth-century culture. If the relational model of masochism resonates with fictional or nonfictional materials from other historical periods or cultures—and its relevance to an enormous range of nineteenth-century British phenomena, from the pained gospel of organicism in Thomas Carlyle or George Eliot to the melancholic late-century dystopias of George Gissing, Thomas Hardy, and H. G. Wells, should be obvious—then so much the better for its general viability as an instrument of analysis. But masochistic fantasy did have an especially powerful role to play in late-Victorian colonial fiction because of the long traditions of masochistic representation that dominated British perspectives on both imperialism and social class. These traditions mixed in strikingly productive ways, as I have tried to demonstrate, when the colonial arena became the subject of serious middle-class fiction.

Besides these specific critical goals, there is always a metacritical yield to the analysis of masochistic fantasy. One cannot study this material, for example, without entertaining the proposition that political idealism always draws on what is usually thought of as perversity. That hypothesis can have a salutary, self-critical effect on those who practice radical politics. Conversely, it can unmask the irrationality of those who claim to be clearsighted instrumentalists. In the current geopolitical moment, it can also help us understand aggressive forms of self-immolation too easily dismissed as "barbarism" when they appear in nonwestern cultures. On a very different scale, there are formal payoffs to studying masochistic fantasy: a new understanding of doubling in Stevenson, of self-consuming narrative energies in Conrad, of the parable or "dream" as a narrative device in Schreiner, or of ambiguous diegetic involvement on the part of Kipling's narrator.

Perhaps the most important metacritical effect of studying masochistic fantasy is that it makes one an enemy of simplicity. On the one hand, it encourages suspicion of either/or arguments about a given work's political orientation, and it demands attention to writers who tend to contest themselves, a habit that inevitably results in their being the object of critical disagreement. On the other hand, though, it makes one resist interpretive pluralism by compelling attention to the psychosocial work any cultural text accomplishes. Masochistic fantasy may be delusional by definition. But it generates delusions in order to change the self and the world in specific ways. The relational paradigm thus offers cultural studies an opportunity for interpretive clarity, encouraging attention to masochistic fantasy's particularized psychosocial work rather than to the inconclusive meditations on reversible master/slave relations or performative distantiations of power that have too often absorbed masochism studies. By the same token, although I recognize that class identifications in literary texts tend to be multiple and unstable and that they lend themselves to unpredictable readerly appropriations, I believe that historicist criticism has a responsibility to name salient ideological forces in the textual field.[1] I believe, too, that the multiple class identifications circulated within literary texts—like those I have described in the work of Kipling and Conrad—often perform peculiar acts of ideological realignment rather than simply defusing a work's political energies.

Critics engaged in masochism studies (and others as well) may be disappointed by this book on methodological grounds for several reasons. The counterintuitive assumptions of relational theory—that masochistic fantasy is rarely about sex and only secondarily about oedipal patterns of conflict—are likely to persuade some that what I have called "masochistic fantasy" is not what most people mean by "masochism." I welcome that distinction, yet I would insist that masochistic fantasy is the more precise analytical instrument, since it enables us to see how cherished pain invokes a more complex intersection of social processes and identity formations than do narrower definitions of masochism. While my broadened definition of masochistic fantasy might also trouble those who worry that it encompasses too many forms of behavior, I can only reply, first, that masochistic fantasy is, in fact, more a part of daily psychosocial experience than many of us have yet realized; and, second, that the concept remains

---

[1] But for a suggestive analysis of the instabilities of class identification in literary texts, see Chris Vanden Bossche, "What Did Jane Eyre Do? Ideology, Agency, Class, and the Novel," *Narrative* 13 (2005), 46–66.

delimited by the relationship it forges between cherished pain and omnipotent fantasy. That delimitation distinguishes masochistic fantasy from forms of self-denial or self-sacrifice that do not necessarily invoke narcissistic delusion: deferred gratification, sublimation, moral choice, or productive self-discipline.

The most bitter disappointment for partisans of masochism studies, however, may be the book's refusal to take a political stand either for or against masochism. My central claims—that masochistic fantasy is a symbolic medium rather than a fixed psychosocial entity and that specific, highly variable political uses were made of it in late-nineteenth-century British culture—hinge on refusing this choice. Certainly, any masochistic practice performs a social action (whether in the subject's immediate interpersonal environment or in the public domain). Particular stagings of masochism, sexual or otherwise, may also seek to have a specific political impact. But it is quite another thing to say that a fixed political intentionality of some kind inhabits masochistic fantasy. A fundamental argument of *Imperial Masochism* is that masochistic fantasy supports an enormous range of ideological rewritings, discursive grafts, and political appropriations.

Finally, I cannot help acknowledging that, in a postmodern age, I will not escape being implicated in my own critiques. It will have occurred to many readers that practicing a stringent critical askesis, in which one suppresses one's own political or moral judgments—or at least gestures toward their suppression—can generate a fantasy of omnipotent detachment: the critic becomes master of all he or she surveys. I have already suggested that there is no political idealism free of perversity. That claim can be extended to critical idealism. But if perverse energies have driven this book (and of course they have), I hope that they will be measured by their productivity and their interpretive yield rather than by the mere fact of their implication in fantasy.

INDEX